& My Brothers

Volume 6

Hari Tokeino

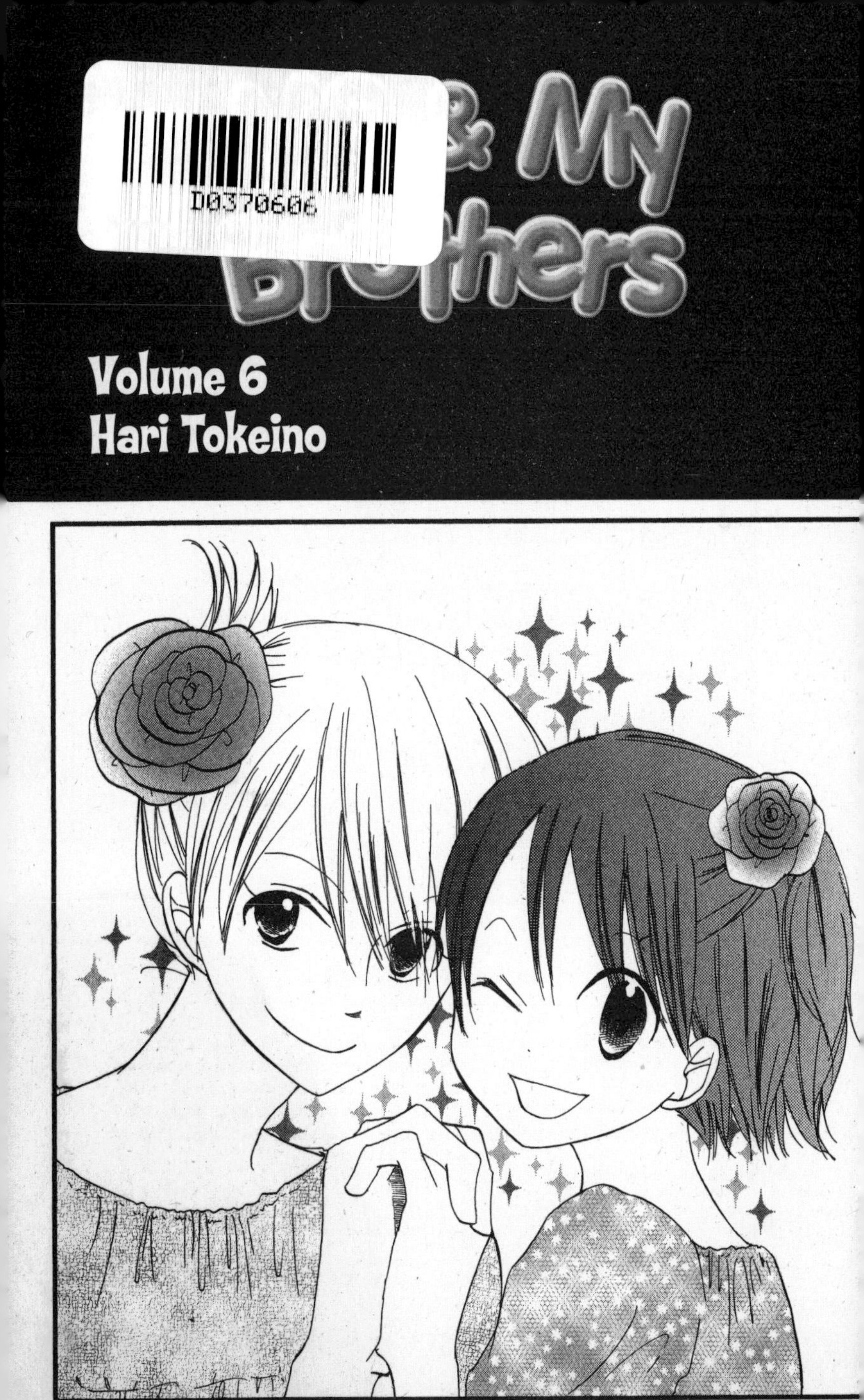

Me & My Brothers Volume 6
Created by Hari Tokeino

Translation - Alethea & Athena Nibley
English Adaptation - Joel Black
Retouch and Lettering - Star Print Brokers
Production Artist - Michael Paolilli
Graphic Designer - Erika Terriquez

Editor - Hyun Joo Kim
Pre-Production Supervisor - Vicente Rivera, Jr.
Pre-Production Specialist - Lucas Rivera
Managing Editor - Vy Nguyen
Senior Designer - Louis Csontos
Senior Designer - James Lee
Senior Editor - Bryce P. Coleman
Senior Editor - Jenna Winterberg
Associate Publisher - Marco F. Pavia
President and C.O.O. - John Parker
C.E.O. and Chief Creative Officer - Stu Levy

A  Manga

TOKYOPOP and 🐷 are trademarks or registered trademarks of TOKYOPOP Inc.

TOKYOPOP Inc.
5900 Wilshire Blvd. Suite 2000
Los Angeles, CA 90036

E-mail: info@TOKYOPOP.com
Come visit us online at www.TOKYOPOP.com

ISBN: 978-1-4278-0684-0

First TOKYOPOP printing: December 2008
10 9 8 7 6 5 4 3
Printed in the USA

Me & My Brothers

Volume 6

Hari Tokeino

TOKYOPOP®

HAMBURG // LONDON // LOS ANGELES // TOKYO

Contents

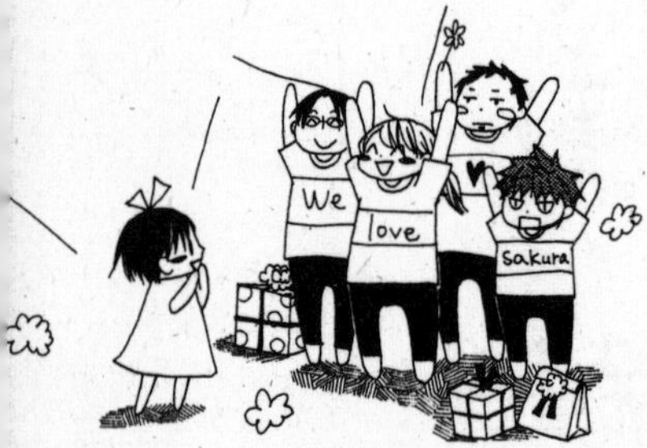
We
love
Sakura

CHARACTERS PROFILE

ME & MY BROTHERS

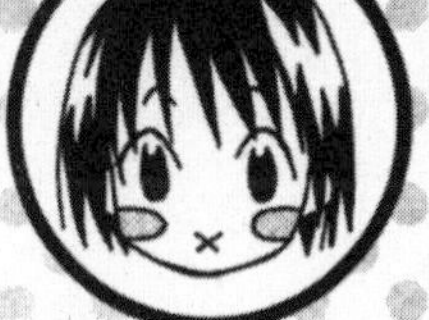

SAKURA MIYASHITA: THE YOUNGEST. A FIRST-YEAR IN HIGH SCHOOL. THE ONLY GIRL IN THE MIYASHITA FAMILY. SHE IS NOT BLOOD RELATED TO HER FOUR BROTHERS. SHE LOVES MASASHI.♥

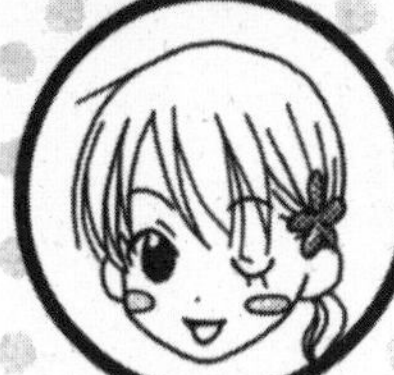

MASASHI MIYASHITA: THE ELDEST. ROMANCE NOVELIST. ACCORDING TO HIM, HE SOUNDS LIKE A WOMAN BECAUSE OF HIS JOB. HE'S THE LEADER OF THE FOUR SAKURA-SPOILERS.

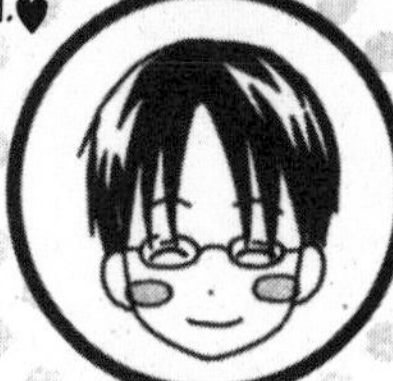

TAKASHI MIYASHITA: THE 2ND BROTHER. A JAPANESE TEACHER. A CALM GENTLEMAN.

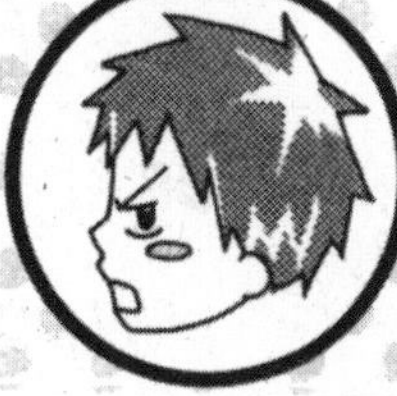

TSUYOSHI MIYASHITA: THE 3RD BROTHER.FULL-TIME PART-TIMER. HE TALKS ROUGH, BUT IS ACTUALLY QUITE BASHFUL.

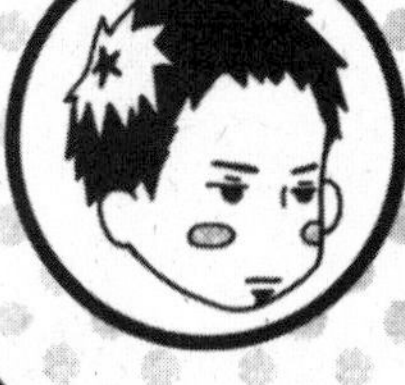

TAKESHI MIYASHITA: THE 4TH BROTHER. COLLEGE FRESHMAN. HE LOOKS OLD, BUT HE IS THE YOUNGEST OF THE FOUR BROTHERS. HE'S QUIET AND LOVES GARDENING.

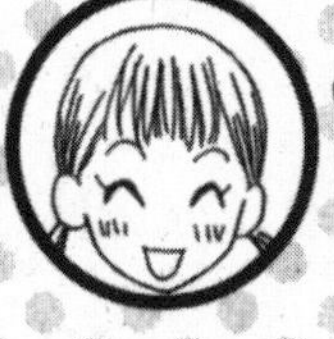

NAKA-CHAN: SAKURA'S BEST FRIEND. HER FAMILY NAME IS TANAKA.

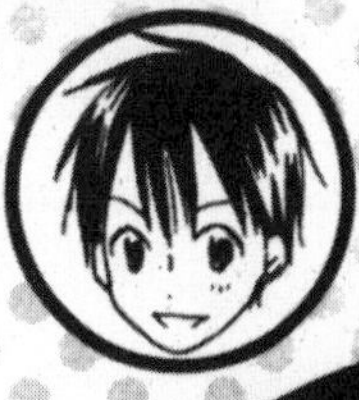

SUZUKI: ON THE SCHOOL SOCCER TEAM. HE HAS A CRUSH ON SAKURA.

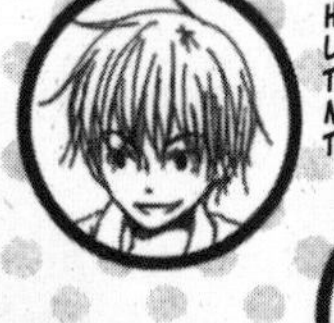

KATAGIRI: HE CONFESSED HIS LOVE TO SAKURA IN THEIR SECOND YEAR OF MIDDLE SCHOOL AND THEN TRANSFERRED AWAY!

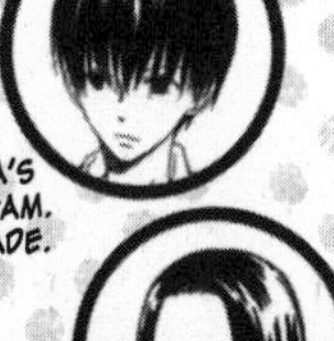

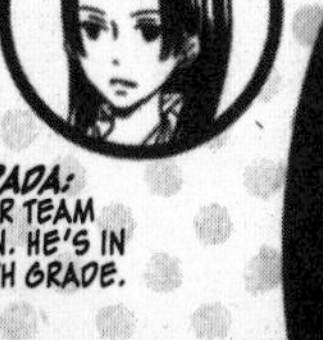

NANA & NENE KOZUKA THE TWINS IN SAKURA'S SCHOOL SOCCER TEAM. BOTH IN THE 11TH GRADE.

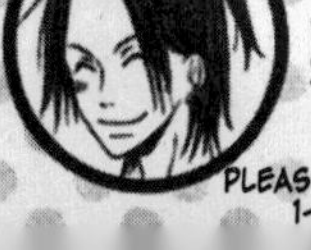

TERADA: SOCCER TEAM CAPTAIN. HE'S IN THE 12TH GRADE.

PLEASE READ *ME & MY BROTHERS* 1-5 FOR MORE DETAILS!

STORY

SAKURA LOST HER PARENTS WHEN SHE WAS 3 AND WAS RAISED BY HER GRANDMOTHER. THEN, WHEN SAKURA WAS 14, HER GRANDMOTHER PASSED AWAY. SHE WAS ALL ALONE UNTIL FOUR STEPBROTHERS SHOWED UP! AFTER 11 YEARS OF SEPARATION, THEY STARTED TO LIVE TOGETHER!♡WHEN WE LAST LEFT OFF, IT WAS VALENTINE'S DAY, AND MASASHI HAD SAID TO SAKURA, "YOU HAD CHOCOLATE ON YOUR FACE," AND KISSED HER CHEEK!

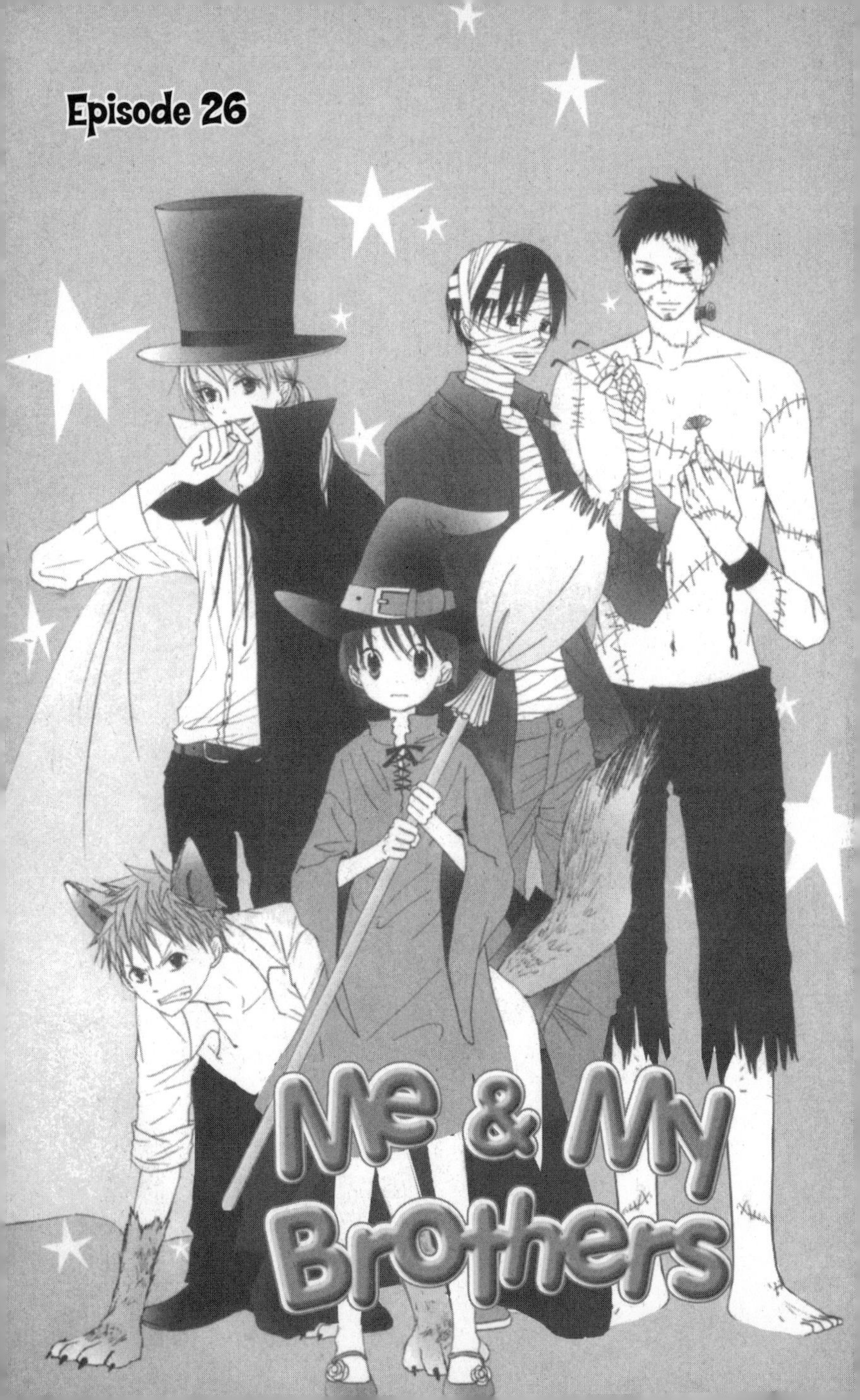
Episode 26
Me & My Brothers

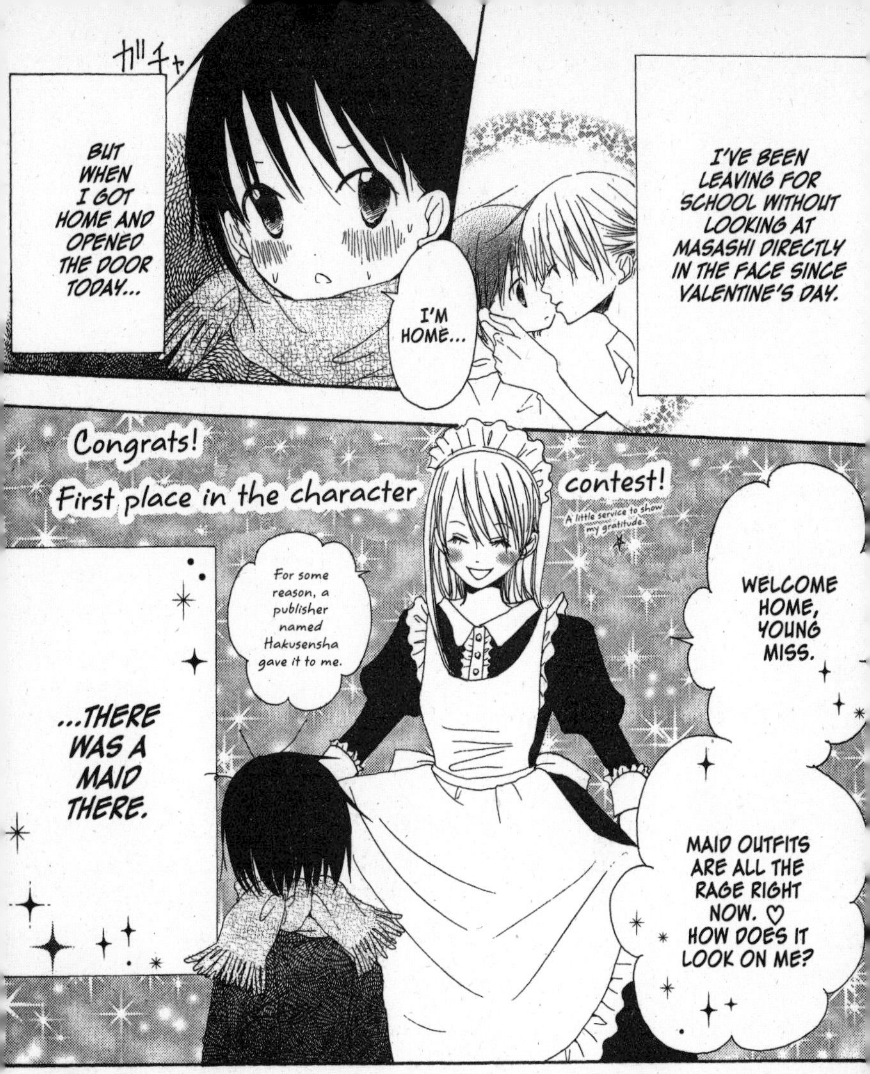
ガチャ
I'VE BEEN LEAVING FOR SCHOOL WITHOUT LOOKING AT MASASHI DIRECTLY IN THE FACE SINCE VALENTINE'S DAY.
BUT WHEN I GOT HOME AND OPENED THE DOOR TODAY...
I'M HOME...
Congrats! First place in the character contest!
A little service to show my gratitude.
WELCOME HOME, YOUNG MISS.
For some reason, a publisher named Hakusensha gave it to me.
...THERE WAS A MAID THERE.
MAID OUTFITS ARE ALL THE RAGE RIGHT NOW. ♡ HOW DOES IT LOOK ON ME?

Favorite Character Contest Results (contest was held in Japan)

First place: Masashi Miyashita	Eighth place: Terada-senpai	15th place: Morishima-kun
Second place: Sakura Miyashita	Ninth place: Nene Kozuka	16th place: Owner of Hamamatsu
Third place: Tsuyoshi Miyashita	10th place: Taizou Fukasawa	17th place: Ume-chan
Fourth place: Nana Kozuka	11th place: Rin Morimoto	18th place: Fumiko-san, Katagiri-kun, Yosuke, the middle-aged men
Fifth place: Takashi Miyashita	12th place: Naka-chan	22nd place: Sakura's grandmother
Sixth place: Suzuki-kun	13th place: The Kozuka Twins	
Seventh place: Takeshi Miyashita	14th place: Fuji-san (the roller coaster guy)	

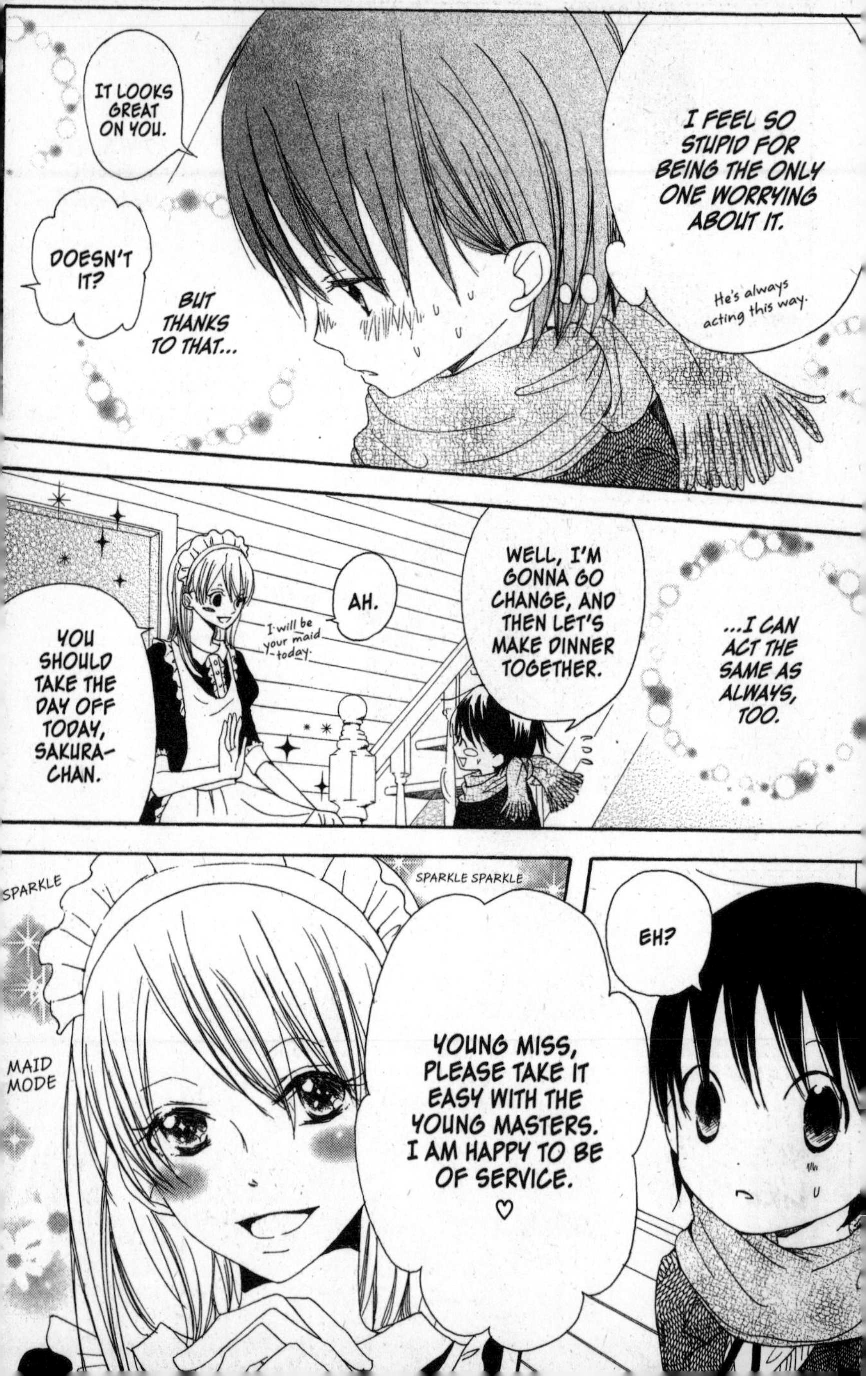
I FEEL SO STUPID FOR BEING THE ONLY ONE WORRYING ABOUT IT.
He's always acting this way.
IT LOOKS GREAT ON YOU.
DOESN'T IT?
BUT THANKS TO THAT...
...I CAN ACT THE SAME AS ALWAYS, TOO.
WELL, I'M GONNA GO CHANGE, AND THEN LET'S MAKE DINNER TOGETHER.
AH.
I will be your maid today.
YOU SHOULD TAKE THE DAY OFF TODAY, SAKURA-CHAN.
EH?
SPARKLE SPARKLE
YOUNG MISS, PLEASE TAKE IT EASY WITH THE YOUNG MASTERS. I AM HAPPY TO BE OF SERVICE. ♡
SPARKLE
MAID MODE

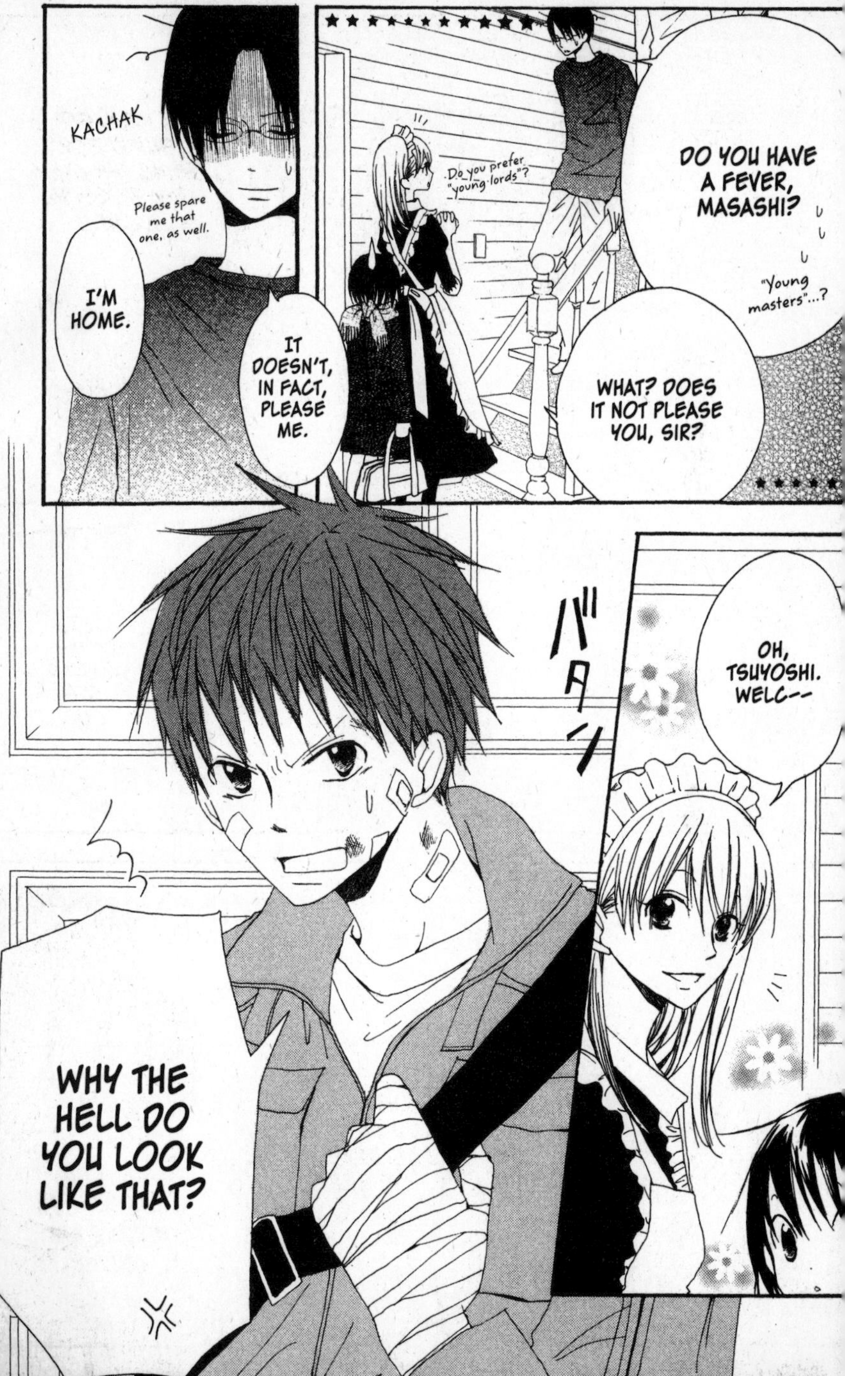
DO YOU HAVE A FEVER, MASASHI?
"Young masters"...?
WHAT? DOES IT NOT PLEASE YOU, SIR?
IT DOESN'T, IN FACT, PLEASE ME.
Do you prefer "young lords"?
KACHAK
Please spare me that one, as well.
I'M HOME.
OH, TSUYOSHI. WELC--
バタン
WHY THE HELL DO YOU LOOK LIKE THAT?

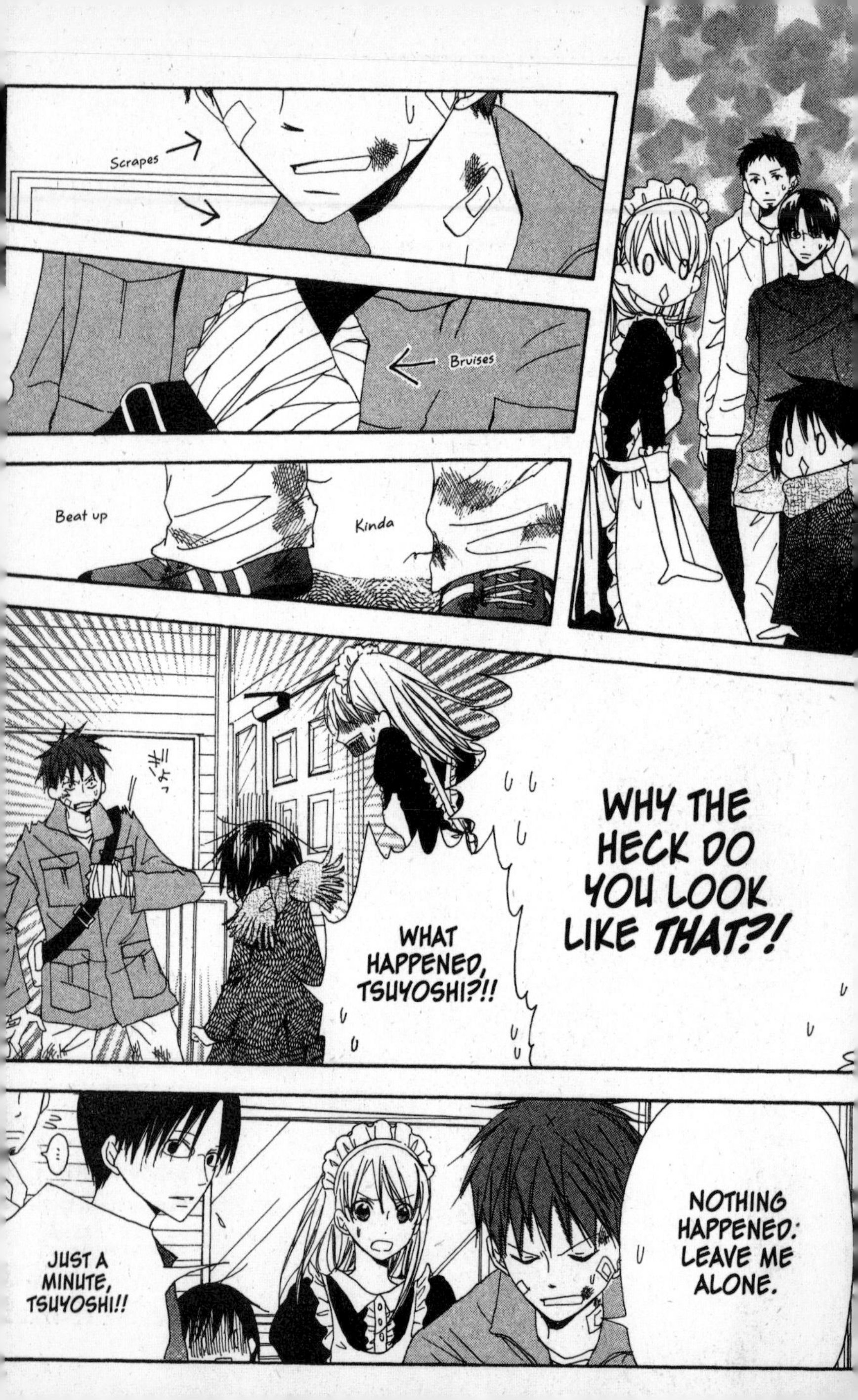
Scrapes
Bruises
Kinda
Beat up
WHY THE HECK DO YOU LOOK LIKE THAT?!
WHAT HAPPENED, TSUYOSHI?!!
NOTHING HAPPENED. LEAVE ME ALONE.
JUST A MINUTE, TSUYOSHI!!
...

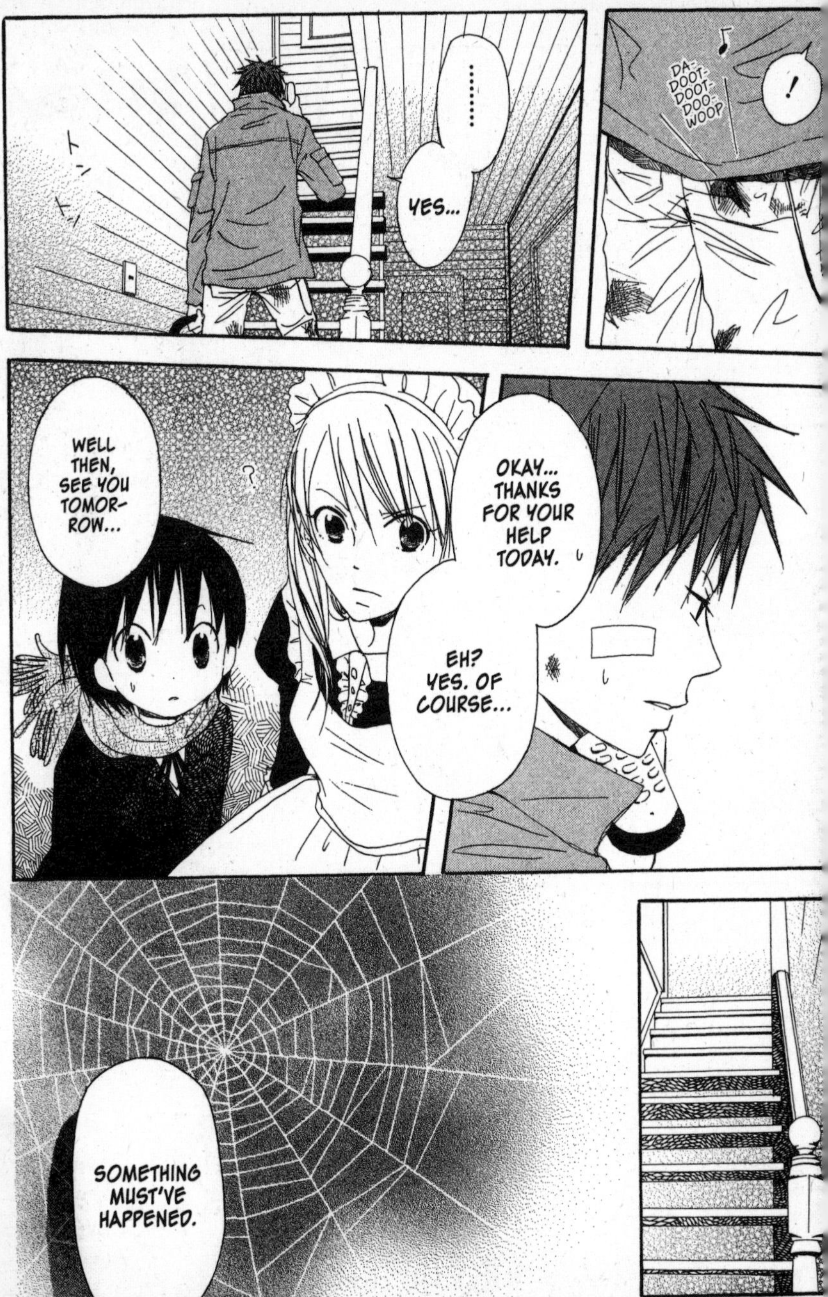
DA-DOOT-DOOT-DOO-WOOP
!
......
YES...
OKAY... THANKS FOR YOUR HELP TODAY.
EH? YES. OF COURSE...
WELL THEN, SEE YOU TOMOR-ROW...
?
SOMETHING MUST'VE HAPPENED.

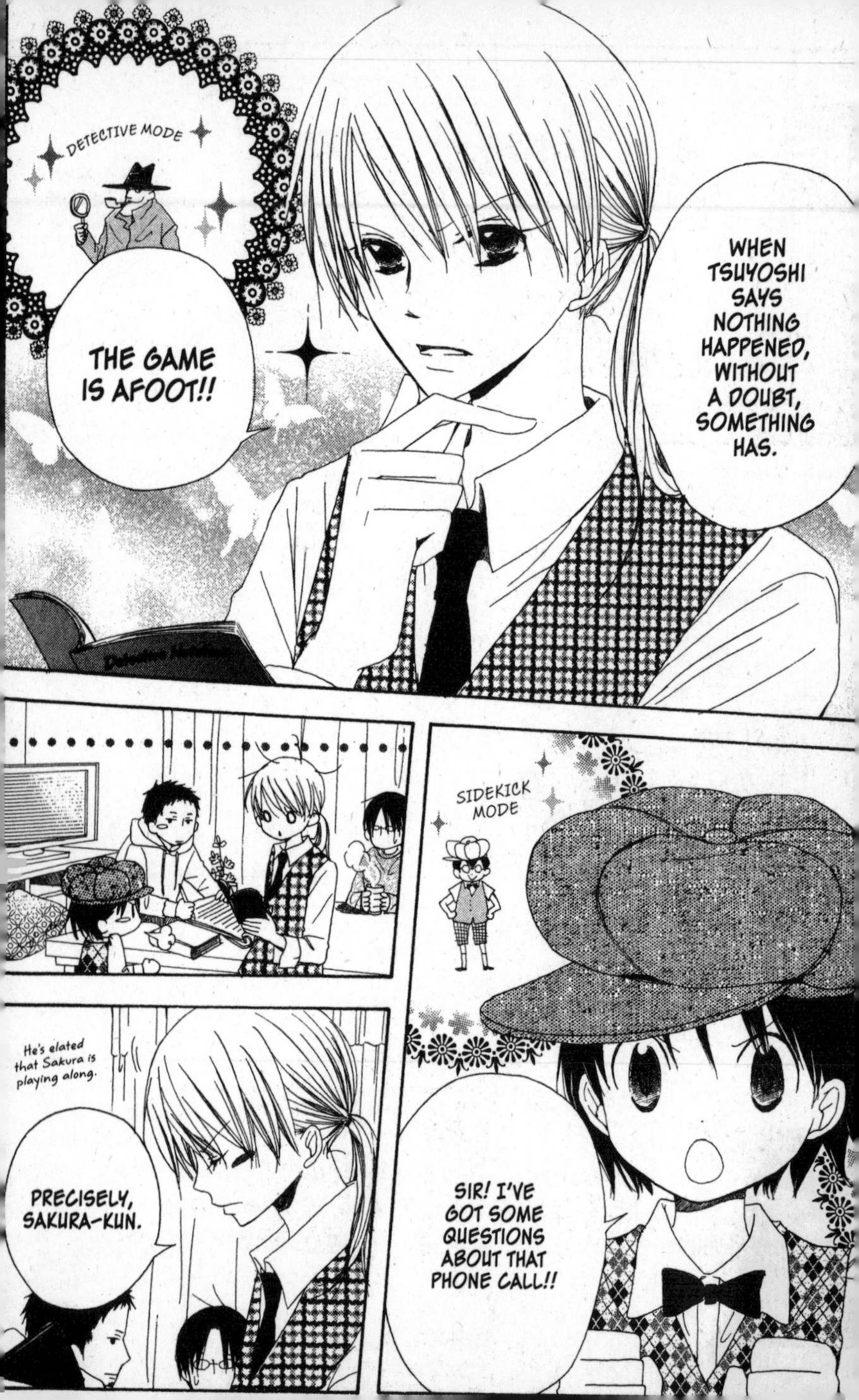
WHEN TSUYOSHI SAYS NOTHING HAPPENED, WITHOUT A DOUBT, SOMETHING HAS.
DETECTIVE MODE
THE GAME IS AFOOT!!
SIDEKICK MODE
SIR! I'VE GOT SOME QUESTIONS ABOUT THAT PHONE CALL!!
He's elated that Sakura is playing along.
PRECISELY, SAKURA-KUN.

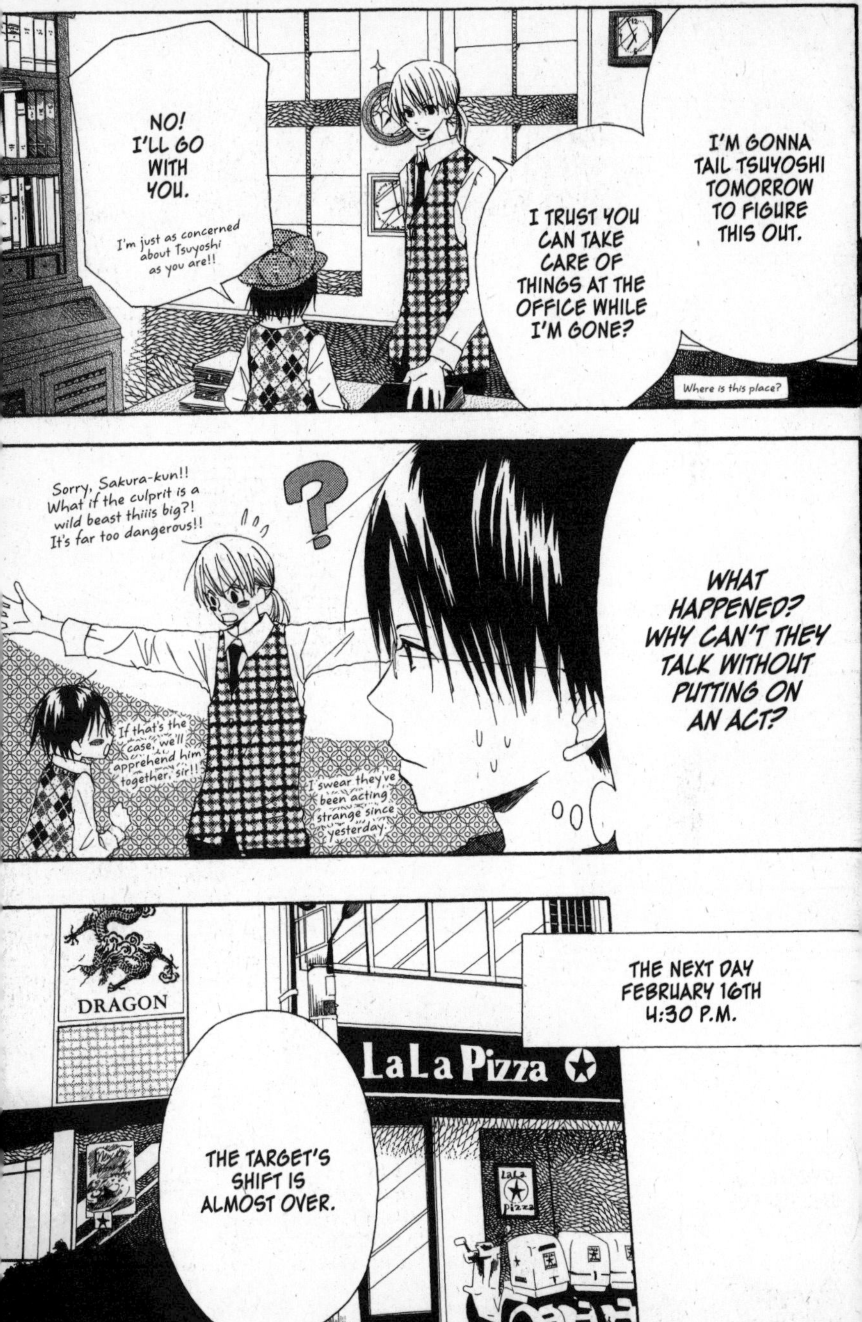
I'M GONNA TAIL TSUYOSHI TOMORROW TO FIGURE THIS OUT.
I TRUST YOU CAN TAKE CARE OF THINGS AT THE OFFICE WHILE I'M GONE?
Where is this place?
NO! I'LL GO WITH YOU.
I'm just as concerned about Tsuyoshi as you are!!
WHAT HAPPENED? WHY CAN'T THEY TALK WITHOUT PUTTING ON AN ACT?
Sorry, Sakura-kun!! What if the culprit is a wild beast thiiis big?! It's far too dangerous!!
I swear they've been acting strange since yesterday.
If that's the case, we'll apprehend him together, sir!!
THE NEXT DAY FEBRUARY 16TH 4:30 P.M.
LaLa Pizza
DRAGON
THE TARGET'S SHIFT IS ALMOST OVER.

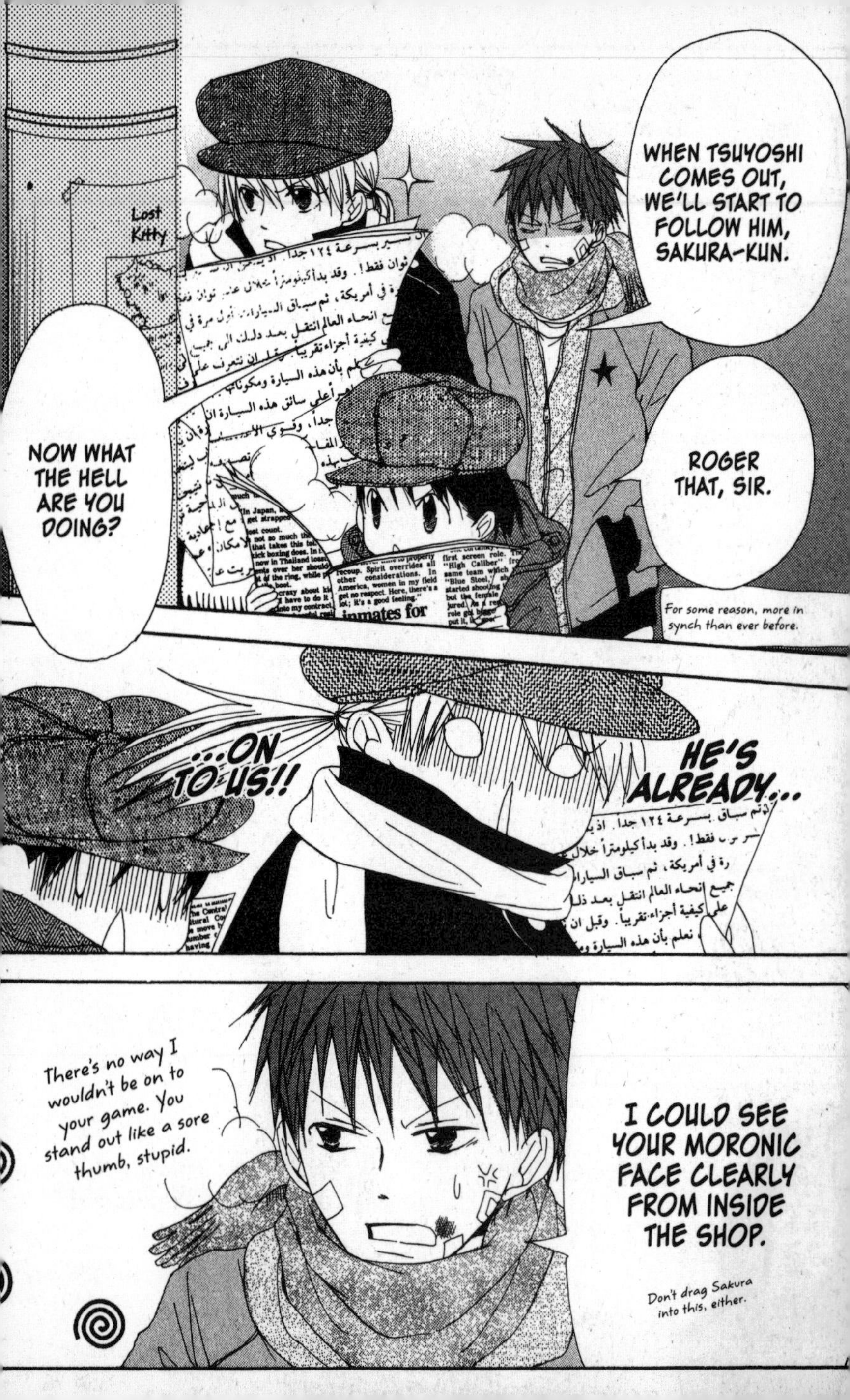
WHEN TSUYOSHI COMES OUT, WE'LL START TO FOLLOW HIM, SAKURA-KUN.
ROGER THAT, SIR.
For some reason, more in synch than ever before.
Lost Kitty
NOW WHAT THE HELL ARE YOU DOING?
HE'S ALREADY...
...ON TO US!!
I COULD SEE YOUR MORONIC FACE CLEARLY FROM INSIDE THE SHOP.
Don't drag Sakura into this, either.
There's no way I wouldn't be on to your game. You stand out like a sore thumb, stupid.

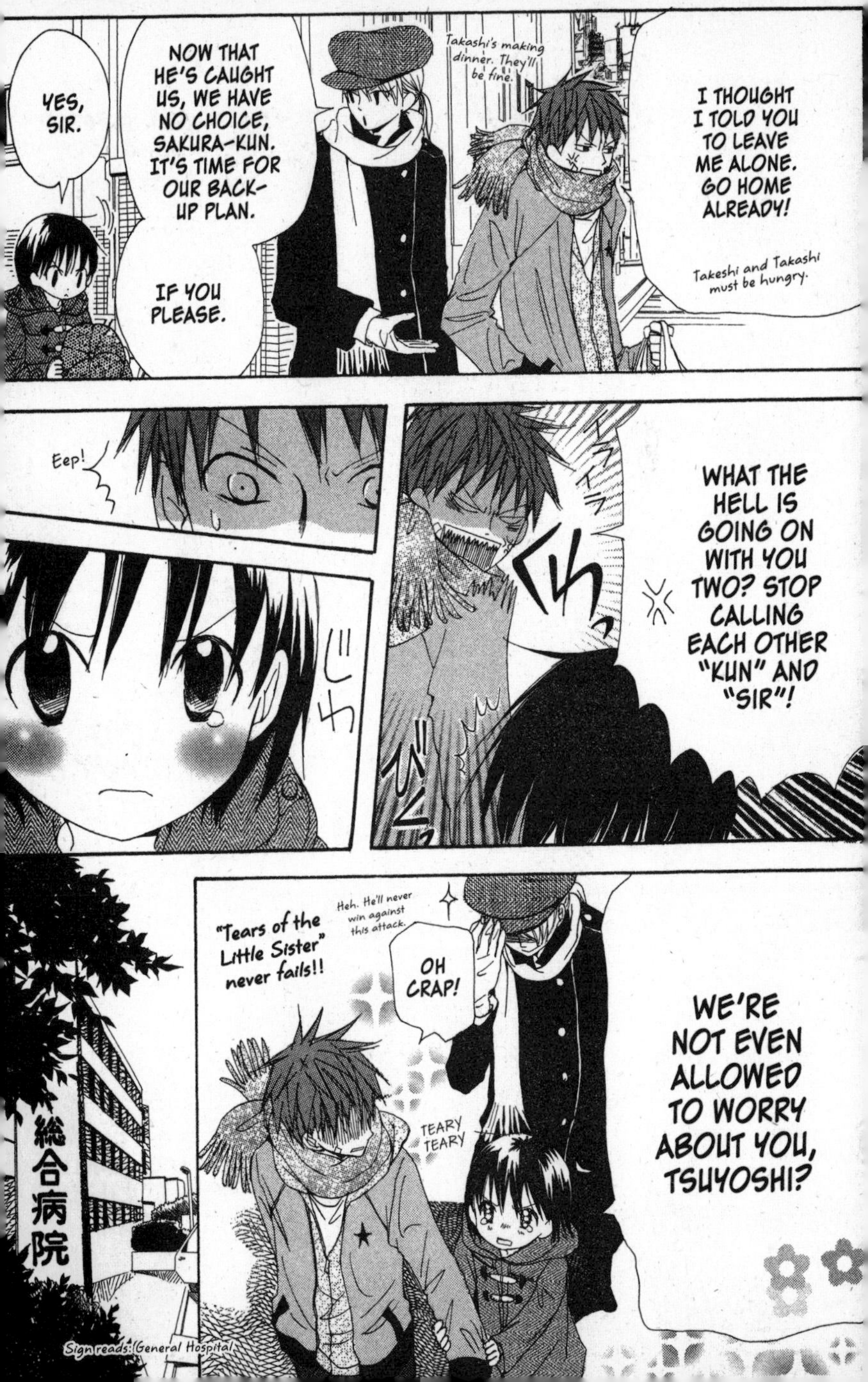
I THOUGHT I TOLD YOU TO LEAVE ME ALONE. GO HOME ALREADY!
Takeshi and Takashi must be hungry.
Takashi's making dinner. They'll be fine.
NOW THAT HE'S CAUGHT US, WE HAVE NO CHOICE, SAKURA-KUN. IT'S TIME FOR OUR BACK-UP PLAN.
YES, SIR.
IF YOU PLEASE.
WHAT THE HELL IS GOING ON WITH YOU TWO? STOP CALLING EACH OTHER "KUN" AND "SIR"!
Eep!
WE'RE NOT EVEN ALLOWED TO WORRY ABOUT YOU, TSUYOSHI?
TEARY TEARY
OH CRAP!
Heh. He'll never win against this attack.
"Tears of the Little Sister" never fails!!
総合病院
Sign reads: General Hospital

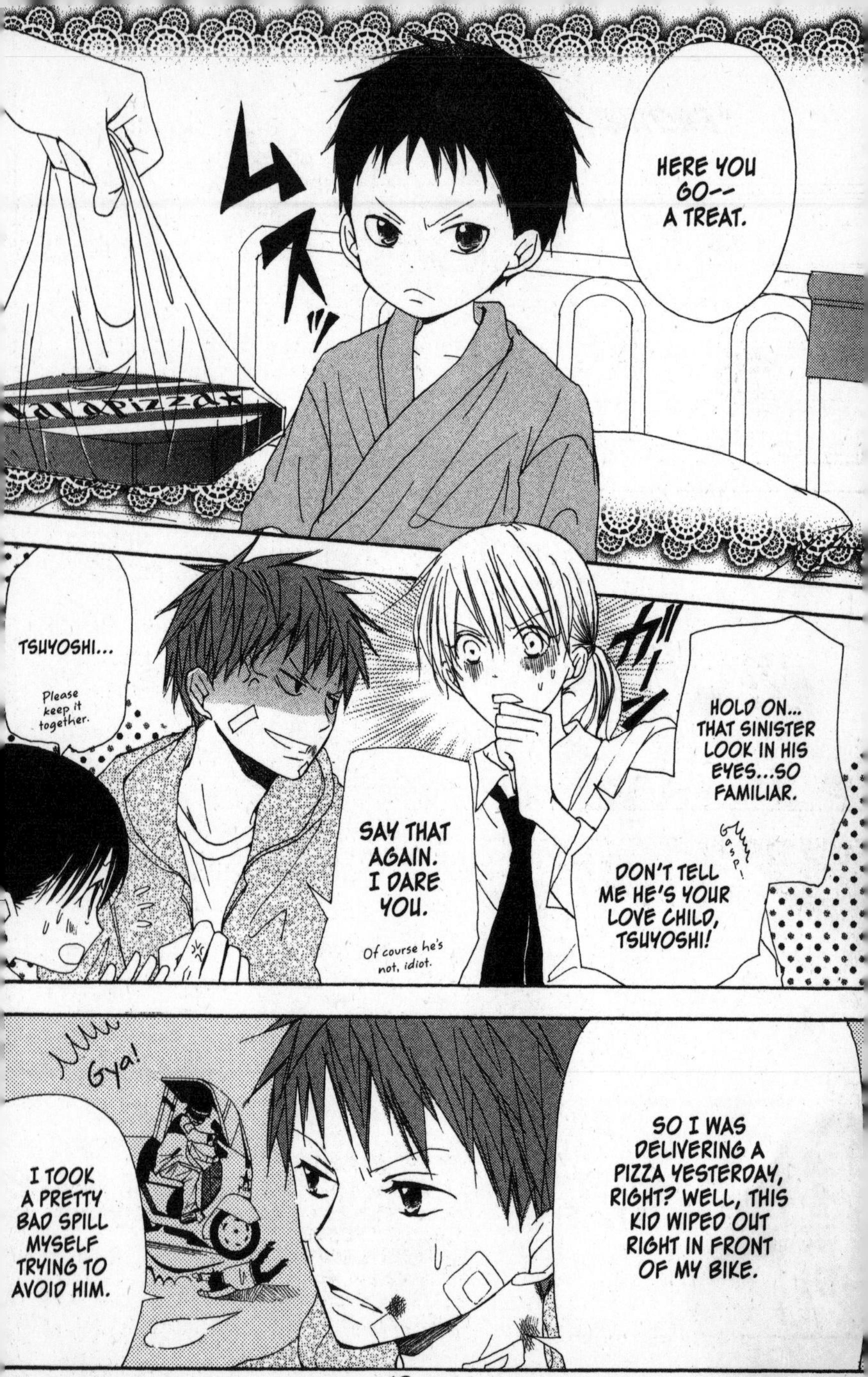
HERE YOU GO-- A TREAT.
HOLD ON... THAT SINISTER LOOK IN HIS EYES...SO FAMILIAR.
Gasp!
DON'T TELL ME HE'S YOUR LOVE CHILD, TSUYOSHI!
SAY THAT AGAIN. I DARE YOU.
Of course he's not, idiot.
TSUYOSHI...
Please keep it together.
SO I WAS DELIVERING A PIZZA YESTERDAY, RIGHT? WELL, THIS KID WIPED OUT RIGHT IN FRONT OF MY BIKE.
I TOOK A PRETTY BAD SPILL MYSELF TRYING TO AVOID HIM.
Gya!

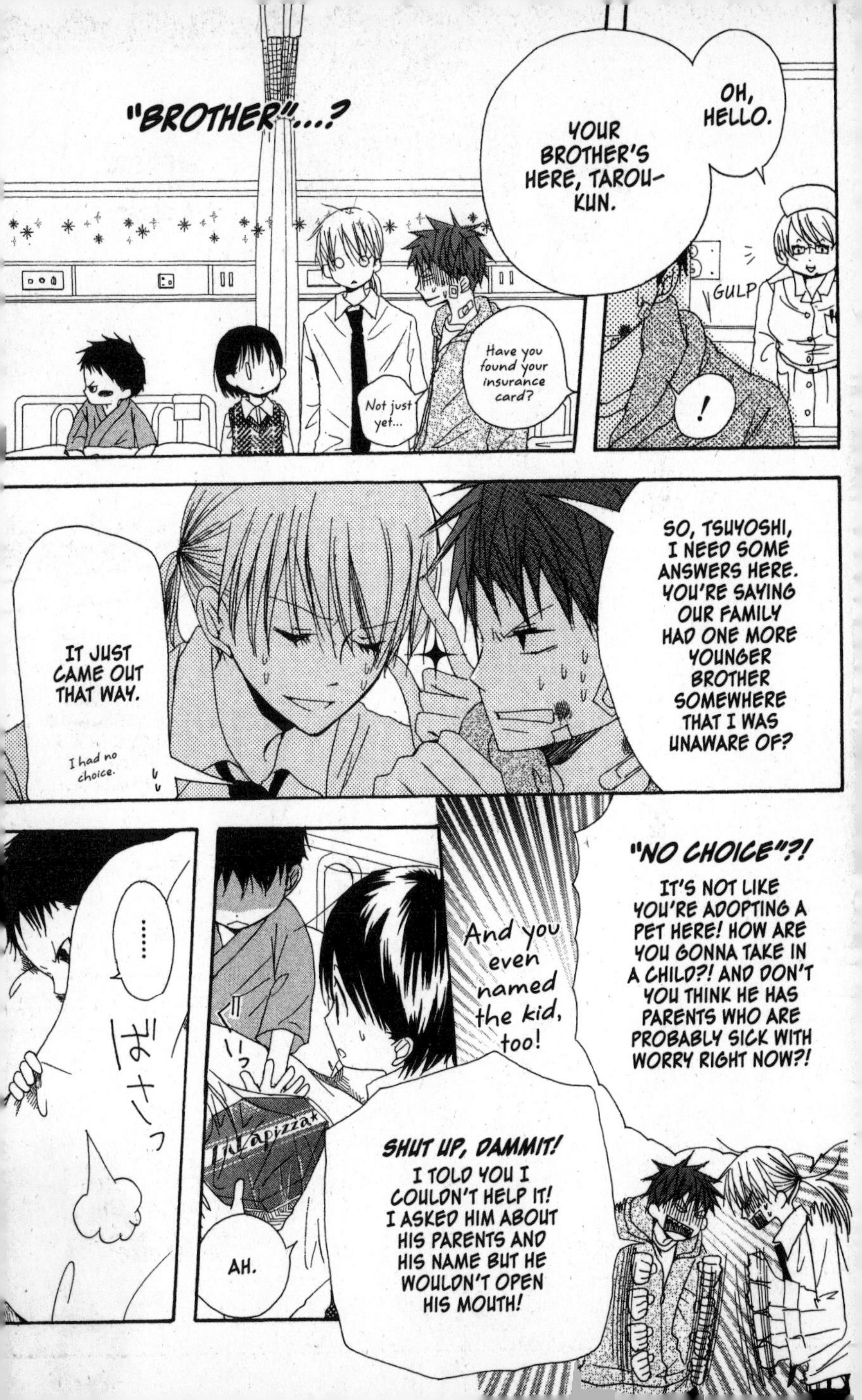
OH, HELLO.
YOUR BROTHER'S HERE, TAROU-KUN.
GULP
!
"BROTHER"...?
Have you found your insurance card?
Not just yet...
SO, TSUYOSHI, I NEED SOME ANSWERS HERE. YOU'RE SAYING OUR FAMILY HAD ONE MORE YOUNGER BROTHER SOMEWHERE THAT I WAS UNAWARE OF?
IT JUST CAME OUT THAT WAY.
I had no choice.
"NO CHOICE"?!
IT'S NOT LIKE YOU'RE ADOPTING A PET HERE! HOW ARE YOU GONNA TAKE IN A CHILD?! AND DON'T YOU THINK HE HAS PARENTS WHO ARE PROBABLY SICK WITH WORRY RIGHT NOW?!
And you even named the kid, too!
SHUT UP, DAMMIT! I TOLD YOU I COULDN'T HELP IT! I ASKED HIM ABOUT HIS PARENTS AND HIS NAME BUT HE WOULDN'T OPEN HIS MOUTH!
AH.
......
ぱさっ

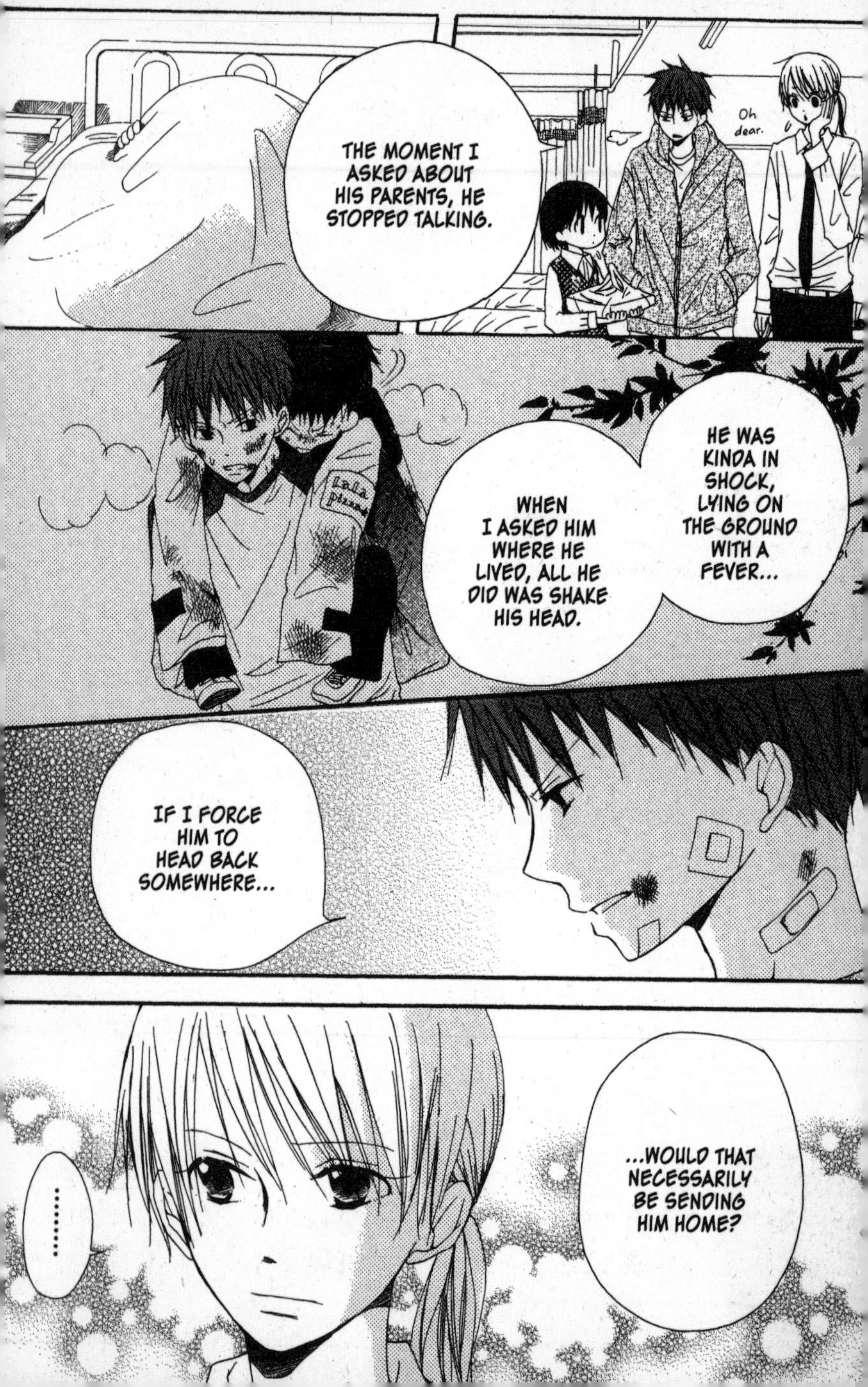
Oh dear.
THE MOMENT I ASKED ABOUT HIS PARENTS, HE STOPPED TALKING.
HE WAS KINDA IN SHOCK, LYING ON THE GROUND WITH A FEVER...
WHEN I ASKED HIM WHERE HE LIVED, ALL HE DID WAS SHAKE HIS HEAD.
IF I FORCE HIM TO HEAD BACK SOMEWHERE...
...WOULD THAT NECESSARILY BE SENDING HIM HOME?
....

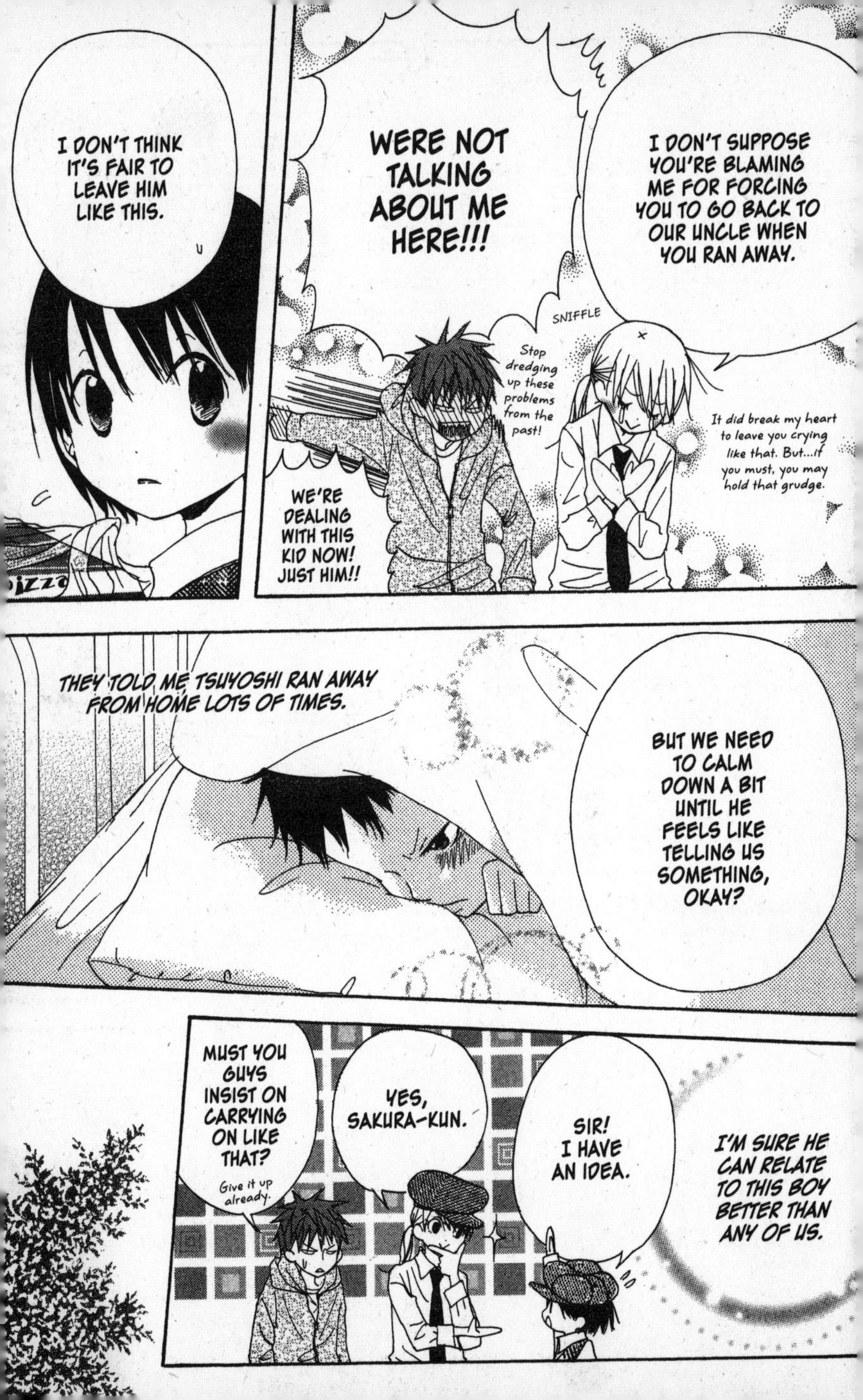
I DON'T SUPPOSE YOU'RE BLAMING ME FOR FORCING YOU TO GO BACK TO OUR UNCLE WHEN YOU RAN AWAY.
WERE NOT TALKING ABOUT ME HERE!!!
SNIFFLE
Stop dredging up these problems from the past!
It did break my heart to leave you crying like that. But...if you must, you may hold that grudge.
WE'RE DEALING WITH THIS KID NOW! JUST HIM!!
I DON'T THINK IT'S FAIR TO LEAVE HIM LIKE THIS.
THEY TOLD ME TSUYOSHI RAN AWAY FROM HOME LOTS OF TIMES.
BUT WE NEED TO CALM DOWN A BIT UNTIL HE FEELS LIKE TELLING US SOMETHING, OKAY?
I'M SURE HE CAN RELATE TO THIS BOY BETTER THAN ANY OF US.
SIR! I HAVE AN IDEA.
YES, SAKURA-KUN.
MUST YOU GUYS INSIST ON CARRYING ON LIKE THAT?
Give it up already.

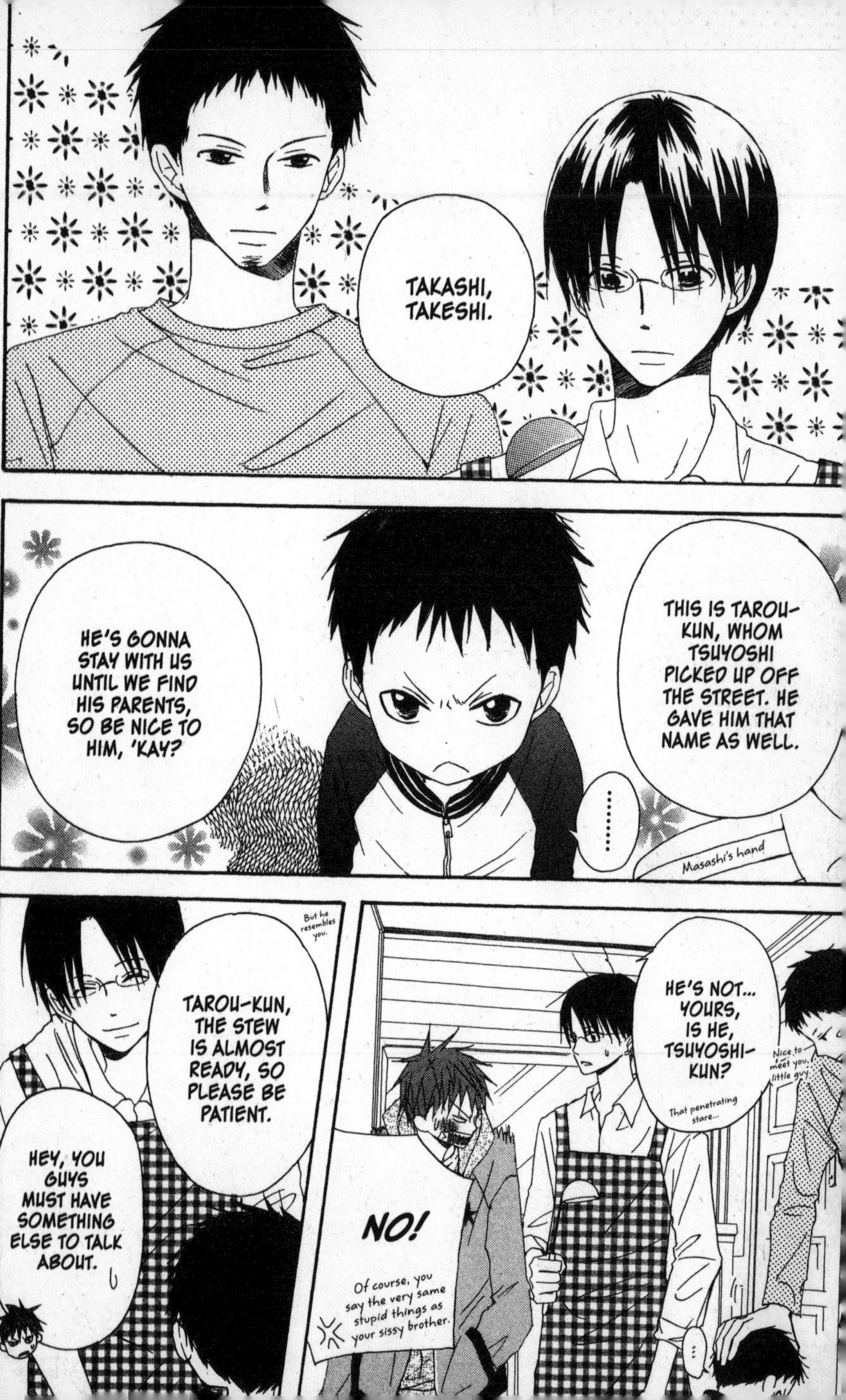
TAKASHI, TAKESHI.
THIS IS TAROU-KUN, WHOM TSUYOSHI PICKED UP OFF THE STREET. HE GAVE HIM THAT NAME AS WELL.
....
Masashi's hand
HE'S GONNA STAY WITH US UNTIL WE FIND HIS PARENTS, SO BE NICE TO HIM, 'KAY?
HE'S NOT... YOURS, IS HE, TSUYOSHI-KUN?
Nice to meet you, little guy.
That penetrating stare...
NO!
Of course, you say the very same stupid things as your sissy brother.
But he resembles you.
TAROU-KUN, THE STEW IS ALMOST READY, SO PLEASE BE PATIENT.
HEY, YOU GUYS MUST HAVE SOMETHING ELSE TO TALK ABOUT.

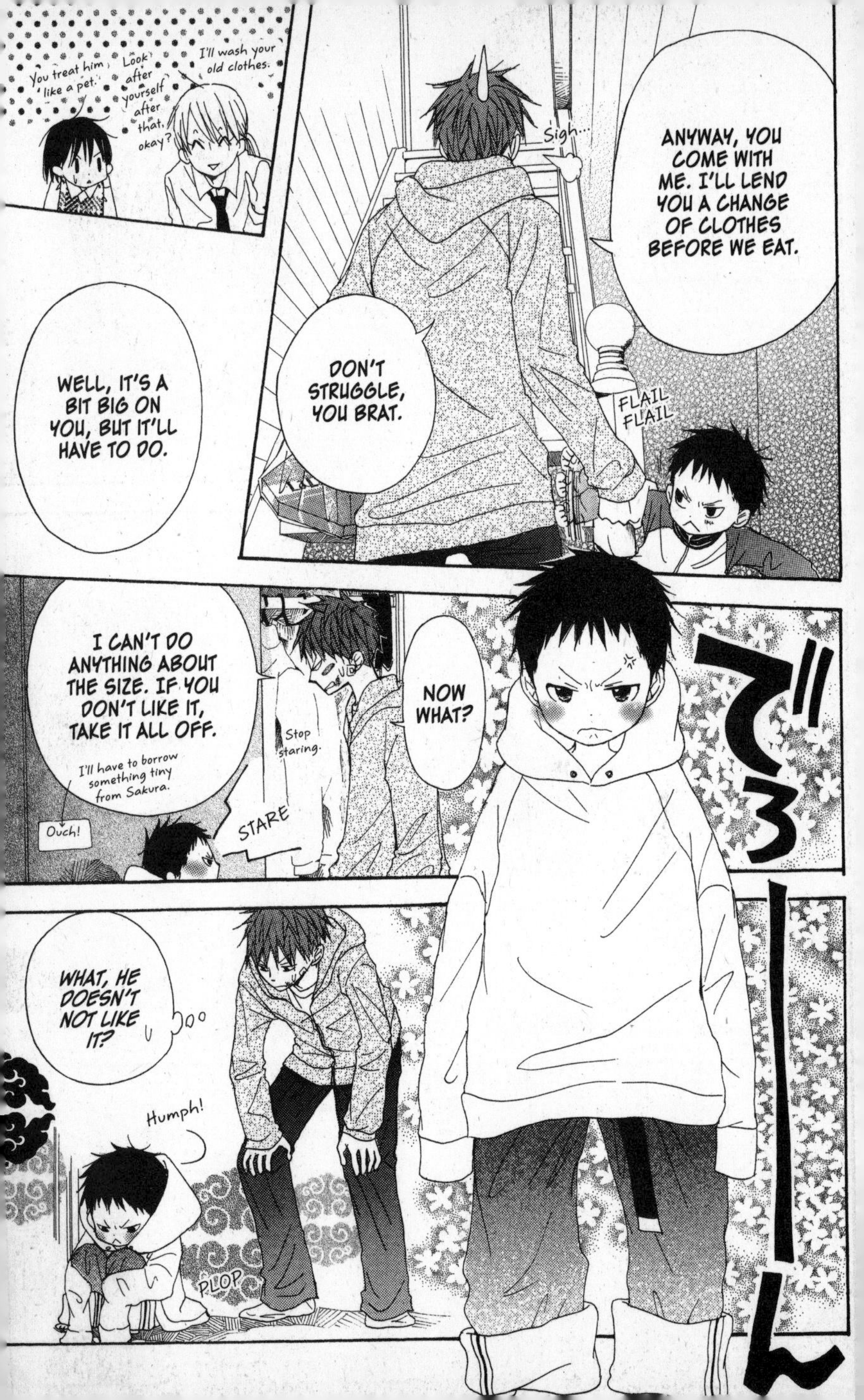
Sigh...
ANYWAY, YOU COME WITH ME. I'LL LEND YOU A CHANGE OF CLOTHES BEFORE WE EAT.
FLAIL FLAIL
DON'T STRUGGLE, YOU BRAT.
I'll wash your old clothes.
Look after yourself after that, okay?
You treat him like a pet.
WELL, IT'S A BIT BIG ON YOU, BUT IT'LL HAVE TO DO.
でーん
NOW WHAT?
I CAN'T DO ANYTHING ABOUT THE SIZE. IF YOU DON'T LIKE IT, TAKE IT ALL OFF.
Stop staring.
STARE
I'll have to borrow something tiny from Sakura.
Ouch!
WHAT, HE DOESN'T NOT LIKE IT?
Humph!
PLOP

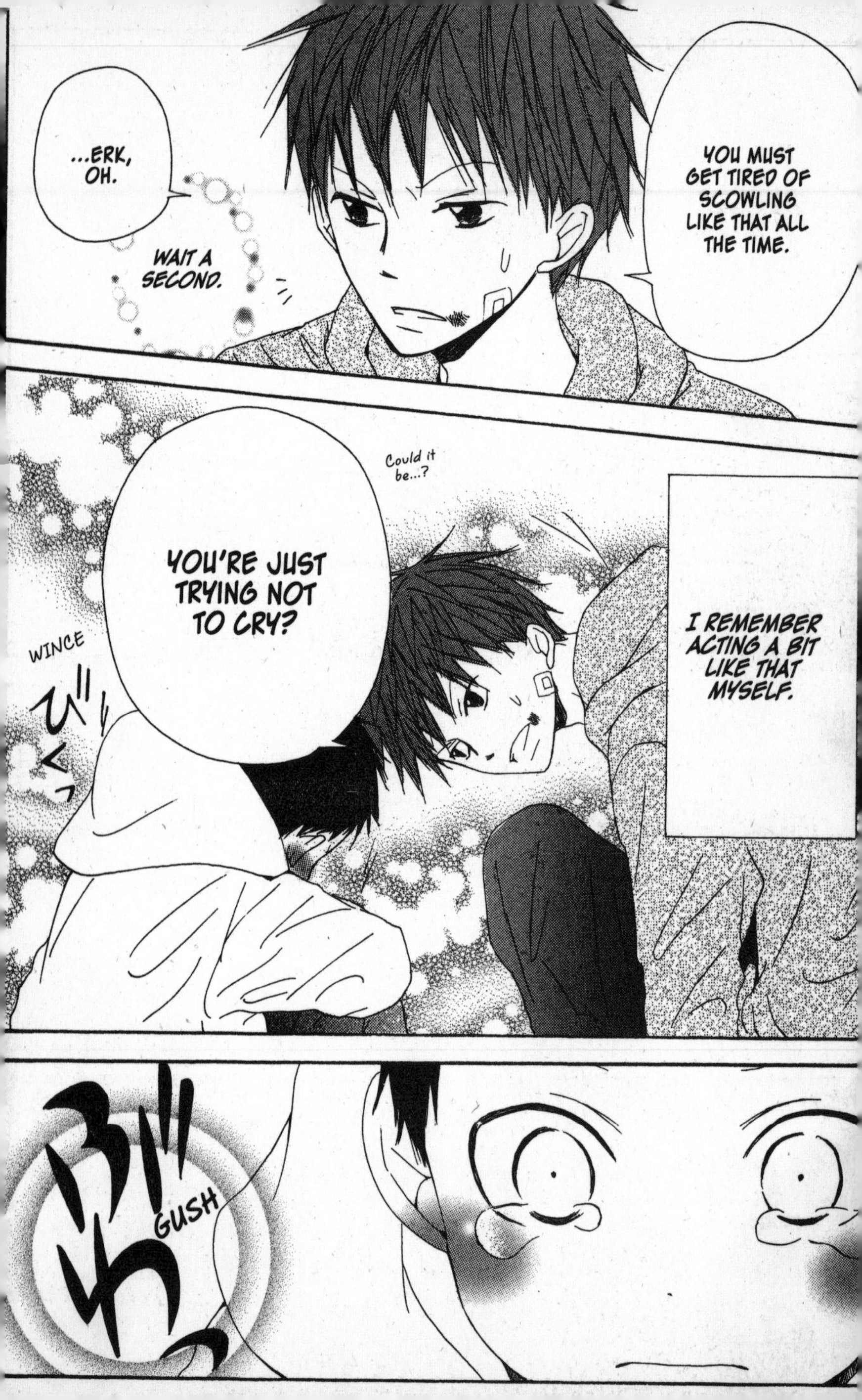
YOU MUST GET TIRED OF SCOWLING LIKE THAT ALL THE TIME.
...ERK, OH.
WAIT A SECOND.
I REMEMBER ACTING A BIT LIKE THAT MYSELF.
Could it be...?
YOU'RE JUST TRYING NOT TO CRY?
WINCE
GUSH

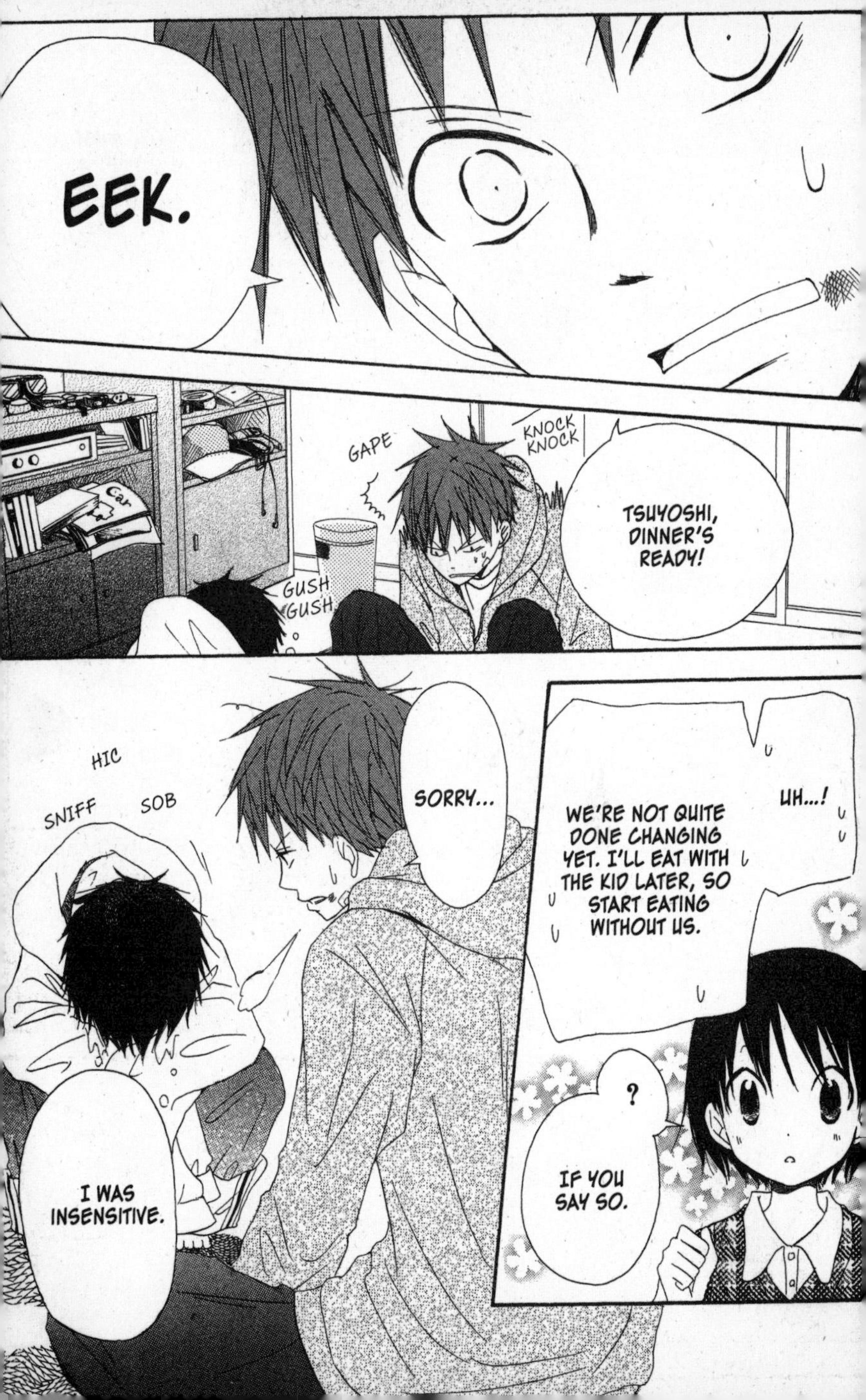
EEK.
TSUYOSHI, DINNER'S READY!
KNOCK KNOCK
GAPE
GUSH GUSH
UH...!
WE'RE NOT QUITE DONE CHANGING YET. I'LL EAT WITH THE KID LATER, SO START EATING WITHOUT US.
?
IF YOU SAY SO.
SORRY...
HIC
SOB
SNIFF
I WAS INSENSITIVE.

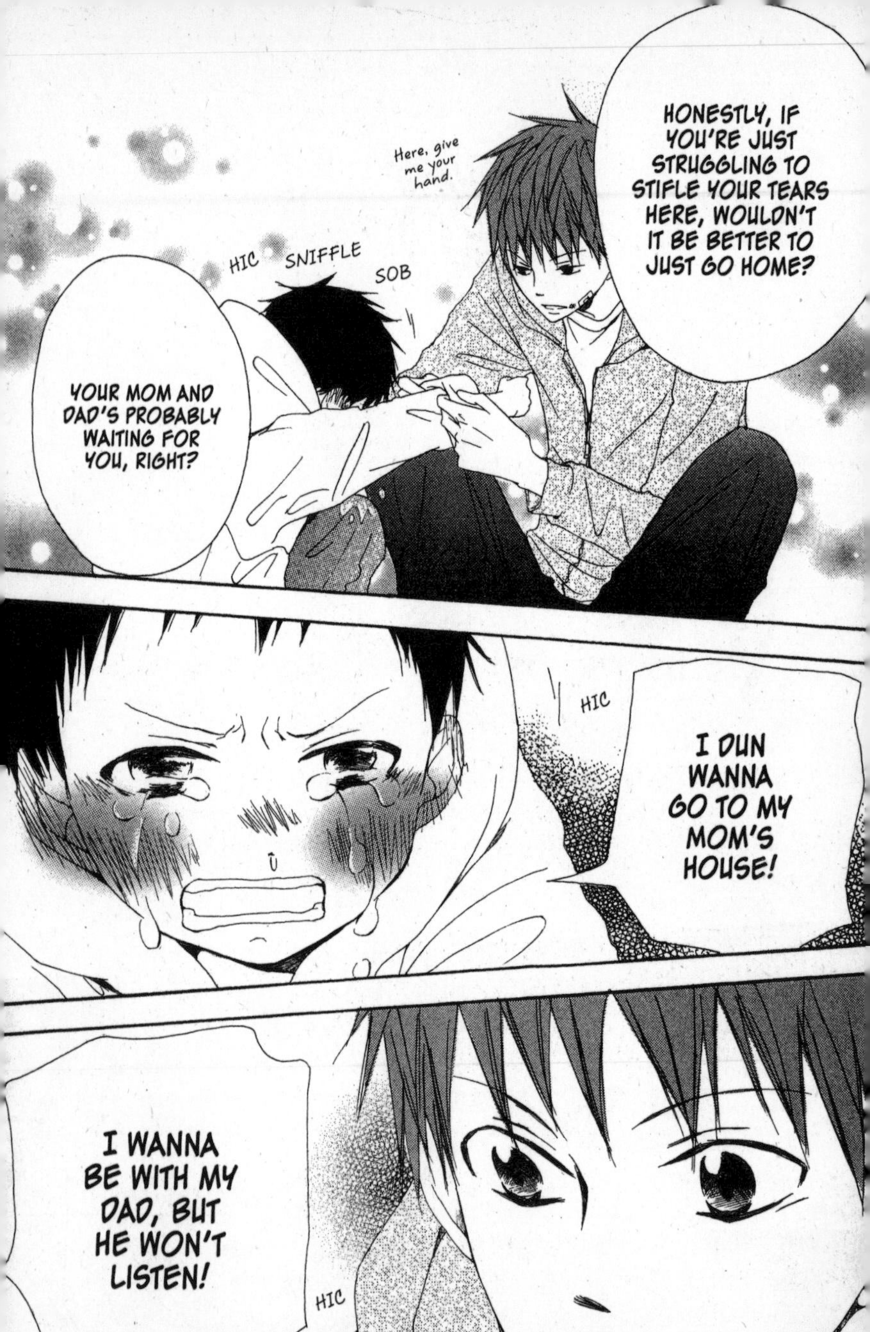
HONESTLY, IF YOU'RE JUST STRUGGLING TO STIFLE YOUR TEARS HERE, WOULDN'T IT BE BETTER TO JUST GO HOME?
Here, give me your hand.
SOB
SNIFFLE
HIC
YOUR MOM AND DAD'S PROBABLY WAITING FOR YOU, RIGHT?
HIC
I DUN WANNA GO TO MY MOM'S HOUSE!
I WANNA BE WITH MY DAD, BUT HE WON'T LISTEN!
HIC

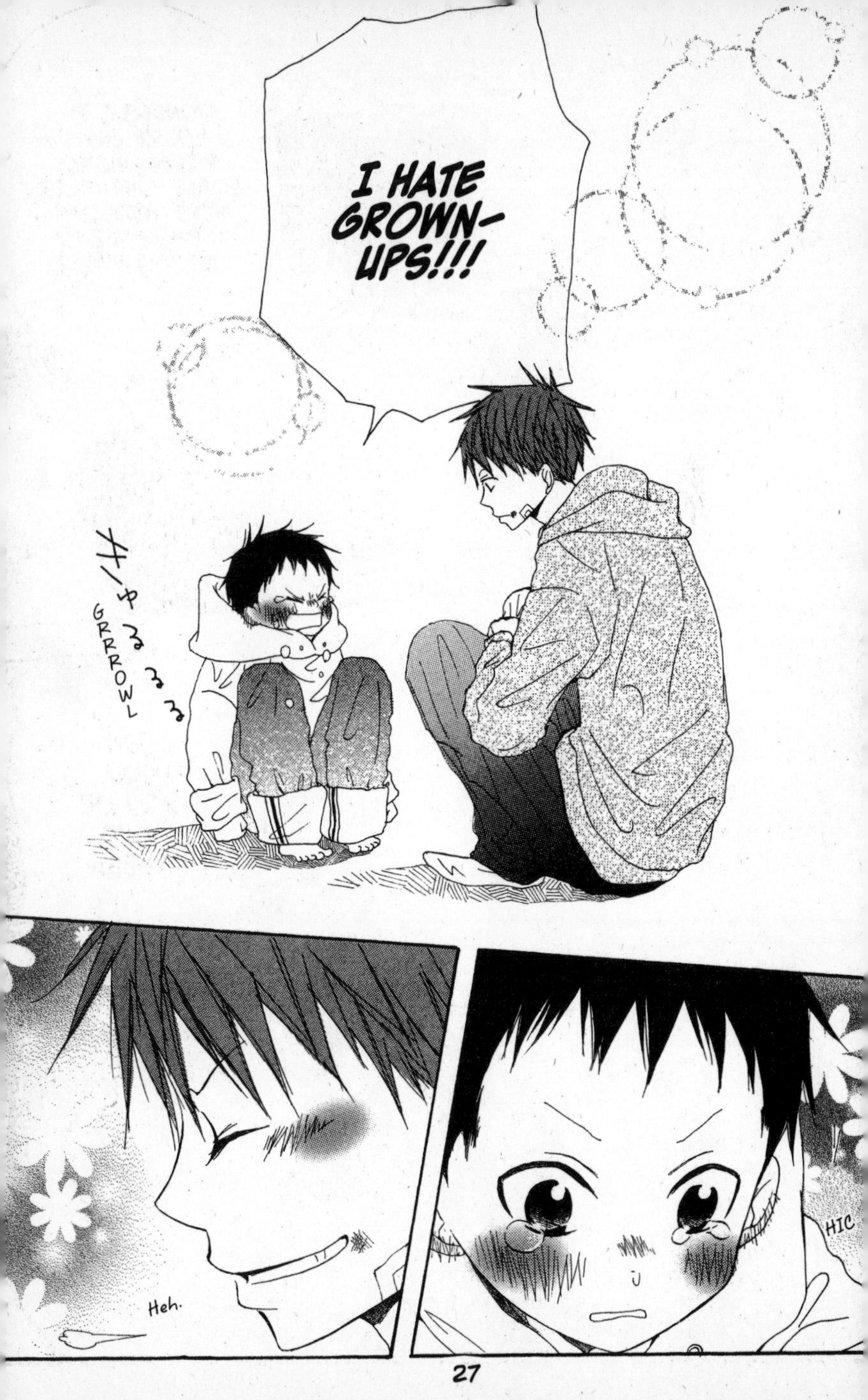
I HATE GROWN-UPS!!!
GRRROWL
HIC
Heh.

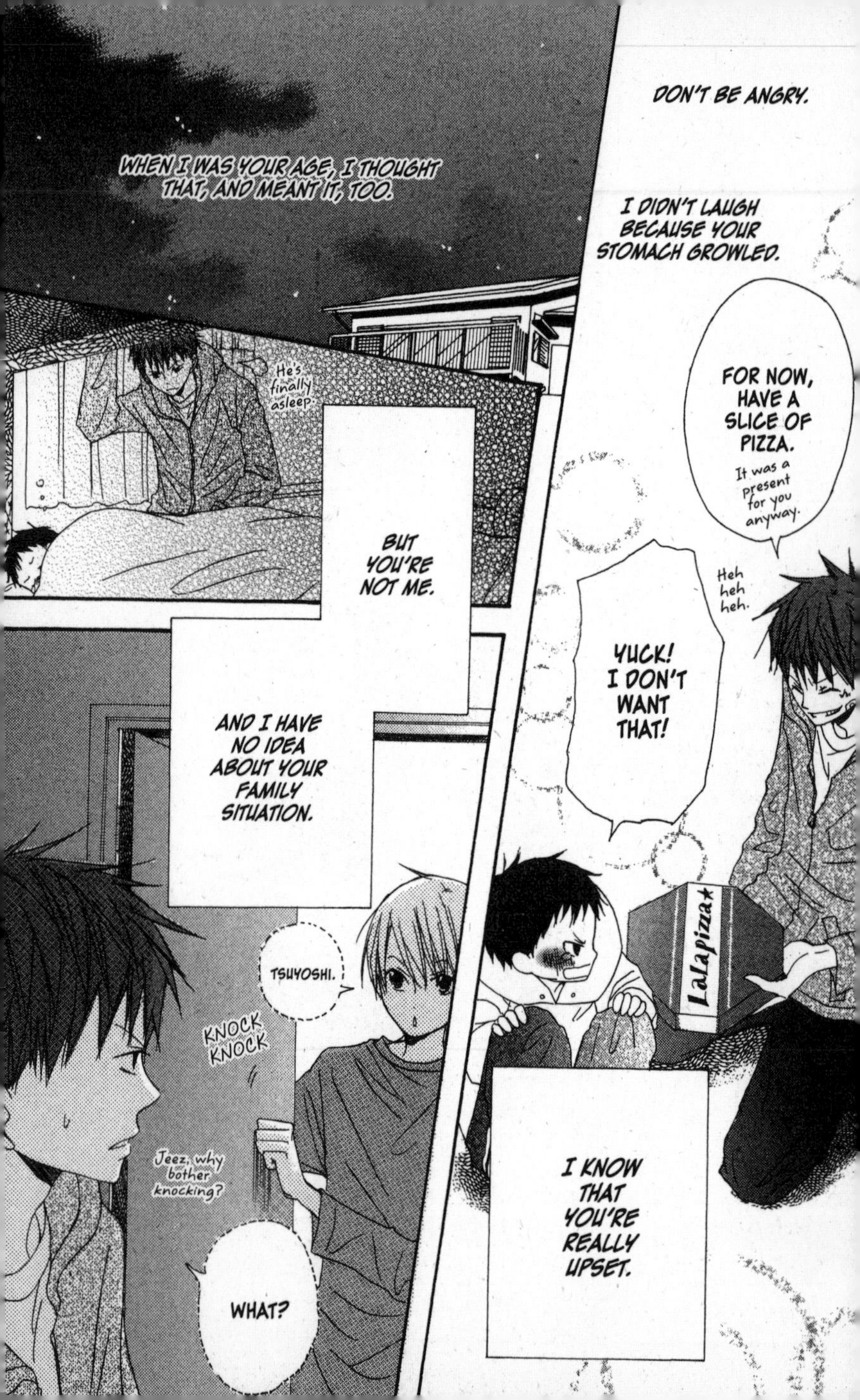

DON'T BE ANGRY.
I DIDN'T LAUGH BECAUSE YOUR STOMACH GROWLED.
FOR NOW, HAVE A SLICE OF PIZZA.
It was a present for you anyway.
Heh heh heh.
YUCK! I DON'T WANT THAT!
LaLapizza★
I KNOW THAT YOU'RE REALLY UPSET.
WHEN I WAS YOUR AGE, I THOUGHT THAT, AND MEANT IT, TOO.
He's finally asleep.
BUT YOU'RE NOT ME.
AND I HAVE NO IDEA ABOUT YOUR FAMILY SITUATION.
TSUYOSHI.
KNOCK KNOCK
Jeez, why bother knocking?
WHAT?

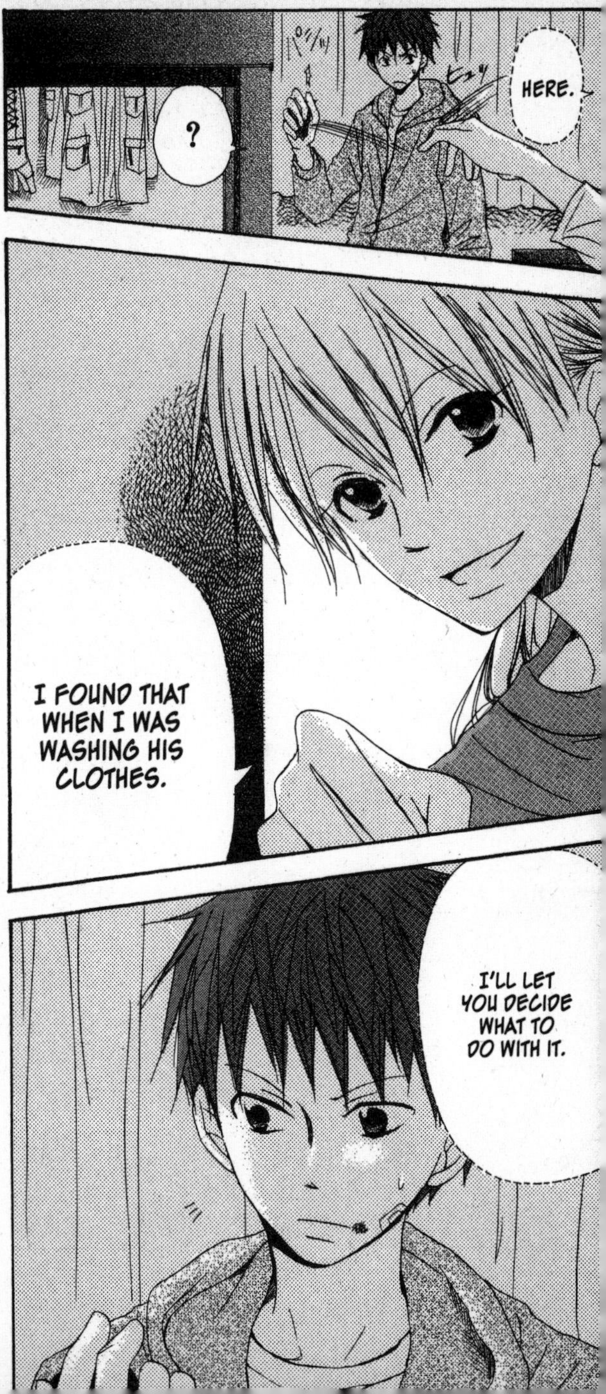
HERE.
?
I FOUND THAT WHEN I WAS WASHING HIS CLOTHES.
I'LL LET YOU DECIDE WHAT TO DO WITH IT.

1
2
3
4
5
6...

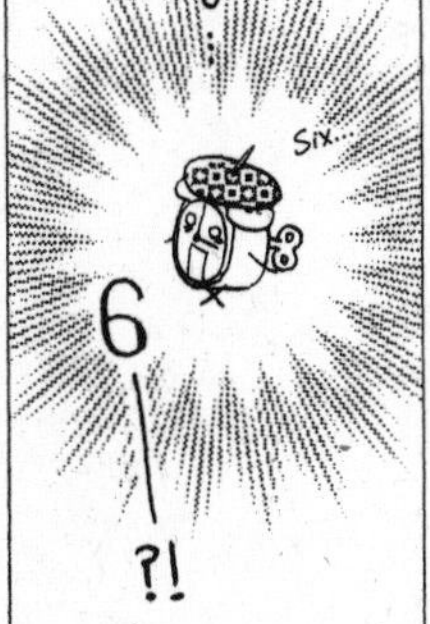
Six...
6
?!

Yes. This is volume six. If you turn it upside down, it's volume nine. It's incredible. I was working on the book and my sister was like, "Which volume's coming out?" and I was like, "Volume six." My sister applauded me, saying, "Wow, that's amazing." So domestic. We're a heartwarming family. Heh heh.

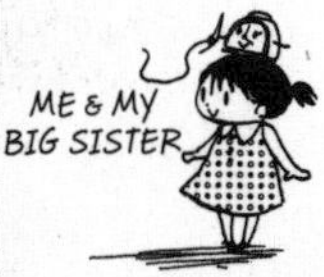
ME & MY BIG SISTER

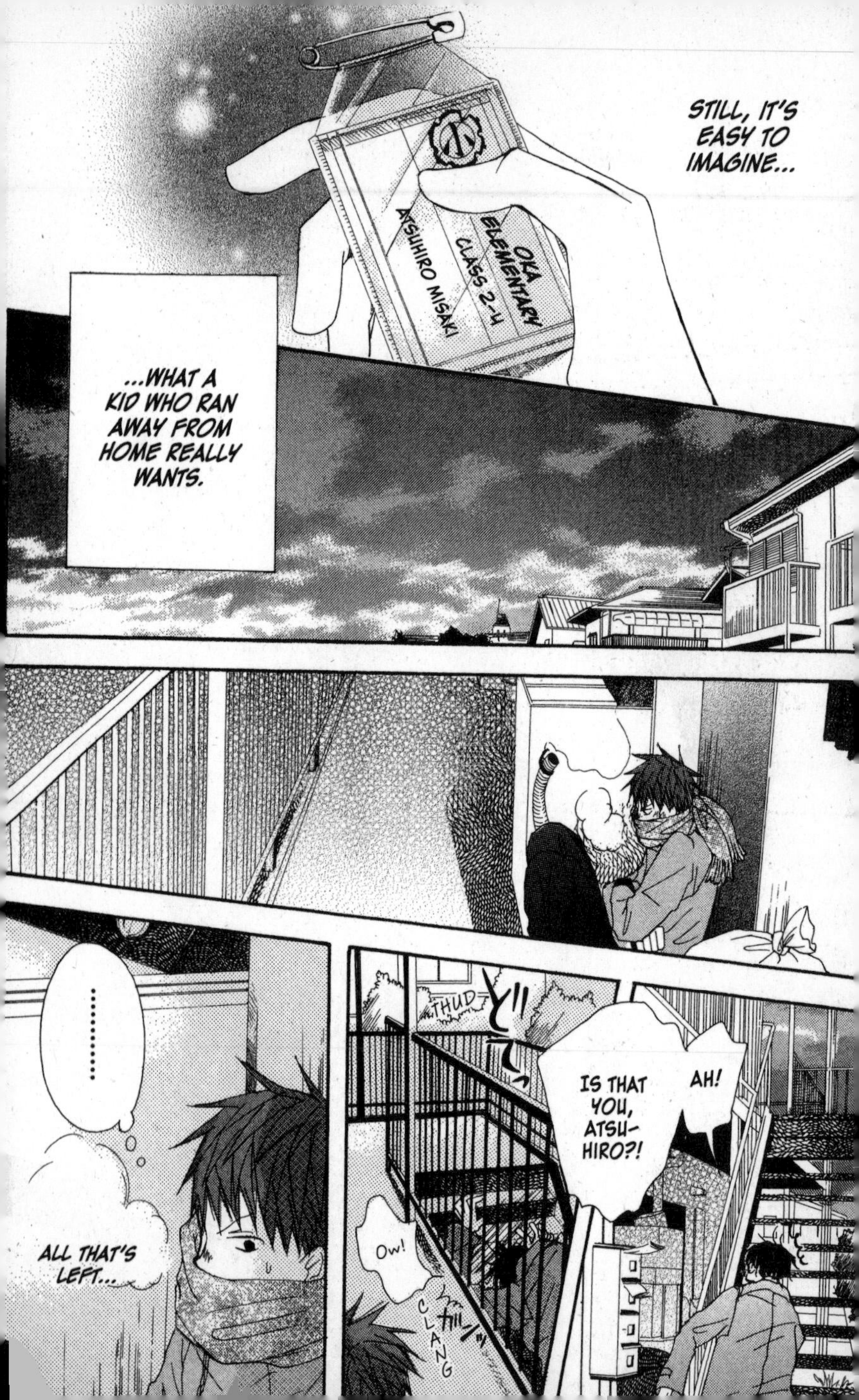
STILL, IT'S EASY TO IMAGINE...
OKA ELEMENTARY
CLASS 2-4
ATSUHIRO MISAKI
...WHAT A KID WHO RAN AWAY FROM HOME REALLY WANTS.
AH!
IS THAT YOU, ATSU-HIRO?!
THUD
Ow!
CLANG
......
ALL THAT'S LEFT...

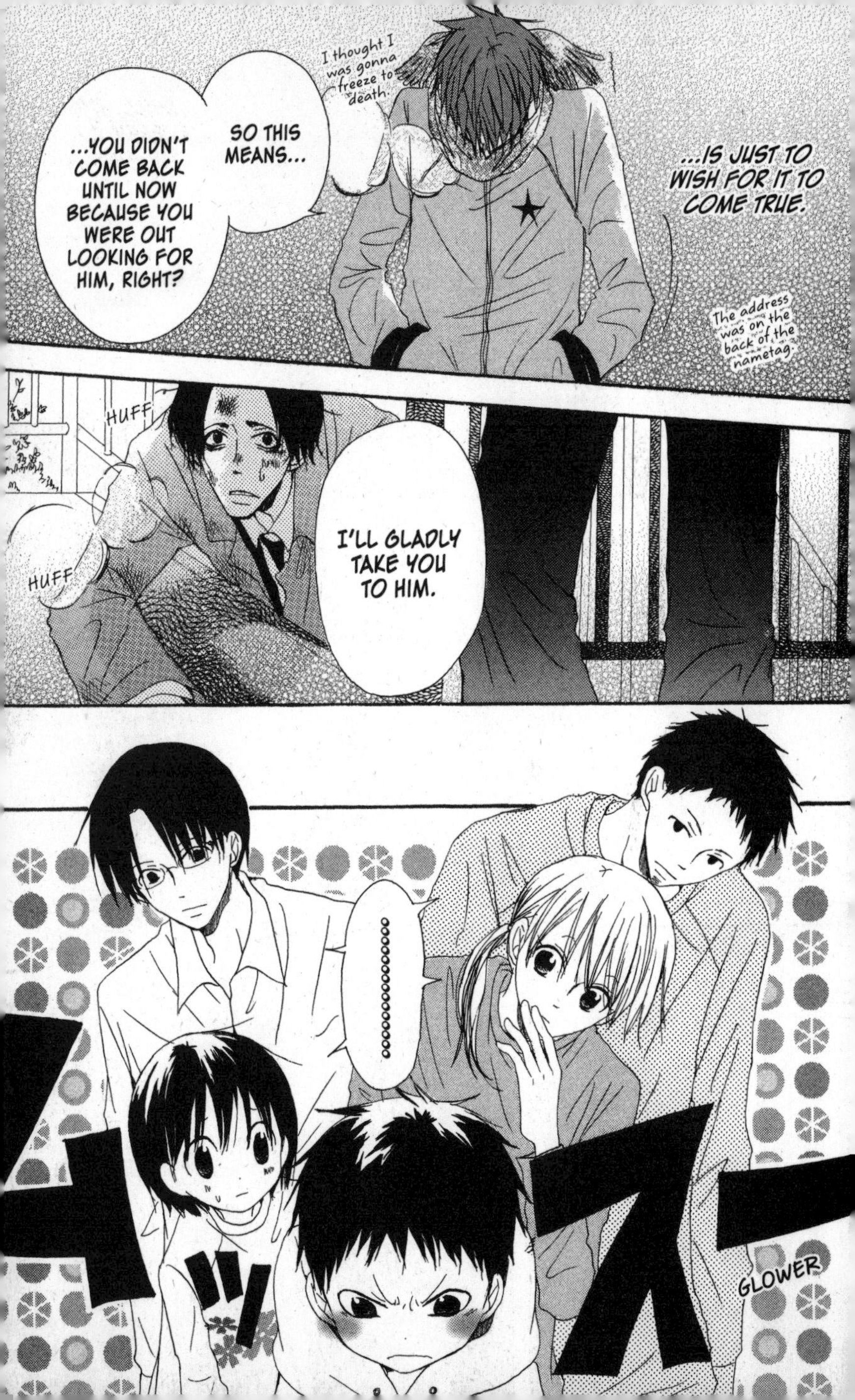
...IS JUST TO WISH FOR IT TO COME TRUE.
The address was on the back of the nametag.
I thought I was gonna freeze to death.
SO THIS MEANS...
...YOU DIDN'T COME BACK UNTIL NOW BECAUSE YOU WERE OUT LOOKING FOR HIM, RIGHT?
I'LL GLADLY TAKE YOU TO HIM.
HUFF
HUFF
....
GLOWER

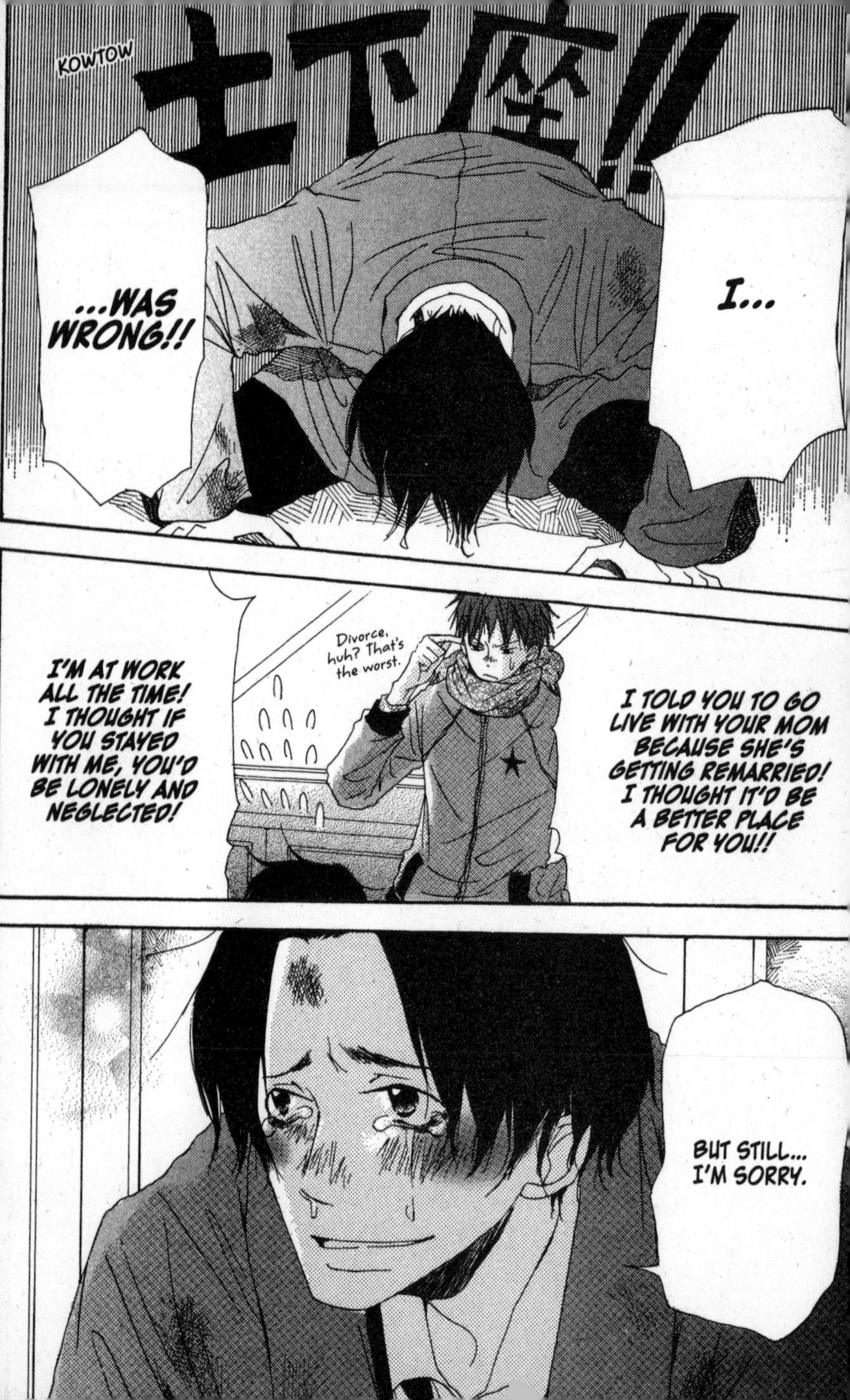
KOWTOW
土下座!!
I...
...WAS WRONG!!
I TOLD YOU TO GO LIVE WITH YOUR MOM BECAUSE SHE'S GETTING REMARRIED! I THOUGHT IT'D BE A BETTER PLACE FOR YOU!!
Divorce, huh? That's the worst.
I'M AT WORK ALL THE TIME! I THOUGHT IF YOU STAYED WITH ME, YOU'D BE LONELY AND NEGLECTED!
BUT STILL... I'M SORRY.

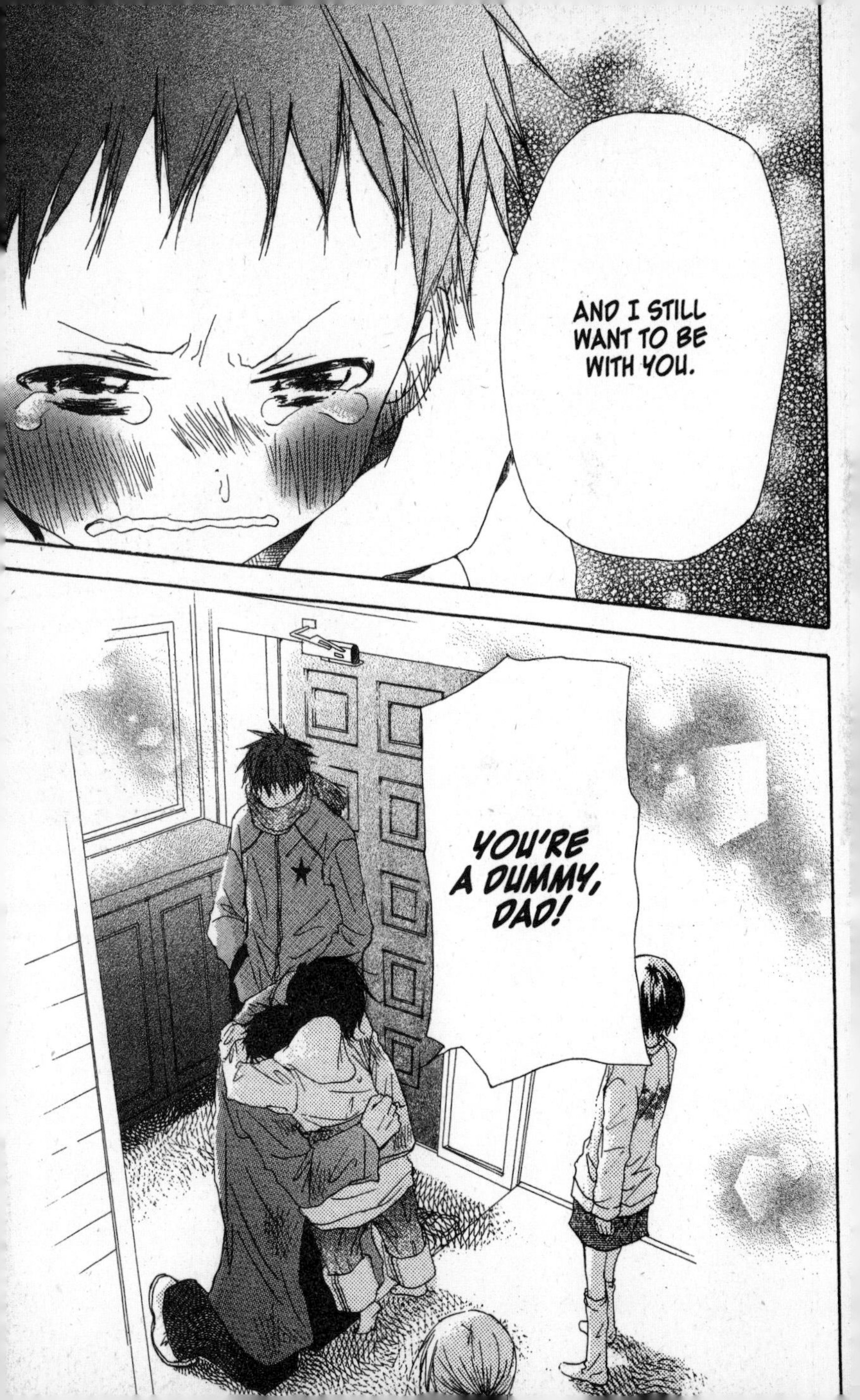
AND I STILL WANT TO BE WITH YOU.
YOU'RE A DUMMY, DAD!

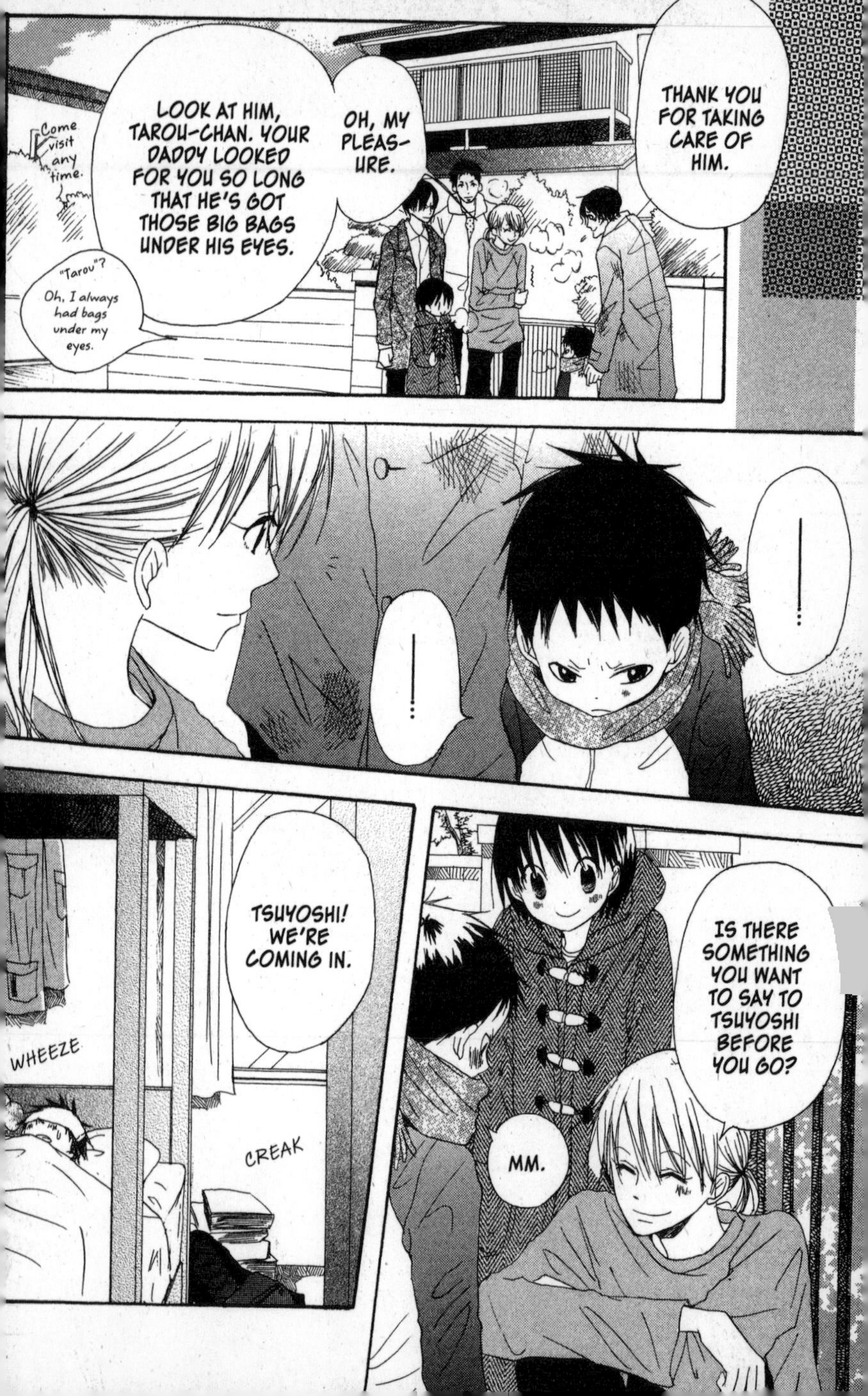
THANK YOU FOR TAKING CARE OF HIM.
OH, MY PLEAS-URE.
LOOK AT HIM, TAROU-CHAN. YOUR DADDY LOOKED FOR YOU SO LONG THAT HE'S GOT THOSE BIG BAGS UNDER HIS EYES.
Come visit any time.
"Tarou"? Oh, I always had bags under my eyes.
......
......
IS THERE SOMETHING YOU WANT TO SAY TO TSUYOSHI BEFORE YOU GO?
MM.
TSUYOSHI! WE'RE COMING IN.
CREAK
WHEEZE

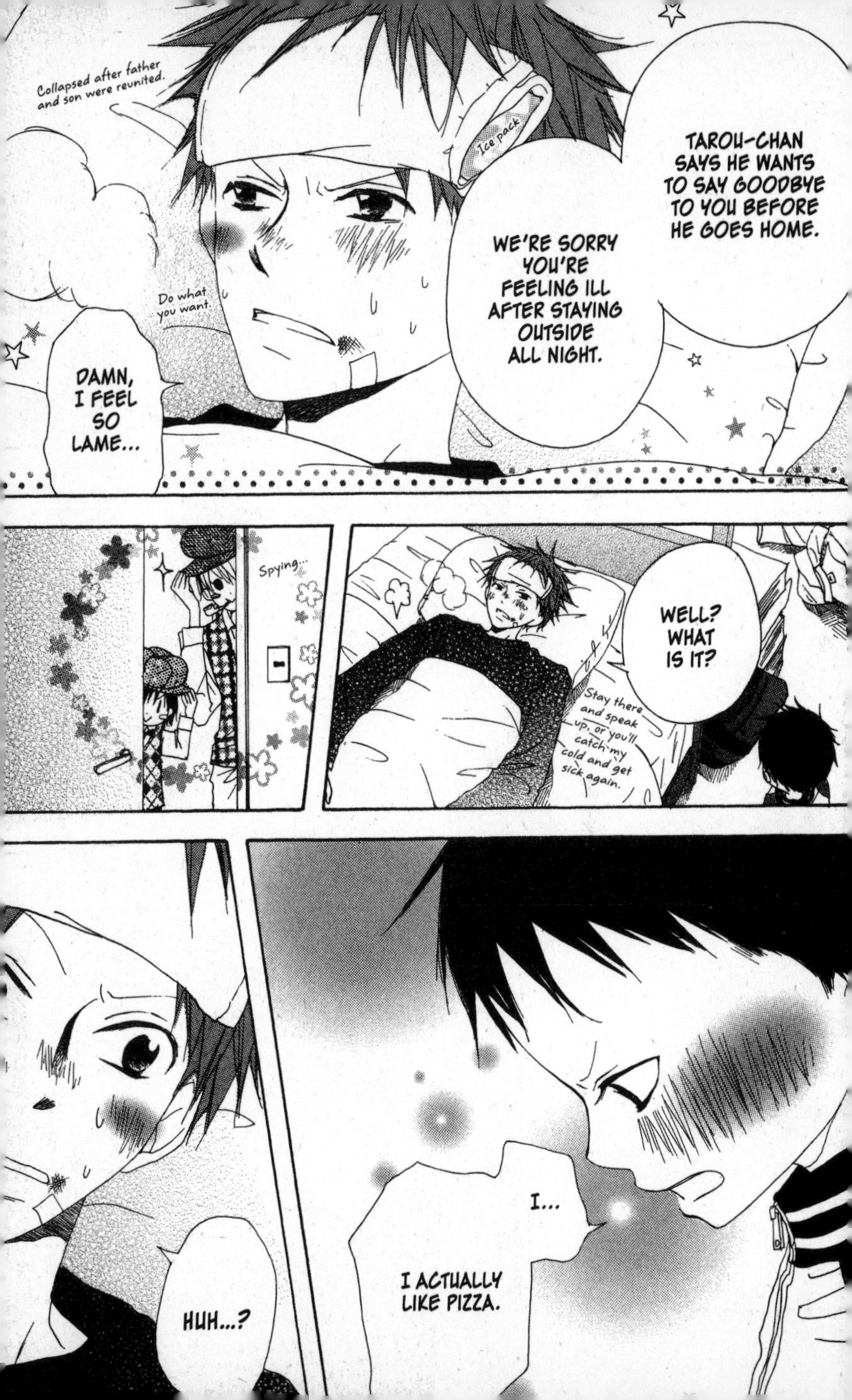
TAROU-CHAN SAYS HE WANTS TO SAY GOODBYE TO YOU BEFORE HE GOES HOME.
WE'RE SORRY YOU'RE FEELING ILL AFTER STAYING OUTSIDE ALL NIGHT.
Ice pack
Collapsed after father and son were reunited.
Do what you want.
DAMN, I FEEL SO LAME...
WELL? WHAT IS IT?
Stay there and speak up, or you'll catch my cold and get sick again.
Spying...
I...
I ACTUALLY LIKE PIZZA.
HUH...?

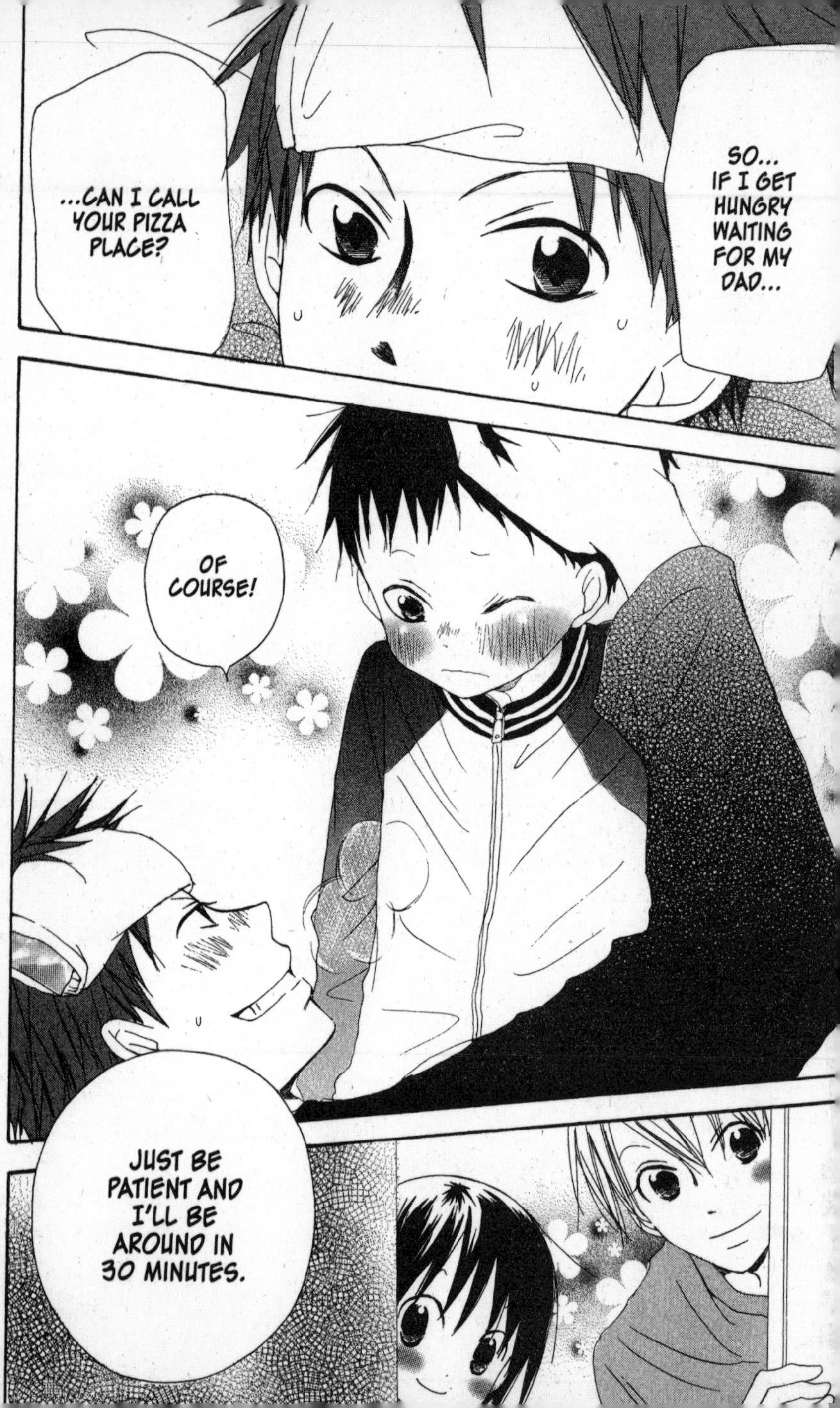
SO... IF I GET HUNGRY WAITING FOR MY DAD...
...CAN I CALL YOUR PIZZA PLACE?
OF COURSE!
JUST BE PATIENT AND I'LL BE AROUND IN 30 MINUTES.

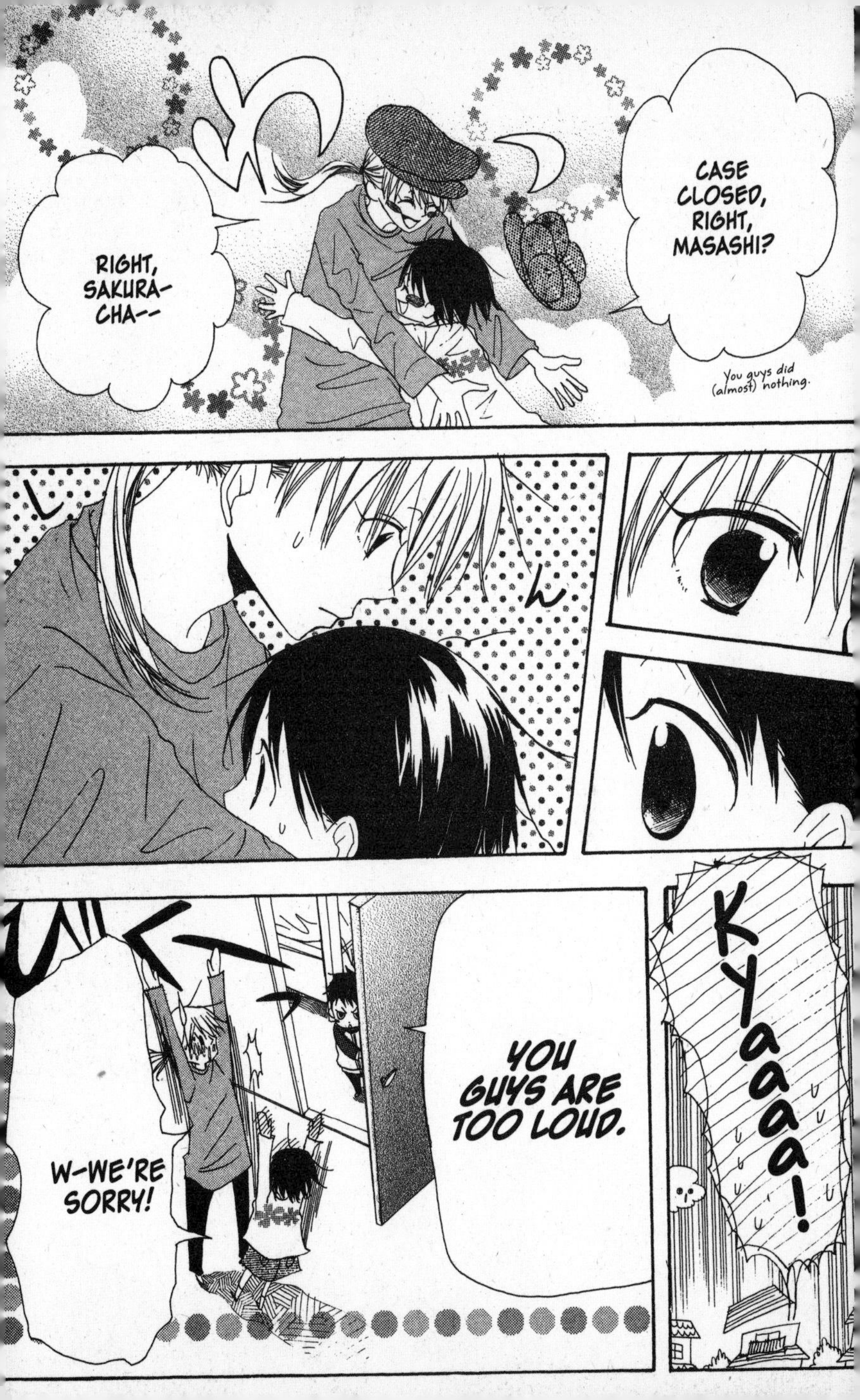
CASE CLOSED, RIGHT, MASASHI?
RIGHT, SAKURA-CHA--
You guys did (almost) nothing.
Kyaaaaa!
YOU GUYS ARE TOO LOUD.
W-WE'RE SORRY!

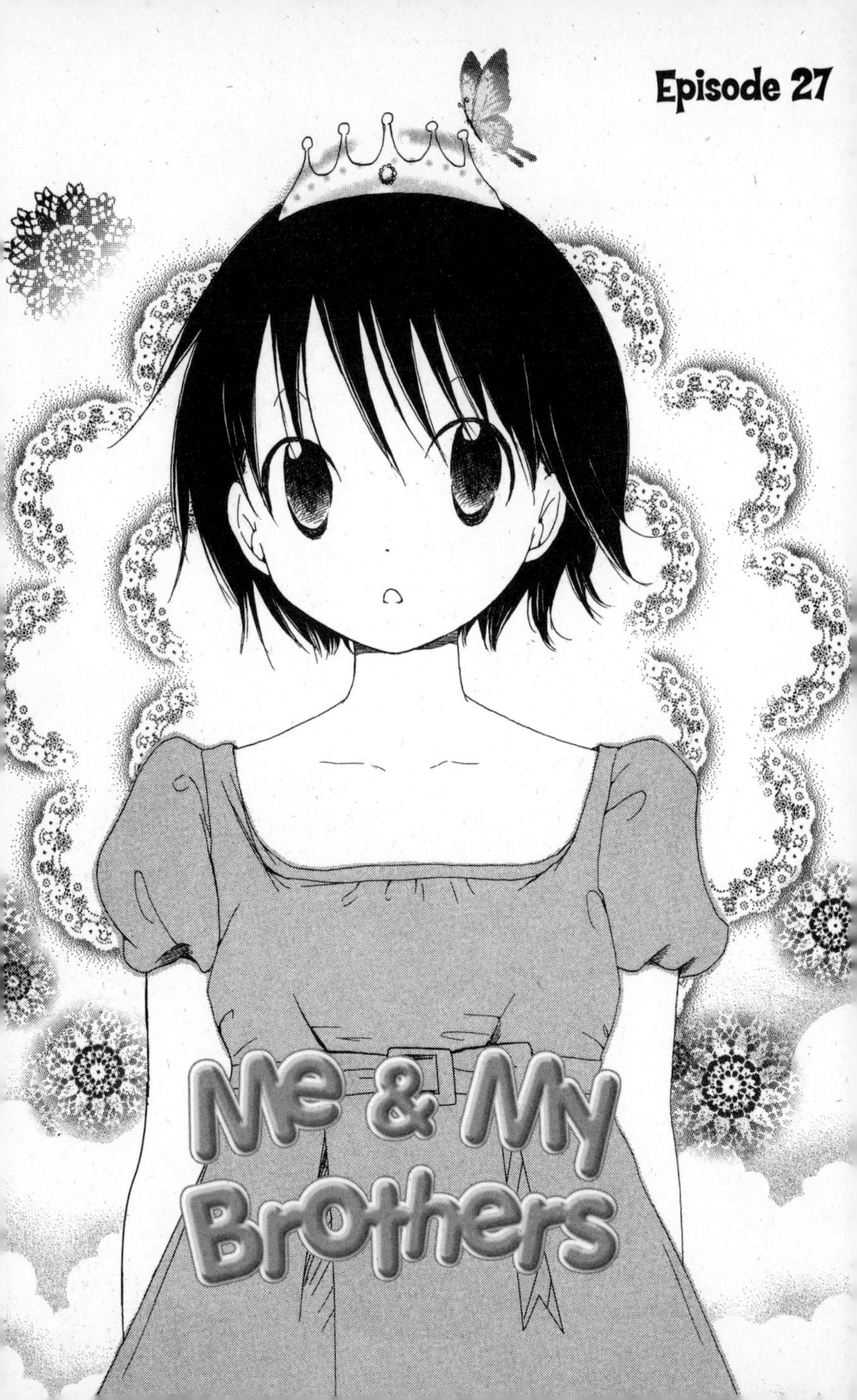
Episode 27
Me & My Brothers

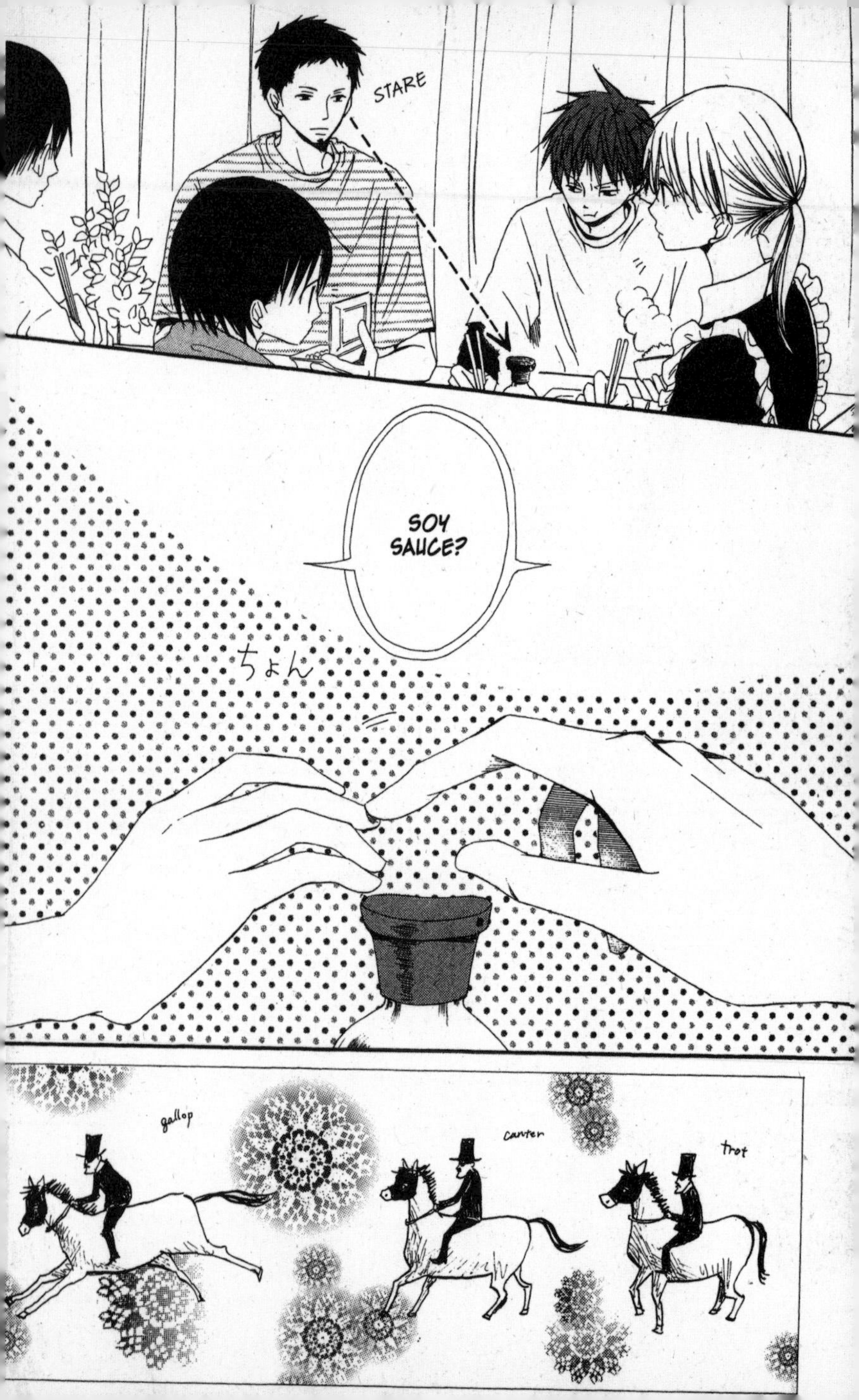
STARE
SOY SAUCE?
ちょん
trot
canter
gallop

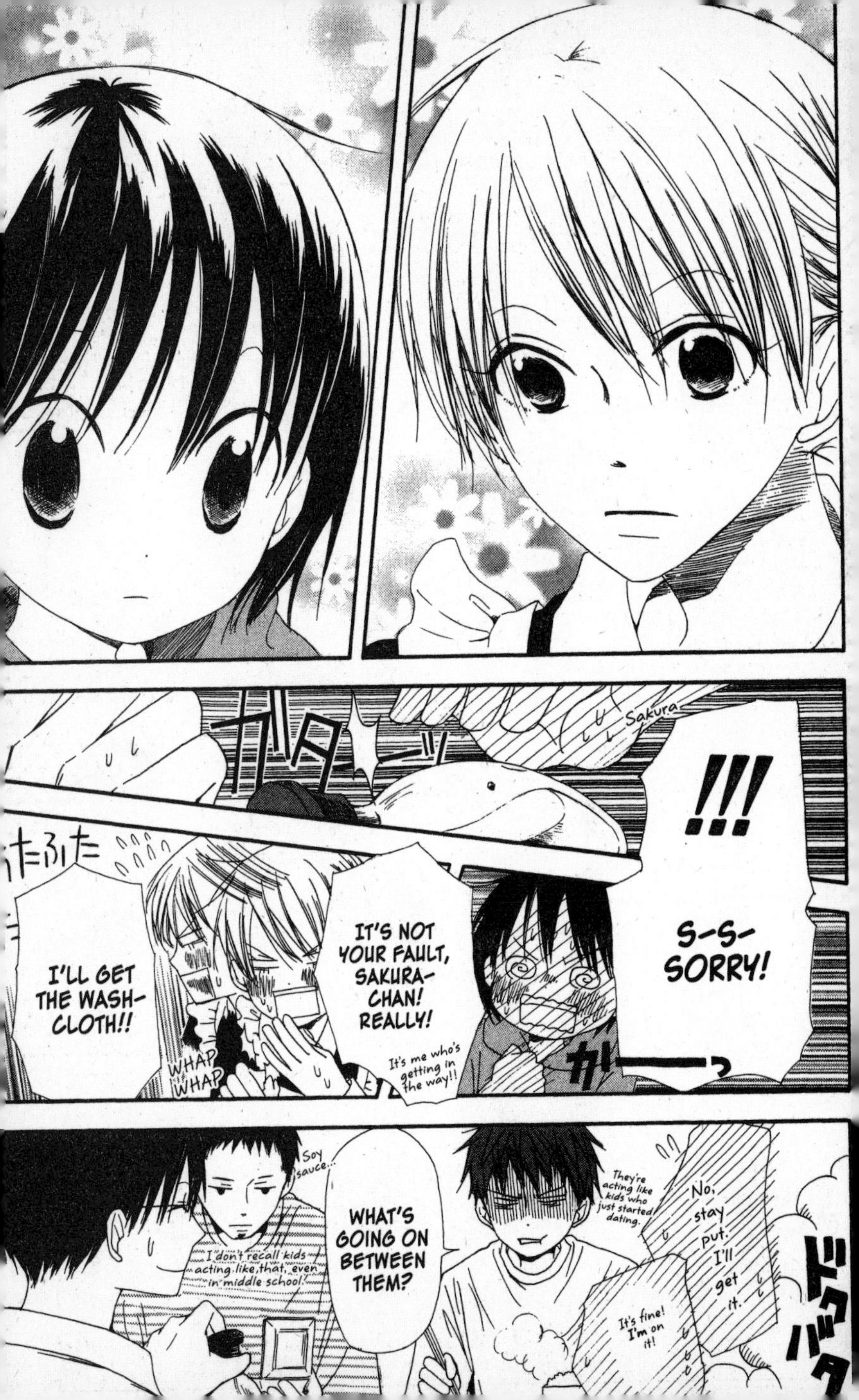
Sakura
!!!
S-S-SORRY!
IT'S NOT YOUR FAULT, SAKURA-CHAN! REALLY!
It's me who's getting in the way!!
WHAP WHAP
I'LL GET THE WASH-CLOTH!!
ドタバタ
No, stay put. I'll get it.
It's fine! I'm on it!
They're acting like kids who just started dating.
WHAT'S GOING ON BETWEEN THEM?
Soy sauce...
I don't recall kids acting like that, even in middle school.

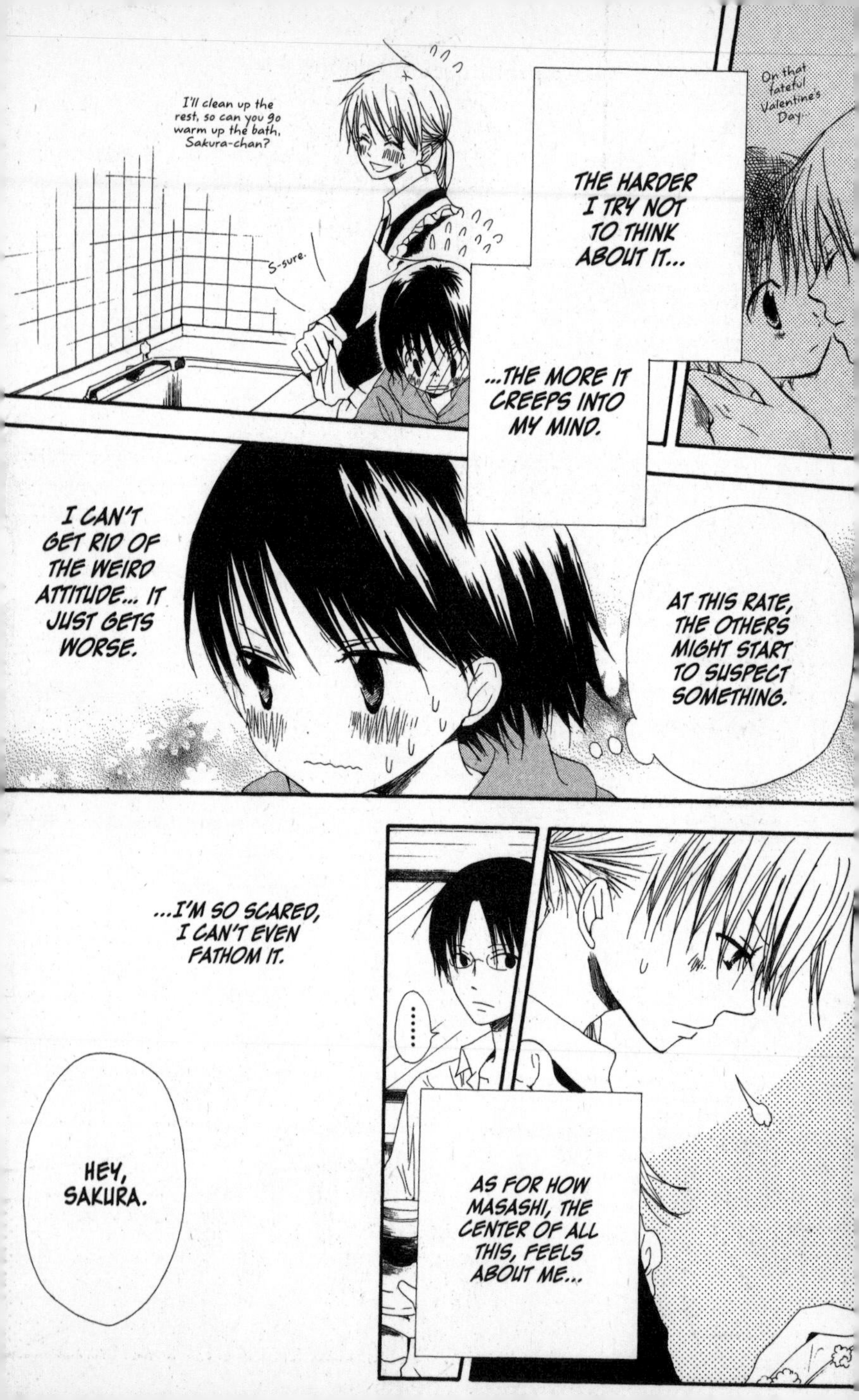
On that fateful Valentine's Day
THE HARDER I TRY NOT TO THINK ABOUT IT...
...THE MORE IT CREEPS INTO MY MIND.
I'll clean up the rest, so can you go warm up the bath, Sakura-chan?
S-sure.
AT THIS RATE, THE OTHERS MIGHT START TO SUSPECT SOMETHING.
I CAN'T GET RID OF THE WEIRD ATTITUDE... IT JUST GETS WORSE.
......
AS FOR HOW MASASHI, THE CENTER OF ALL THIS, FEELS ABOUT ME...
...I'M SO SCARED, I CAN'T EVEN FATHOM IT.
HEY, SAKURA.

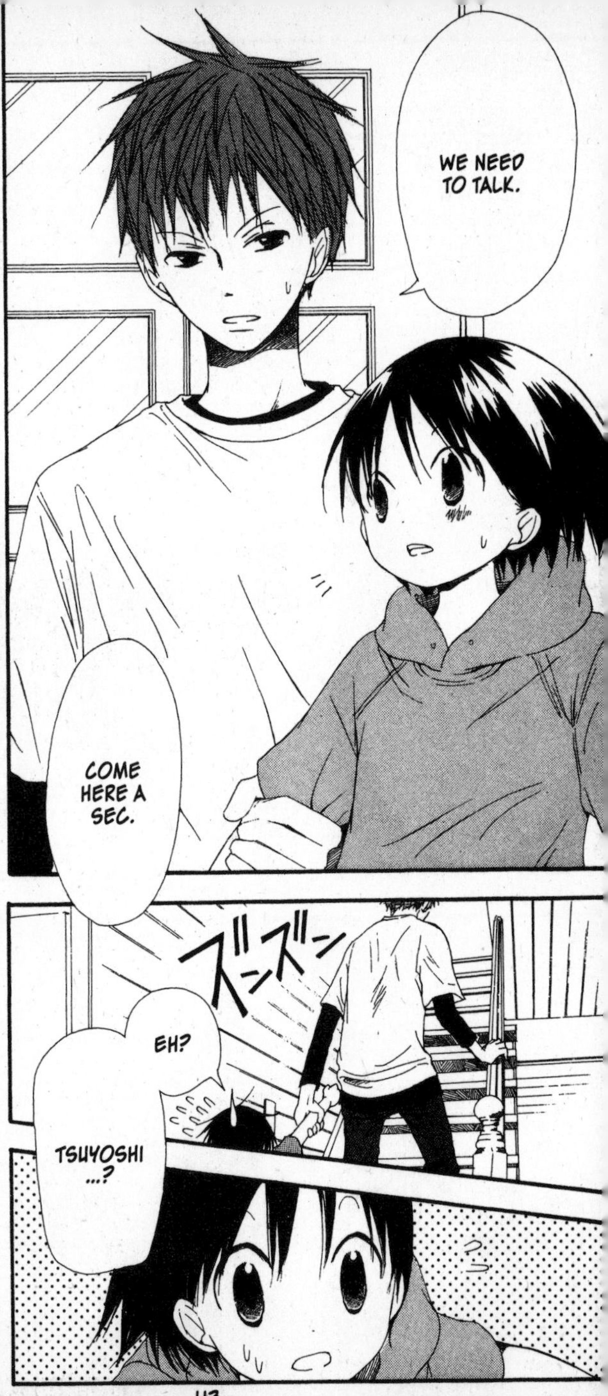
WE NEED TO TALK.
COME HERE A SEC.
ズンズン
EH?
TSUYOSHI ...?

2

They had a character contest in *Lala*. I posted the results in the bottom one-fourth space in Episode 26.

First Place: Masashi!

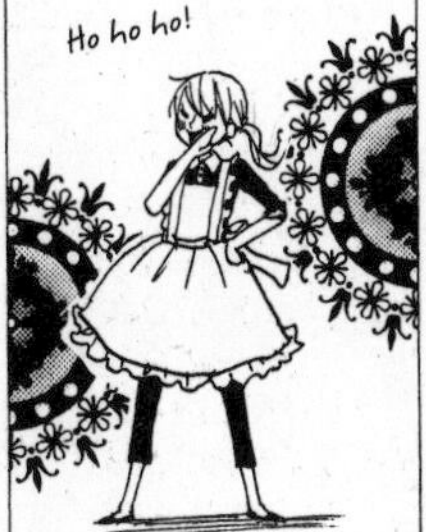
Ho ho ho!

I had been a bit worried, thinking, "I don't know about this guy. Will he be okay?" So I'm glad.

He's finally getting to an age where I can't say it anymore...

Fourth Place: Nana Kozuka-kun!

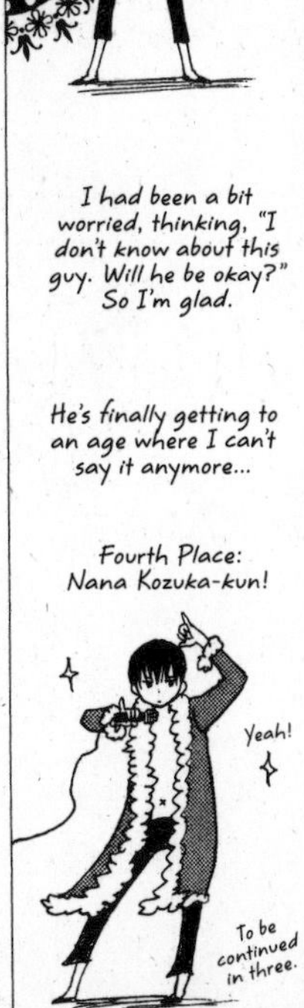
Yeah!
To be continued in three.

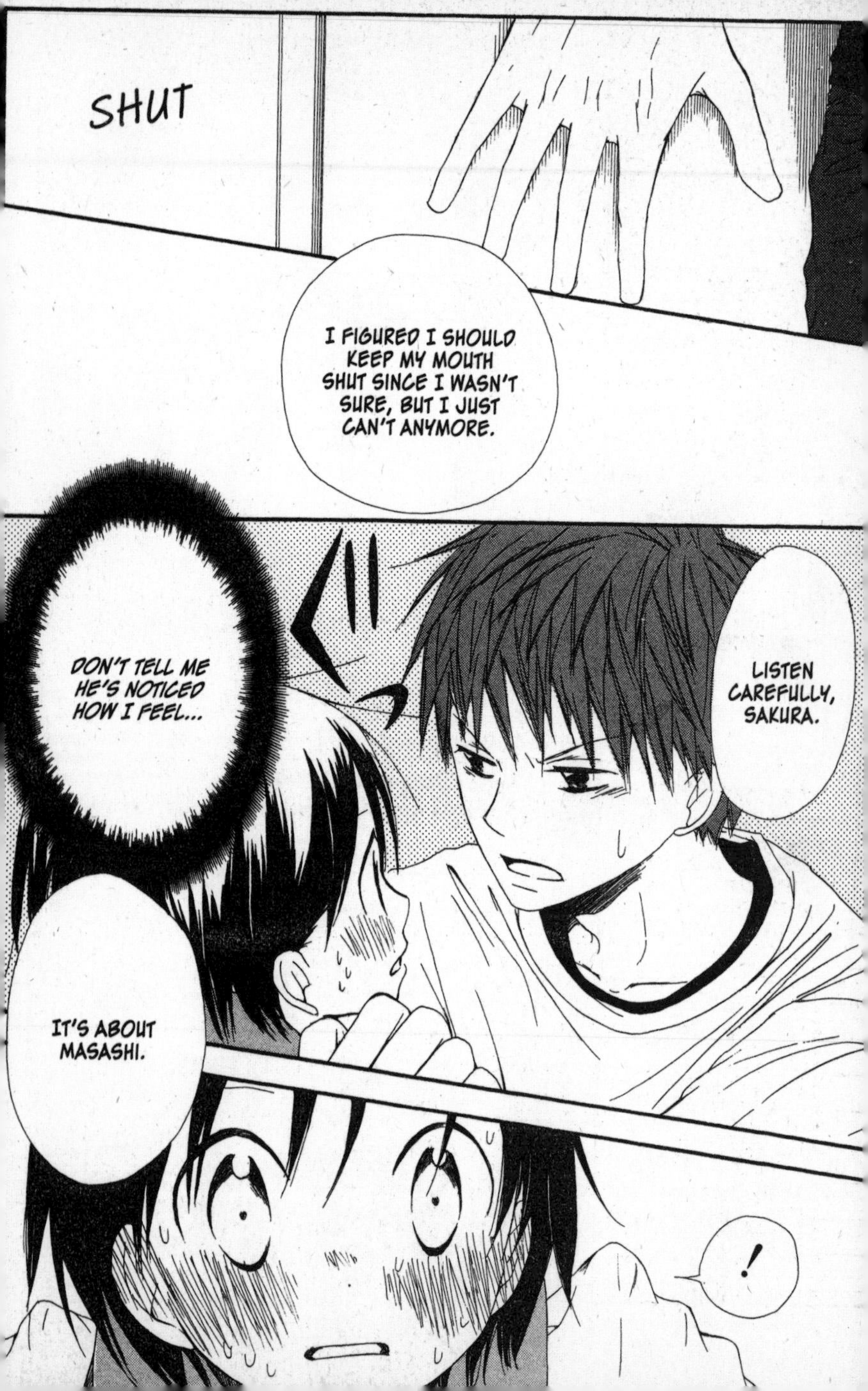
SHUT
I FIGURED I SHOULD KEEP MY MOUTH SHUT SINCE I WASN'T SURE, BUT I JUST CAN'T ANYMORE.
LISTEN CAREFULLY, SAKURA.
DON'T TELL ME HE'S NOTICED HOW I FEEL...
IT'S ABOUT MASASHI.
!

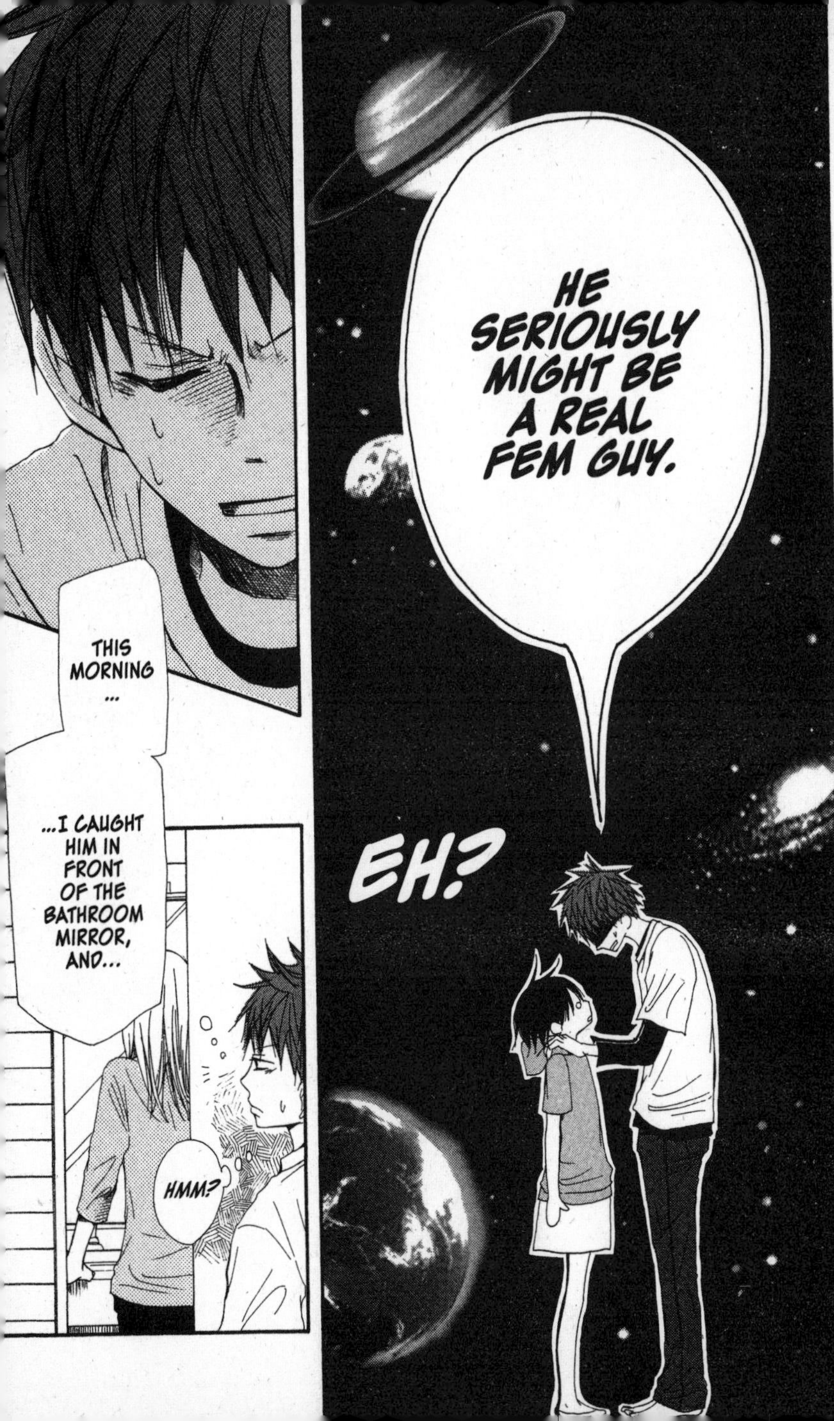
HE SERIOUSLY MIGHT BE A REAL FEM GUY.
EH?
THIS MORNING...
...I CAUGHT HIM IN FRONT OF THE BATHROOM MIRROR, AND...
HMM?

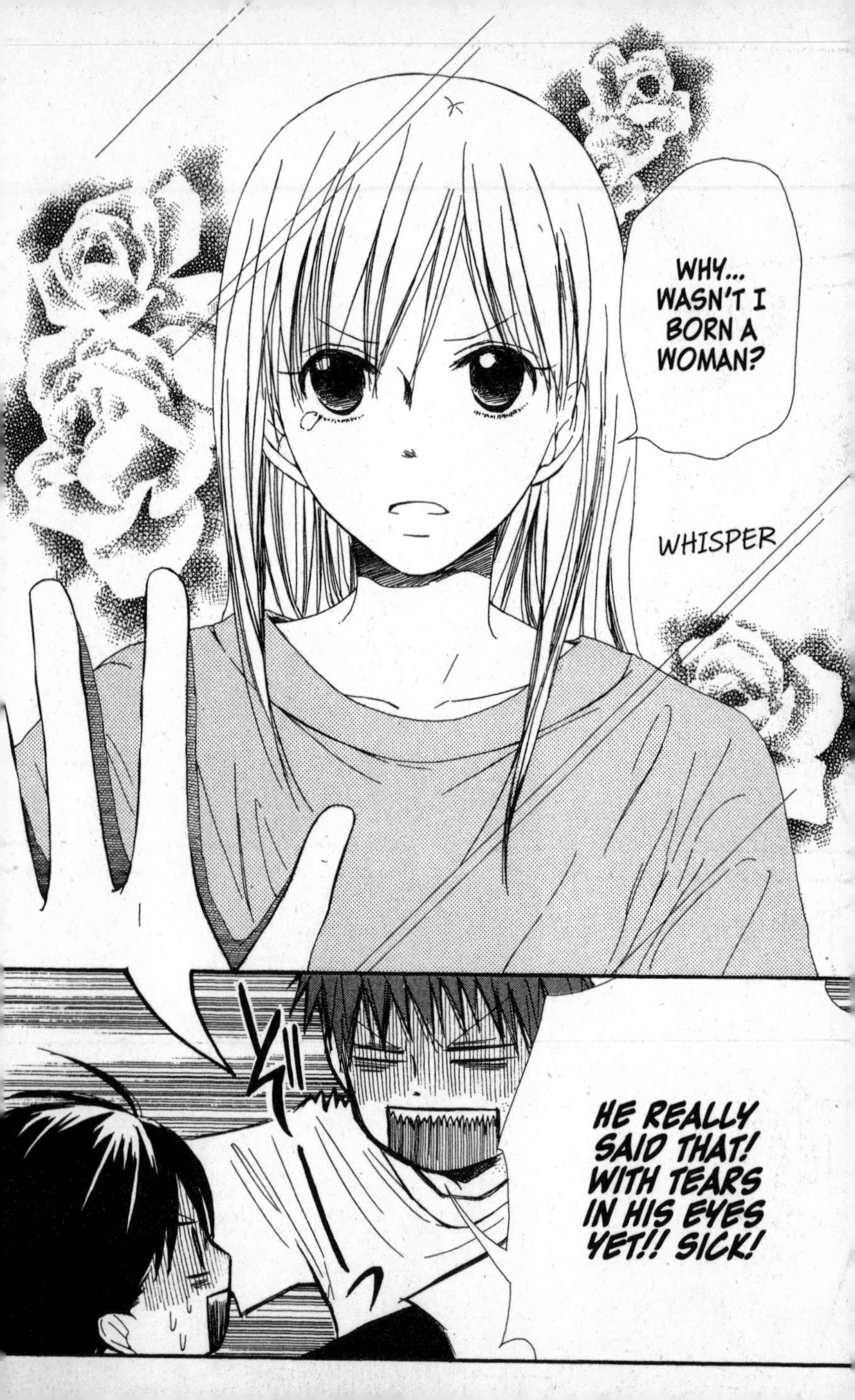
WHY... WASN'T I BORN A WOMAN?
WHISPER
HE REALLY SAID THAT! WITH TEARS IN HIS EYES YET!! SICK!

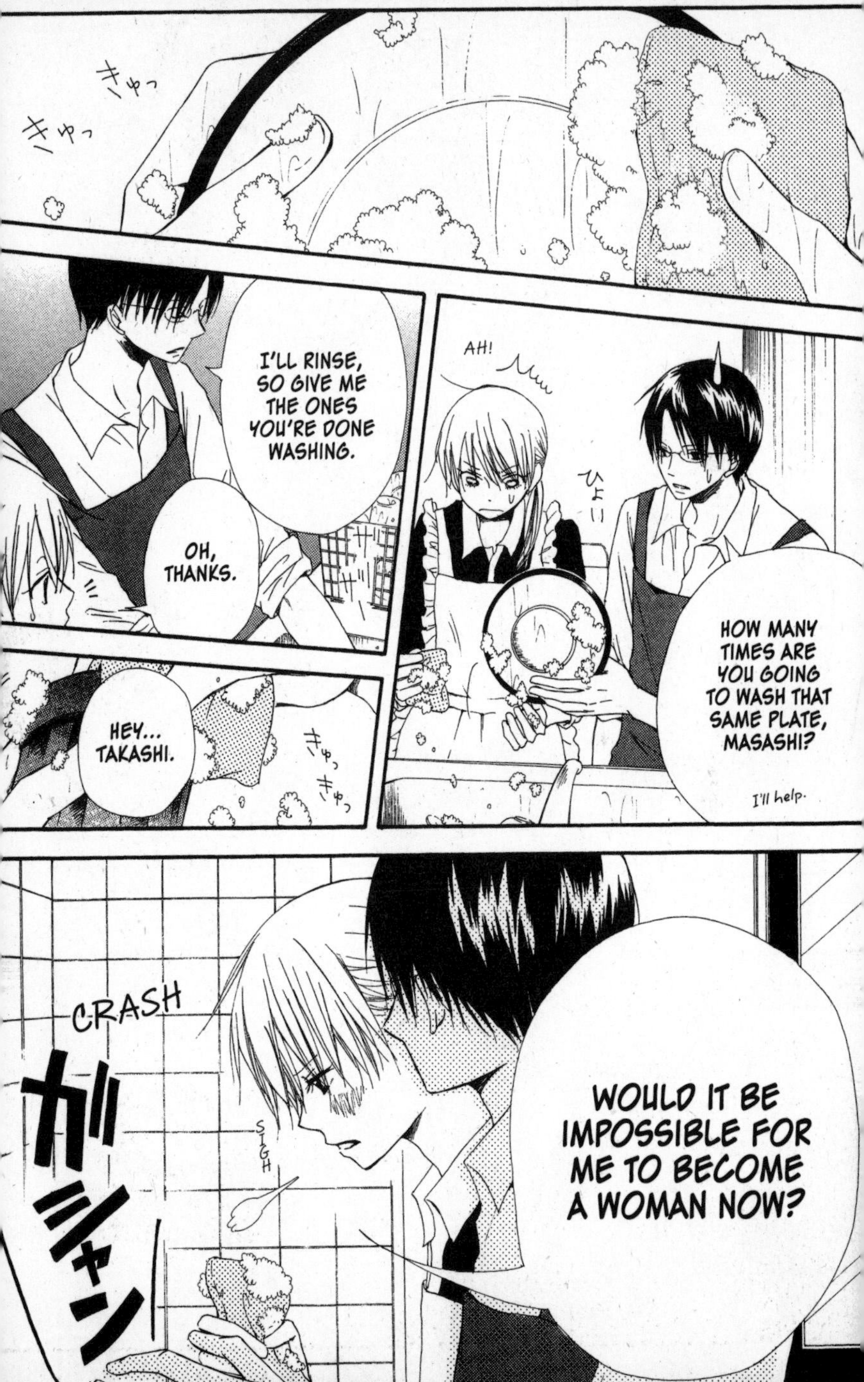
きゅっ
きゅっ
AH!
ひょい
HOW MANY TIMES ARE YOU GOING TO WASH THAT SAME PLATE, MASASHI?
I'll help.
I'LL RINSE, SO GIVE ME THE ONES YOU'RE DONE WASHING.
OH, THANKS.
HEY... TAKASHI.
きゅっ きゅっ
WOULD IT BE IMPOSSIBLE FOR ME TO BECOME A WOMAN NOW?
SIGH
CRASH
ガシャン

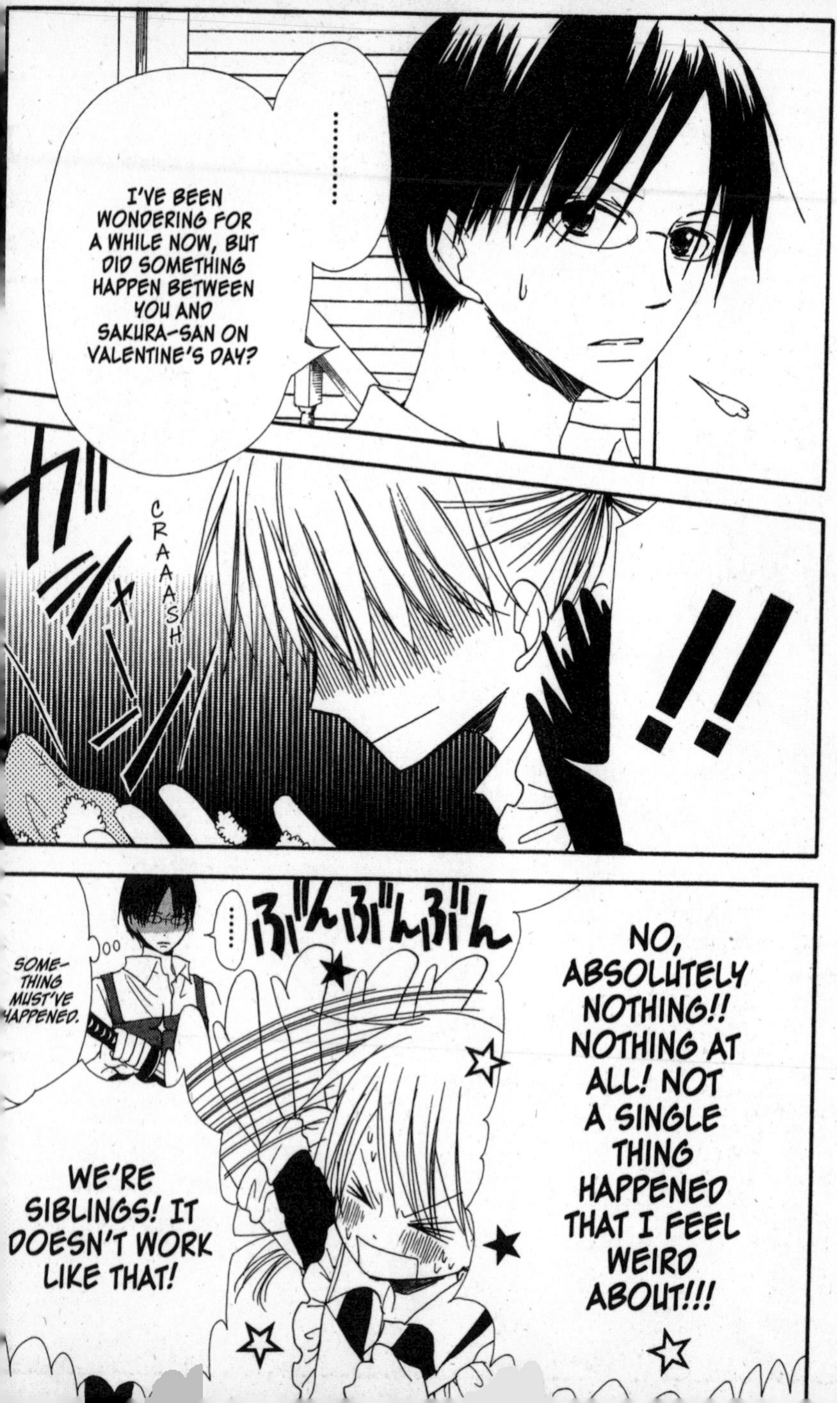
......
I'VE BEEN WONDERING FOR A WHILE NOW, BUT DID SOMETHING HAPPEN BETWEEN YOU AND SAKURA-SAN ON VALENTINE'S DAY?
ガシャー
CRAAASH
!!
NO, ABSOLUTELY NOTHING!! NOTHING AT ALL! NOT A SINGLE THING HAPPENED THAT I FEEL WEIRD ABOUT!!!
ぶんぶんぶん
WE'RE SIBLINGS! IT DOESN'T WORK LIKE THAT!
......
SOME-THING MUST'VE HAPPENED.

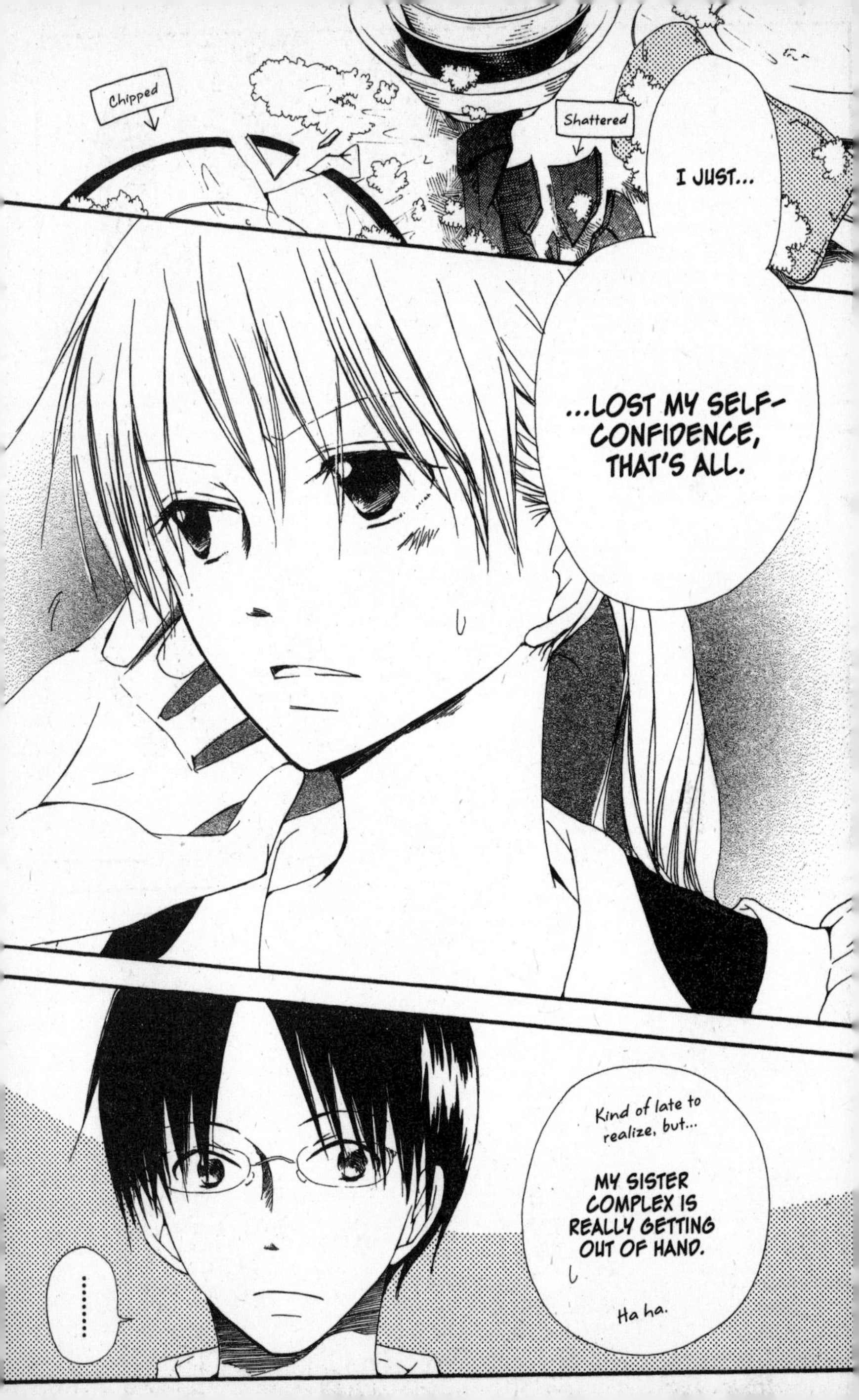
I JUST...
Shattered
Chipped
...LOST MY SELF-CONFIDENCE, THAT'S ALL.
Kind of late to realize, but...
MY SISTER COMPLEX IS REALLY GETTING OUT OF HAND.
Ha ha.
....

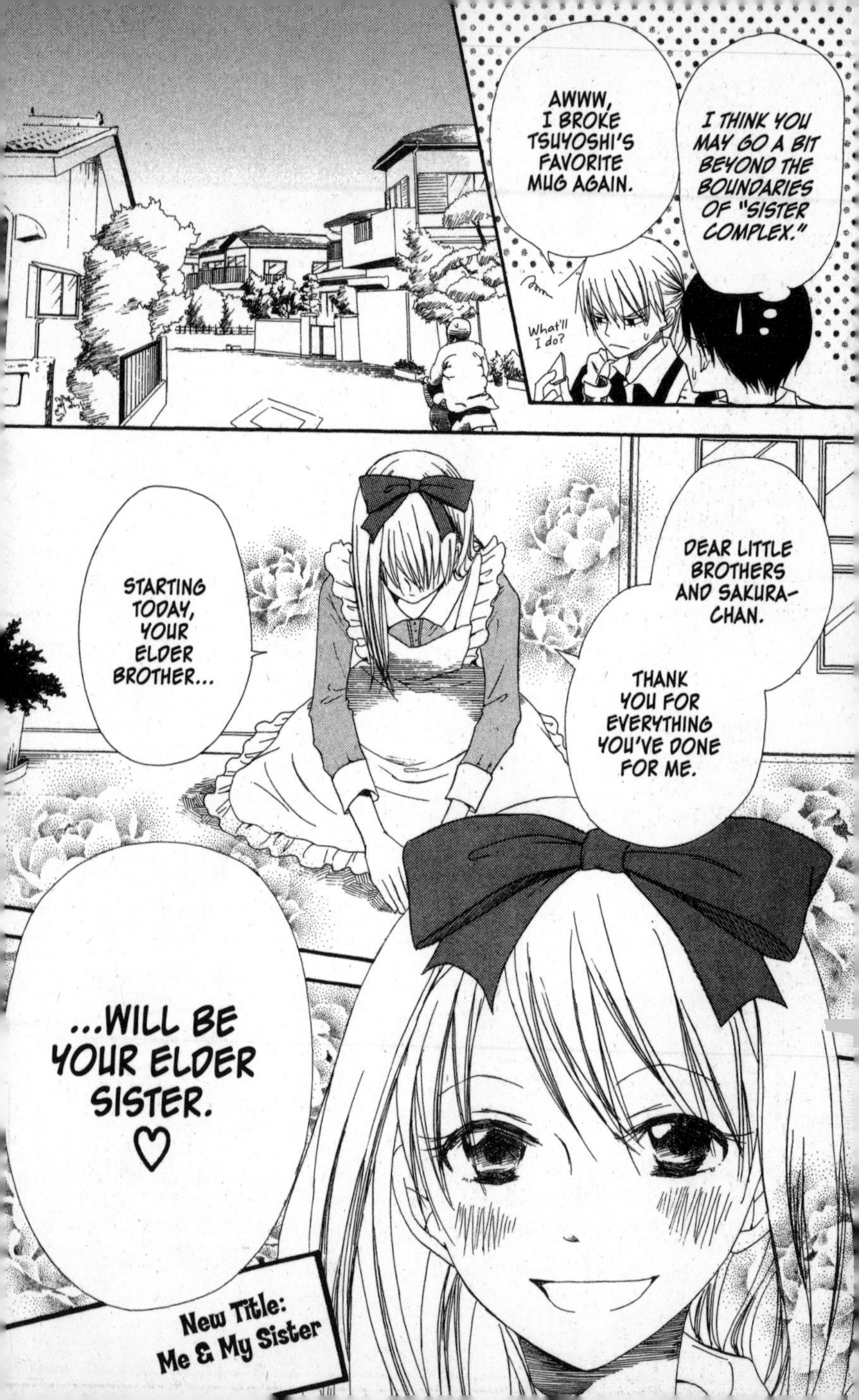
I THINK YOU MAY GO A BIT BEYOND THE BOUNDARIES OF "SISTER COMPLEX."
AWWW, I BROKE TSUYOSHI'S FAVORITE MUG AGAIN.
What'll I do?
DEAR LITTLE BROTHERS AND SAKURA-CHAN.
THANK YOU FOR EVERYTHING YOU'VE DONE FOR ME.
STARTING TODAY, YOUR ELDER BROTHER...
...WILL BE YOUR ELDER SISTER. ♡
New Title: Me & My Sister

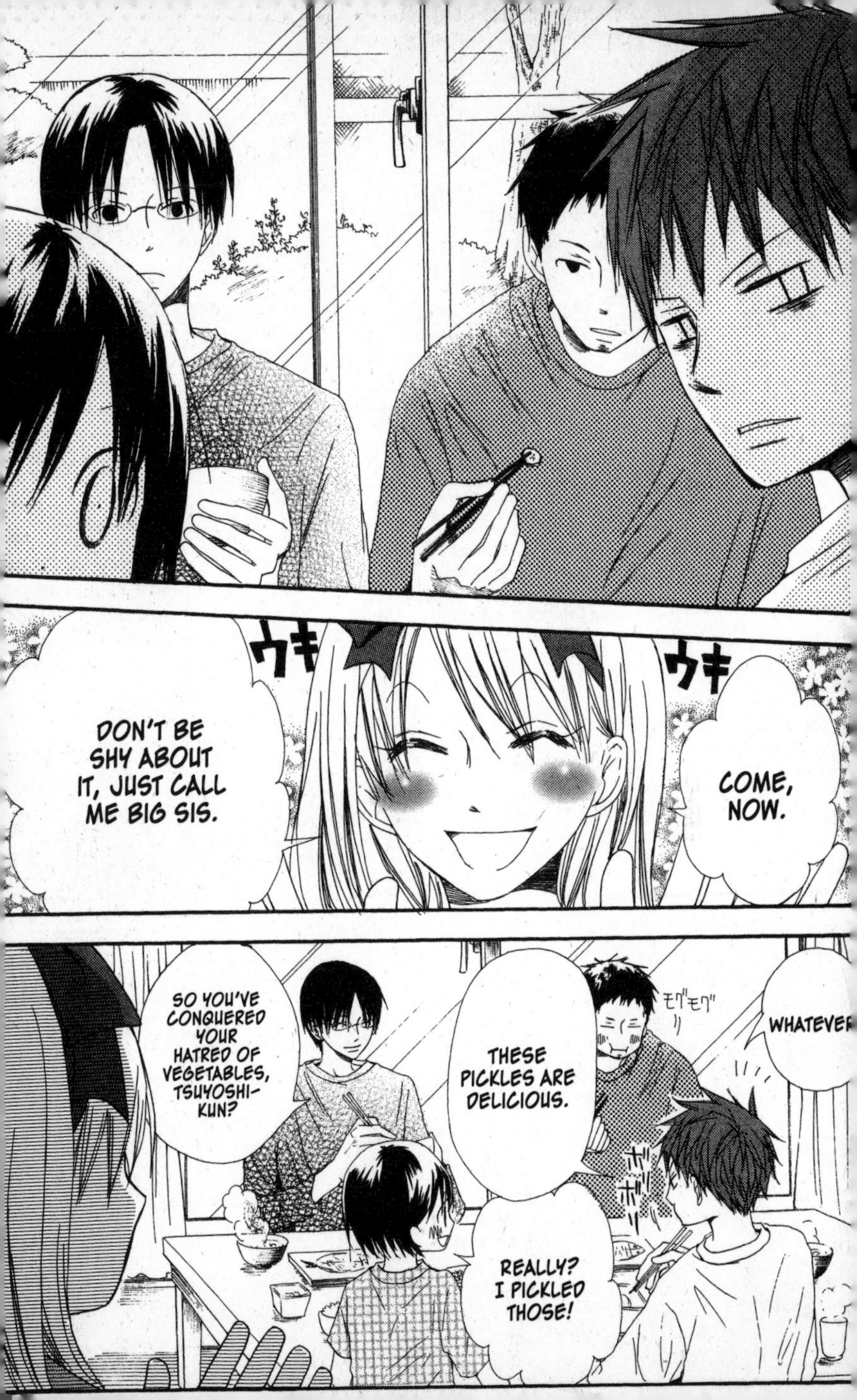
ウキ
COME, NOW.
ウキ
DON'T BE SHY ABOUT IT, JUST CALL ME BIG SIS.
WHATEVER
モグモグ
THESE PICKLES ARE DELICIOUS.
SO YOU'VE CONQUERED YOUR HATRED OF VEGETABLES, TSUYOSHI-KUN?
ボリボリ
REALLY? I PICKLED THOSE!

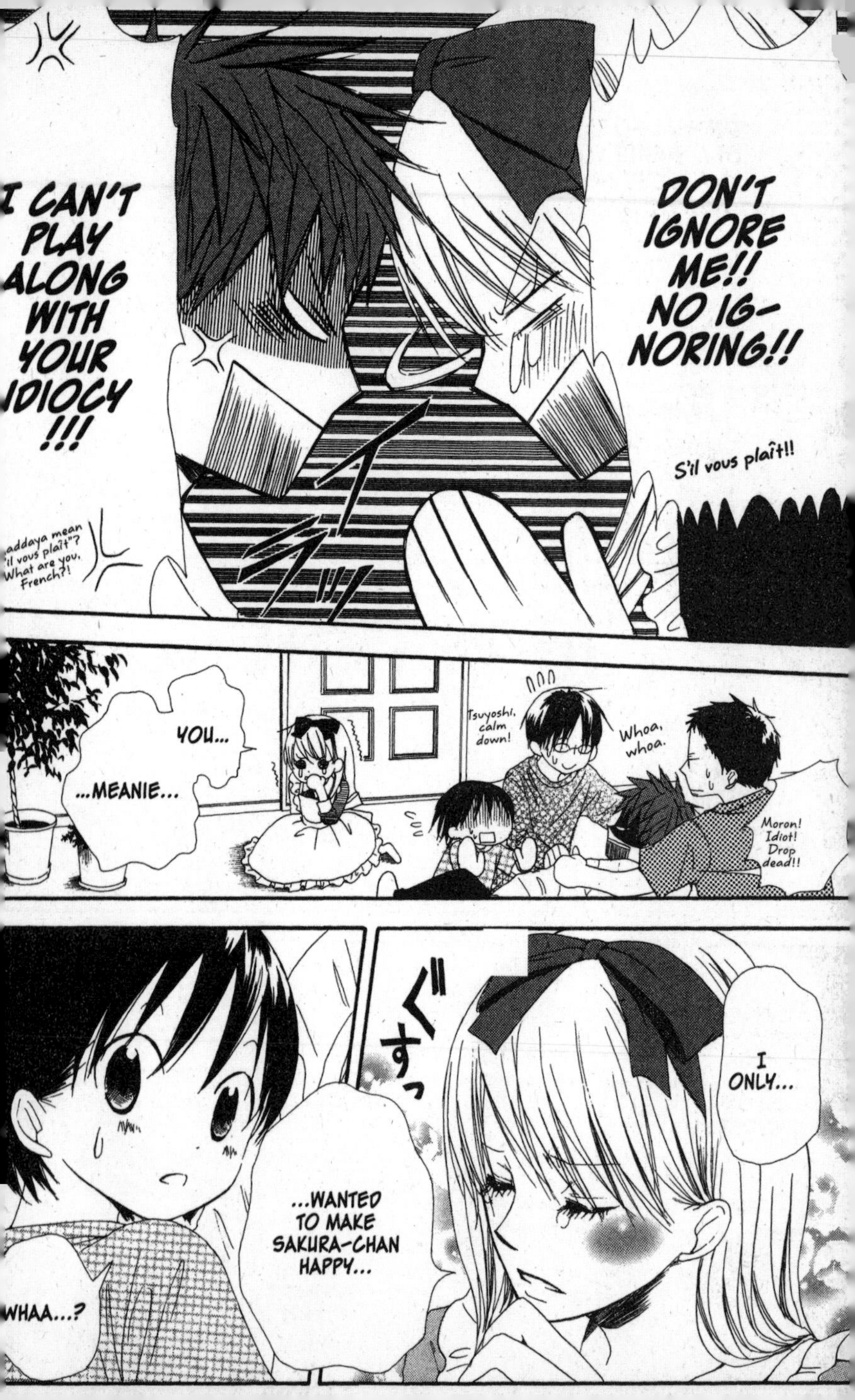
DON'T IGNORE ME!! NO IG- NORING!!
S'il vous plaît!!
I CAN'T PLAY ALONG WITH YOUR IDIOCY!!!
addaya mean 'il vous plaît"? What are you, French?!
Moron! Idiot! Drop dead!!
Whoa, whoa.
Tsuyoshi, calm down!
YOU...
...MEANIE...
I ONLY...
ぐすっ
...WANTED TO MAKE SAKURA-CHAN HAPPY...
WHAA...?

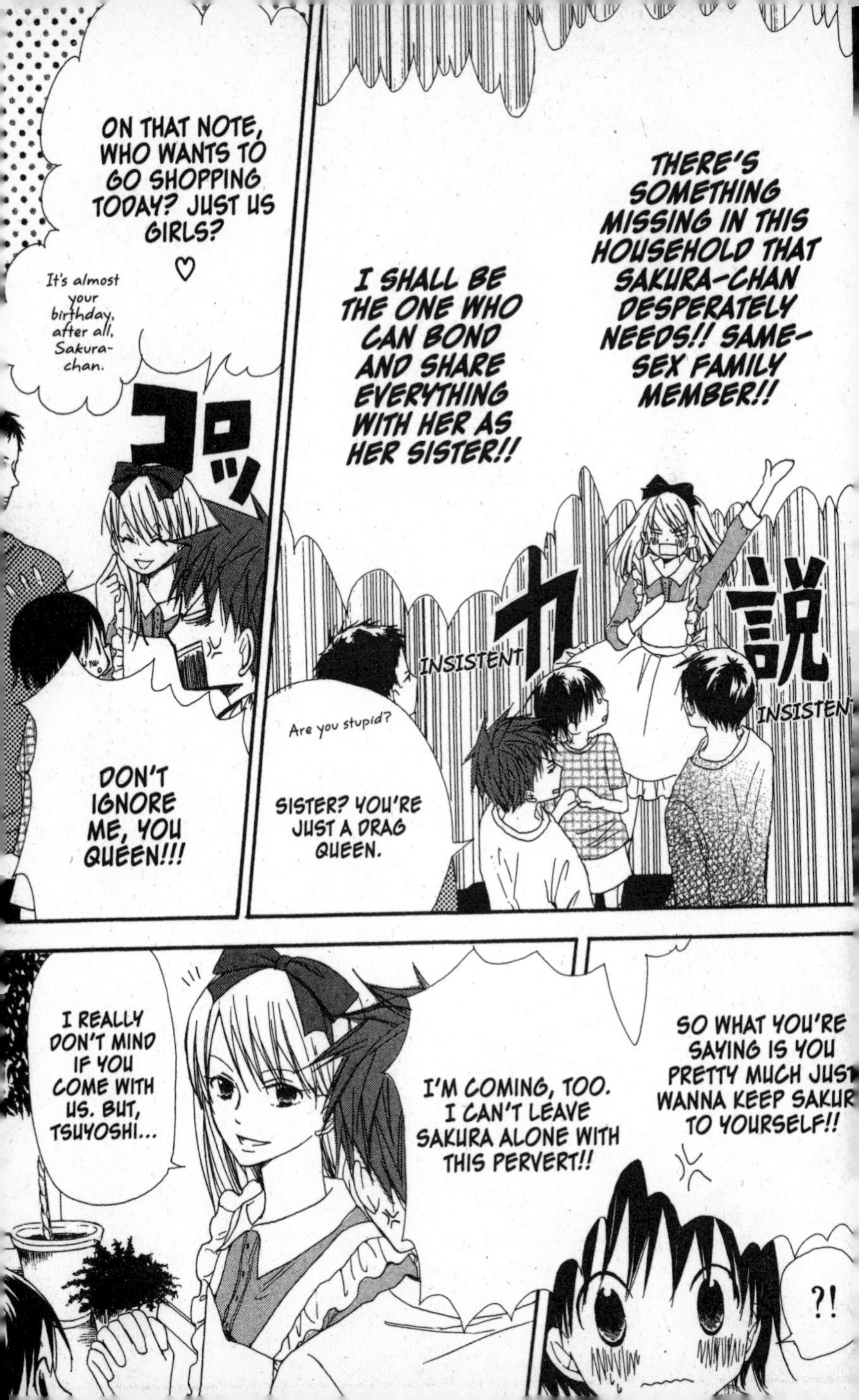
THERE'S SOMETHING MISSING IN THIS HOUSEHOLD THAT SAKURA-CHAN DESPERATELY NEEDS!! SAME-SEX FAMILY MEMBER!!
I SHALL BE THE ONE WHO CAN BOND AND SHARE EVERYTHING WITH HER AS HER SISTER!!
力説
INSISTENT
INSISTENT
Are you stupid?
SISTER? YOU'RE JUST A DRAG QUEEN.
ON THAT NOTE, WHO WANTS TO GO SHOPPING TODAY? JUST US GIRLS? ♡
It's almost your birthday, after all, Sakura-chan.
コロッ
DON'T IGNORE ME, YOU QUEEN!!!
SO WHAT YOU'RE SAYING IS YOU PRETTY MUCH JUST WANNA KEEP SAKUR TO YOURSELF!!
?!
I'M COMING, TOO. I CAN'T LEAVE SAKURA ALONE WITH THIS PERVERT!!
I REALLY DON'T MIND IF YOU COME WITH US. BUT, TSUYOSHI...

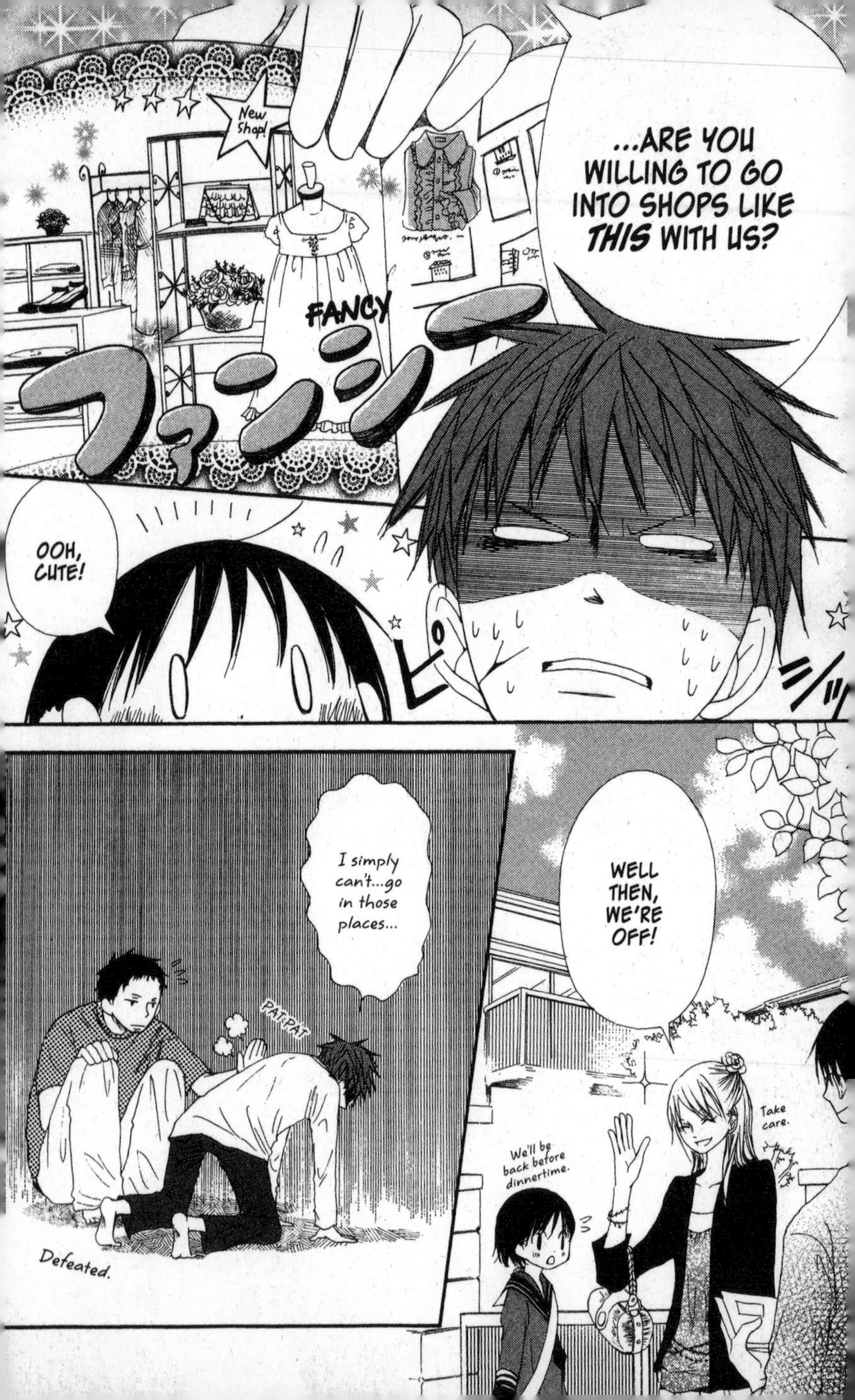
...ARE YOU WILLING TO GO INTO SHOPS LIKE THIS WITH US?
New Shop!
FANCY
OOH, CUTE!
WELL THEN, WE'RE OFF!
Take care.
We'll be back before dinnertime.
I simply can't...go in those places...
PAT PAT
Defeated.

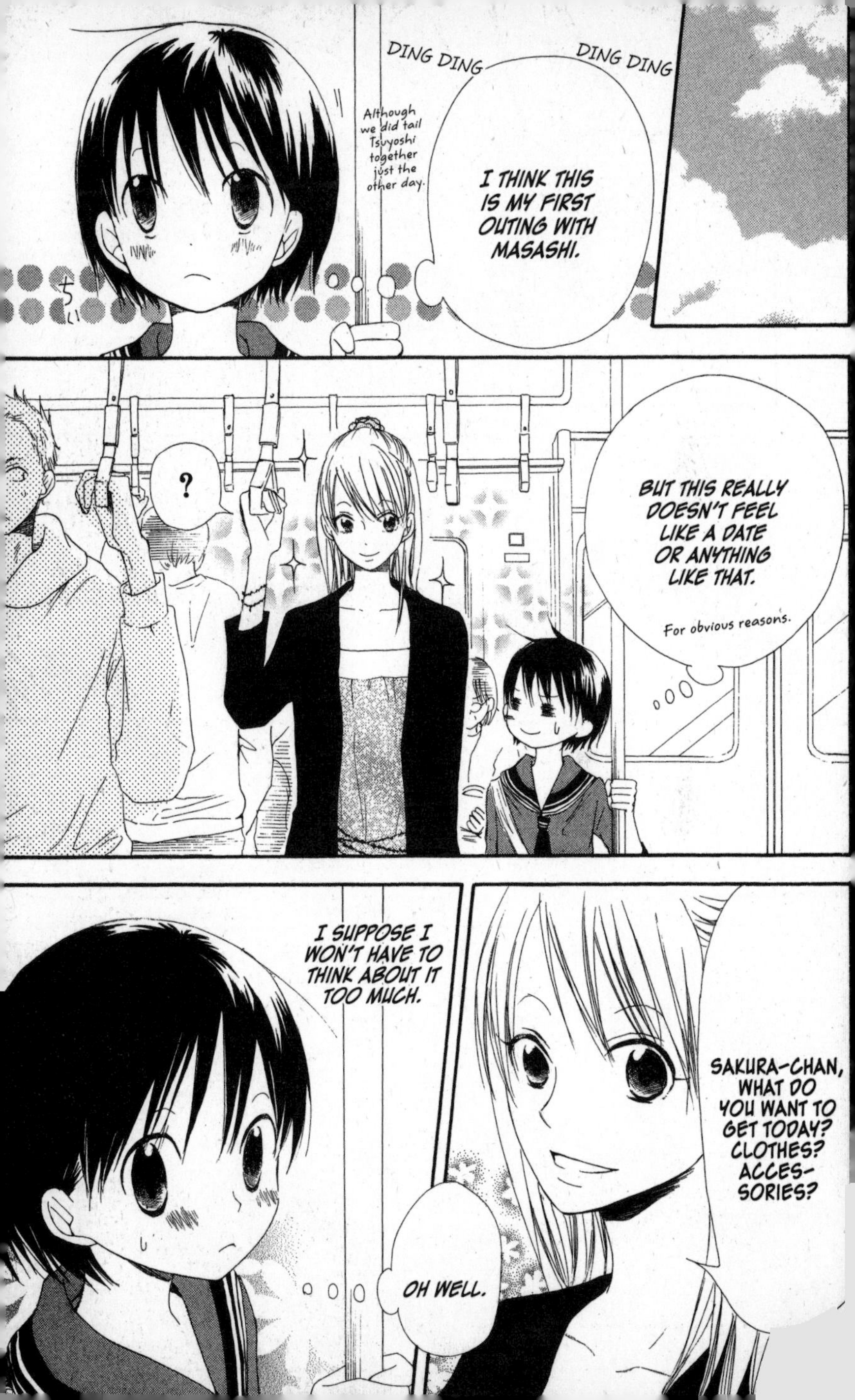
DING DING
DING DING
I THINK THIS IS MY FIRST OUTING WITH MASASHI.
Although we did tail Tsuyoshi together just the other day.
BUT THIS REALLY DOESN'T FEEL LIKE A DATE OR ANYTHING LIKE THAT.
For obvious reasons.
?
SAKURA-CHAN, WHAT DO YOU WANT TO GET TODAY? CLOTHES? ACCES-SORIES?
I SUPPOSE I WON'T HAVE TO THINK ABOUT IT TOO MUCH.
OH WELL.

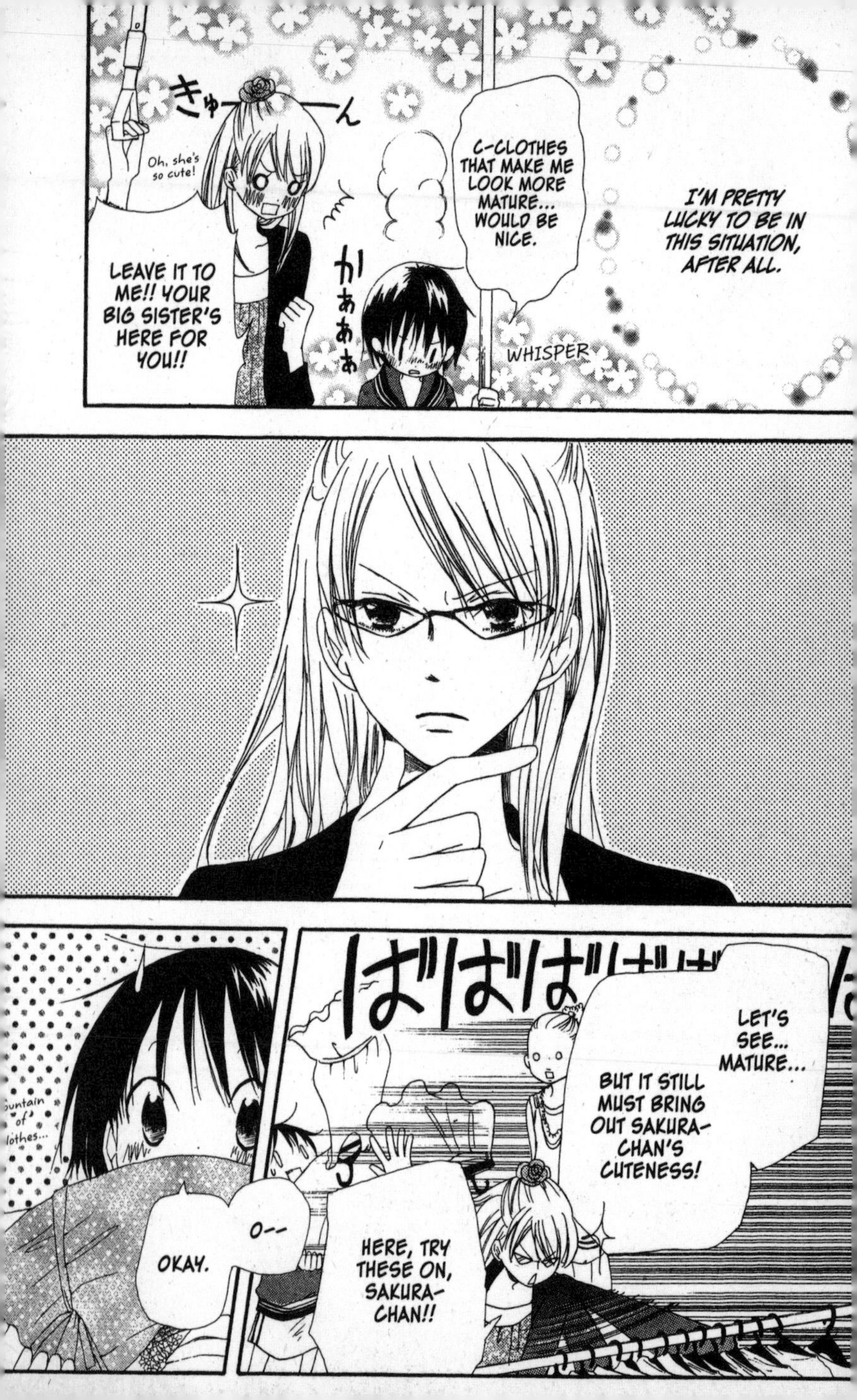
I'M PRETTY LUCKY TO BE IN THIS SITUATION, AFTER ALL.
C-CLOTHES THAT MAKE ME LOOK MORE MATURE... WOULD BE NICE.
WHISPER
かぁぁぁ
きゅーーん
Oh, she's so cute!
LEAVE IT TO ME!! YOUR BIG SISTER'S HERE FOR YOU!!
ばばば
LET'S SEE... MATURE...
BUT IT STILL MUST BRING OUT SAKURA-CHAN'S CUTENESS!
HERE, TRY THESE ON, SAKURA-CHAN!!
O--
OKAY.
ountain of lothes...

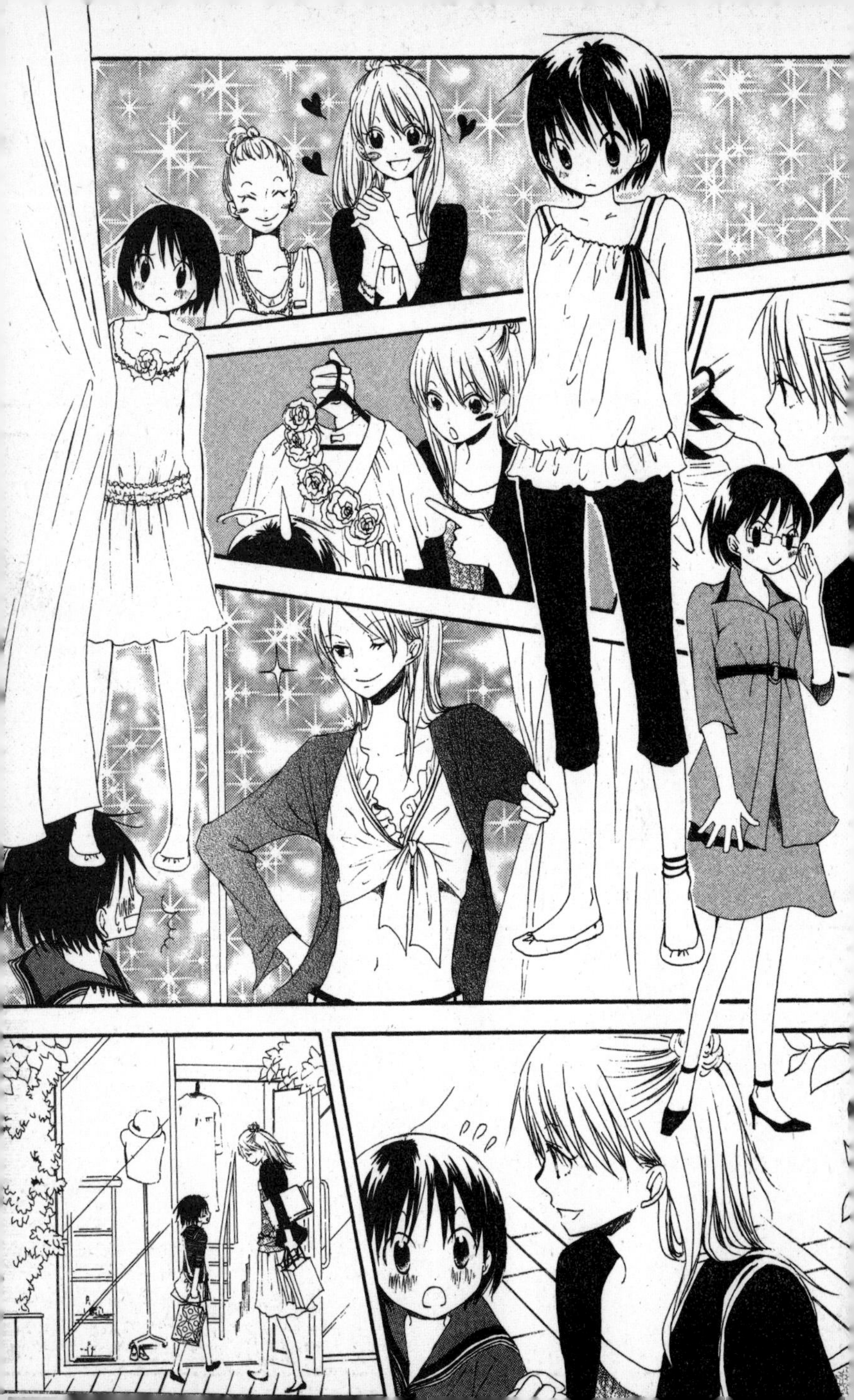

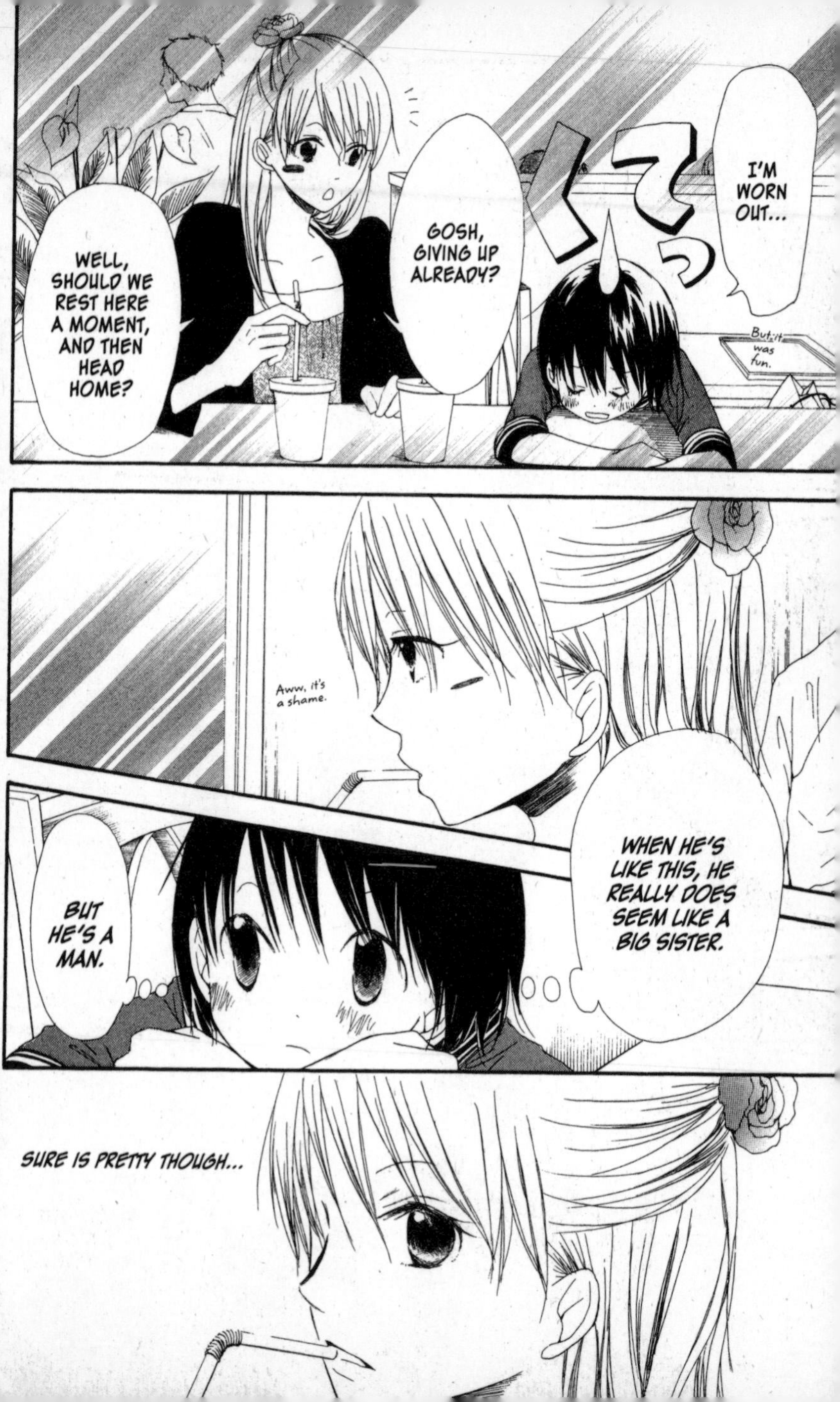
I'M WORN OUT...
くてっ
But it was fun.
GOSH, GIVING UP ALREADY?
WELL, SHOULD WE REST HERE A MOMENT, AND THEN HEAD HOME?
Aww, it's a shame.
WHEN HE'S LIKE THIS, HE REALLY DOES SEEM LIKE A BIG SISTER.
BUT HE'S A MAN.
SURE IS PRETTY THOUGH...

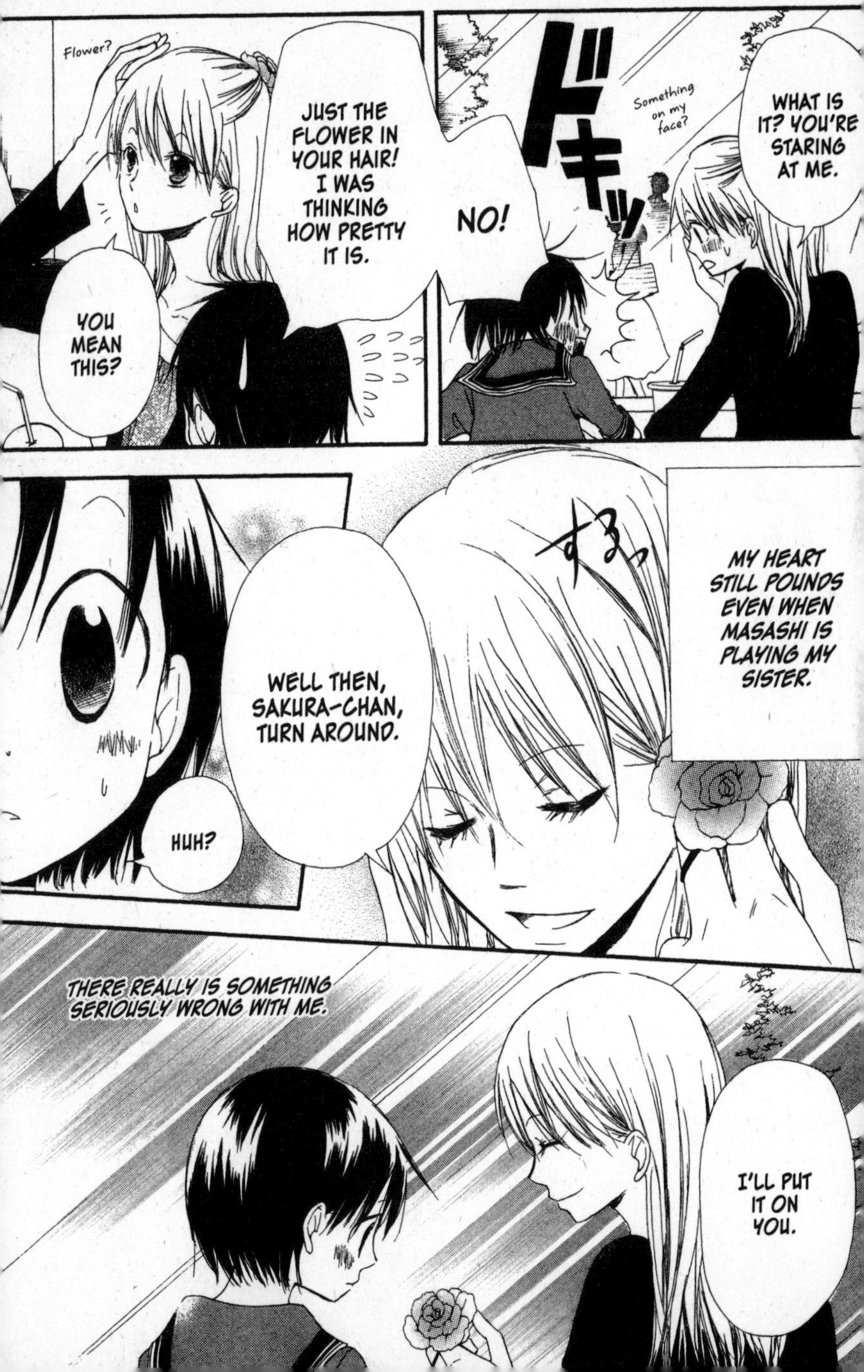
WHAT IS IT? YOU'RE STARING AT ME.
Something on my face?
ドキッ
NO!
JUST THE FLOWER IN YOUR HAIR! I WAS THINKING HOW PRETTY IT IS.
Flower?
YOU MEAN THIS?
MY HEART STILL POUNDS EVEN WHEN MASASHI IS PLAYING MY SISTER.
するっ
WELL THEN, SAKURA-CHAN, TURN AROUND.
HUH?
I'LL PUT IT ON YOU.
THERE REALLY IS SOMETHING SERIOUSLY WRONG WITH ME.

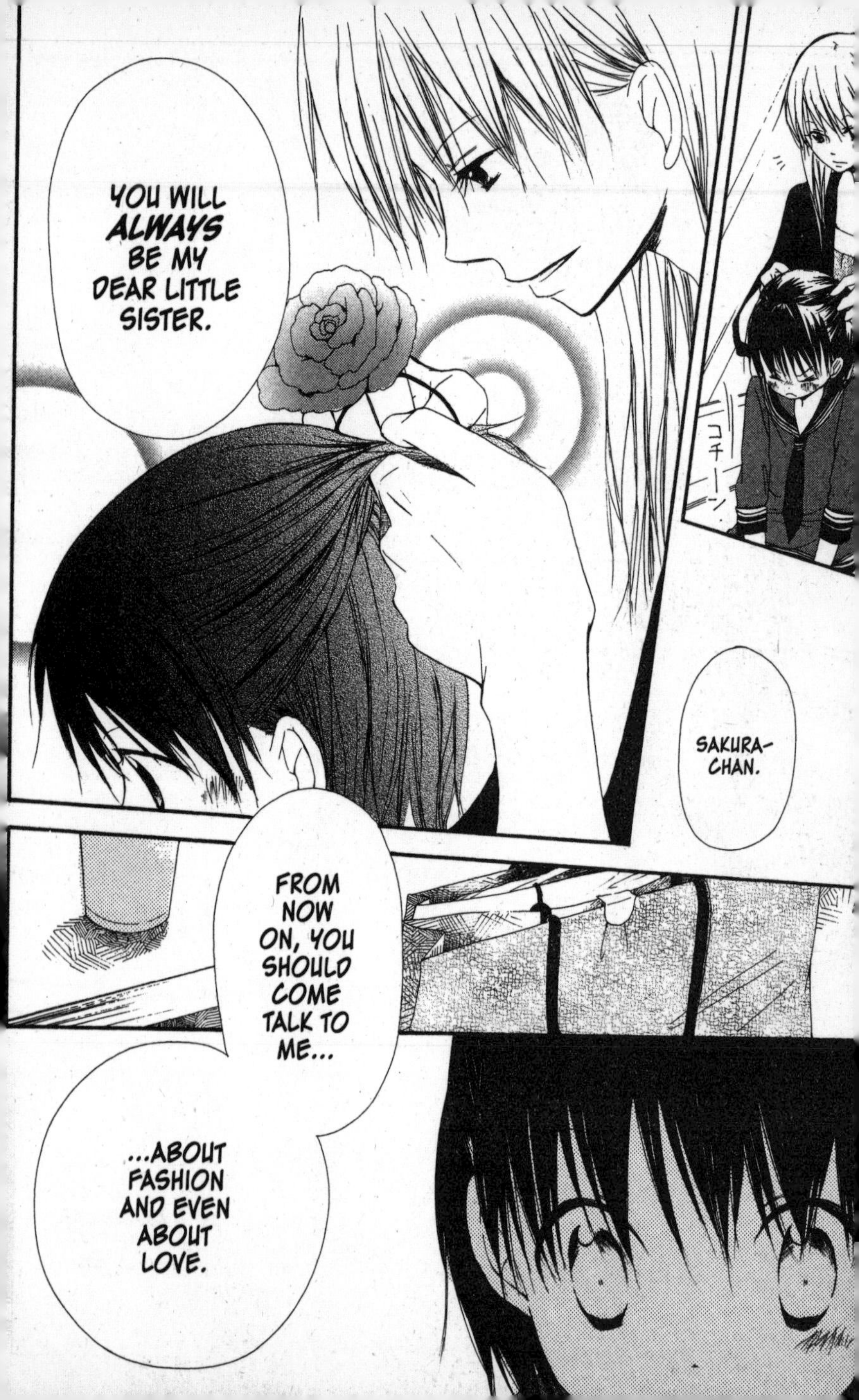
コチーン
SAKURA-CHAN.
YOU WILL ALWAYS BE MY DEAR LITTLE SISTER.
FROM NOW ON, YOU SHOULD COME TALK TO ME...
...ABOUT FASHION AND EVEN ABOUT LOVE.

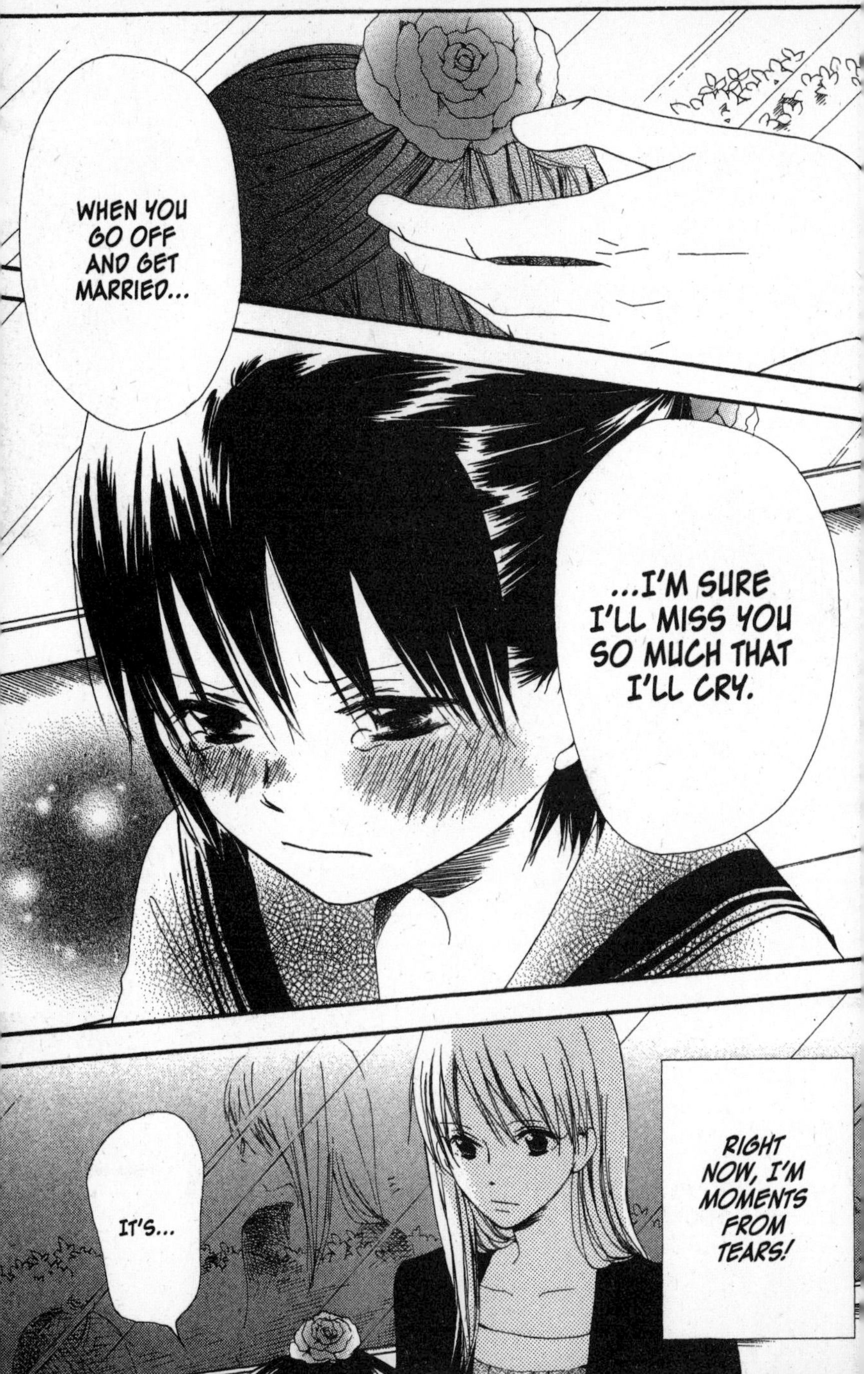
WHEN YOU GO OFF AND GET MARRIED...
...I'M SURE I'LL MISS YOU SO MUCH THAT I'LL CRY.
RIGHT NOW, I'M MOMENTS FROM TEARS!
IT'S...

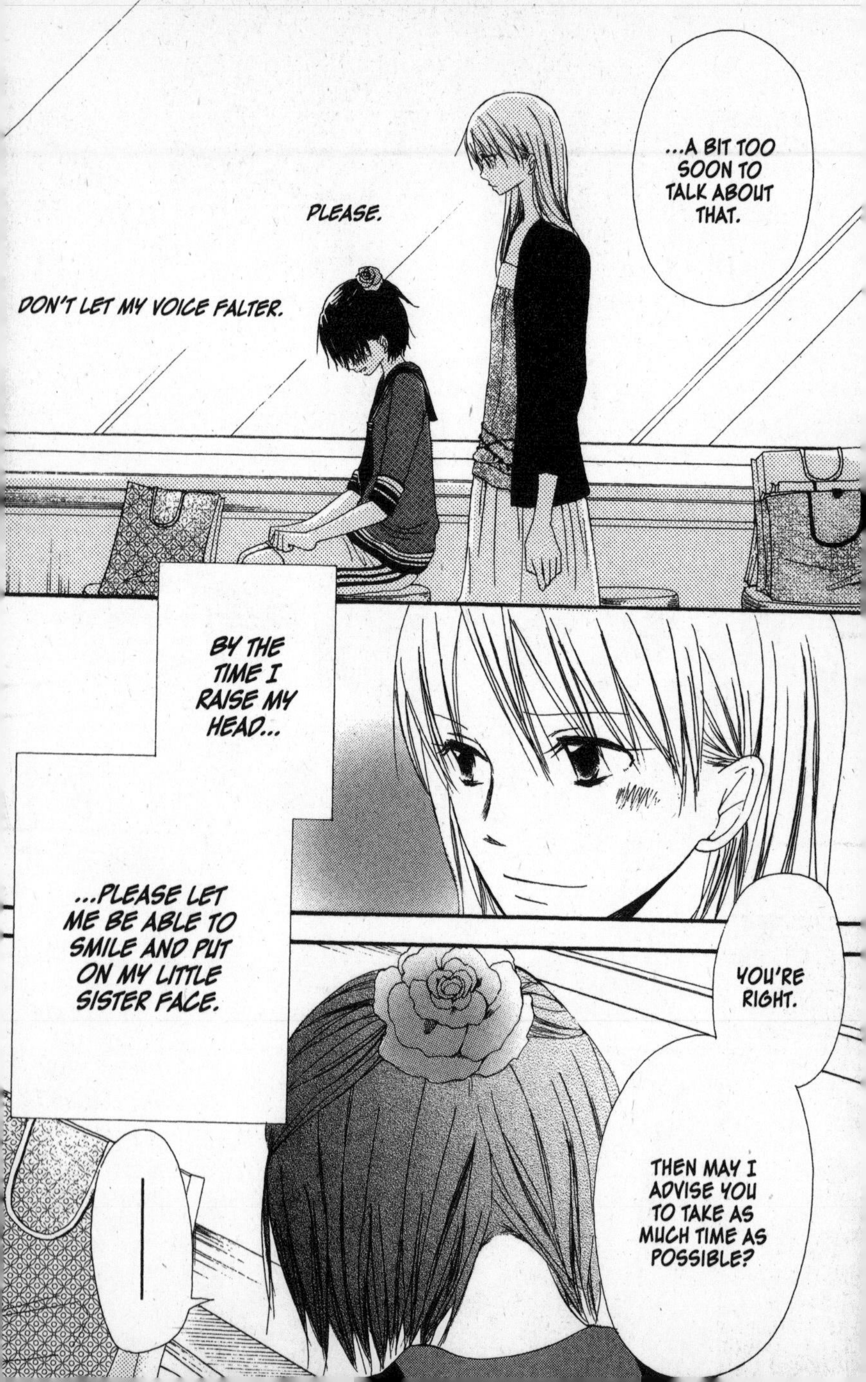
...A BIT TOO SOON TO TALK ABOUT THAT.
PLEASE.
DON'T LET MY VOICE FALTER.
BY THE TIME I RAISE MY HEAD...
...PLEASE LET ME BE ABLE TO SMILE AND PUT ON MY LITTLE SISTER FACE.
YOU'RE RIGHT.
THEN MAY I ADVISE YOU TO TAKE AS MUCH TIME AS POSSIBLE?
—

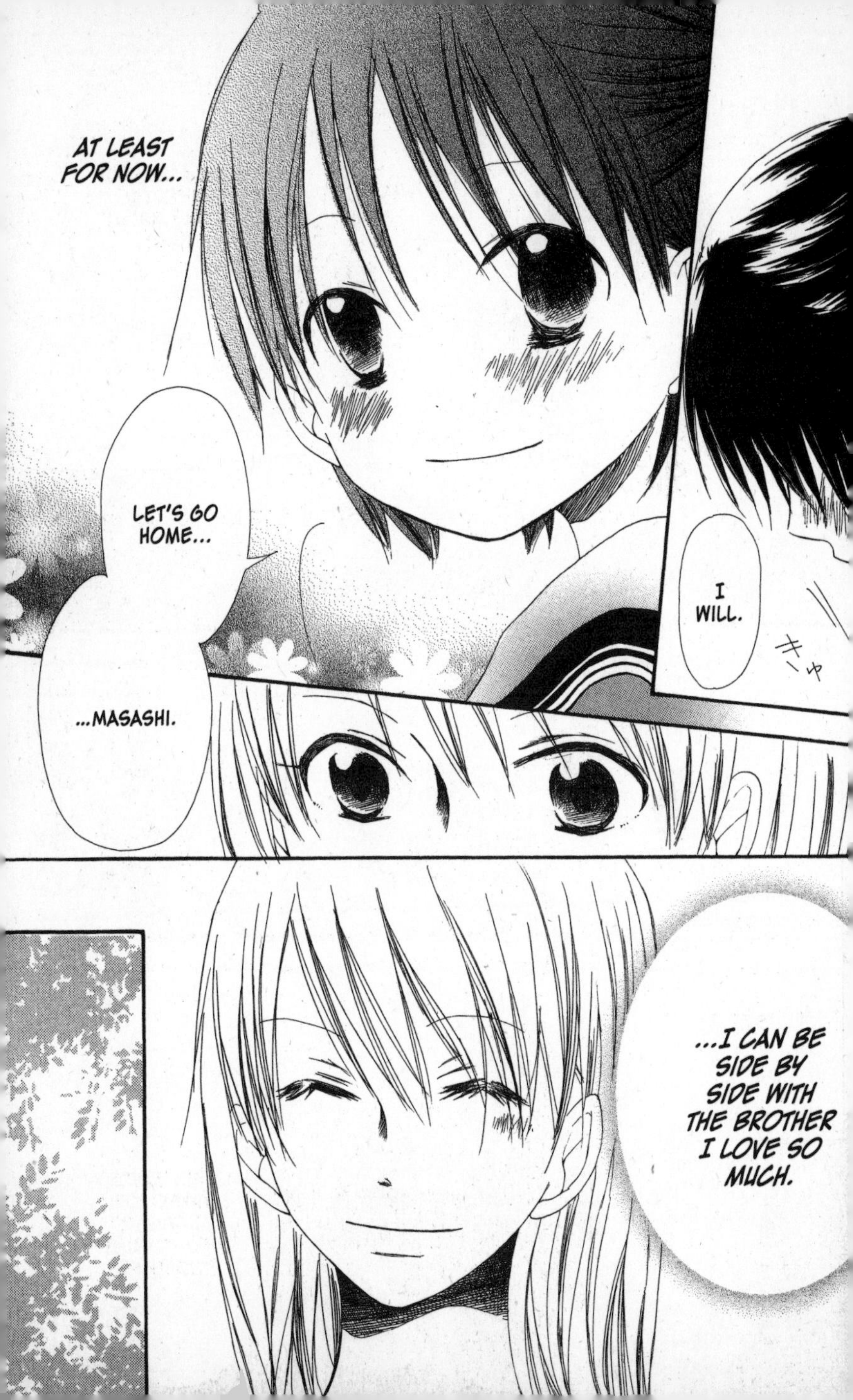
I WILL.
キュ
AT LEAST FOR NOW...
LET'S GO HOME...
...MASASHI.
...I CAN BE SIDE BY SIDE WITH THE BROTHER I LOVE SO MUCH.

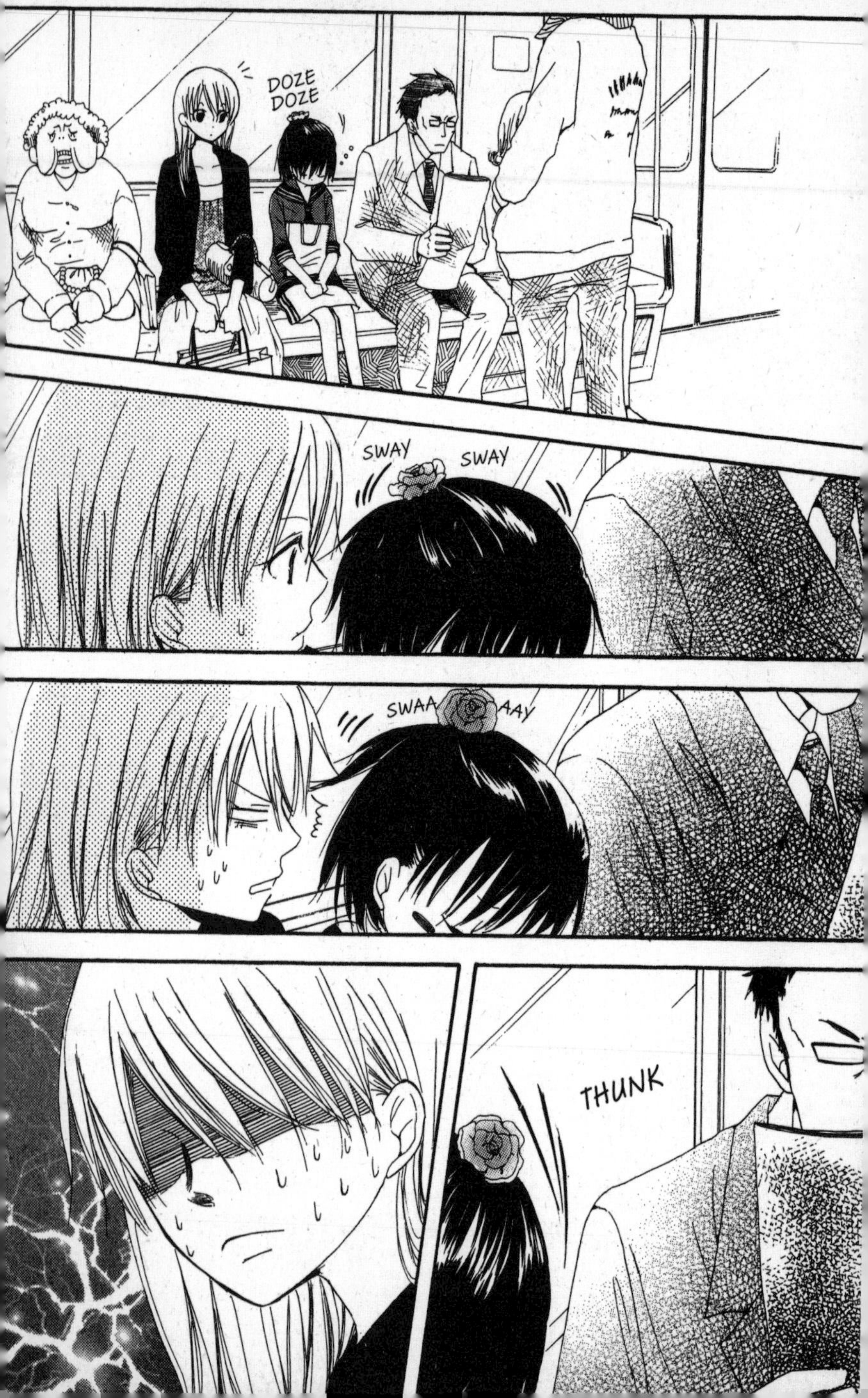
DOZE DOZE
SWAY
SWAY
SWAAAAY
THUNK

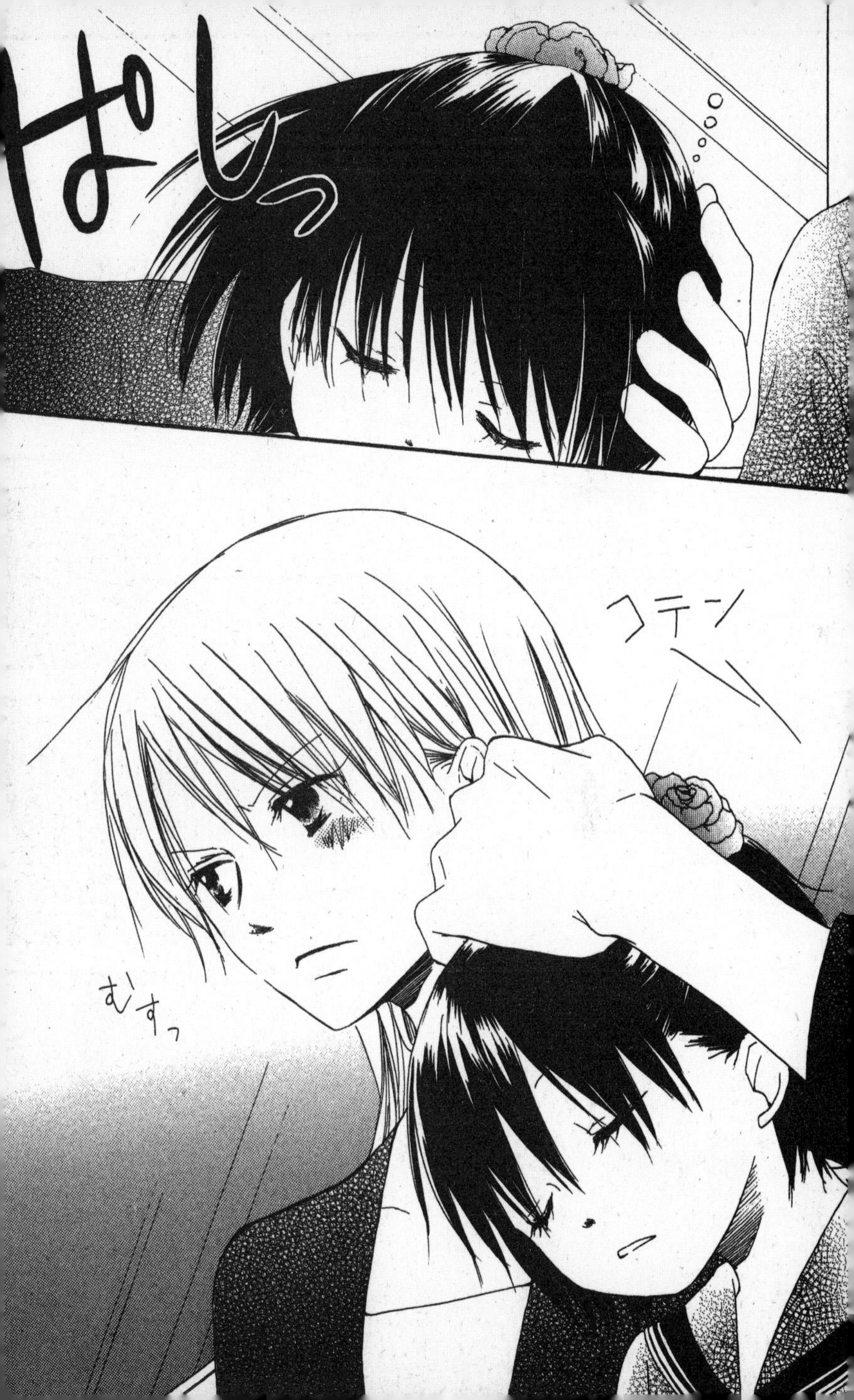
はしっ
コテン
むすっ

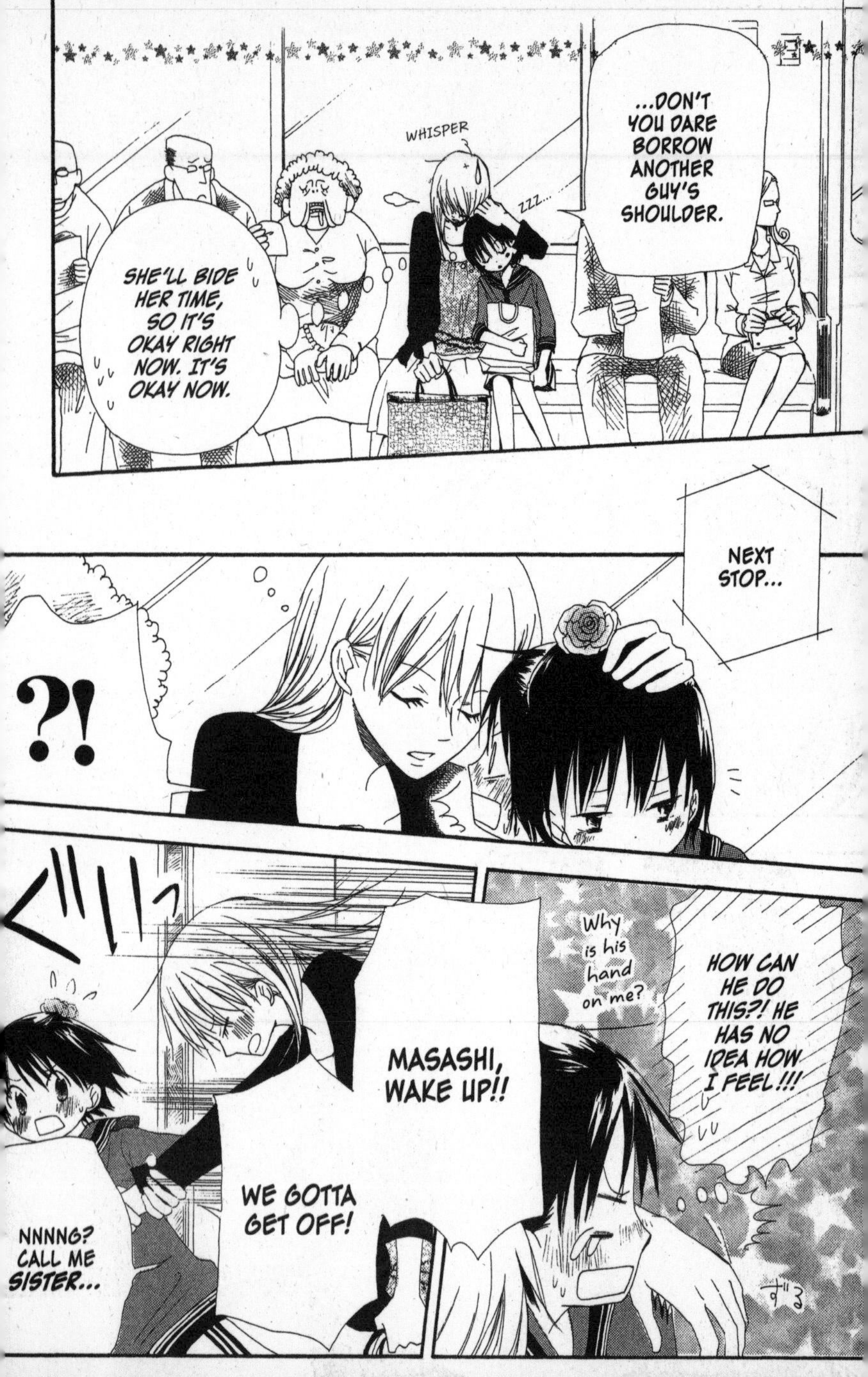
...DON'T YOU DARE BORROW ANOTHER GUY'S SHOULDER.
ZZZ...
WHISPER
SHE'LL BIDE HER TIME, SO IT'S OKAY RIGHT NOW. IT'S OKAY NOW.
NEXT STOP...
?!
HOW CAN HE DO THIS?! HE HAS NO IDEA HOW I FEEL!!!
Why is his hand on me?
MASASHI, WAKE UP!!
WE GOTTA GET OFF!
NNNNG? CALL ME SISTER...

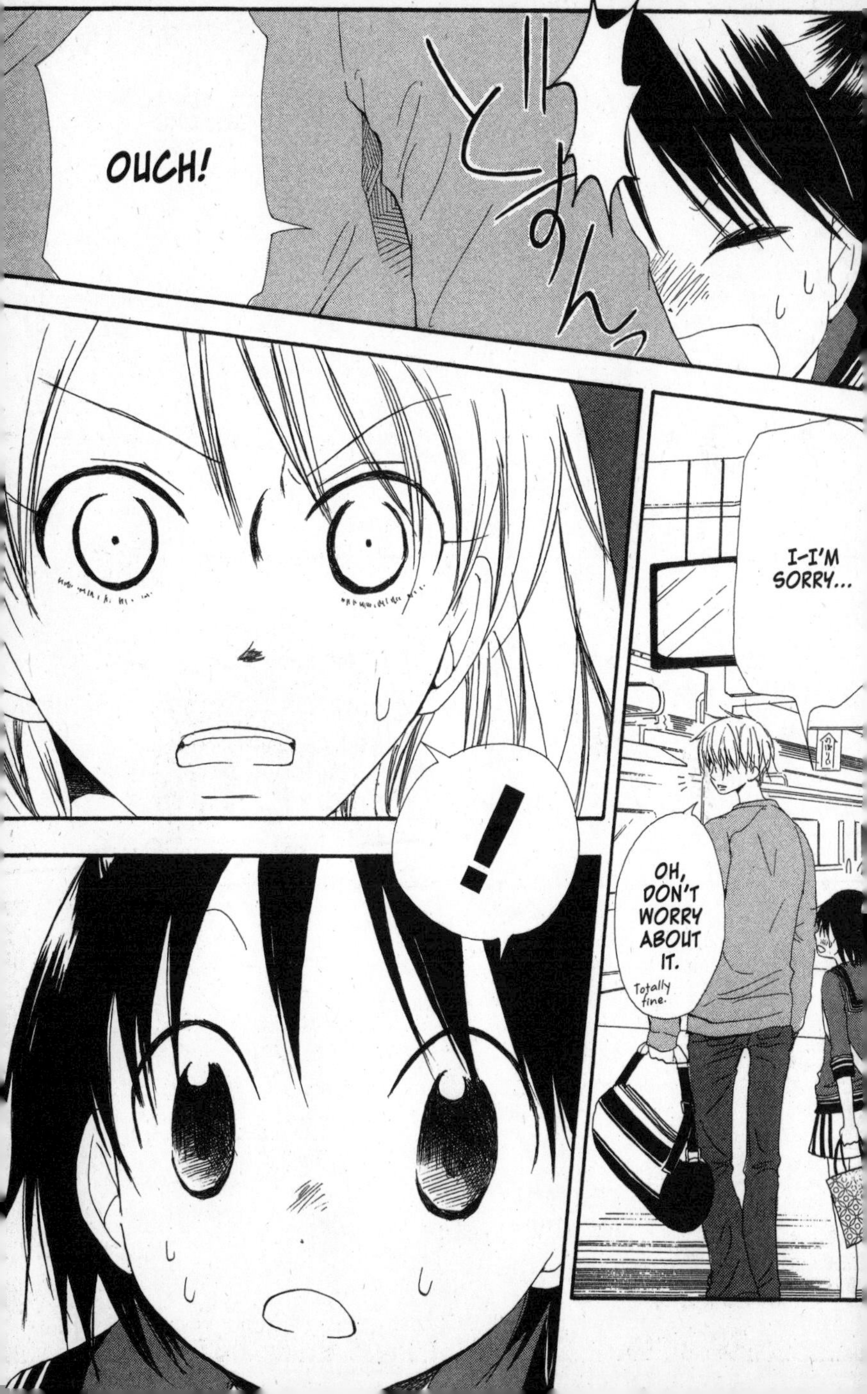

どすんっ
OUCH!
I-I'M SORRY...
OH, DON'T WORRY ABOUT IT.
Totally fine.
!

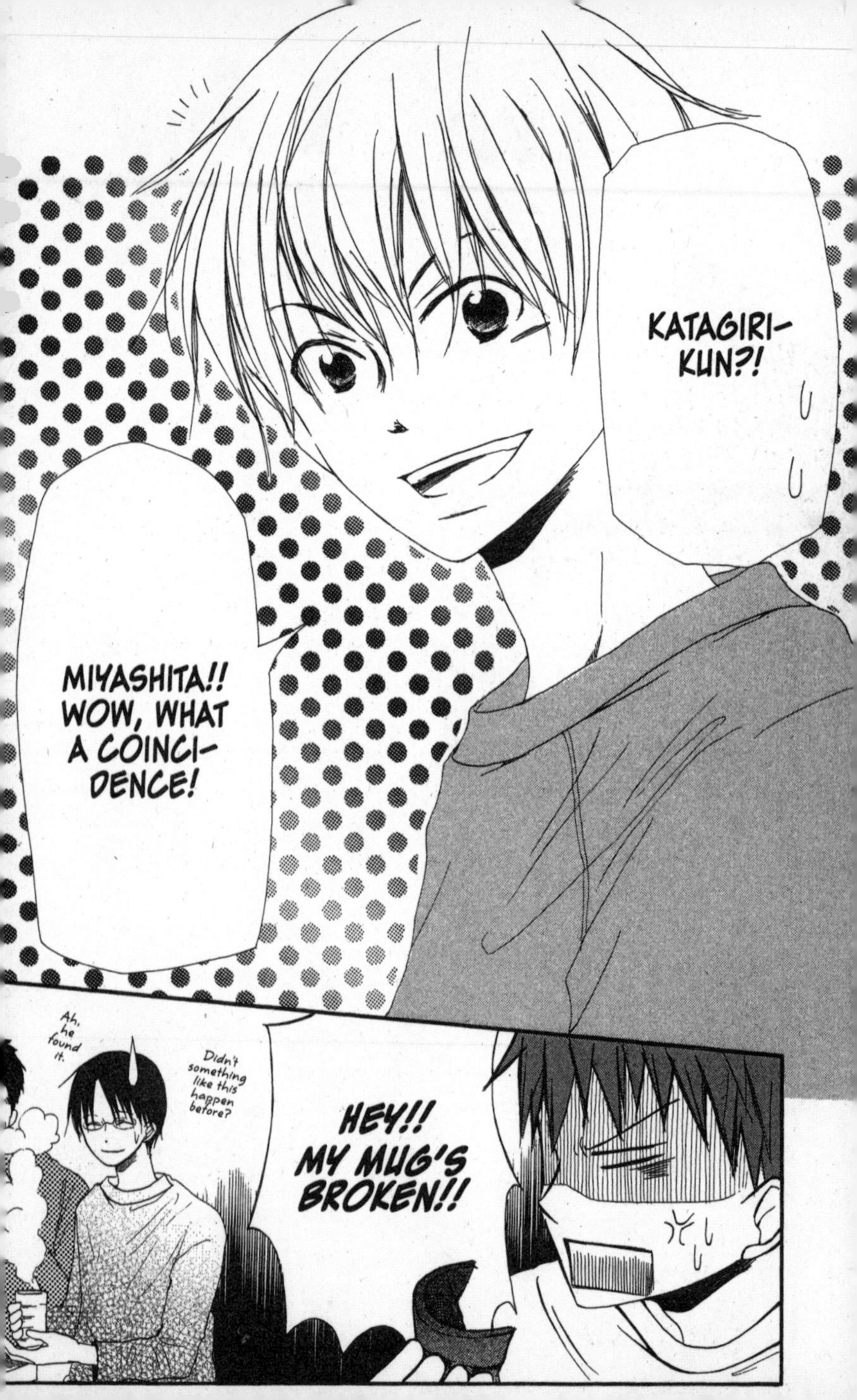
KATAGIRI-KUN?!
MIYASHITA!! WOW, WHAT A COINCIDENCE!
HEY!! MY MUG'S BROKEN!!
Didn't something like this happen before?
Ah, he found it.

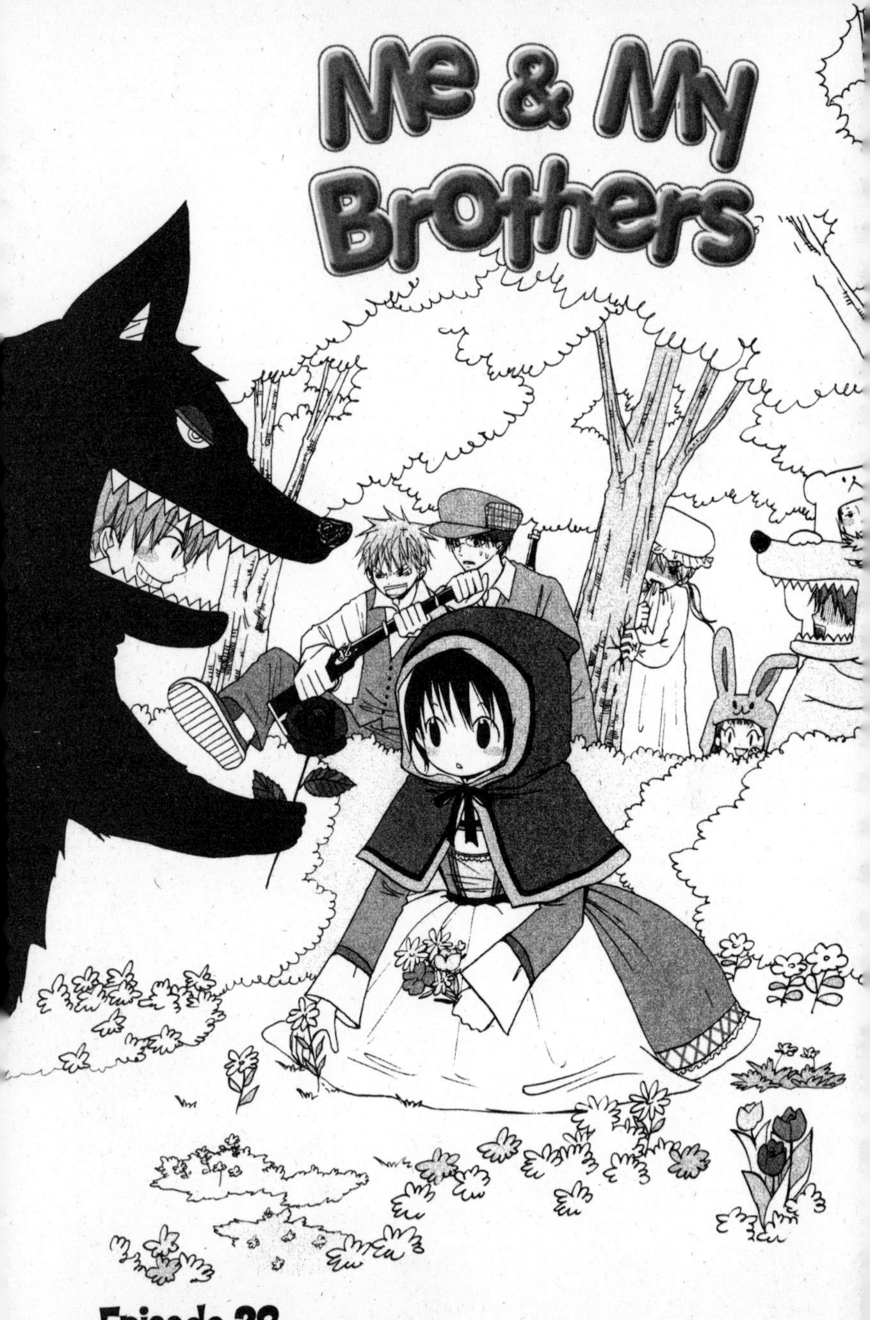
Me & My Brothers

Episode 28

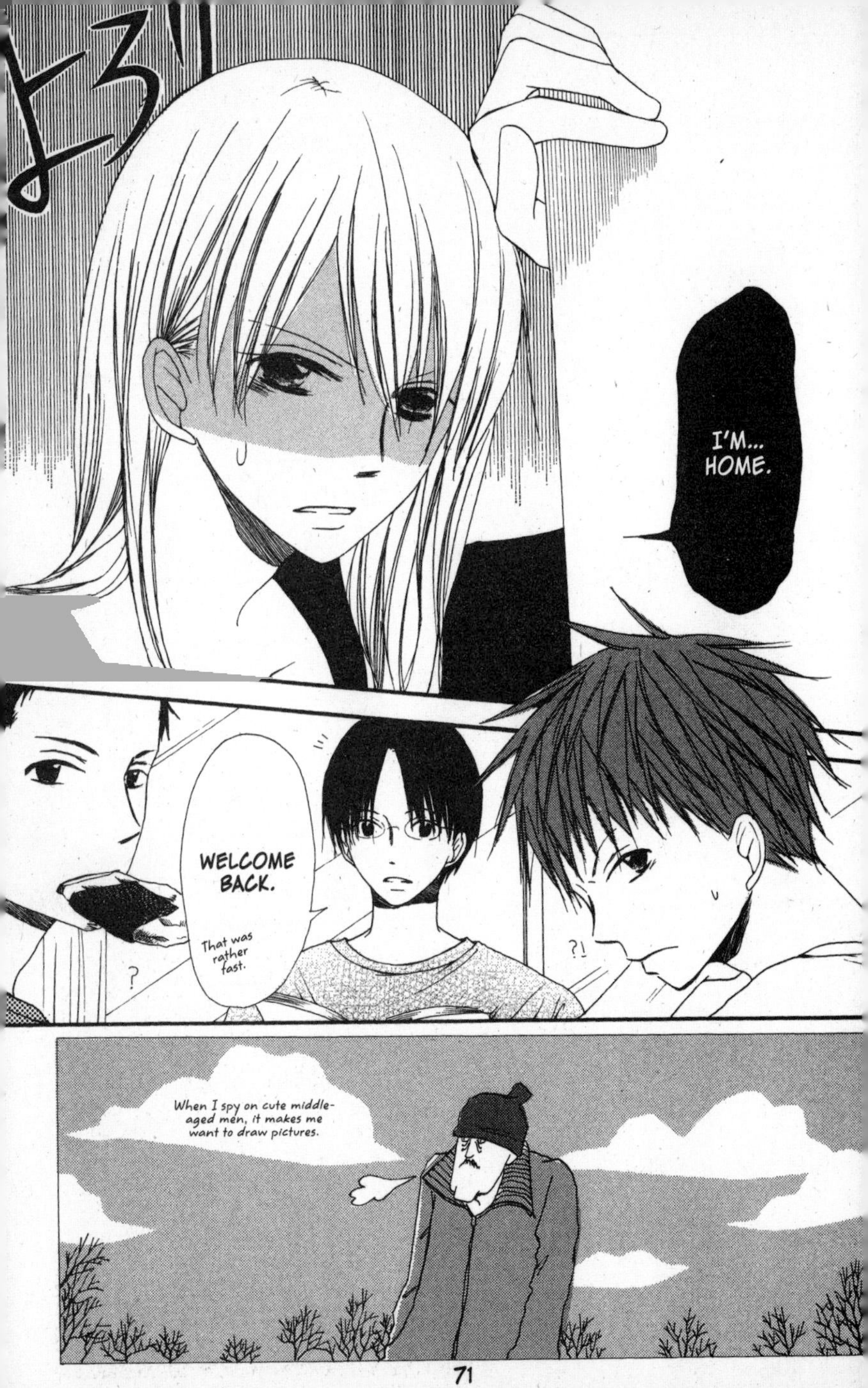
よろ
I'M... HOME.
?!
WELCOME BACK.
That was rather fast.
?
When I spy on cute middle-aged men, it makes me want to draw pictures.

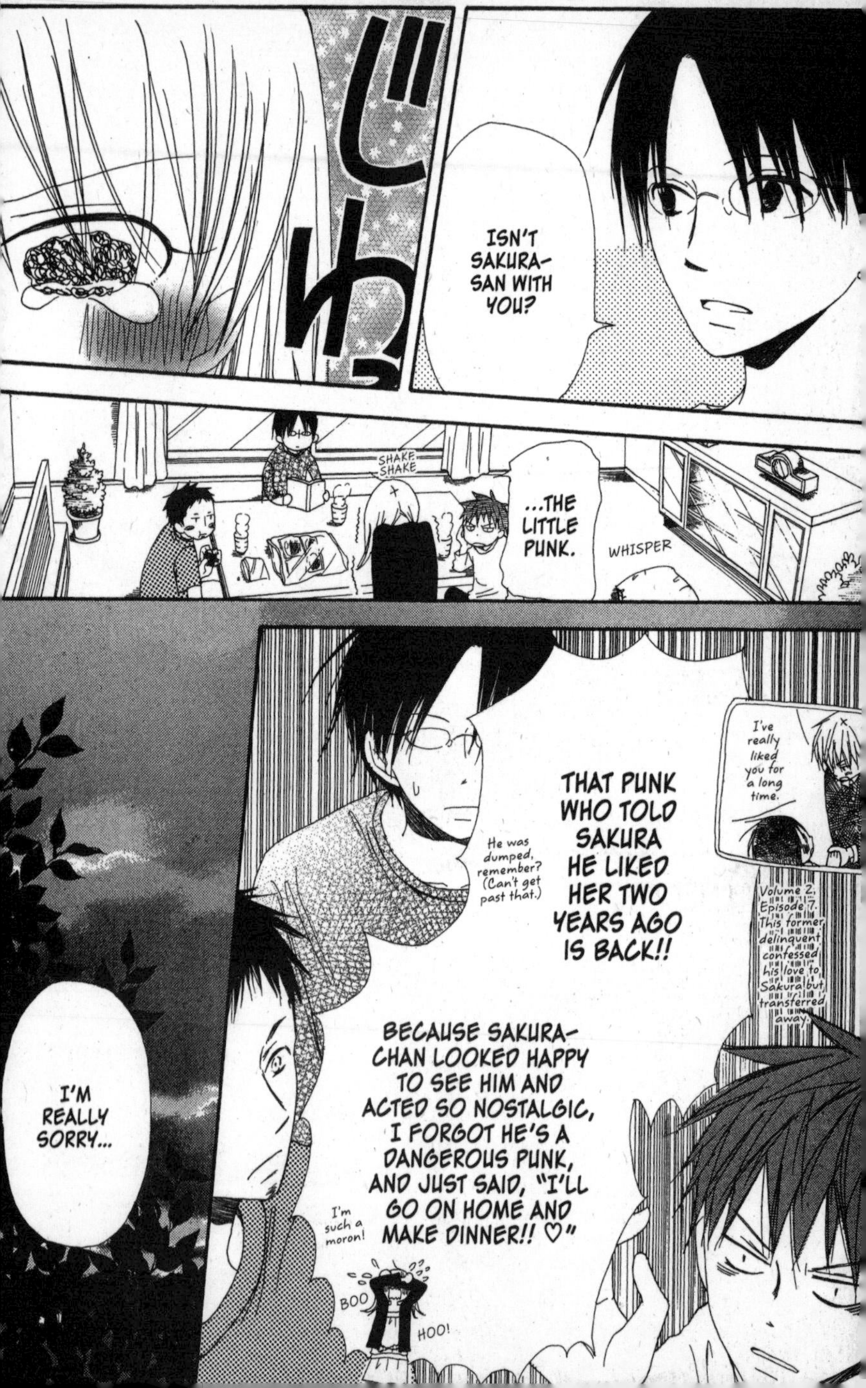
ISN'T SAKURA-SAN WITH YOU?
SHAKE SHAKE
...THE LITTLE PUNK.
WHISPER
I've really liked you for a long time.
Volume 2, Episode 7. This former delinquent confessed his love to Sakura but transferred away.
THAT PUNK WHO TOLD SAKURA HE LIKED HER TWO YEARS AGO IS BACK!!
He was dumped, remember? (Can't get past that.)
BECAUSE SAKURA-CHAN LOOKED HAPPY TO SEE HIM AND ACTED SO NOSTALGIC, I FORGOT HE'S A DANGEROUS PUNK, AND JUST SAID, "I'LL GO ON HOME AND MAKE DINNER!! ♡"
I'm such a moron!
BOO HOO!
I'M REALLY SORRY...

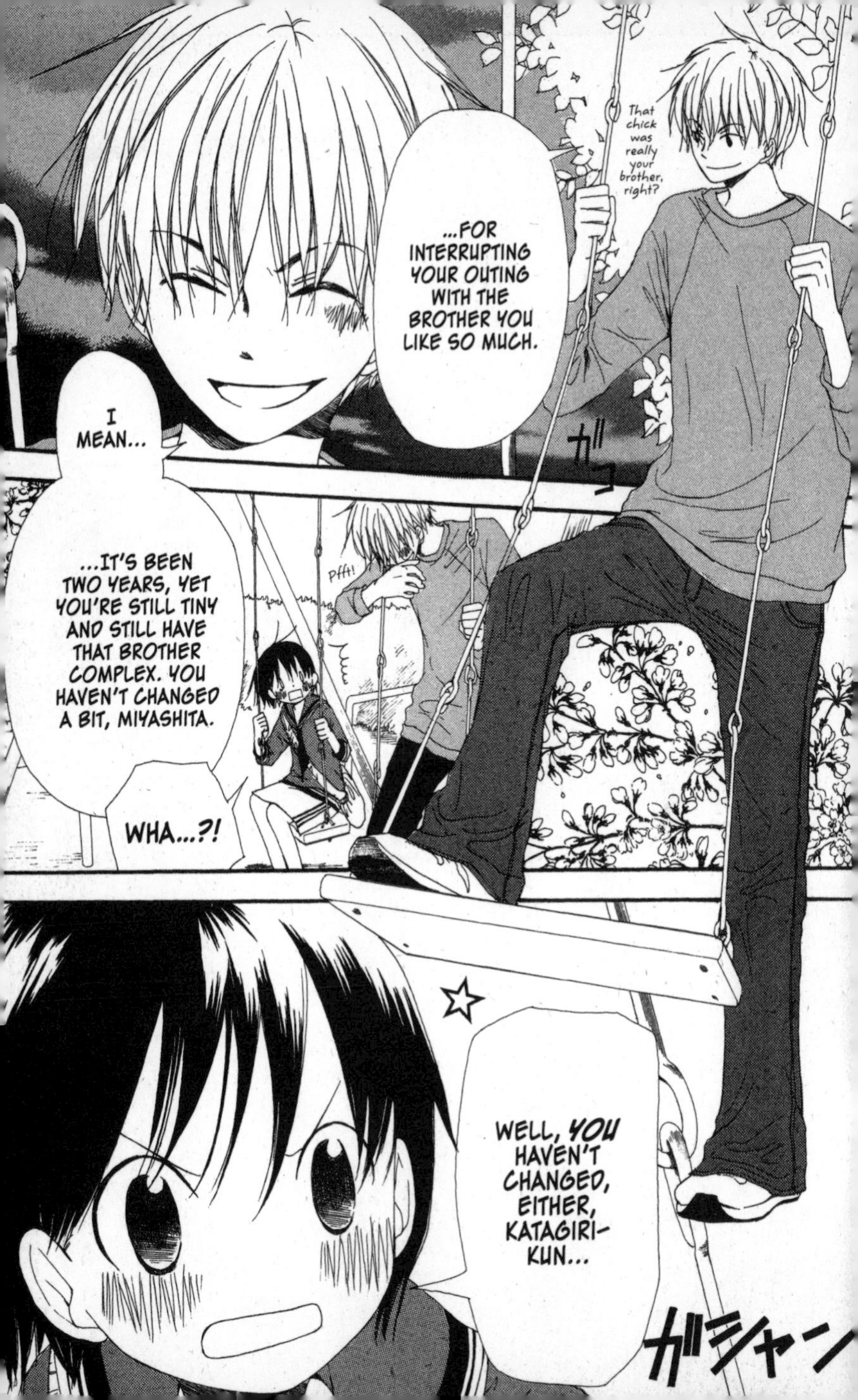

That chick was really your brother, right?
...FOR INTERRUPTING YOUR OUTING WITH THE BROTHER YOU LIKE SO MUCH.
ガッ
I MEAN...
...IT'S BEEN TWO YEARS, YET YOU'RE STILL TINY AND STILL HAVE THAT BROTHER COMPLEX. YOU HAVEN'T CHANGED A BIT, MIYASHITA.
Pfft!
WHA...?!
WELL, *YOU* HAVEN'T CHANGED, EITHER, KATAGIRI-KUN...
ガシャン

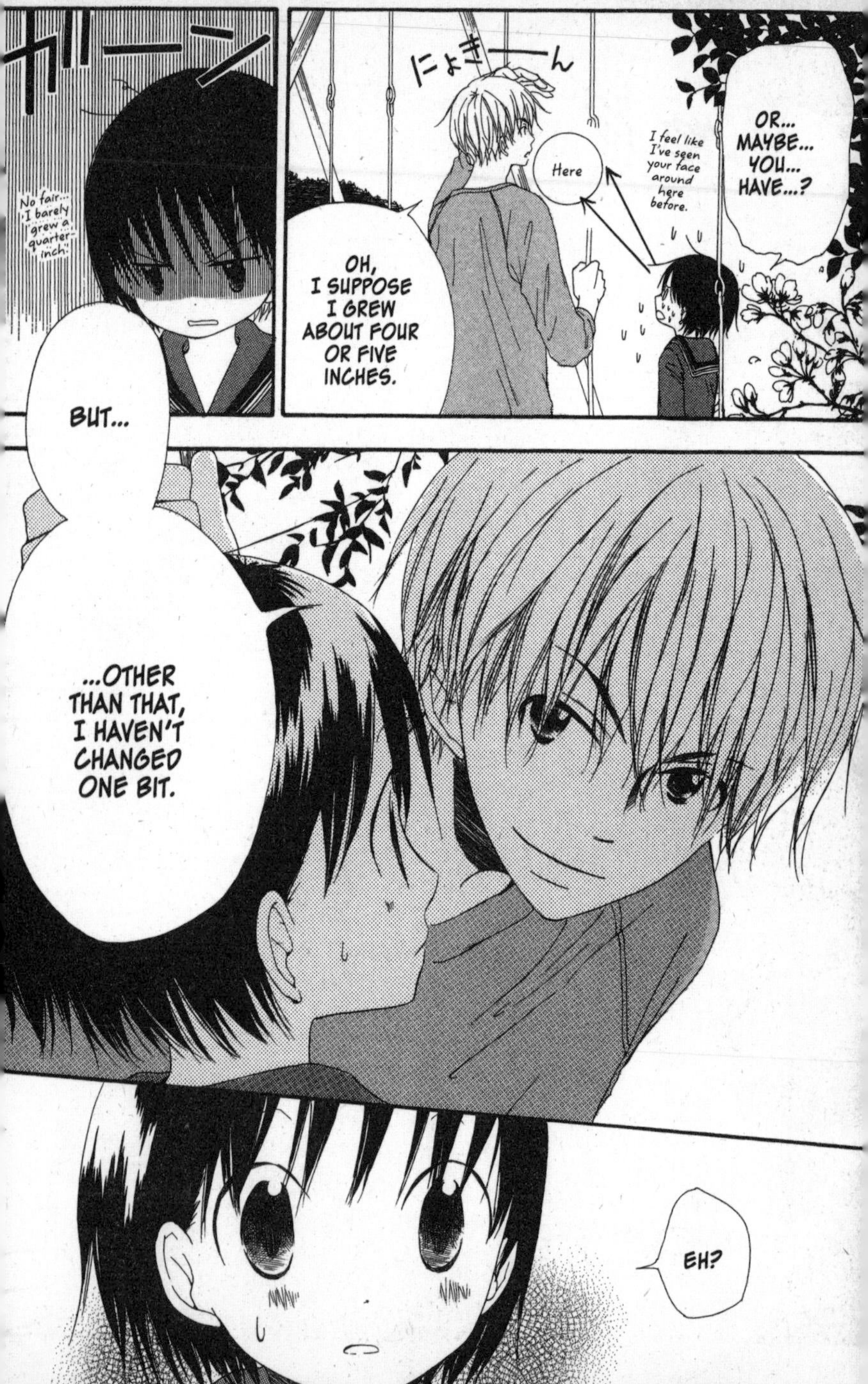
OR... MAYBE... YOU... HAVE...?
I feel like I've seen your face around here before.
にょきーーん
Here
OH, I SUPPOSE I GREW ABOUT FOUR OR FIVE INCHES.
ガーーン
No fair... I barely grew a quarter-inch.
BUT...
...OTHER THAN THAT, I HAVEN'T CHANGED ONE BIT.
EH?

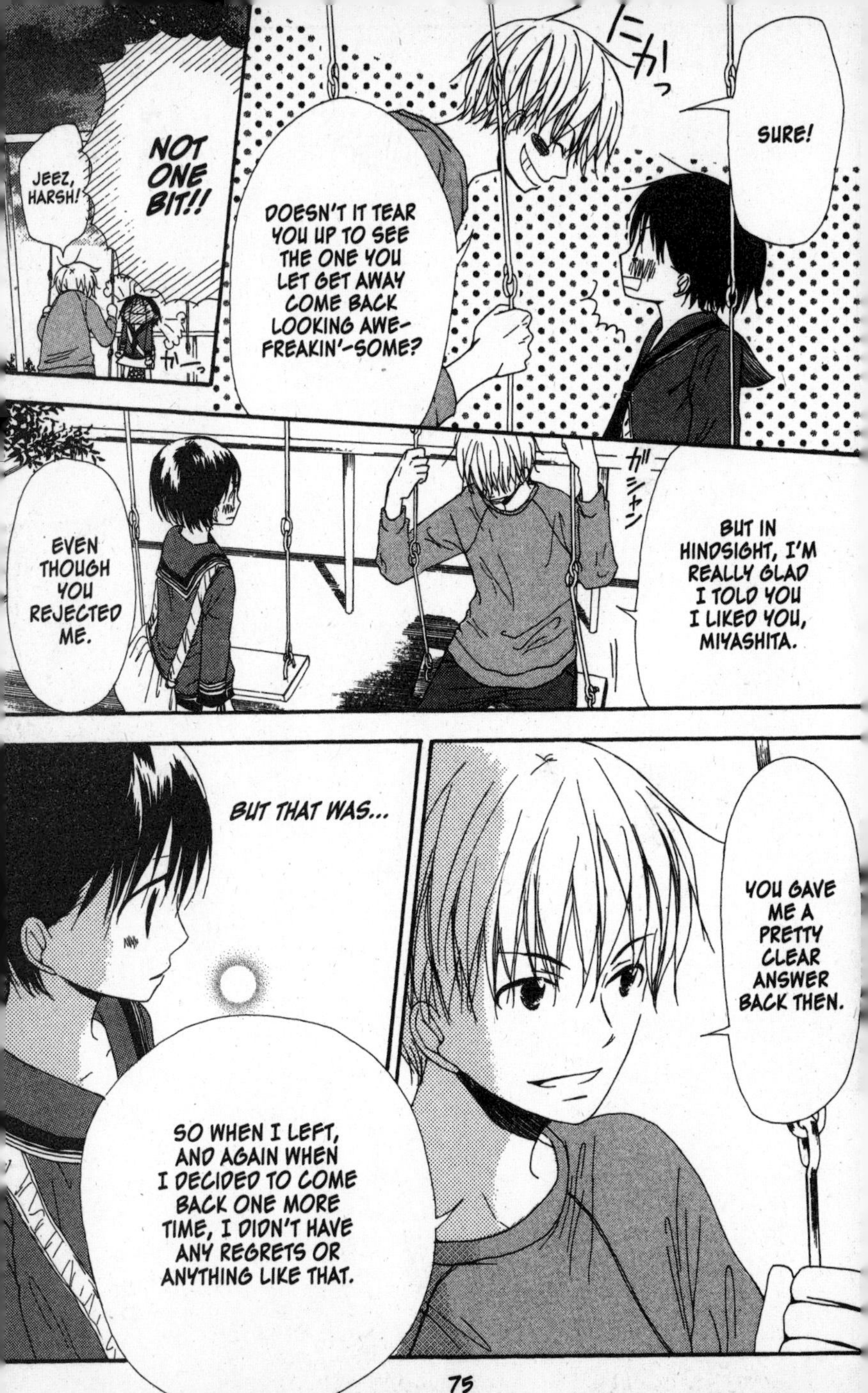

にかっ
SURE!
DOESN'T IT TEAR YOU UP TO SEE THE ONE YOU LET GET AWAY COME BACK LOOKING AWE-FREAKIN'-SOME?
NOT ONE BIT!!
JEEZ, HARSH!
ガシャン
BUT IN HINDSIGHT, I'M REALLY GLAD I TOLD YOU I LIKED YOU, MIYASHITA.
EVEN THOUGH YOU REJECTED ME.
YOU GAVE ME A PRETTY CLEAR ANSWER BACK THEN.
BUT THAT WAS...
SO WHEN I LEFT, AND AGAIN WHEN I DECIDED TO COME BACK ONE MORE TIME, I DIDN'T HAVE ANY REGRETS OR ANYTHING LIKE THAT.

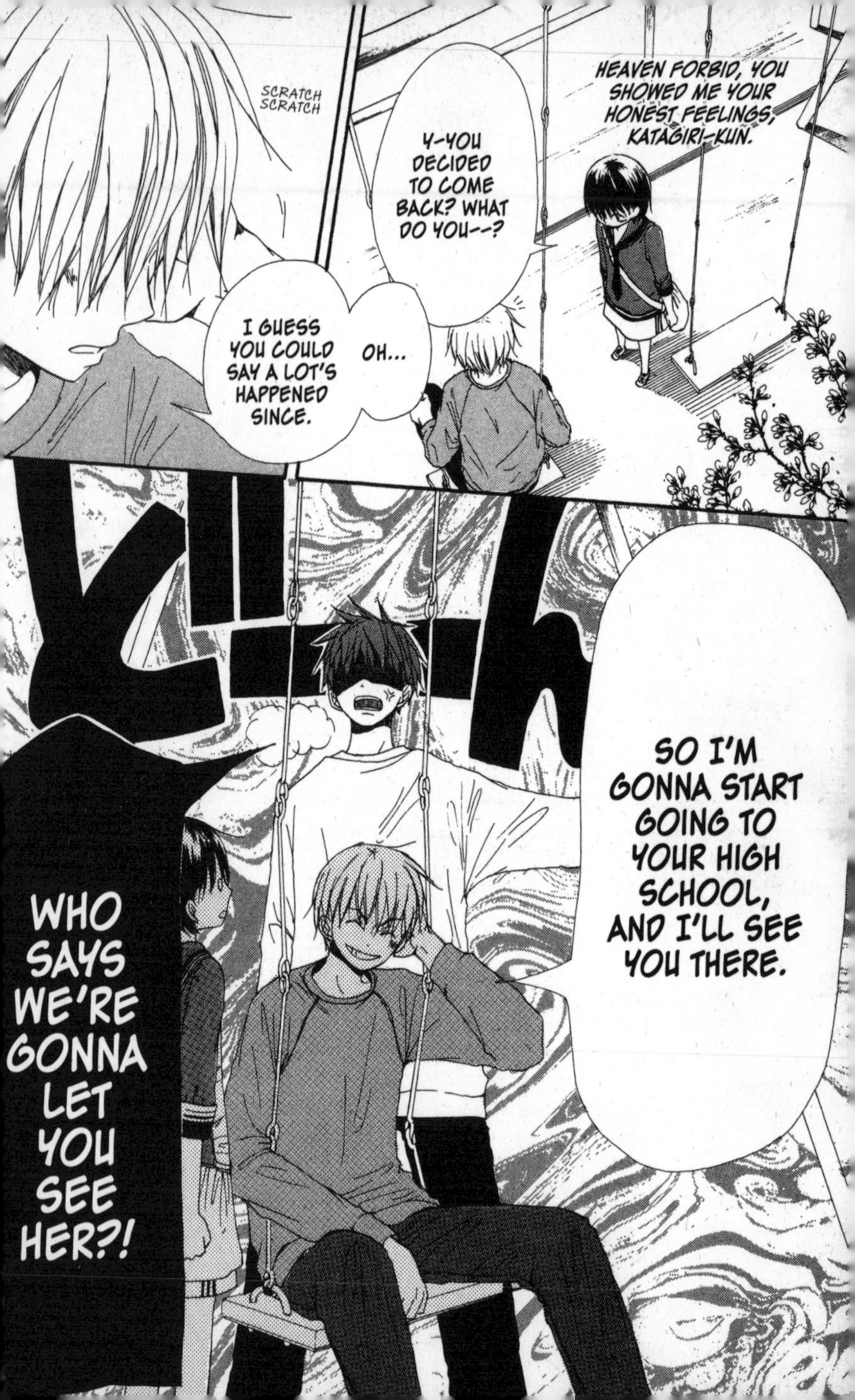
HEAVEN FORBID, YOU SHOWED ME YOUR HONEST FEELINGS, KATAGIRI-KUN.
Y-YOU DECIDED TO COME BACK? WHAT DO YOU--?
OH...
I GUESS YOU COULD SAY A LOT'S HAPPENED SINCE.
SCRATCH SCRATCH
SO I'M GONNA START GOING TO YOUR HIGH SCHOOL, AND I'LL SEE YOU THERE.
WHO SAYS WE'RE GONNA LET YOU SEE HER?!

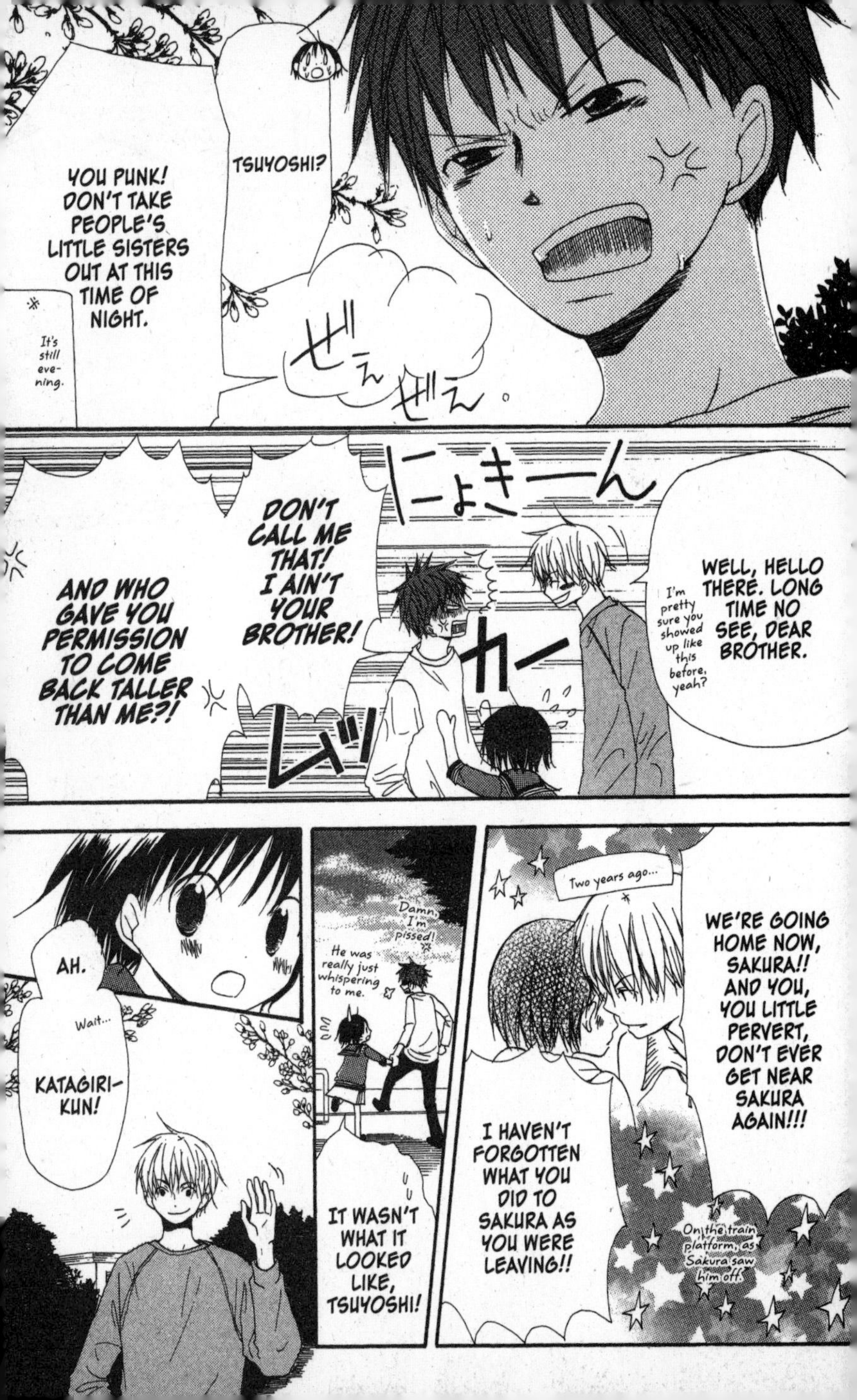
TSUYOSHI?
YOU PUNK! DON'T TAKE PEOPLE'S LITTLE SISTERS OUT AT THIS TIME OF NIGHT.
ぜぇ ぜぇ。
※ It's still evening.
にょきーん
WELL, HELLO THERE. LONG TIME NO SEE, DEAR BROTHER.
I'm pretty sure you showed up like this before, yeah?
DON'T CALL ME THAT! I AIN'T YOUR BROTHER!
カー
AND WHO GAVE YOU PERMISSION TO COME BACK TALLER THAN ME?!
ムッ
Two years ago...
WE'RE GOING HOME NOW, SAKURA!! AND YOU, YOU LITTLE PERVERT, DON'T EVER GET NEAR SAKURA AGAIN!!!
I HAVEN'T FORGOTTEN WHAT YOU DID TO SAKURA AS YOU WERE LEAVING!!
On the train platform, as Sakura saw him off.
Damn, I'm pissed!
He was really just whispering to me.
IT WASN'T WHAT IT LOOKED LIKE, TSUYOSHI!
AH.
Wait...
KATAGIRI-KUN!

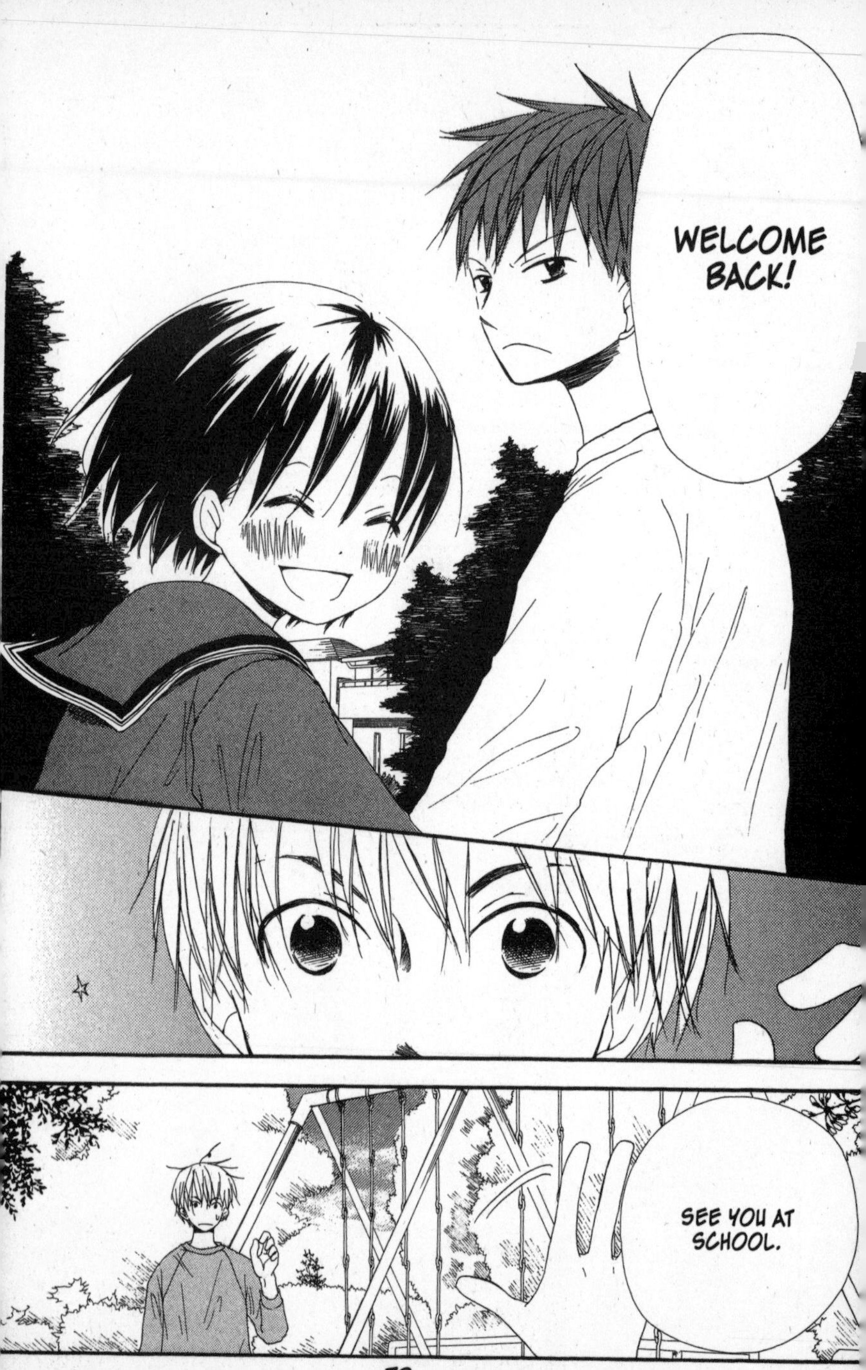
WELCOME BACK!
SEE YOU AT SCHOOL.

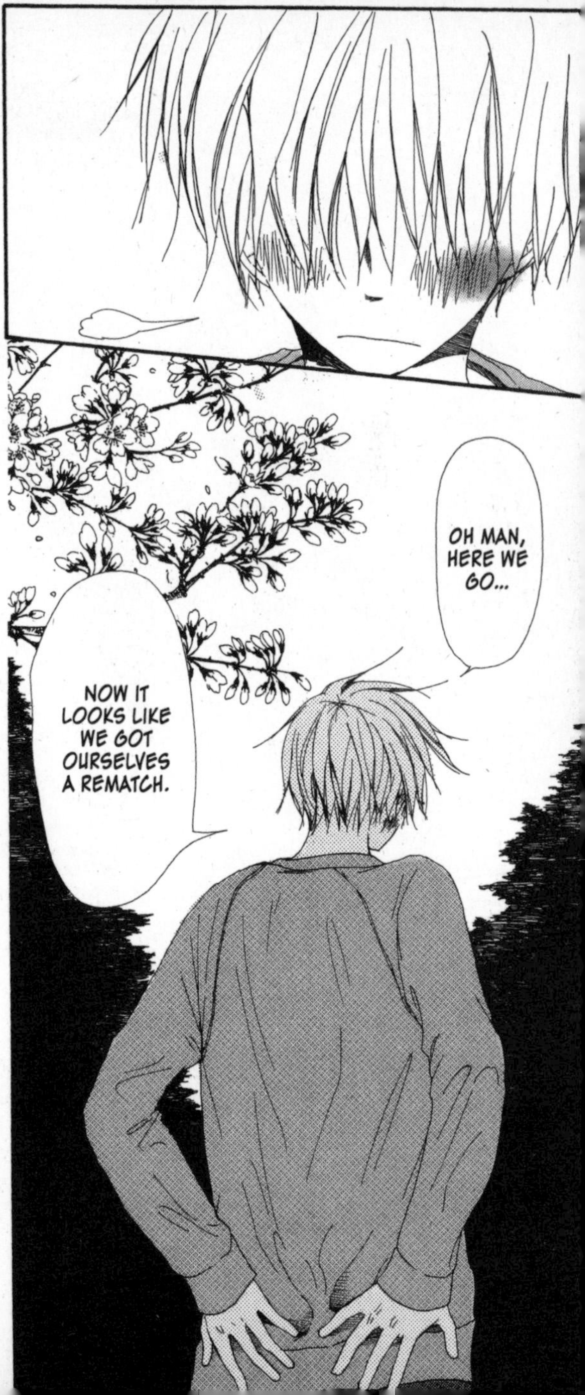
OH MAN, HERE WE GO...
NOW IT LOOKS LIKE WE GOT OURSELVES A REMATCH.

3

Ninth Place:
Nene Kozuka-chan

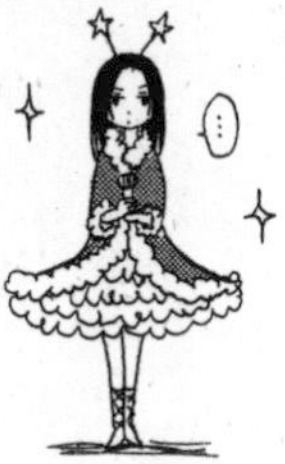
...

And for some strange reason, the Kozuka Twins won 13th place as a set, but they don't show up in this volume at all. As for Terada, who won eighth place, he graduated at some time that didn't show up in the manga...

And so, this time, I made a bonus manga about Terada-senpai's graduation.

It's really fun to draw these kids.

14th Place:
Fuji-san

When we were taking votes, he was the one I was pushing for the most.

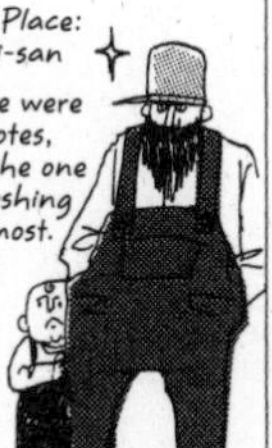

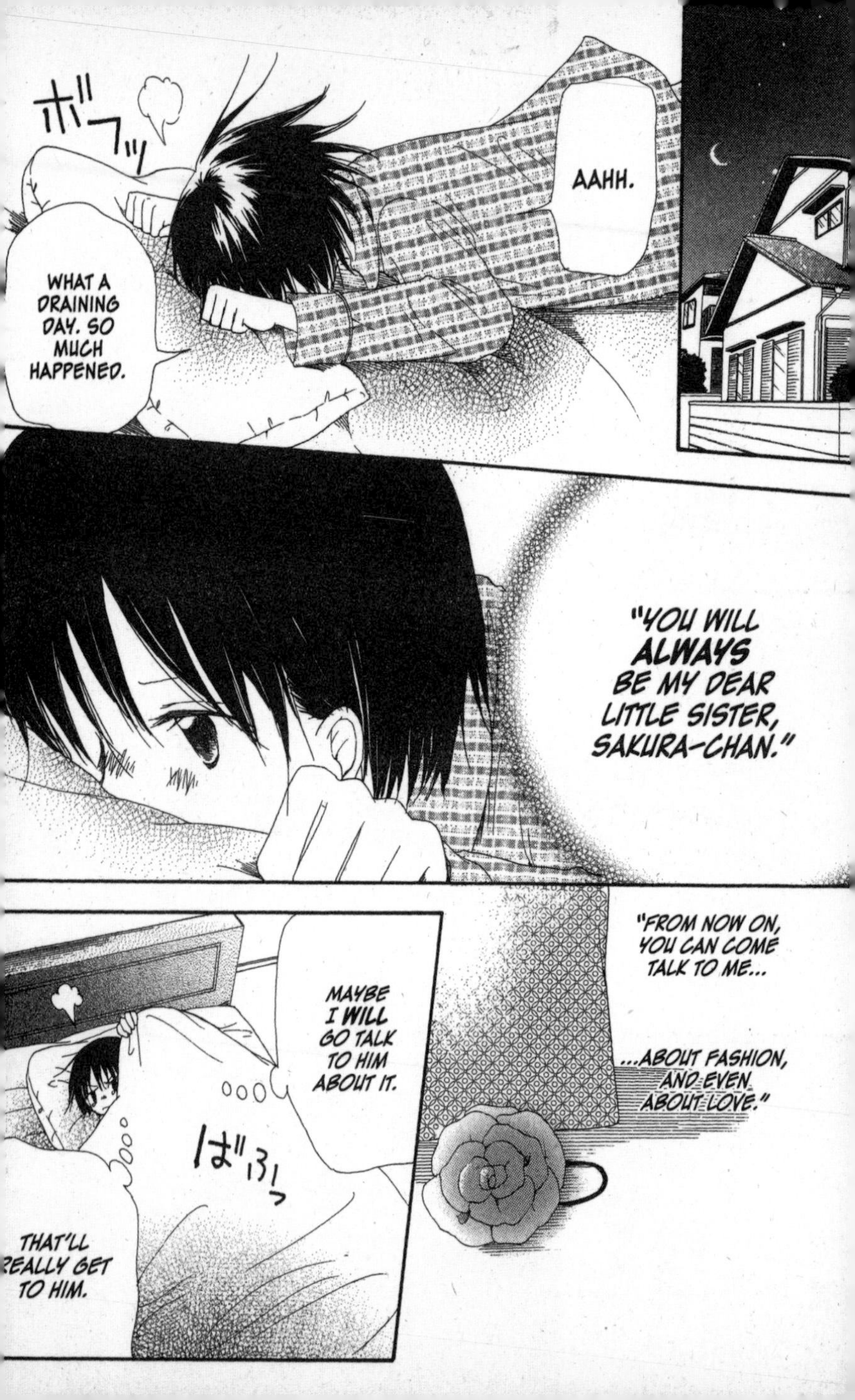
AAHH.
ボフッ
WHAT A DRAINING DAY. SO MUCH HAPPENED.
"YOU WILL ALWAYS BE MY DEAR LITTLE SISTER, SAKURA-CHAN."
"FROM NOW ON, YOU CAN COME TALK TO ME...
...ABOUT FASHION, AND EVEN ABOUT LOVE."
MAYBE I WILL GO TALK TO HIM ABOUT IT.
ばふっ
THAT'LL REALLY GET TO HIM.

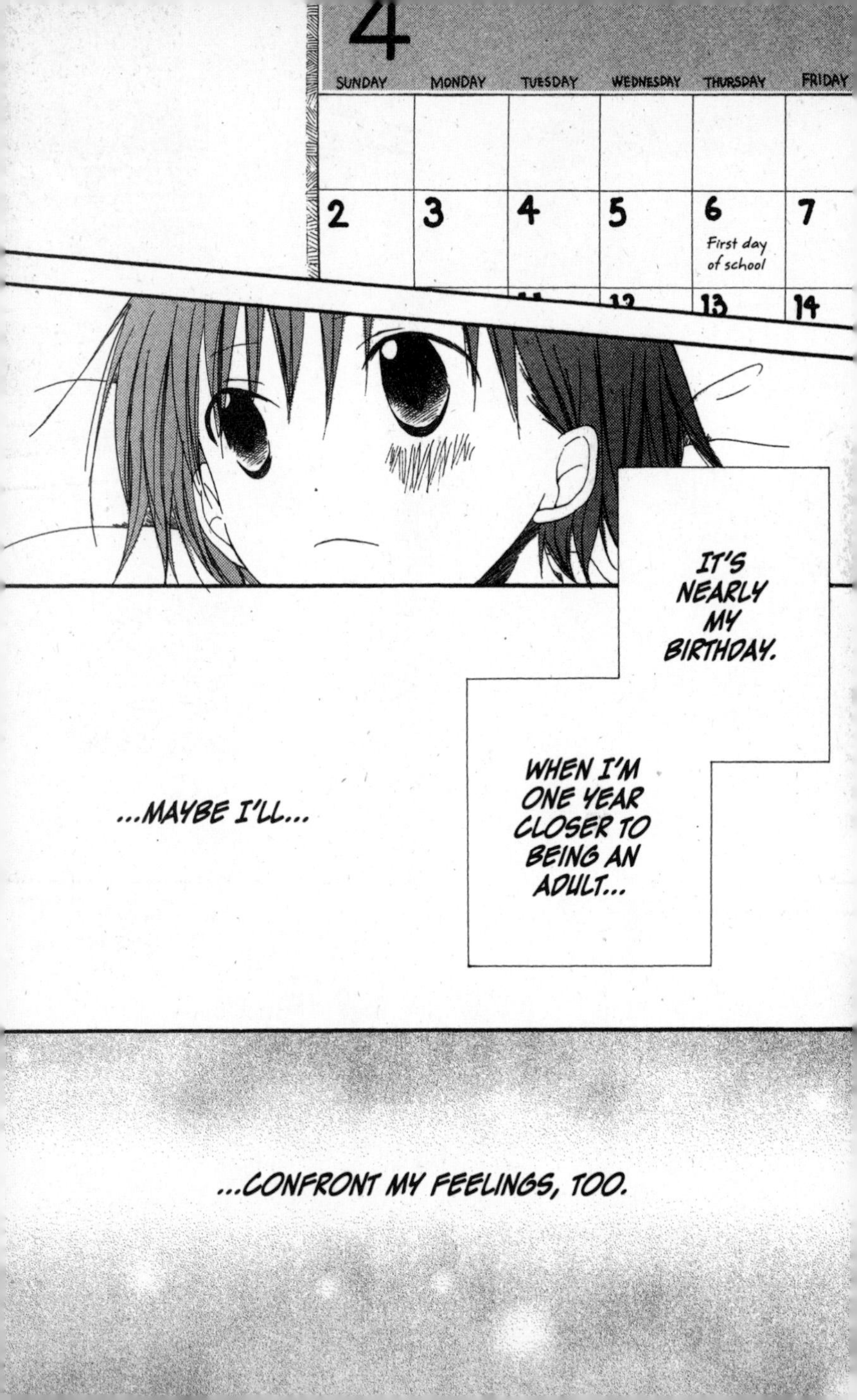
4
SUNDAY
MONDAY
TUESDAY
WEDNESDAY
THURSDAY
FRIDAY
2
3
4
5
6
7
First day of school
13
14
IT'S NEARLY MY BIRTHDAY.
WHEN I'M ONE YEAR CLOSER TO BEING AN ADULT...
...MAYBE I'LL...
...CONFRONT MY FEELINGS, TOO.

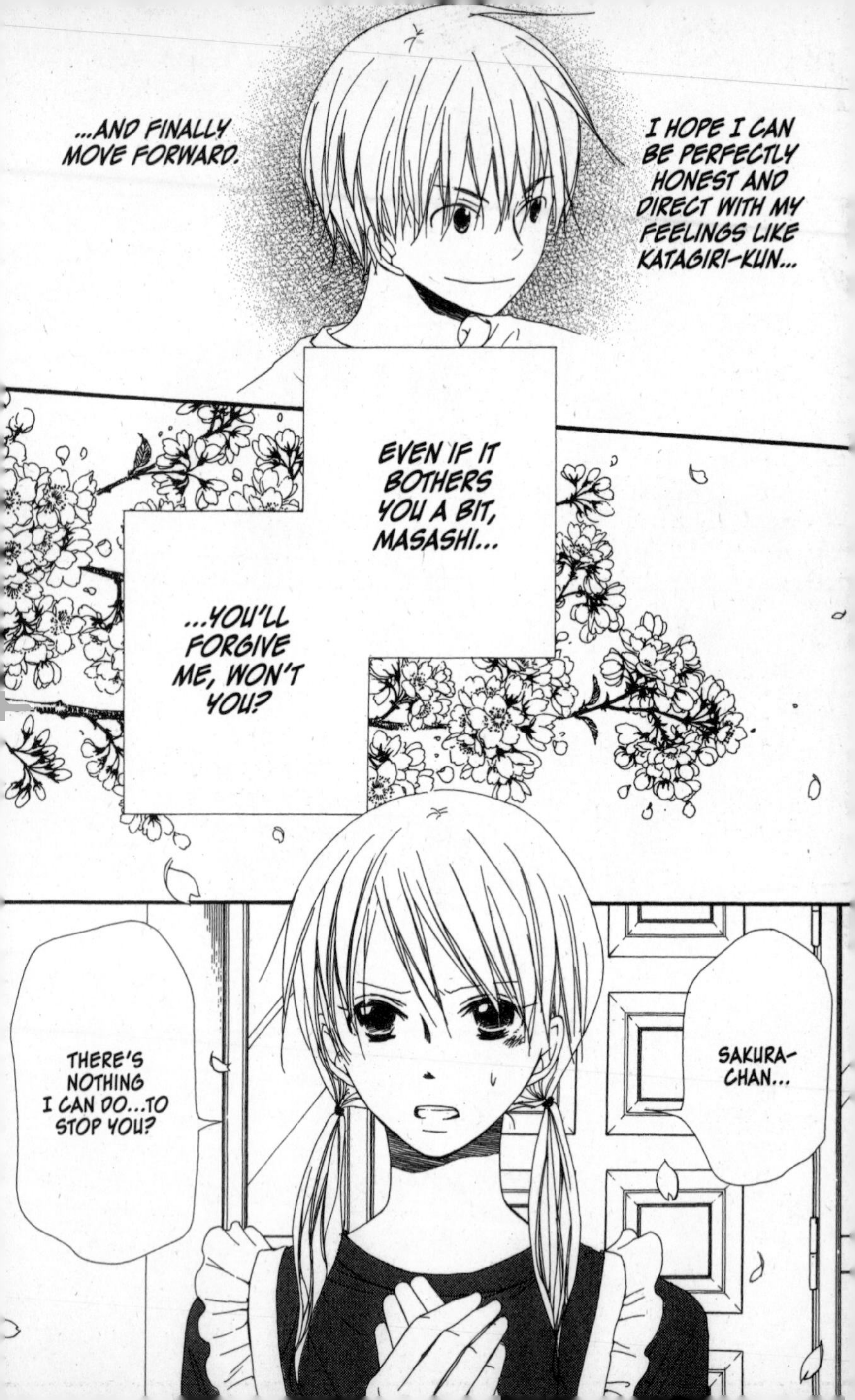
I HOPE I CAN BE PERFECTLY HONEST AND DIRECT WITH MY FEELINGS LIKE KATAGIRI-KUN...
...AND FINALLY MOVE FORWARD.
EVEN IF IT BOTHERS YOU A BIT, MASASHI...
...YOU'LL FORGIVE ME, WON'T YOU?
SAKURA-CHAN...
THERE'S NOTHING I CAN DO...TO STOP YOU?

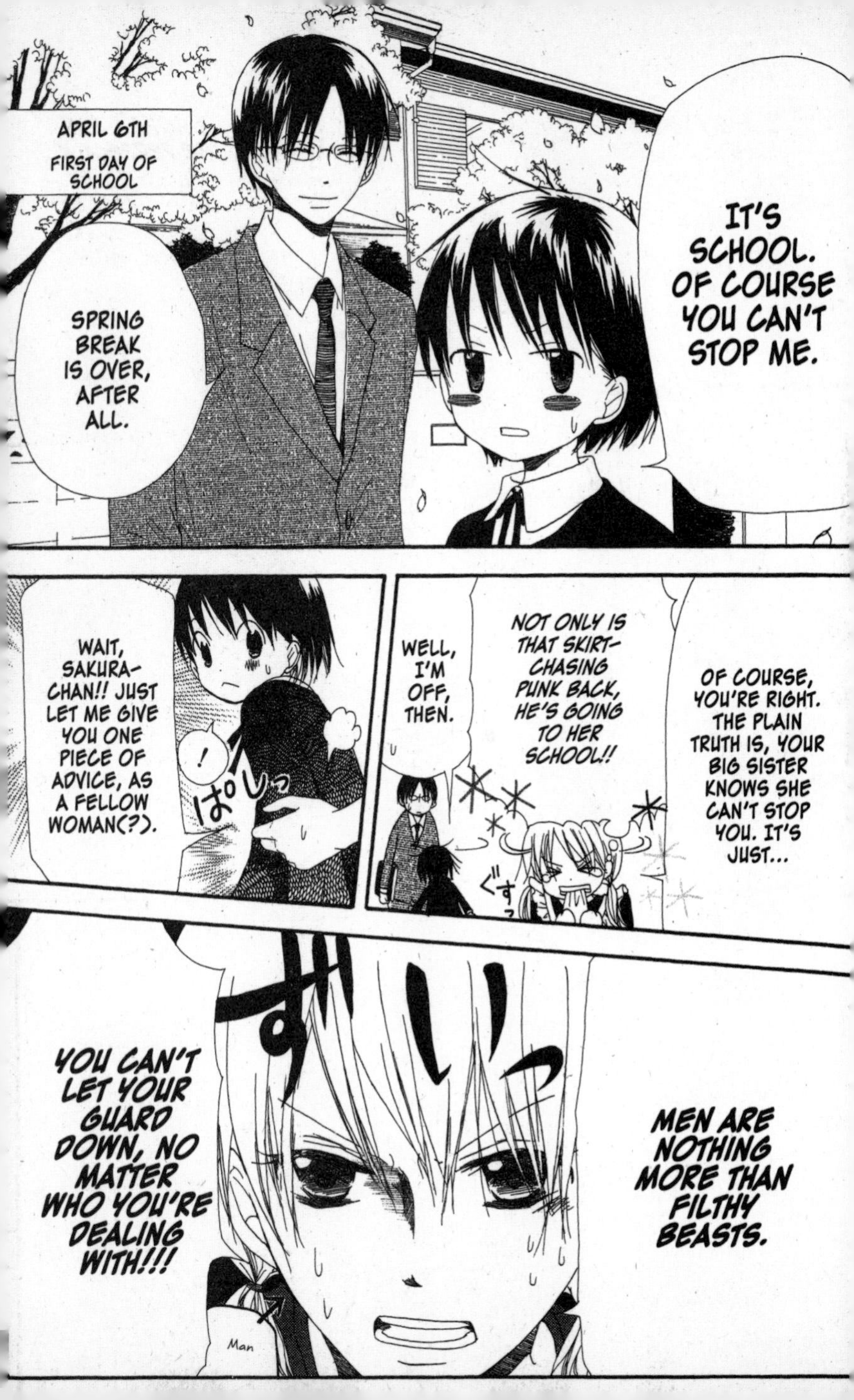

IT'S SCHOOL. OF COURSE YOU CAN'T STOP ME.
APRIL 6TH
FIRST DAY OF SCHOOL
SPRING BREAK IS OVER, AFTER ALL.
OF COURSE, YOU'RE RIGHT. THE PLAIN TRUTH IS, YOUR BIG SISTER KNOWS SHE CAN'T STOP YOU. IT'S JUST...
NOT ONLY IS THAT SKIRT-CHASING PUNK BACK, HE'S GOING TO HER SCHOOL!!
WELL, I'M OFF, THEN.
ぐすっ
WAIT, SAKURA-CHAN!! JUST LET ME GIVE YOU ONE PIECE OF ADVICE, AS A FELLOW WOMAN(?).
!
ぱしっ
MEN ARE NOTHING MORE THAN FILTHY BEASTS.
すいっ
YOU CAN'T LET YOUR GUARD DOWN, NO MATTER WHO YOU'RE DEALING WITH!!!
Man

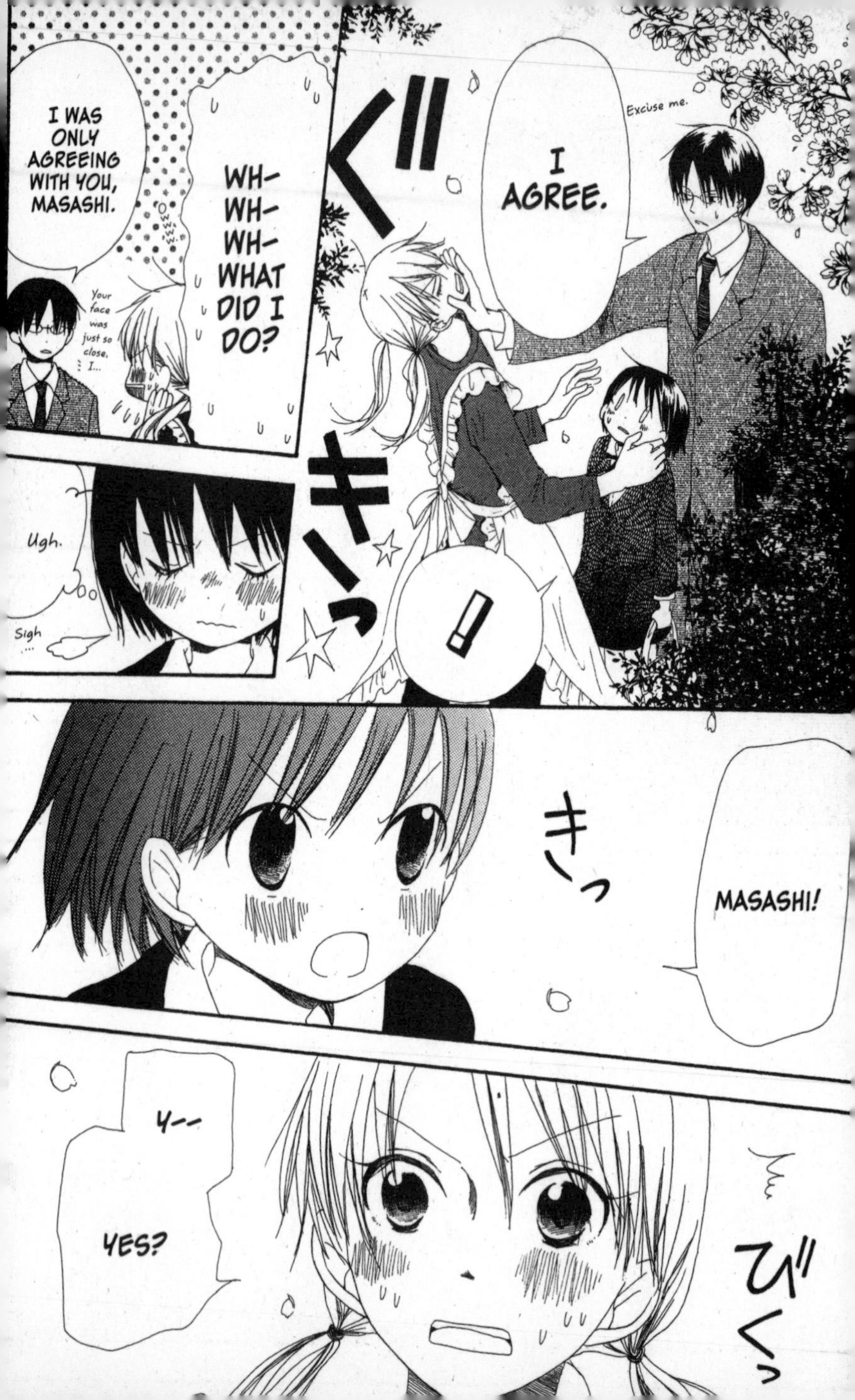

Excuse me.
I AGREE.
きっ
!
WH-WH-WH-WHAT DID I DO?
OWWW.
I WAS ONLY AGREEING WITH YOU, MASASHI.
Your face was just so close, I...
Ugh.
Sigh....
きっ
MASASHI!
Y-- YES?

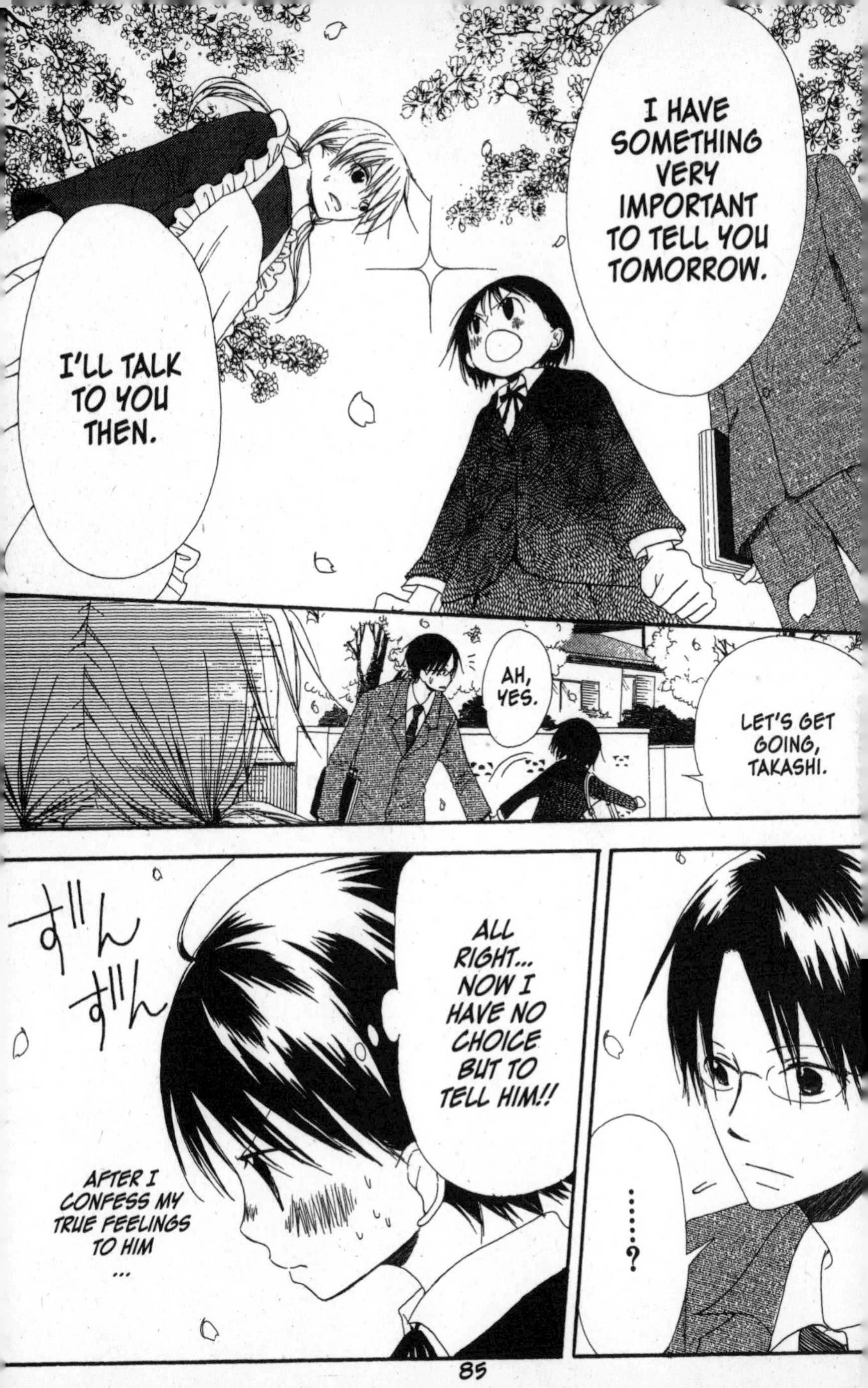
I HAVE SOMETHING VERY IMPORTANT TO TELL YOU TOMORROW.
I'LL TALK TO YOU THEN.
LET'S GET GOING, TAKASHI.
AH, YES.
......?
ALL RIGHT... NOW I HAVE NO CHOICE BUT TO TELL HIM!!
ずん ずん
AFTER I CONFESS MY TRUE FEELINGS TO HIM ...

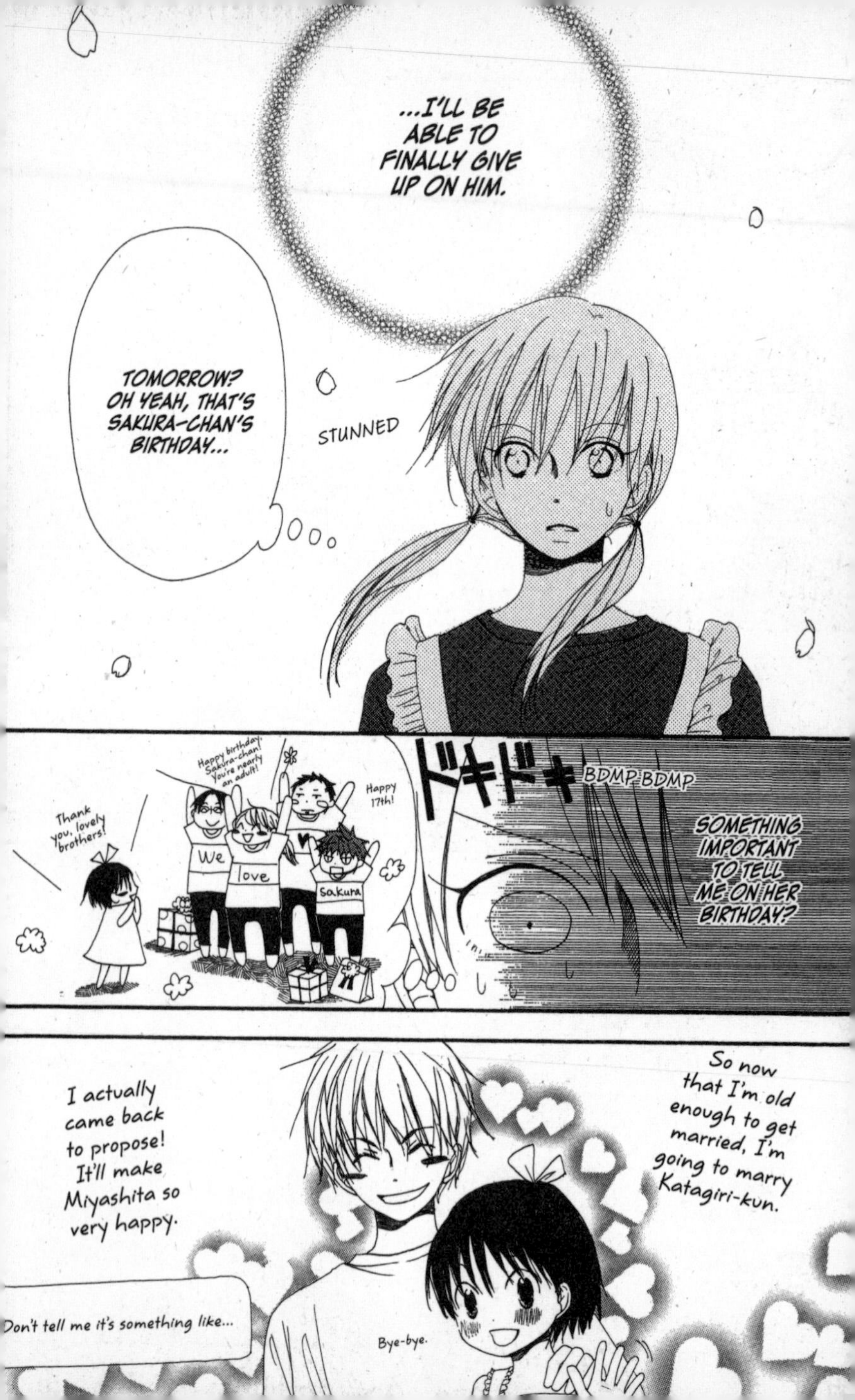
...I'LL BE ABLE TO FINALLY GIVE UP ON HIM.
STUNNED
TOMORROW? OH YEAH, THAT'S SAKURA-CHAN'S BIRTHDAY...
ドキドキ BDMP BDMP
SOMETHING IMPORTANT TO TELL ME ON HER BIRTHDAY?
Happy 17th!
Happy birthday, Sakura-chan! You're nearly an adult!
We love sakura
Thank you, lovely brothers!
So now that I'm old enough to get married, I'm going to marry Katagiri-kun.
I actually came back to propose! It'll make Miyashita so very happy.
Bye-bye.
Don't tell me it's something like...

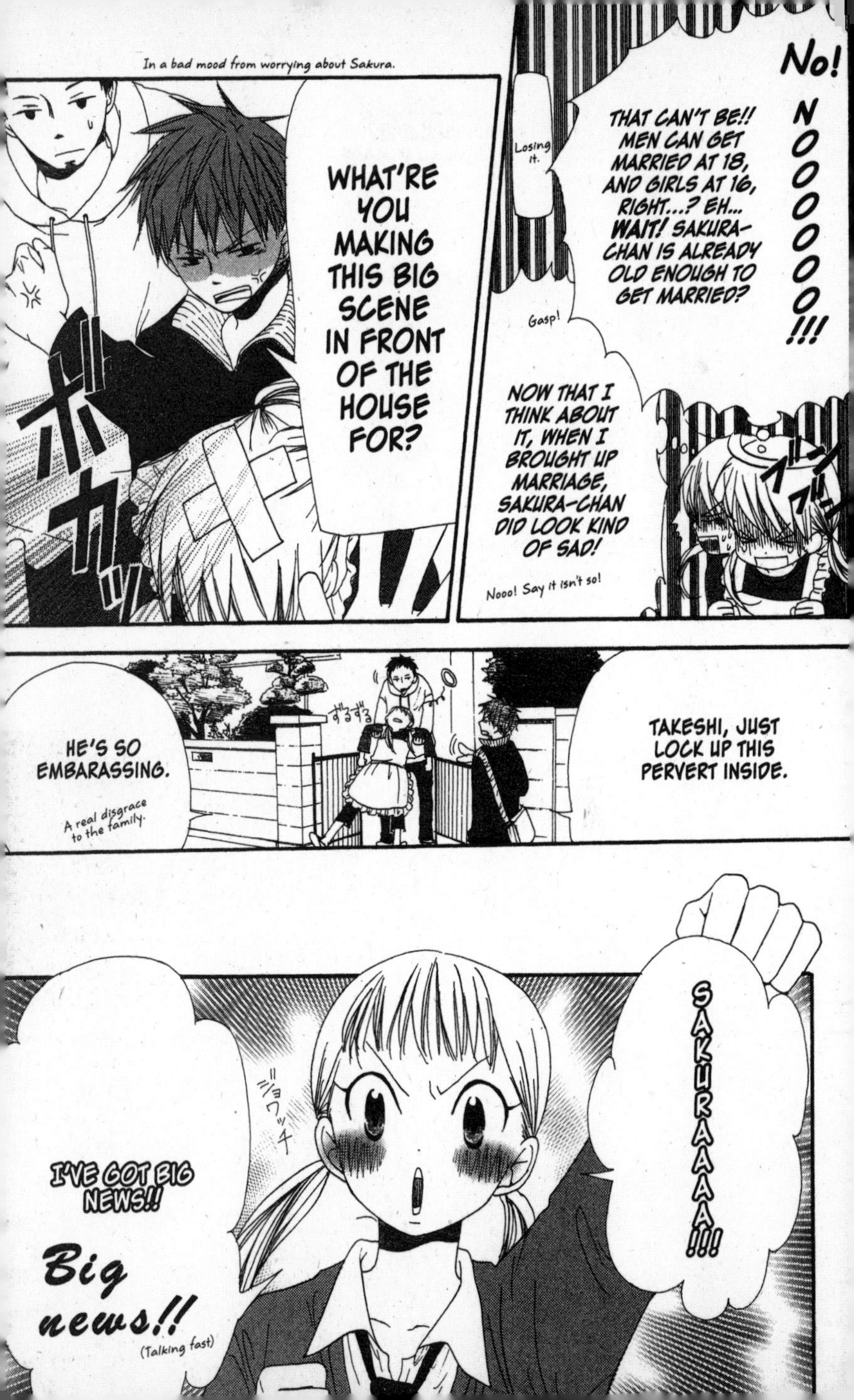

No!
NOOOOOOOO!!!
THAT CAN'T BE!! MEN CAN GET MARRIED AT 18, AND GIRLS AT 16, RIGHT...? EH... WAIT! SAKURA-CHAN IS ALREADY OLD ENOUGH TO GET MARRIED?
Losing it.
Gasp!
NOW THAT I THINK ABOUT IT, WHEN I BROUGHT UP MARRIAGE, SAKURA-CHAN DID LOOK KIND OF SAD!
Nooo! Say it isn't so!
In a bad mood from worrying about Sakura.
WHAT'RE YOU MAKING THIS BIG SCENE IN FRONT OF THE HOUSE FOR?
TAKESHI, JUST LOCK UP THIS PERVERT INSIDE.
HE'S SO EMBARASSING.
A real disgrace to the family.
SAKURAAAAAA!!!
I'VE GOT BIG NEWS!!
Big news!!
(Talking fast)

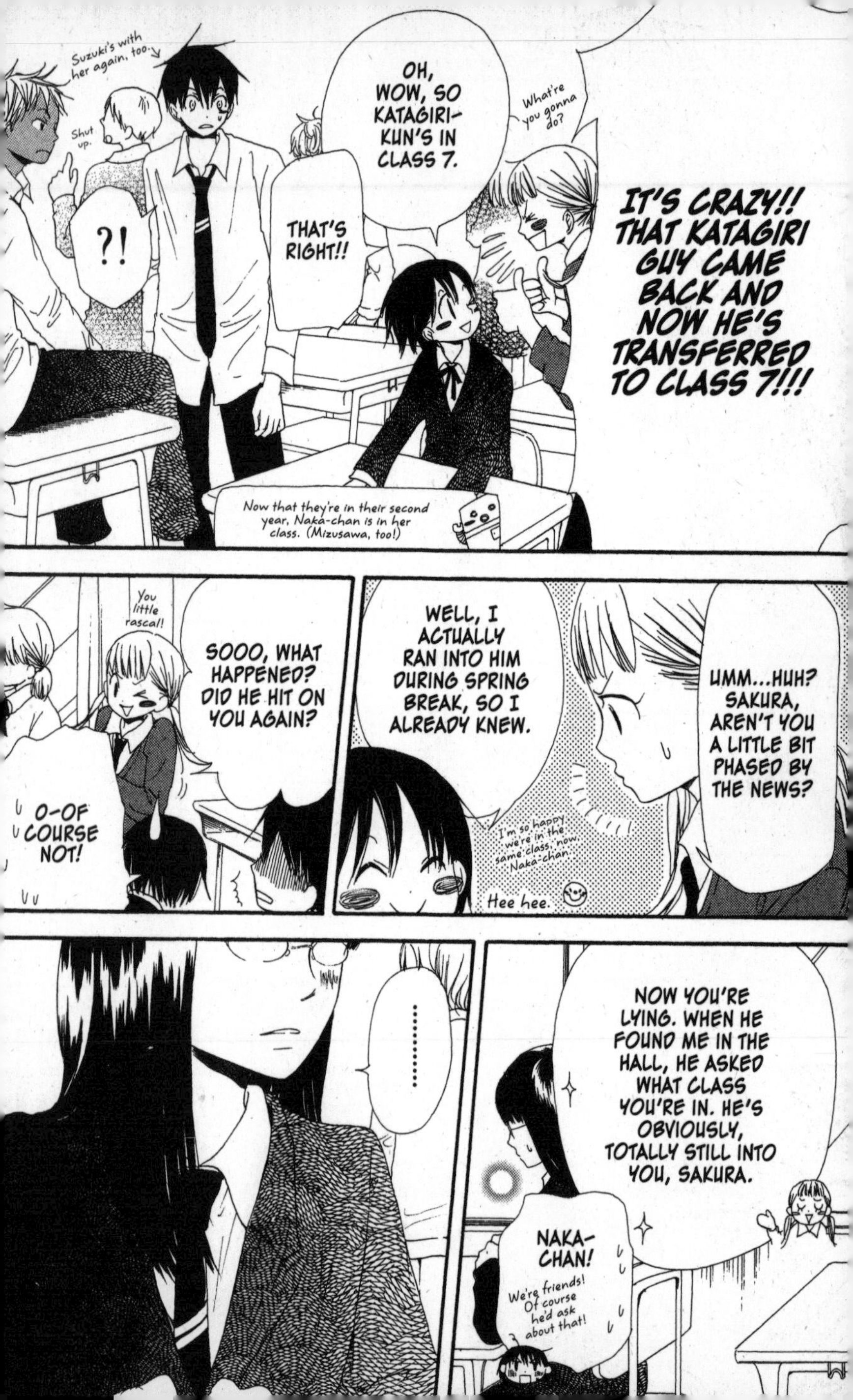
What're you gonna do?
IT'S CRAZY!! THAT KATAGIRI GUY CAME BACK AND NOW HE'S TRANSFERRED TO CLASS 7!!!
OH, WOW, SO KATAGIRI-KUN'S IN CLASS 7.
THAT'S RIGHT!!
Suzuki's with her again, too.
Shut up.
?!
Now that they're in their second year, Naka-chan is in her class. (Mizusawa, too!)
UMM...HUH? SAKURA, AREN'T YOU A LITTLE BIT PHASED BY THE NEWS?
WELL, I ACTUALLY RAN INTO HIM DURING SPRING BREAK, SO I ALREADY KNEW.
I'm so happy we're in the same class now, Naka-chan.
Hee hee.
You little rascal!
SOOO, WHAT HAPPENED? DID HE HIT ON YOU AGAIN?
O-OF COURSE NOT!
NOW YOU'RE LYING. WHEN HE FOUND ME IN THE HALL, HE ASKED WHAT CLASS YOU'RE IN. HE'S OBVIOUSLY, TOTALLY STILL INTO YOU, SAKURA.
NAKA-CHAN!
We're friends! Of course he'd ask about that!
....

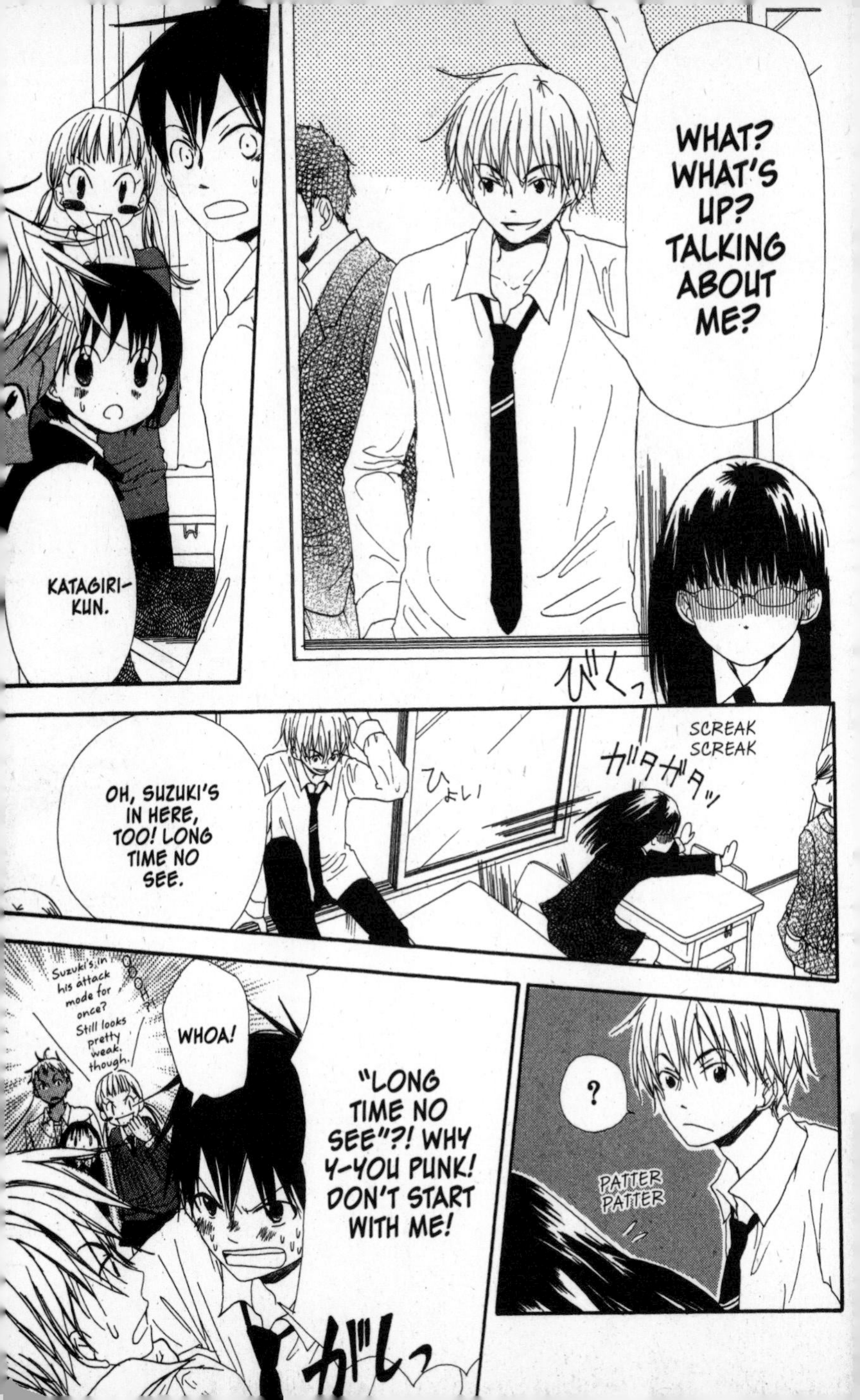
WHAT? WHAT'S UP? TALKING ABOUT ME?
びくっ
KATAGIRI-KUN.
SCREAK SCREAK
ガタガタッ
ひょい
OH, SUZUKI'S IN HERE, TOO! LONG TIME NO SEE.
?
PATTER PATTER
"LONG TIME NO SEE"?! WHY Y-YOU PUNK! DON'T START WITH ME!
WHOA!
Suzuki's in his attack mode for once? Still looks pretty weak, though.
がしっ

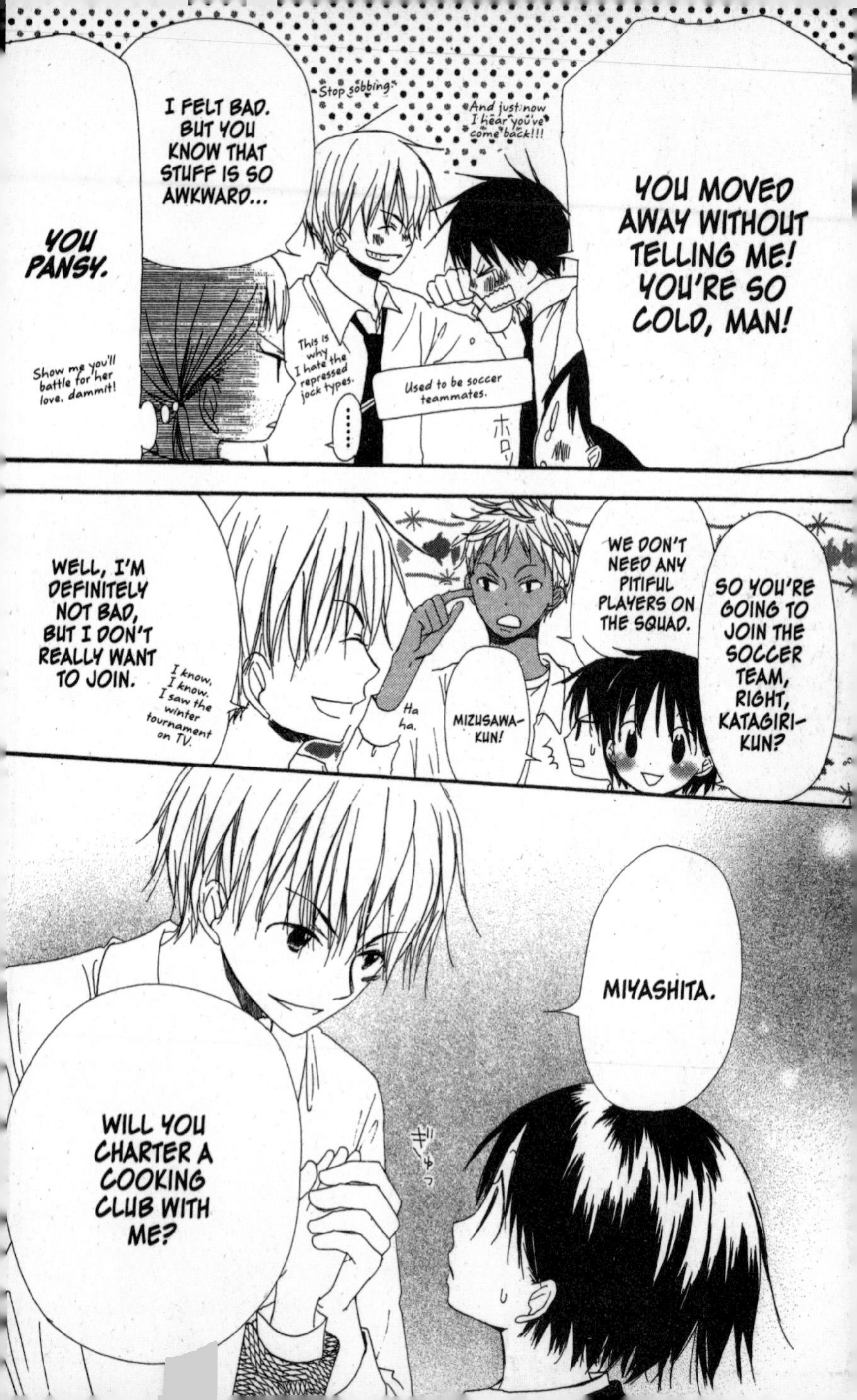
YOU MOVED AWAY WITHOUT TELLING ME! YOU'RE SO COLD, MAN!
And just now I hear you've come back!!!
Stop sobbing.
I FELT BAD. BUT YOU KNOW THAT STUFF IS SO AWKWARD...
YOU PANSY.
Used to be soccer teammates.
This is why I hate the repressed jock types.
......
Show me you'll battle for her love, dammit!
SO YOU'RE GOING TO JOIN THE SOCCER TEAM, RIGHT, KATAGIRI-KUN?
WE DON'T NEED ANY PITIFUL PLAYERS ON THE SQUAD.
MIZUSAWA-KUN!
Ha ha.
I know, I know. I saw the winter tournament on TV.
WELL, I'M DEFINITELY NOT BAD, BUT I DON'T REALLY WANT TO JOIN.
MIYASHITA.
WILL YOU CHARTER A COOKING CLUB WITH ME?

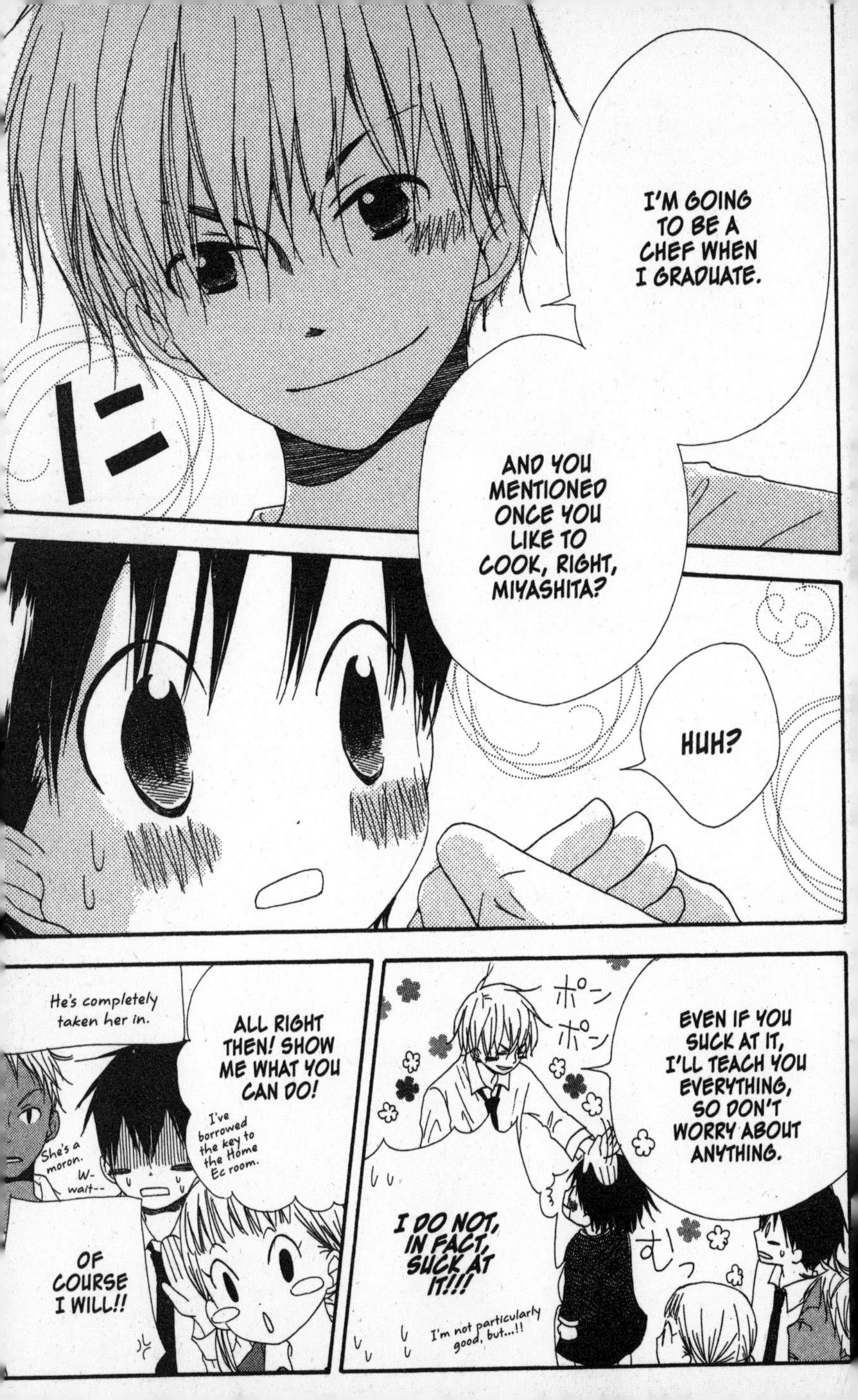
I'M GOING TO BE A CHEF WHEN I GRADUATE.
AND YOU MENTIONED ONCE YOU LIKE TO COOK, RIGHT, MIYASHITA?
HUH?
EVEN IF YOU SUCK AT IT, I'LL TEACH YOU EVERYTHING, SO DON'T WORRY ABOUT ANYTHING.
ポン
ポン
むっ
I DO NOT, IN FACT, SUCK AT IT!!!
I'm not particularly good, but...!!
He's completely taken her in.
ALL RIGHT THEN! SHOW ME WHAT YOU CAN DO!
I've borrowed the key to the Home Ec room.
She's a moron.
W-wait--
OF COURSE I WILL!!

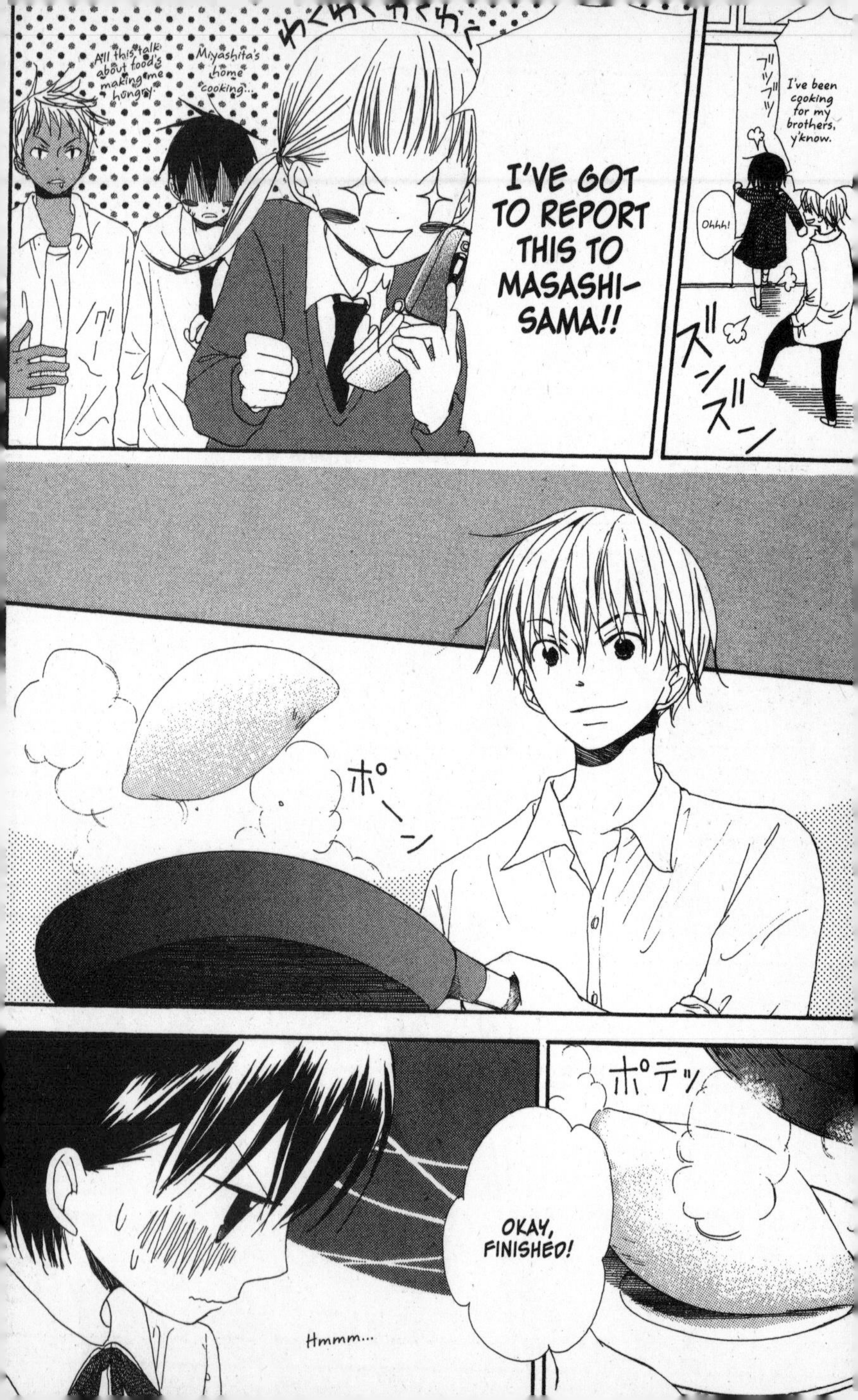
ブツブツ
I've been cooking for my brothers, y'know.
Ohhh!
ズシズーン
わくわくわくわく
All this talk about food's making me hungry.
Miyashita's home cooking...
I'VE GOT TO REPORT THIS TO MASASHI-SAMA!!
ポーン
ポテッ
OKAY, FINISHED!
Hmmm...

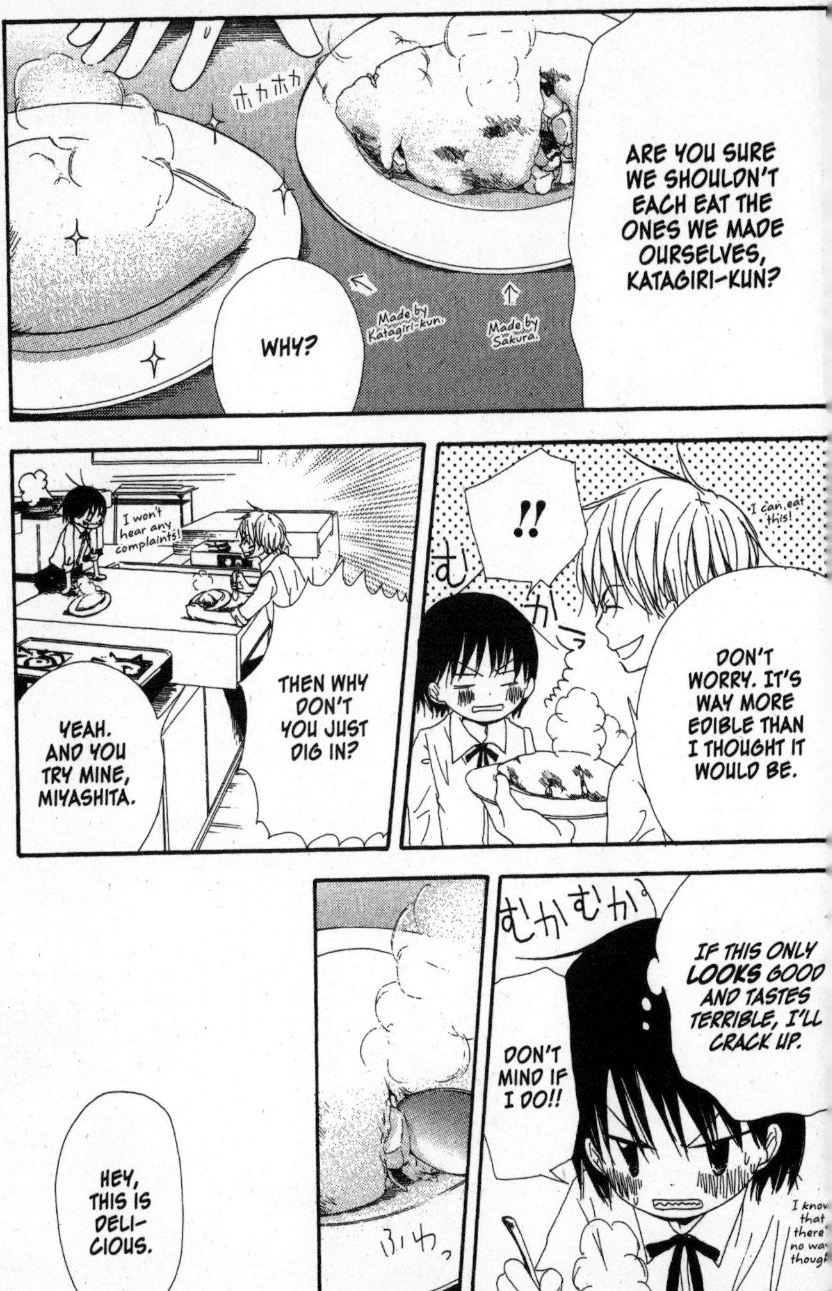
ARE YOU SURE WE SHOULDN'T EACH EAT THE ONES WE MADE OURSELVES, KATAGIRI-KUN?
Made by Sakura.
Made by Katagiri-kun.
ホカホカ
WHY?
!!
むか
I can eat this!
DON'T WORRY. IT'S WAY MORE EDIBLE THAN I THOUGHT IT WOULD BE.
THEN WHY DON'T YOU JUST DIG IN?
I won't hear any complaints!
YEAH. AND YOU TRY MINE, MIYASHITA.
むかむか
IF THIS ONLY LOOKS GOOD AND TASTES TERRIBLE, I'LL CRACK UP.
DON'T MIND IF I DO!!
ふわっ
HEY, THIS IS DELI- CIOUS.

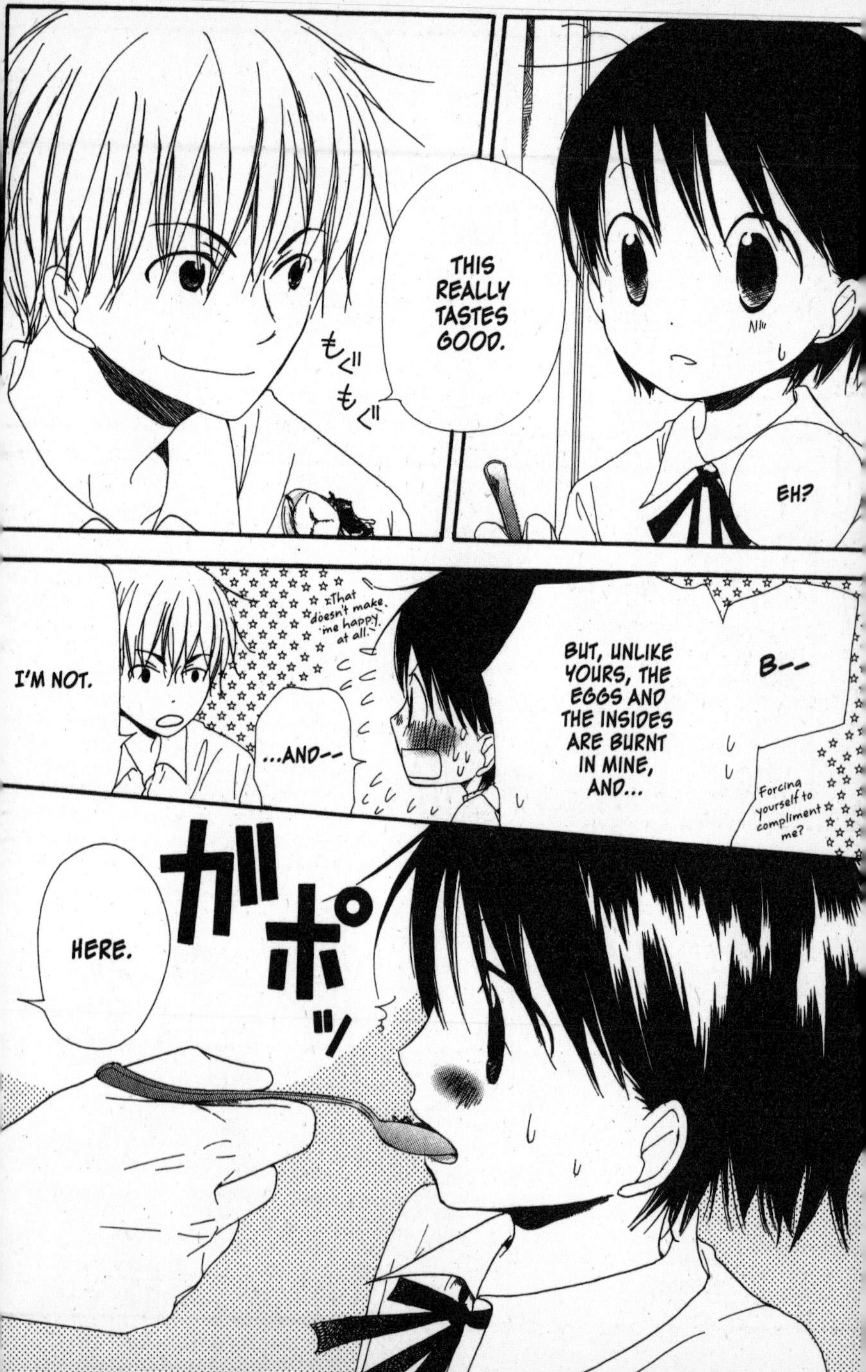
EH?
THIS REALLY TASTES GOOD.
もぐもぐ
B--
Forcing yourself to compliment me?
BUT, UNLIKE YOURS, THE EGGS AND THE INSIDES ARE BURNT IN MINE, AND...
...AND--
That doesn't make me happy at all.
I'M NOT.
ガポッ
HERE.

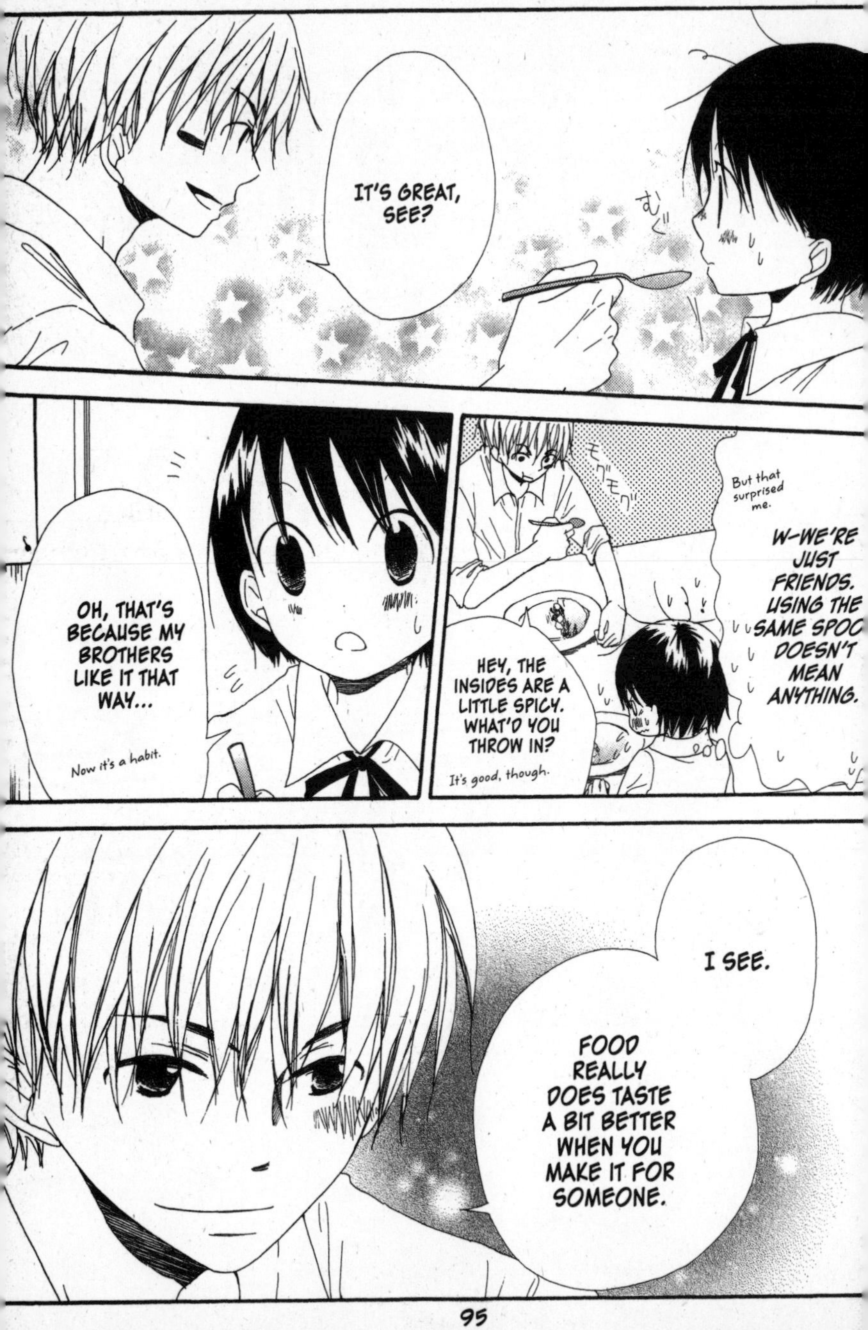
IT'S GREAT, SEE?
むぐ
モグモグ
But that surprised me.
W-WE'RE JUST FRIENDS. USING THE SAME SPOO DOESN'T MEAN ANYTHING.
HEY, THE INSIDES ARE A LITTLE SPICY. WHAT'D YOU THROW IN?
It's good, though.
OH, THAT'S BECAUSE MY BROTHERS LIKE IT THAT WAY...
Now it's a habit.
I SEE.
FOOD REALLY DOES TASTE A BIT BETTER WHEN YOU MAKE IT FOR SOMEONE.

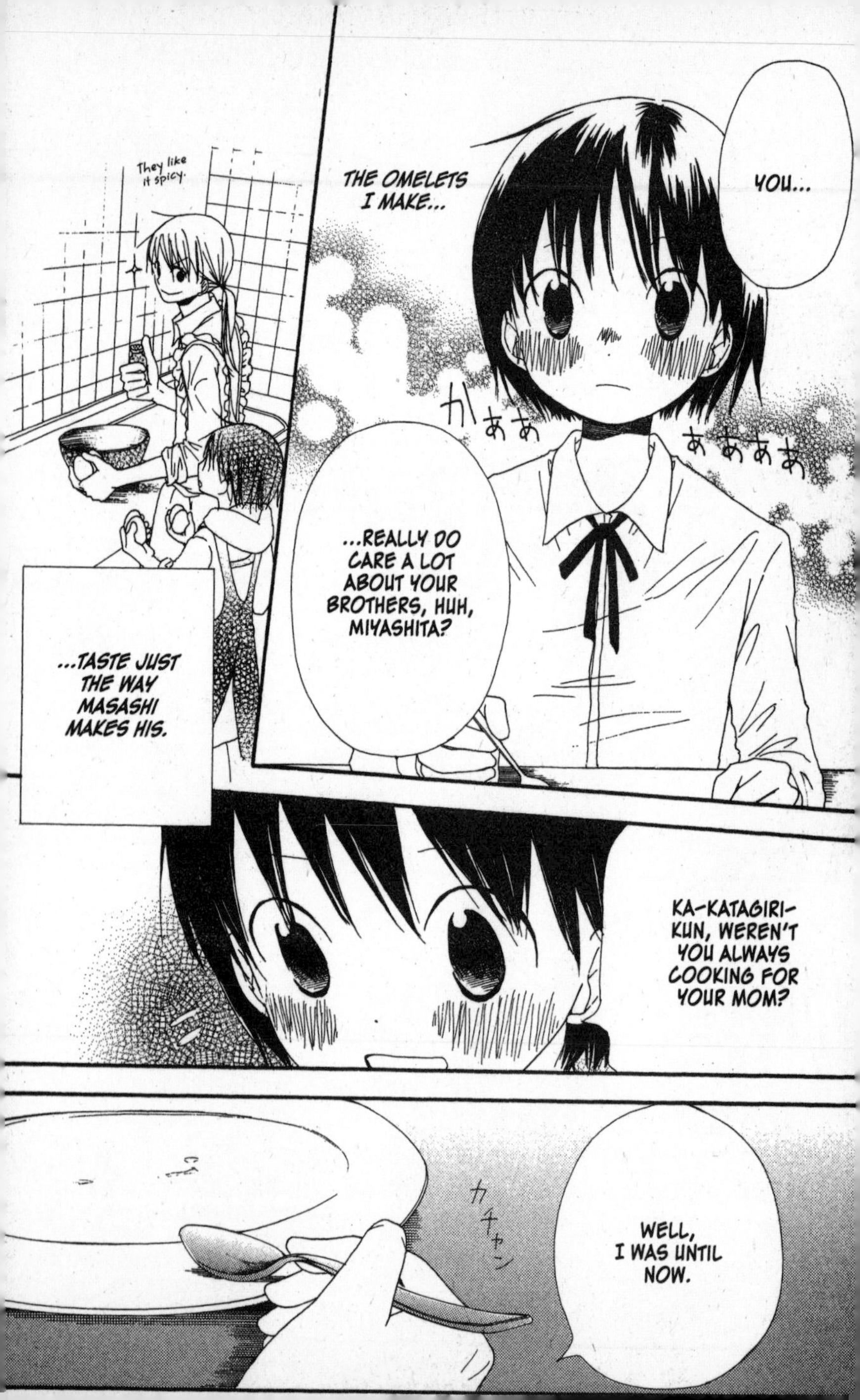
YOU...
THE OMELETS I MAKE...
かああ
ああああ
...REALLY DO CARE A LOT ABOUT YOUR BROTHERS, HUH, MIYASHITA?
They like it spicy.
...TASTE JUST THE WAY MASASHI MAKES HIS.
KA-KATAGIRI-KUN, WEREN'T YOU ALWAYS COOKING FOR YOUR MOM?
カチャン
WELL, I WAS UNTIL NOW.

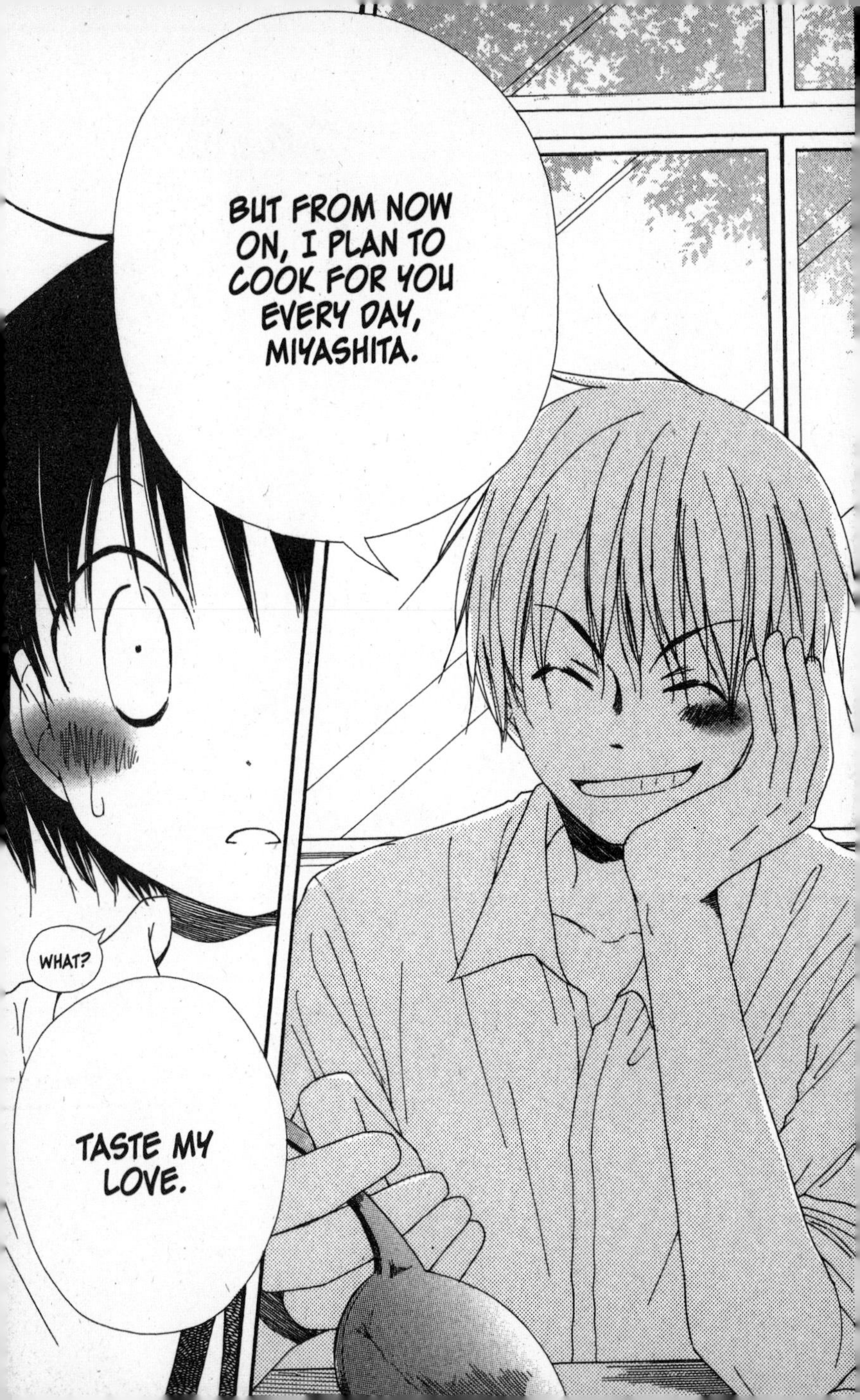
BUT FROM NOW ON, I PLAN TO COOK FOR YOU EVERY DAY, MIYASHITA.
WHAT?
TASTE MY LOVE.

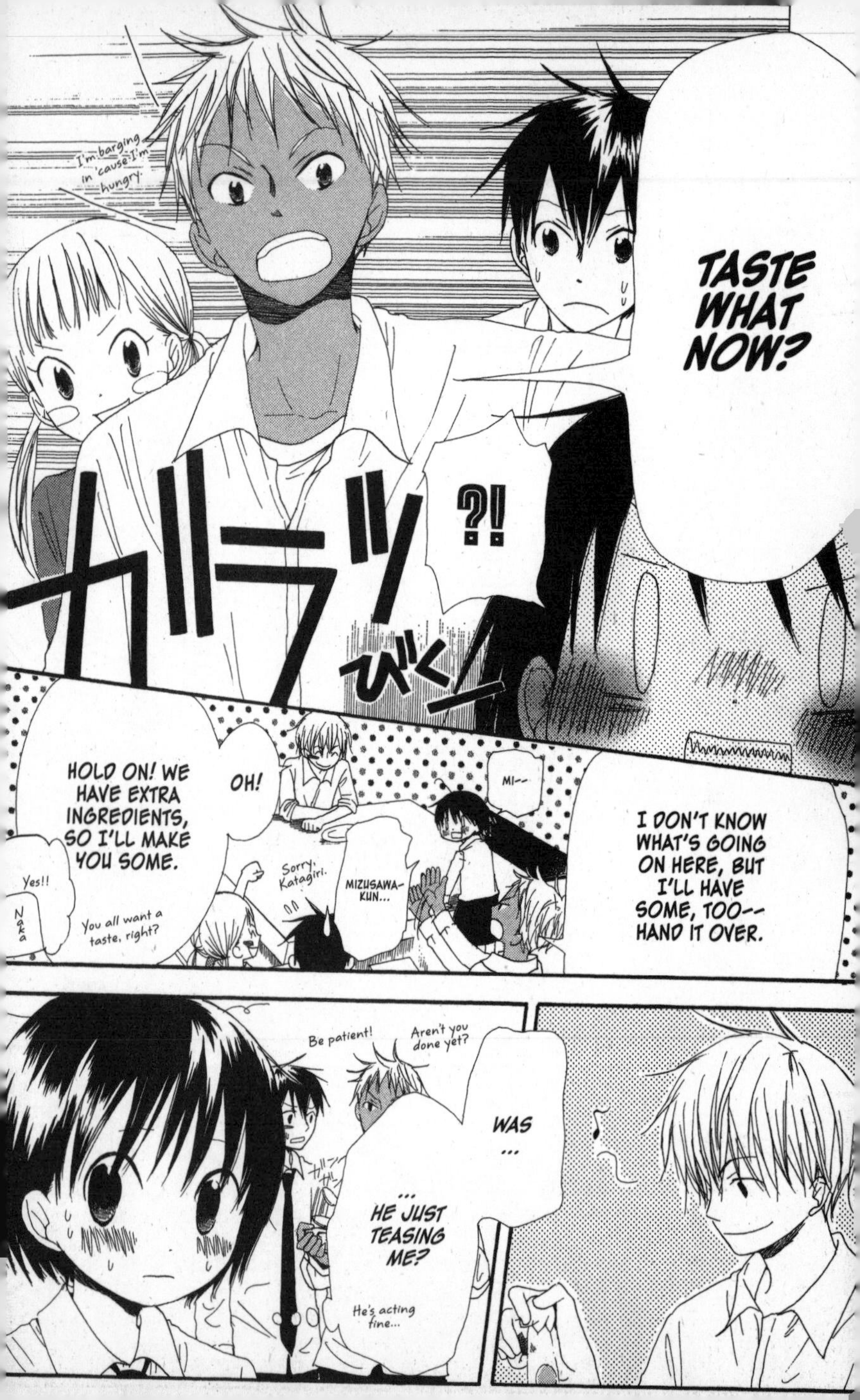
TASTE WHAT NOW?
?!
I'm barging in 'cause I'm hungry.
ガラッ
びくっ
I DON'T KNOW WHAT'S GOING ON HERE, BUT I'LL HAVE SOME, TOO--HAND IT OVER.
MI--
MIZUSAWA-KUN...
Sorry, Katagiri.
OH!
HOLD ON! WE HAVE EXTRA INGREDIENTS, SO I'LL MAKE YOU SOME.
You all want a taste, right?
Yes!!
Naka
WAS ...
... HE JUST TEASING ME?
Aren't you done yet?
Be patient!
He's acting fine...

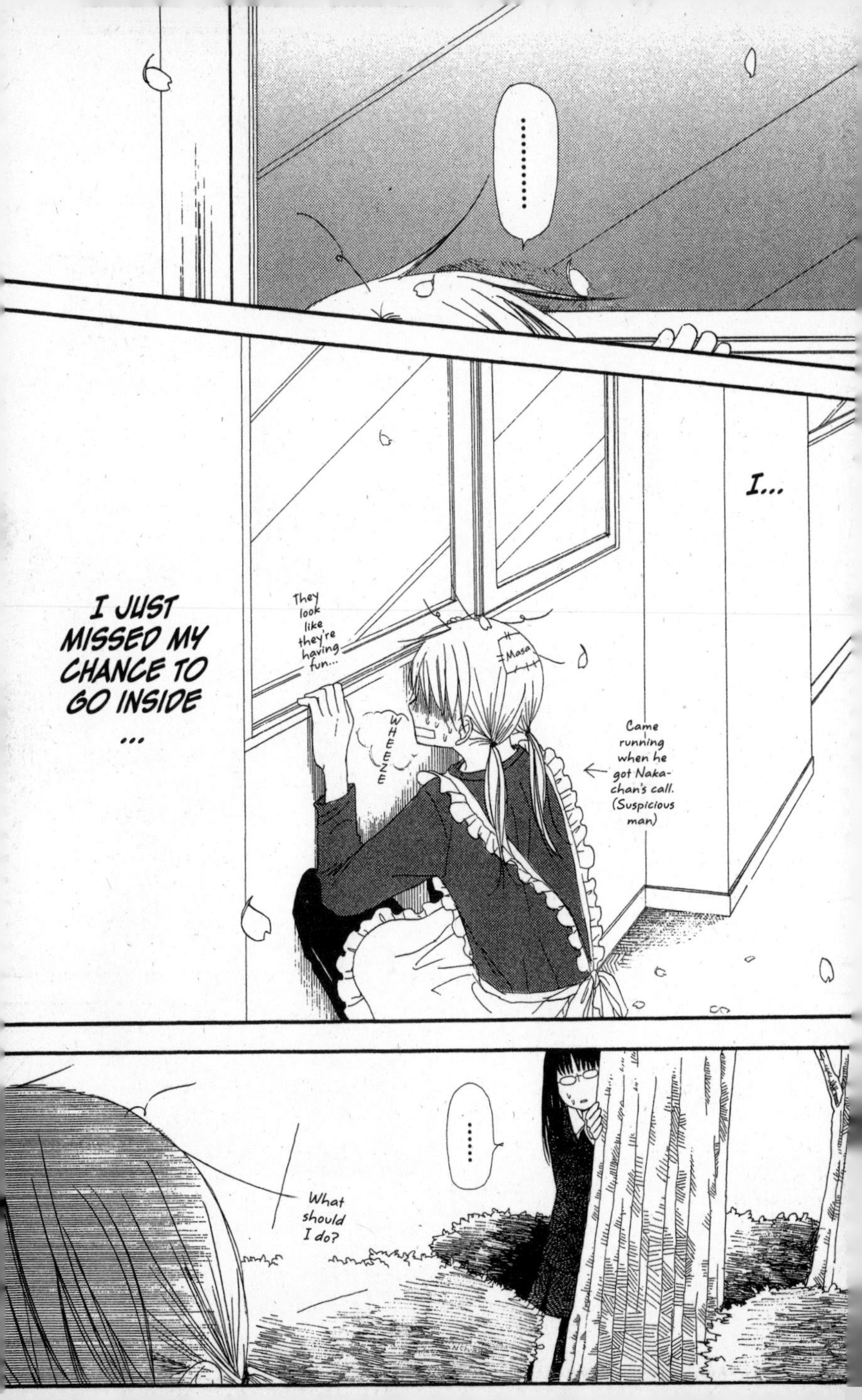
......
I...
Came running when he got Naka-chan's call. (Suspicious man)
Masa
WHEEZE
They look like they're having fun...
I JUST MISSED MY CHANCE TO GO INSIDE ...
......
What should I do?

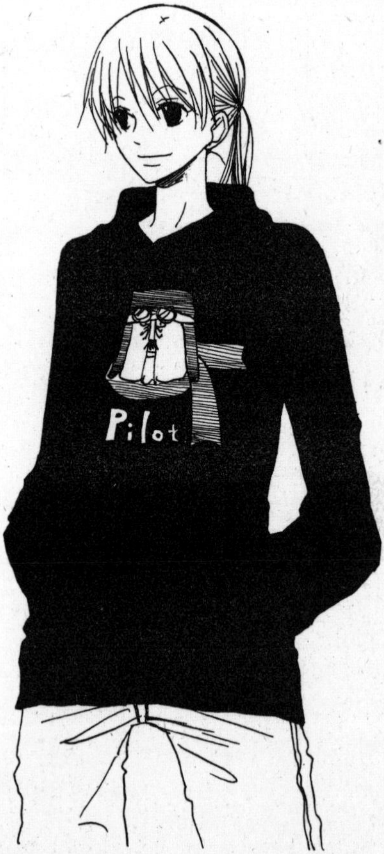
Pilot

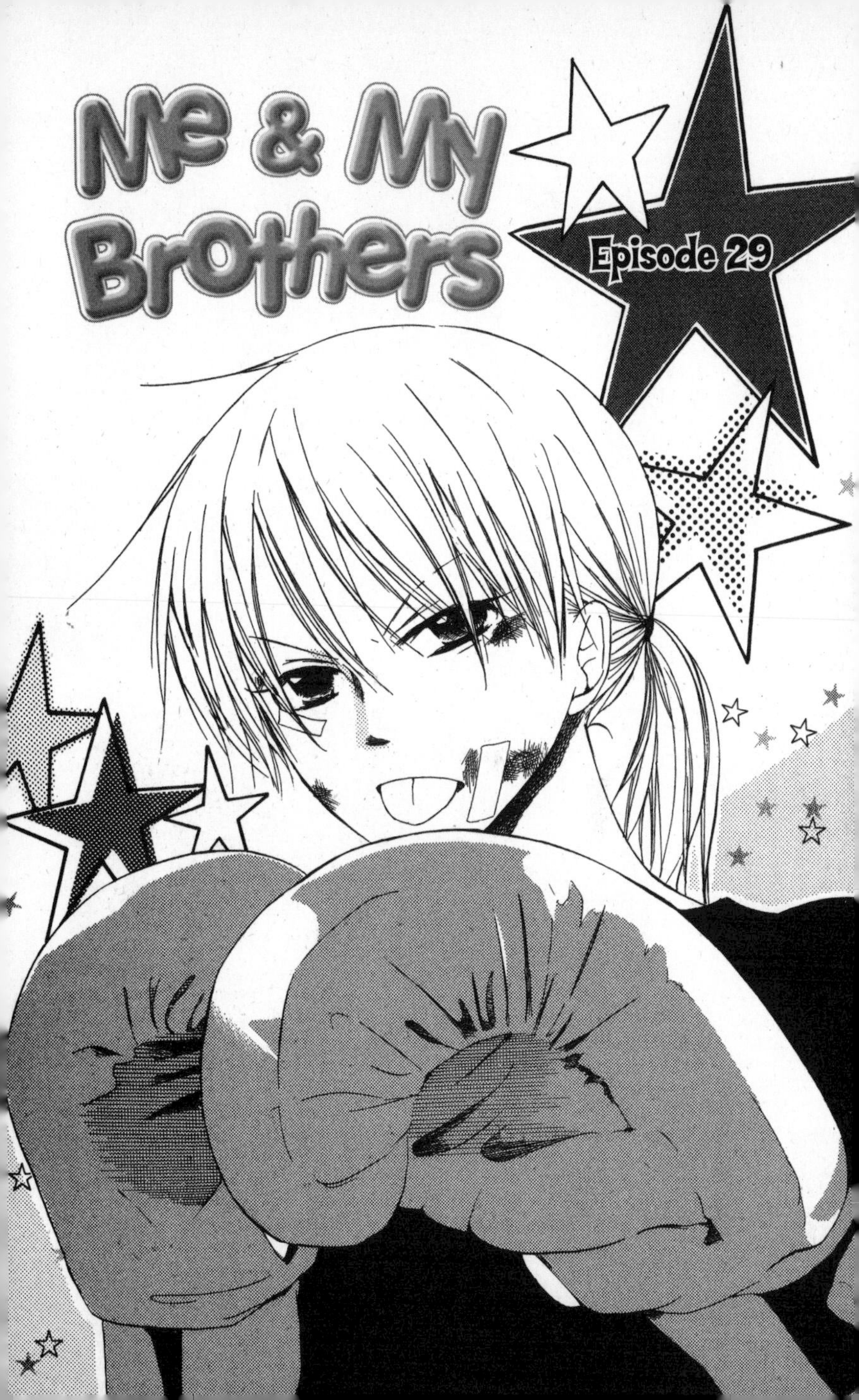
Me & My Brothers
Episode 29

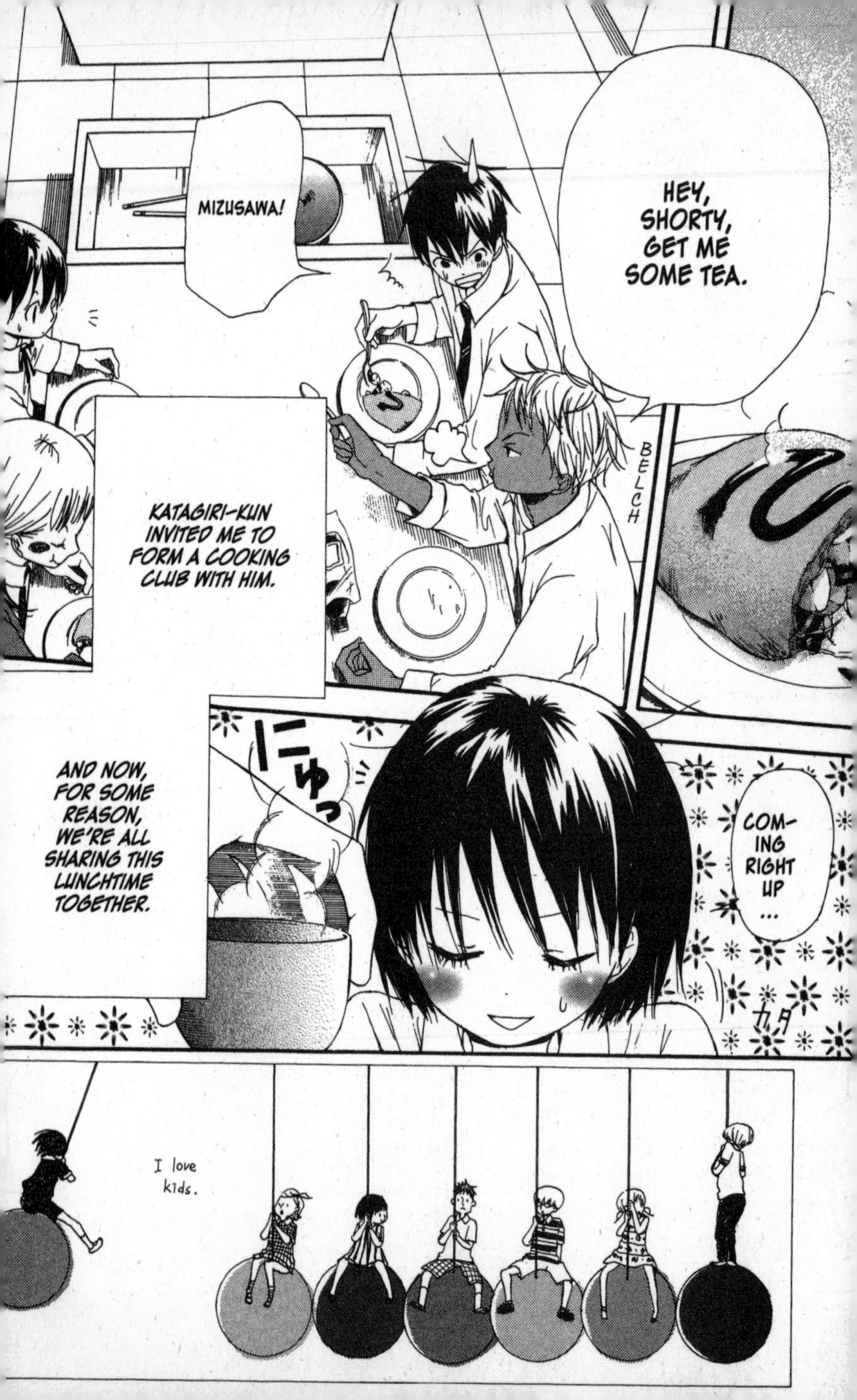

HEY, SHORTY, GET ME SOME TEA.
MIZUSAWA!
BELCH
KATAGIRI-KUN INVITED ME TO FORM A COOKING CLUB WITH HIM.
COMING RIGHT UP ...
カタ
にゅっ
AND NOW, FOR SOME REASON, WE'RE ALL SHARING THIS LUNCHTIME TOGETHER.
I love kids.

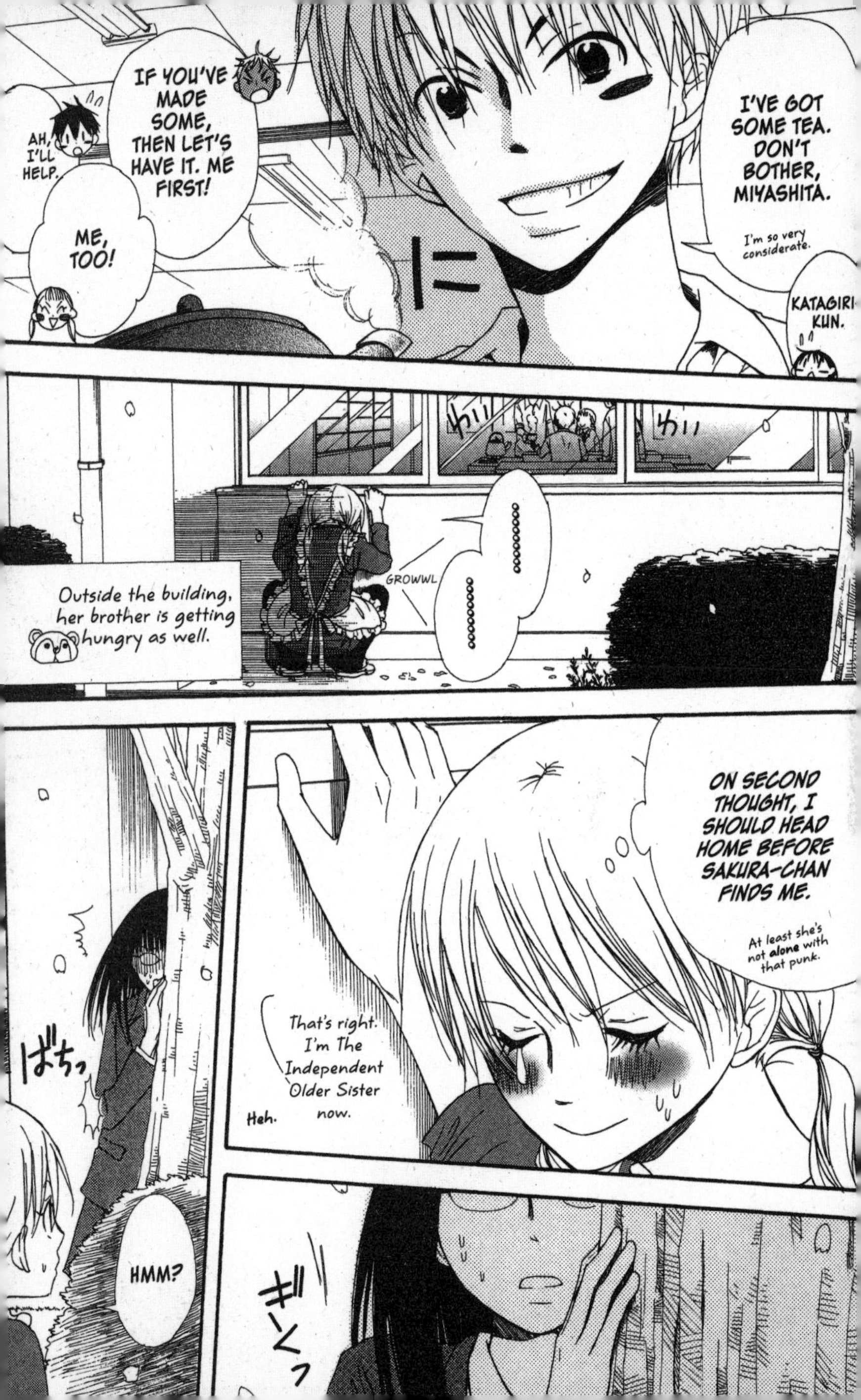
I'VE GOT SOME TEA. DON'T BOTHER, MIYASHITA.
I'm so very considerate.
KATAGIRI-KUN.
IF YOU'VE MADE SOME, THEN LET'S HAVE IT. ME FIRST!
AH, I'LL HELP.
ME, TOO!
......
......
GROWWL
Outside the building, her brother is getting hungry as well.
ON SECOND THOUGHT, I SHOULD HEAD HOME BEFORE SAKURA-CHAN FINDS ME.
At least she's not alone with that punk.
That's right. I'm The Independent Older Sister now.
Heh.
ぎくっ
ばちっ
HMM?

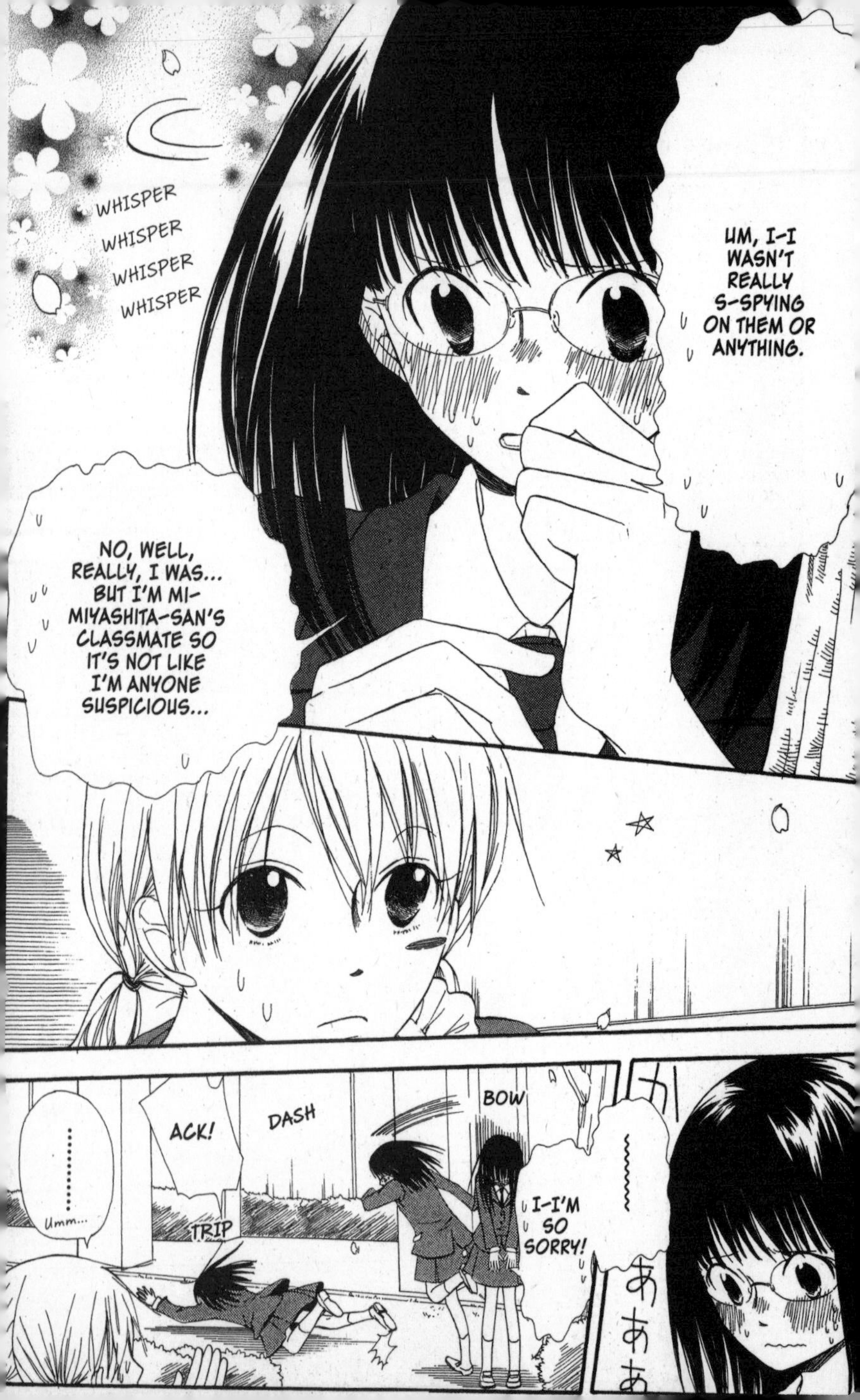
UM, I-I WASN'T REALLY S-SPYING ON THEM OR ANYTHING.
WHISPER
WHISPER
WHISPER
WHISPER
NO, WELL, REALLY, I WAS... BUT I'M MI-MIYASHITA-SAN'S CLASSMATE SO IT'S NOT LIKE I'M ANYONE SUSPICIOUS...
ああ
~~~~
I-I'M SO SORRY!
BOW
DASH
ACK!
TRIP
..........
Umm...
~~~~

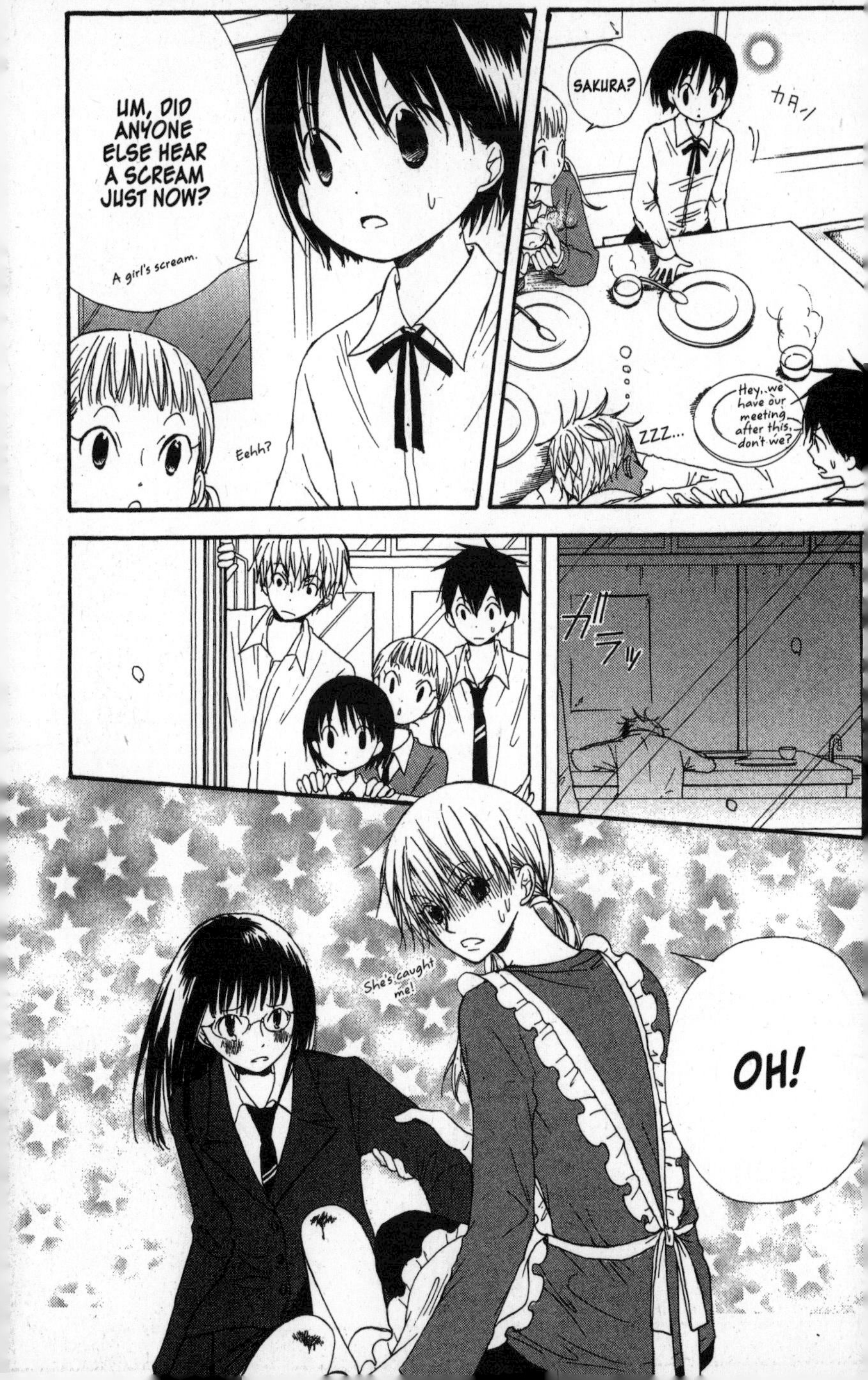
SAKURA?
カタン
Hey, we have our meeting after this, don't we?
ZZZ...
UM, DID ANYONE ELSE HEAR A SCREAM JUST NOW?
A girl's scream.
Eehh?
ガラッ
OH!
She's caught me!

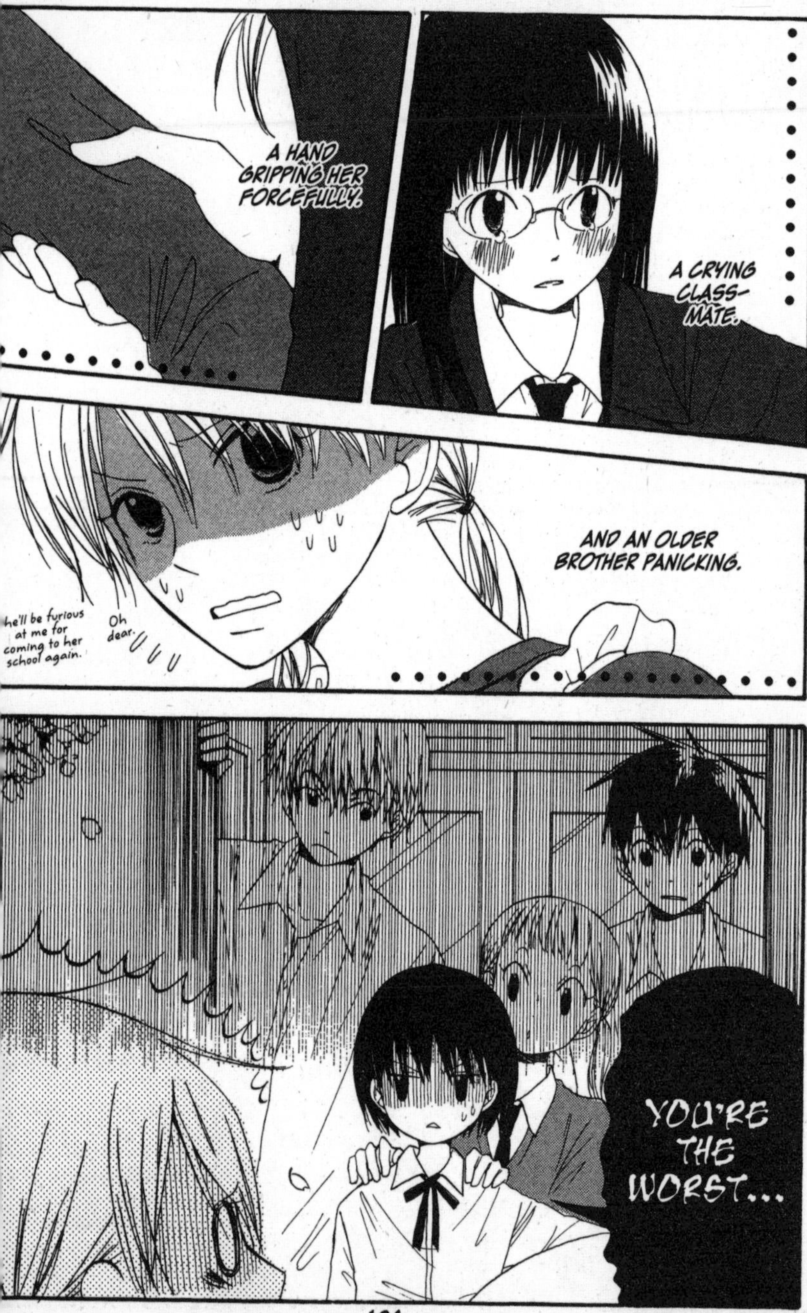

A CRYING CLASS-MATE.
A HAND GRIPPING HER FORCEFULLY.
AND AN OLDER BROTHER PANICKING.
Oh dear.
he'll be furious at me for coming to her school again.
YOU'RE THE WORST...

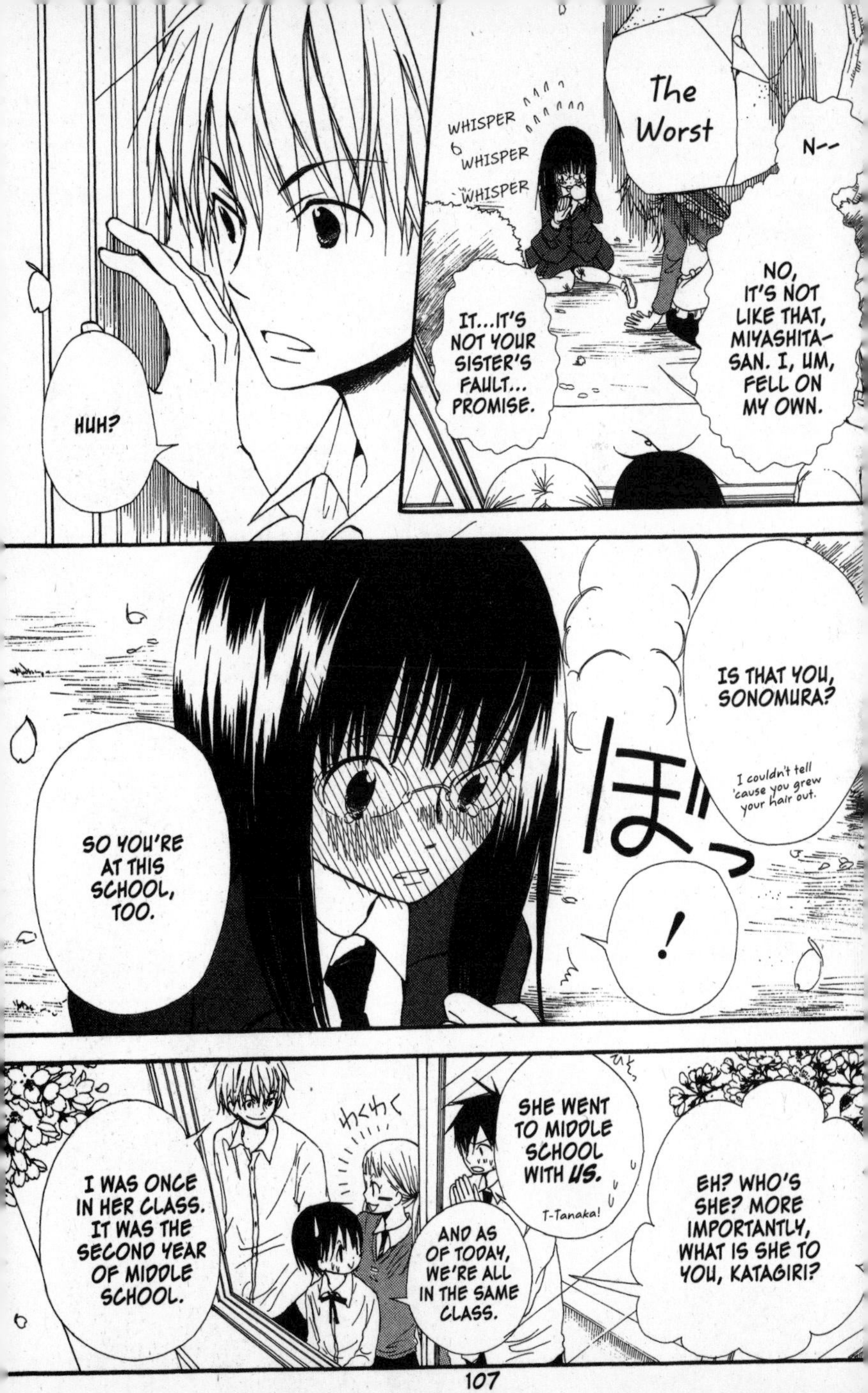
The Worst
N--
WHISPER WHISPER WHISPER
NO, IT'S NOT LIKE THAT, MIYASHITA-SAN. I, UM, FELL ON MY OWN.
IT...IT'S NOT YOUR SISTER'S FAULT... PROMISE.
HUH?
IS THAT YOU, SONOMURA?
I couldn't tell 'cause you grew your hair out.
ぽっ
!
SO YOU'RE AT THIS SCHOOL, TOO.
EH? WHO'S SHE? MORE IMPORTANTLY, WHAT IS SHE TO YOU, KATAGIRI?
SHE WENT TO MIDDLE SCHOOL WITH *US*.
T-Tanaka!
わくわく
I WAS ONCE IN HER CLASS. IT WAS THE SECOND YEAR OF MIDDLE SCHOOL.
AND AS OF TODAY, WE'RE ALL IN THE SAME CLASS.

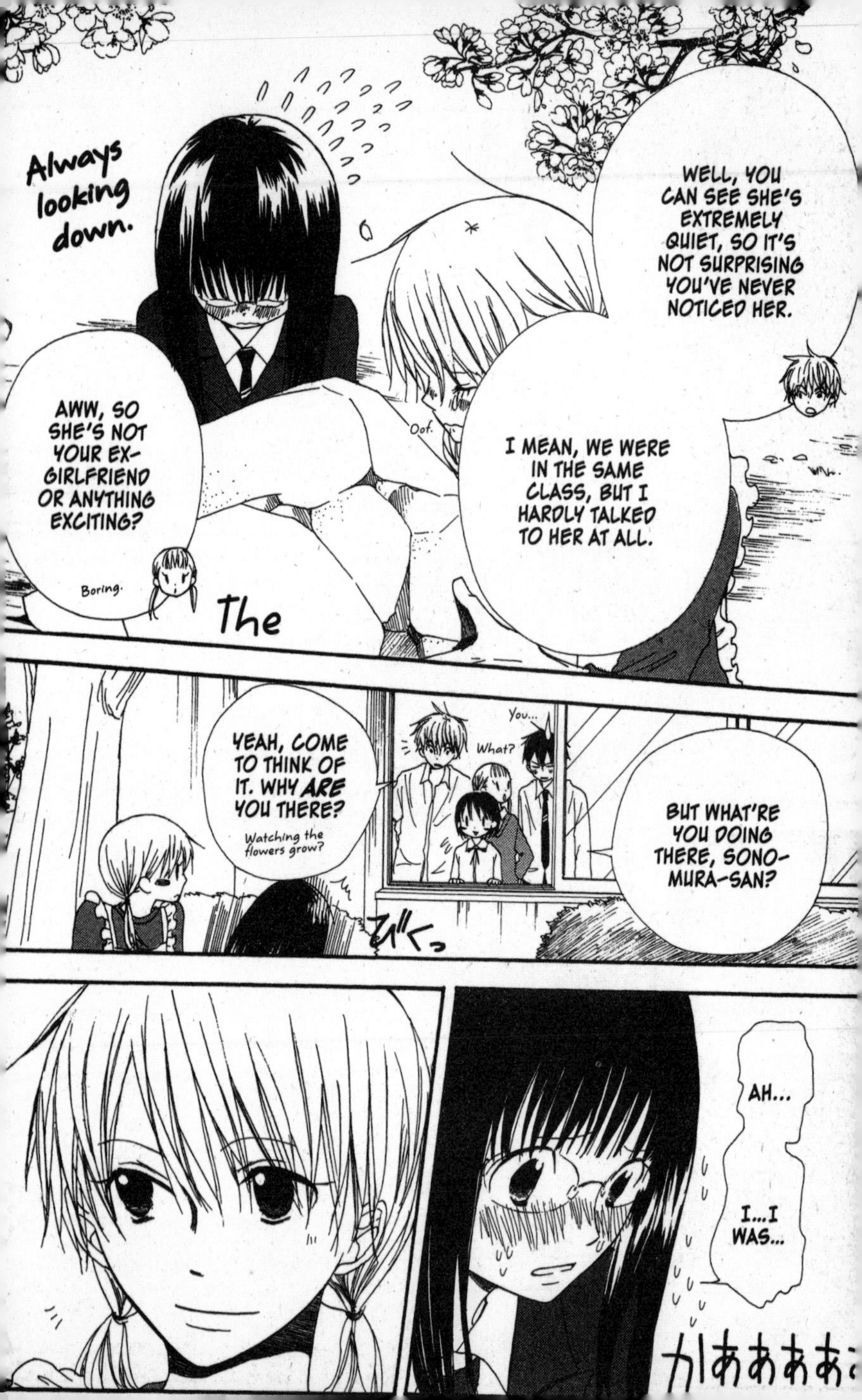
WELL, YOU CAN SEE SHE'S EXTREMELY QUIET, SO IT'S NOT SURPRISING YOU'VE NEVER NOTICED HER.
I MEAN, WE WERE IN THE SAME CLASS, BUT I HARDLY TALKED TO HER AT ALL.
Oof.
Always looking down.
AWW, SO SHE'S NOT YOUR EX-GIRLFRIEND OR ANYTHING EXCITING?
Boring.
The
BUT WHAT'RE YOU DOING THERE, SONO-MURA-SAN?
You...
What?
YEAH, COME TO THINK OF IT. WHY ARE YOU THERE?
Watching the flowers grow?
びくっ
AH...
I...I WAS...
かあああああ

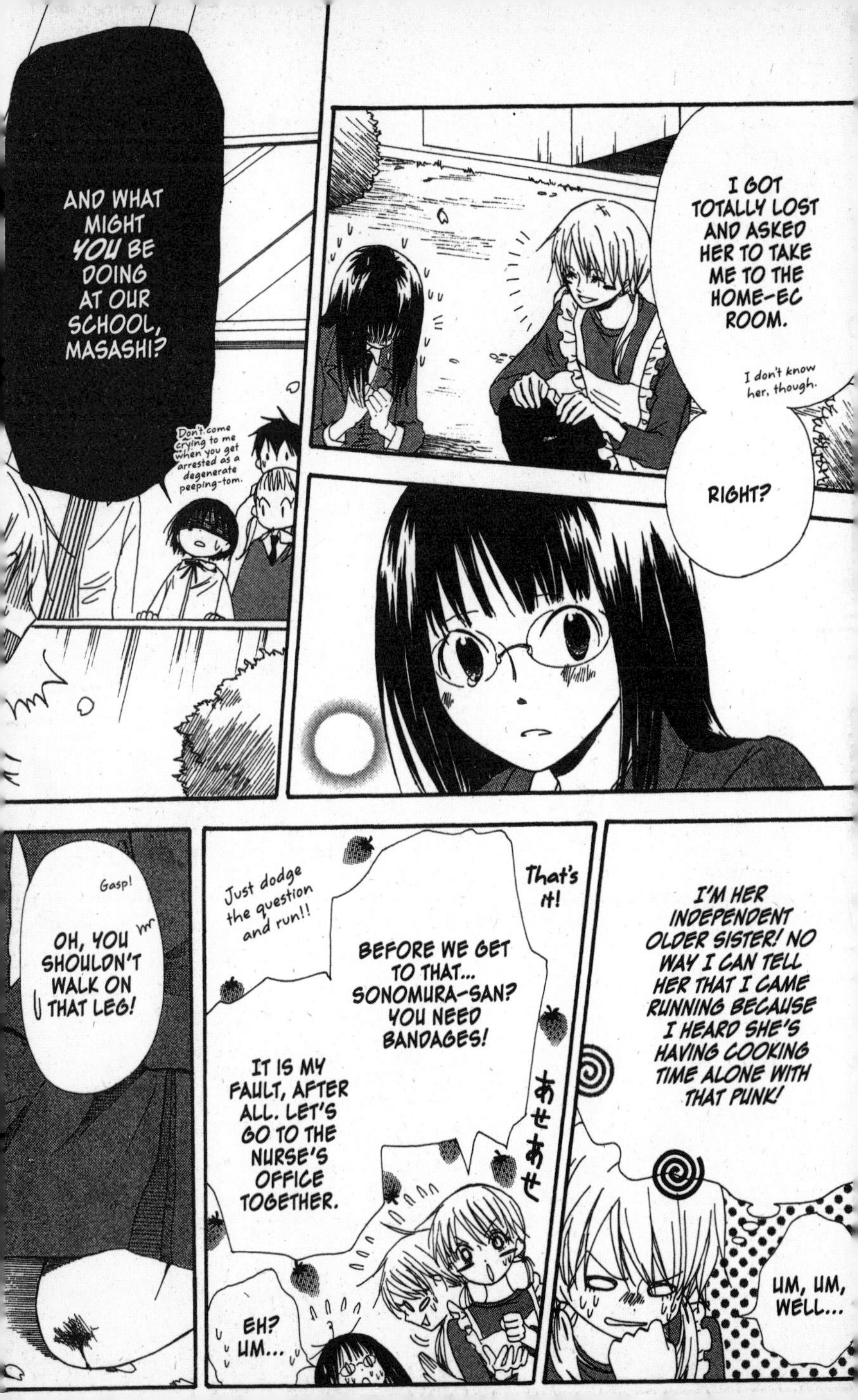

I GOT TOTALLY LOST AND ASKED HER TO TAKE ME TO THE HOME-EC ROOM.
I don't know her, though.
RIGHT?
AND WHAT MIGHT *YOU* BE DOING AT OUR SCHOOL, MASASHI?
Don't come crying to me when you get arrested as a degenerate peeping-tom.
I'M HER INDEPENDENT OLDER SISTER! NO WAY I CAN TELL HER THAT I CAME RUNNING BECAUSE I HEARD SHE'S HAVING COOKING TIME ALONE WITH THAT PUNK!
UM, UM, WELL...
That's it!
Just dodge the question and run!!
BEFORE WE GET TO THAT... SONOMURA-SAN? YOU NEED BANDAGES!
あせあせ
IT IS MY FAULT, AFTER ALL. LET'S GO TO THE NURSE'S OFFICE TOGETHER.
EH? UM...
Gasp!
OH, YOU SHOULDN'T WALK ON THAT LEG!

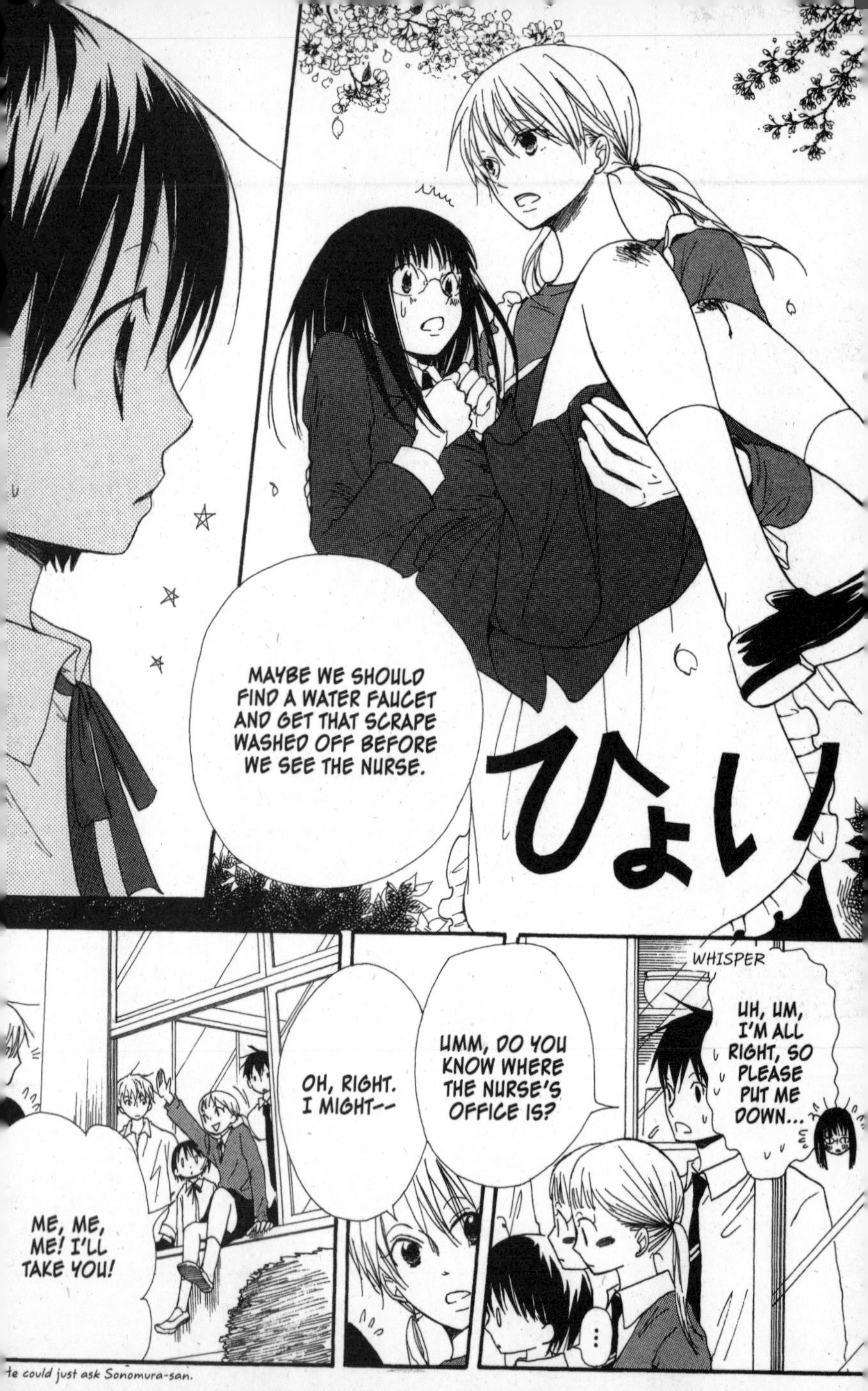
ひょい
MAYBE WE SHOULD FIND A WATER FAUCET AND GET THAT SCRAPE WASHED OFF BEFORE WE SEE THE NURSE.
WHISPER
UH, UM, I'M ALL RIGHT, SO PLEASE PUT ME DOWN...
UMM, DO YOU KNOW WHERE THE NURSE'S OFFICE IS?
OH, RIGHT. I MIGHT--
...
ME, ME, ME! I'LL TAKE YOU!

te could just ask Sonomura-san.

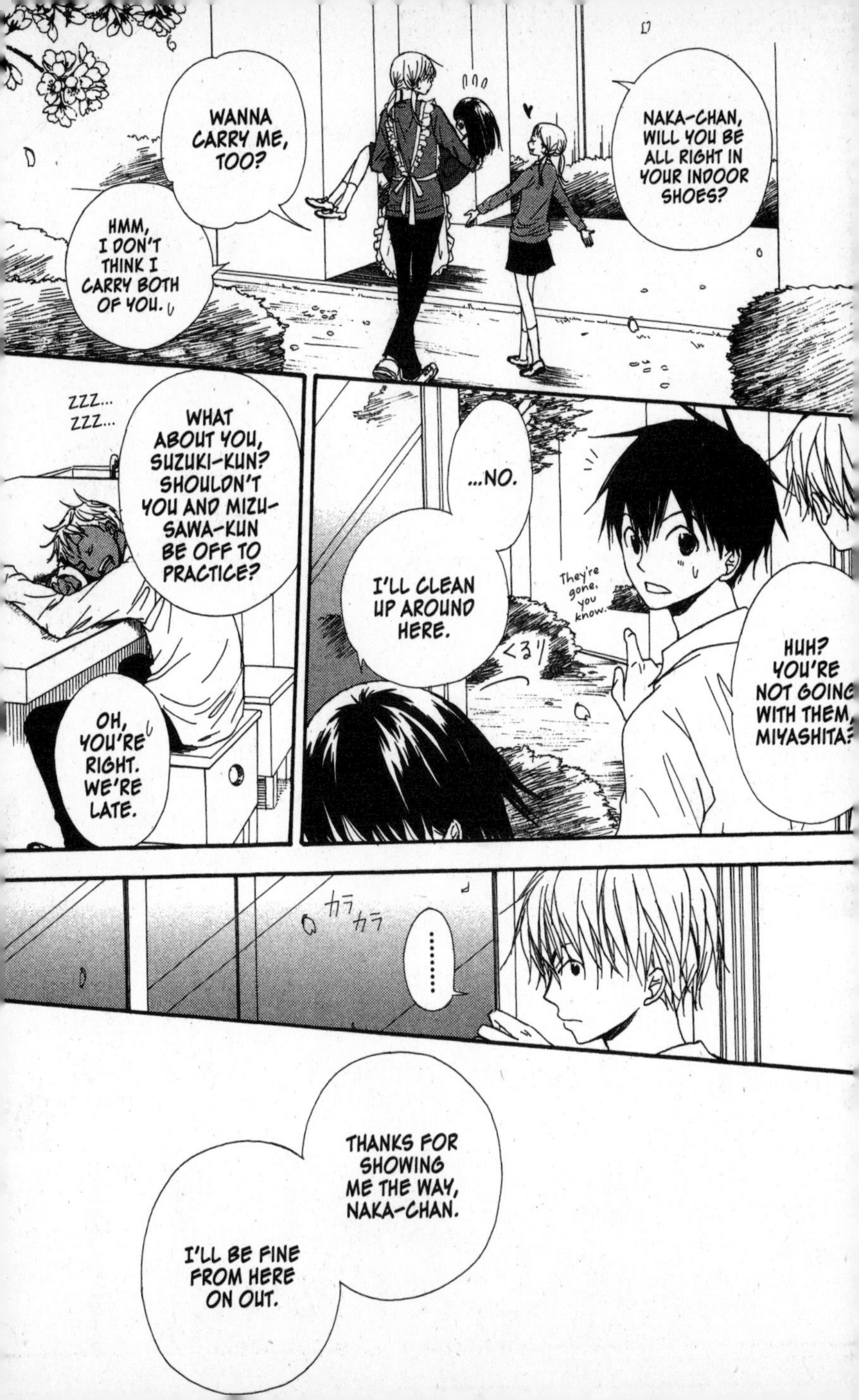
NAKA-CHAN, WILL YOU BE ALL RIGHT IN YOUR INDOOR SHOES?
WANNA CARRY ME, TOO?
HMM, I DON'T THINK I CARRY BOTH OF YOU.
HUH? YOU'RE NOT GOING WITH THEM, MIYASHITA?
They're gone, you know.
...NO.
I'LL CLEAN UP AROUND HERE.
くるり
ZZZ... ZZZ...
WHAT ABOUT YOU, SUZUKI-KUN? SHOULDN'T YOU AND MIZU-SAWA-KUN BE OFF TO PRACTICE?
OH, YOU'RE RIGHT. WE'RE LATE.
カラ カラ
....
THANKS FOR SHOWING ME THE WAY, NAKA-CHAN.
I'LL BE FINE FROM HERE ON OUT.

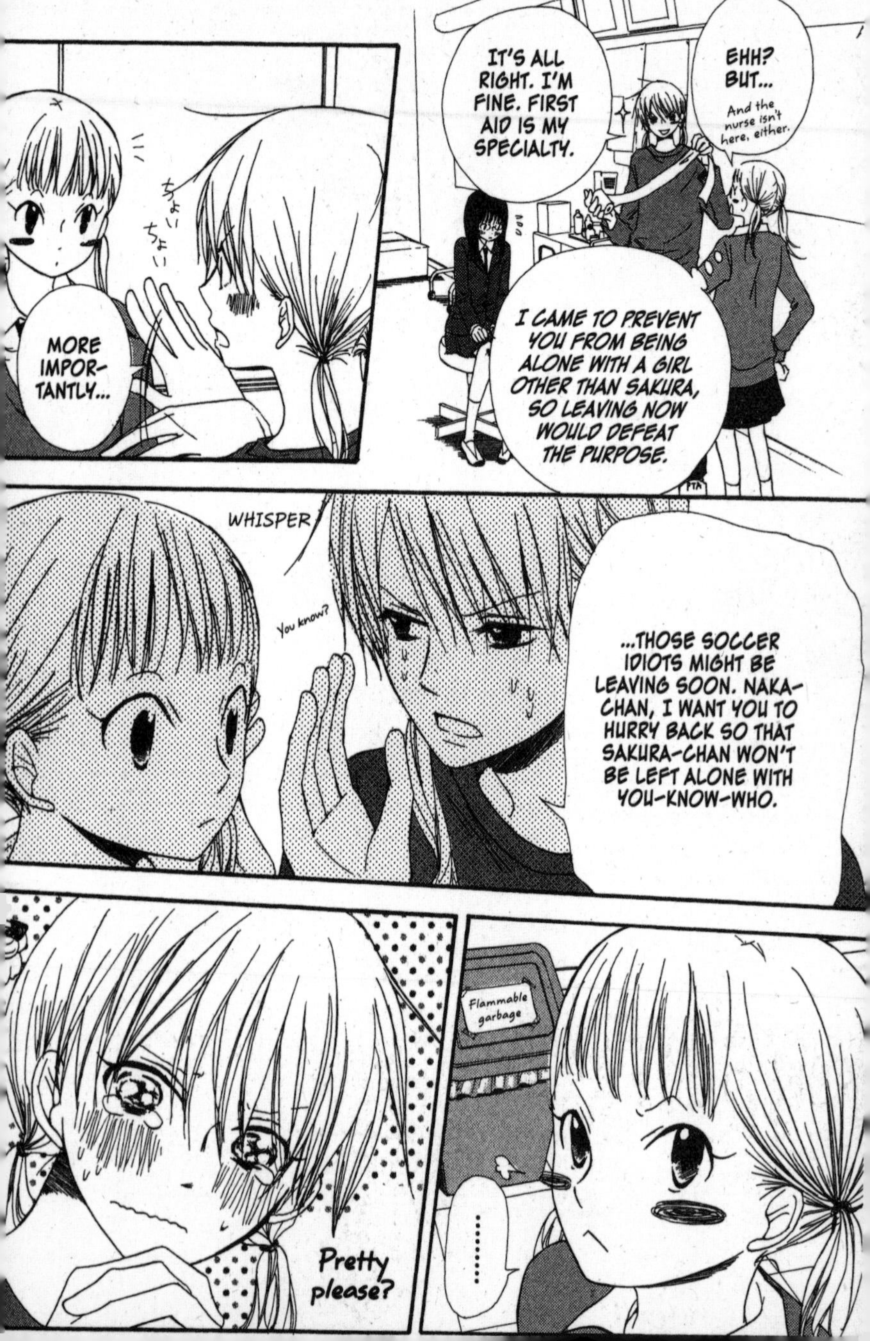
EHH? BUT...
And the nurse isn't here, either.
IT'S ALL RIGHT. I'M FINE. FIRST AID IS MY SPECIALTY.
I CAME TO PREVENT YOU FROM BEING ALONE WITH A GIRL OTHER THAN SAKURA, SO LEAVING NOW WOULD DEFEAT THE PURPOSE.
ちょいちょい
MORE IMPORTANTLY...
...THOSE SOCCER IDIOTS MIGHT BE LEAVING SOON. NAKA-CHAN, I WANT YOU TO HURRY BACK SO THAT SAKURA-CHAN WON'T BE LEFT ALONE WITH YOU-KNOW-WHO.
WHISPER
You know?
Flammable garbage
......
Pretty please?

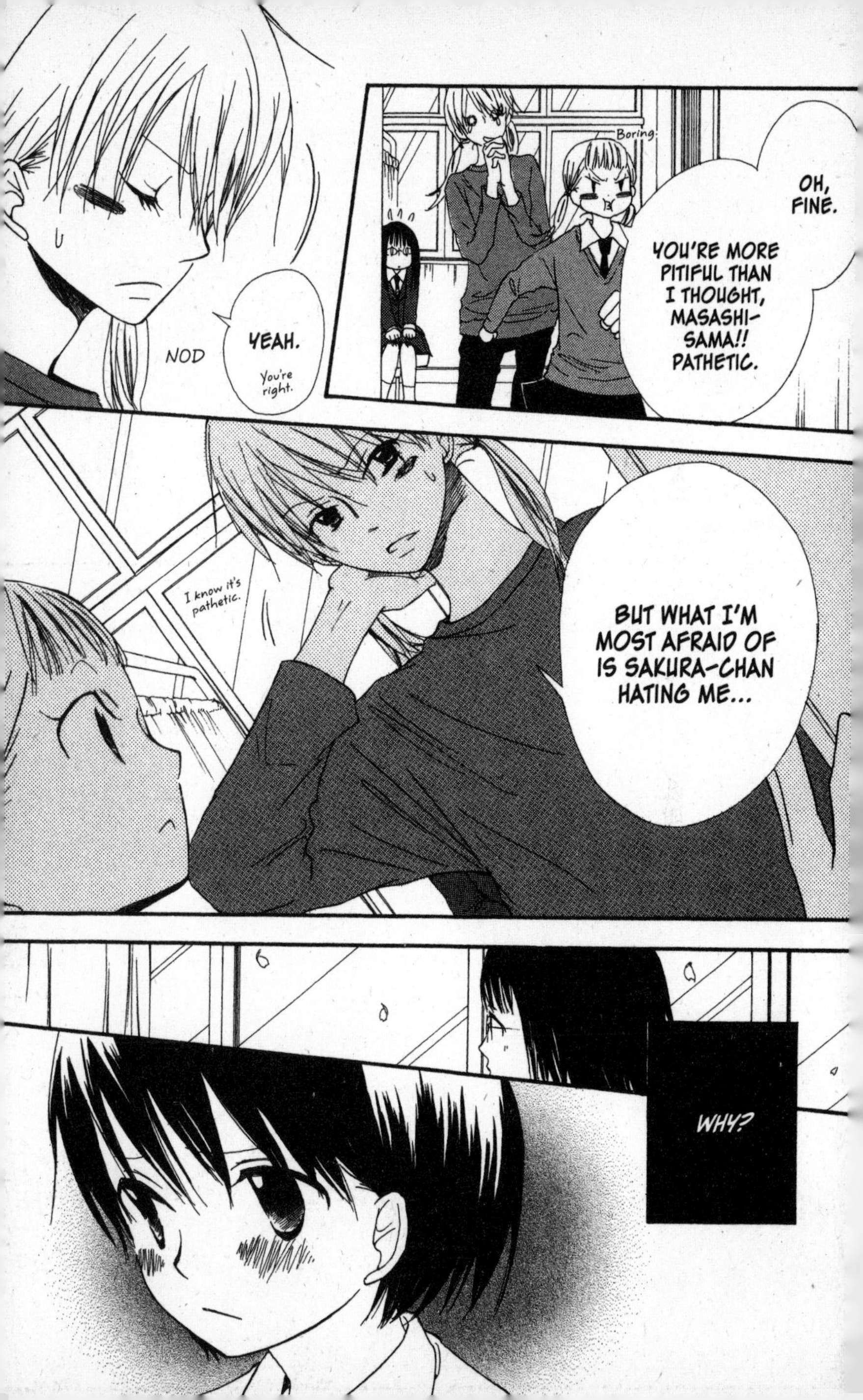
OH, FINE.
YOU'RE MORE PITIFUL THAN I THOUGHT, MASASHI-SAMA!! PATHETIC.
Boring.
YEAH.
You're right.
NOD
BUT WHAT I'M MOST AFRAID OF IS SAKURA-CHAN HATING ME...
I know it's pathetic.
WHY?

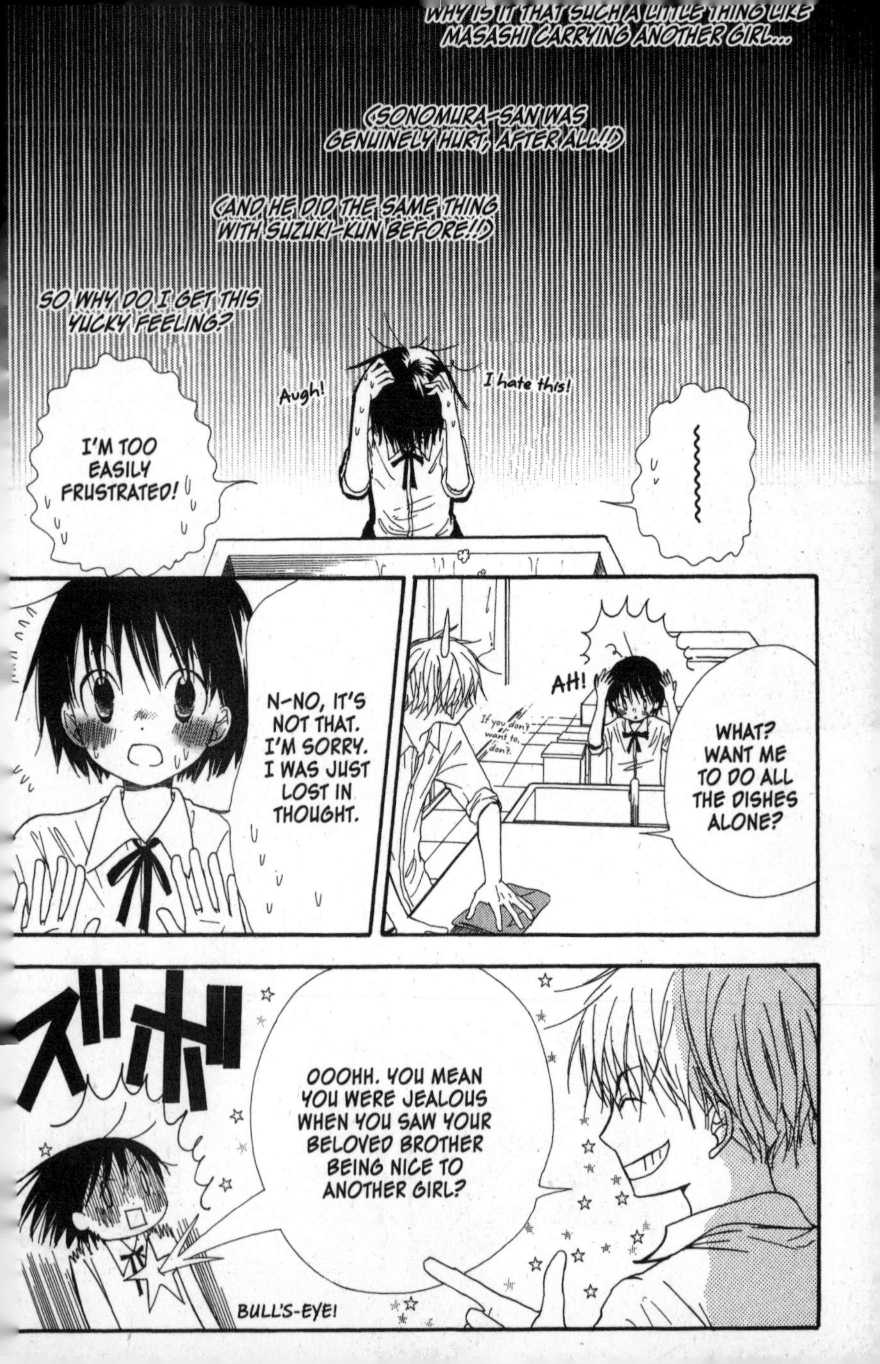
WHY IS IT THAT SUCH A LITTLE THING LIKE MASASHI CARRYING ANOTHER GIRL...
(SONOMURA-SAN WAS GENUINELY HURT, AFTER ALL!)
(AND HE DID THE SAME THING WITH SUZUKI-KUN BEFORE!!)
SO WHY DO I GET THIS YUCKY FEELING?
......
I hate this!
Augh!
I'M TOO EASILY FRUSTRATED!
WHAT? WANT ME TO DO ALL THE DISHES ALONE?
AH!
If you don't want to, don't.
N-NO, IT'S NOT THAT. I'M SORRY. I WAS JUST LOST IN THOUGHT.
OOOHH. YOU MEAN YOU WERE JEALOUS WHEN YOU SAW YOUR BELOVED BROTHER BEING NICE TO ANOTHER GIRL?
ズボ
BULL'S-EYE!

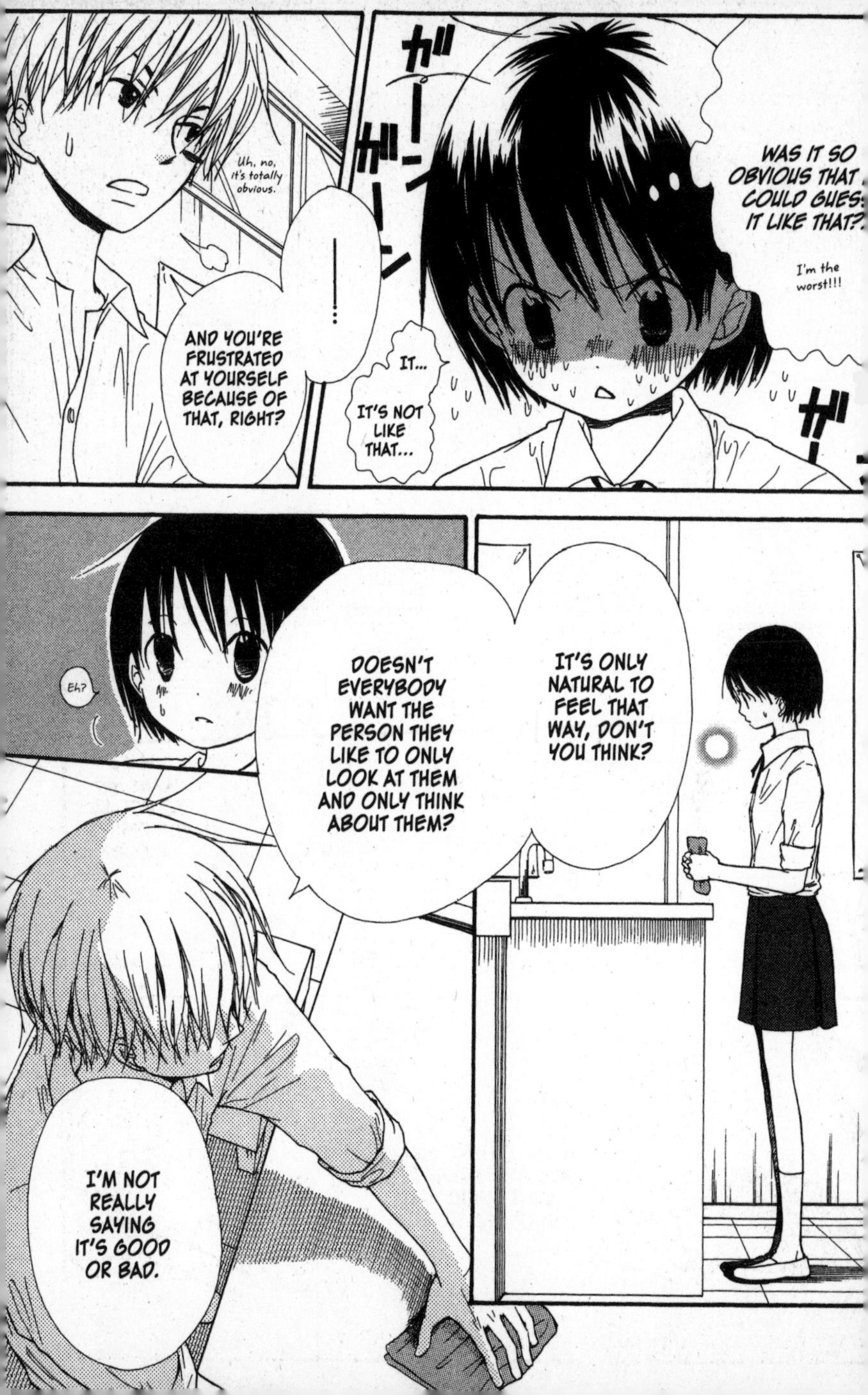

WAS IT SO OBVIOUS THAT COULD GUES IT LIKE THAT?!
I'm the worst!!!
IT...
IT'S NOT LIKE THAT...
......
Uh, no, it's totally obvious.
AND YOU'RE FRUSTRATED AT YOURSELF BECAUSE OF THAT, RIGHT?
IT'S ONLY NATURAL TO FEEL THAT WAY, DON'T YOU THINK?
DOESN'T EVERYBODY WANT THE PERSON THEY LIKE TO ONLY LOOK AT THEM AND ONLY THINK ABOUT THEM?
Eh?
I'M NOT REALLY SAYING IT'S GOOD OR BAD.

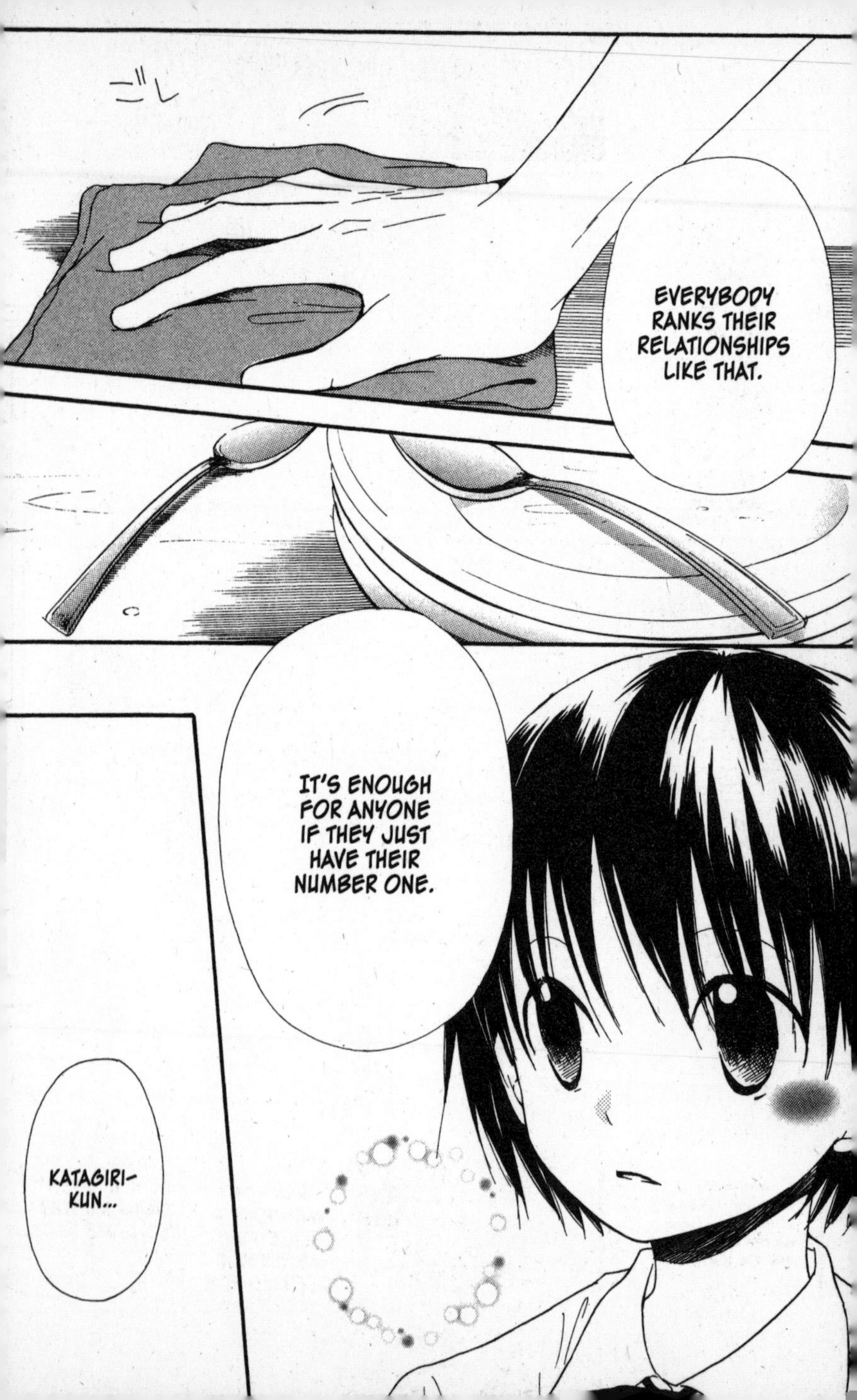
ごし
EVERYBODY RANKS THEIR RELATIONSHIPS LIKE THAT.
IT'S ENOUGH FOR ANYONE IF THEY JUST HAVE THEIR NUMBER ONE.
KATAGIRI-KUN...

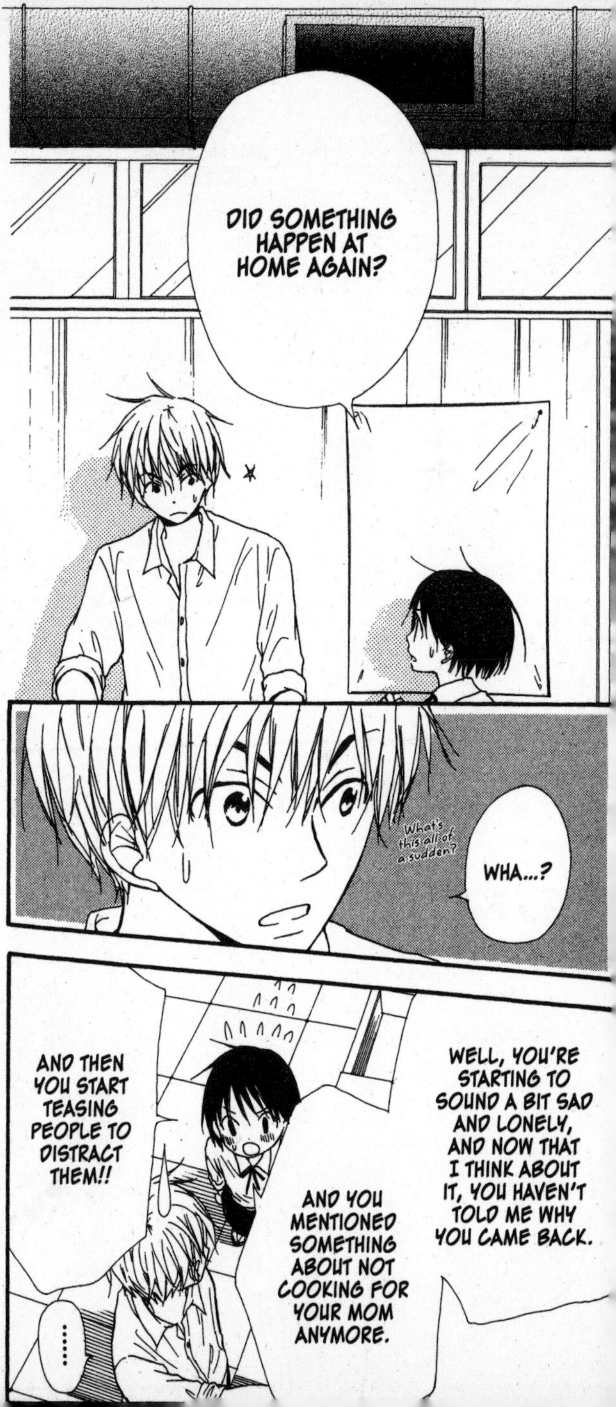
DID SOMETHING HAPPEN AT HOME AGAIN?
WHA...?
What's this all of a sudden?
WELL, YOU'RE STARTING TO SOUND A BIT SAD AND LONELY, AND NOW THAT I THINK ABOUT IT, YOU HAVEN'T TOLD ME WHY YOU CAME BACK.
AND YOU MENTIONED SOMETHING ABOUT NOT COOKING FOR YOUR MOM ANYMORE.
AND THEN YOU START TEASING PEOPLE TO DISTRACT THEM!!
......

4

15th place:
Morishima-kun

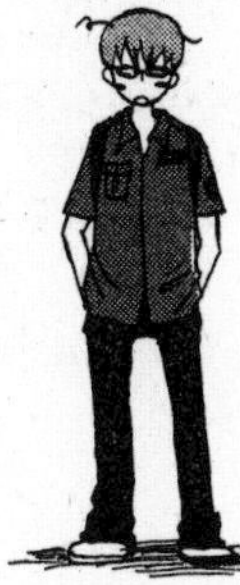

I secretly think I want to bring him in again, by force if necessary. I was happy that he got some votes!

17th place:
Ume-chan

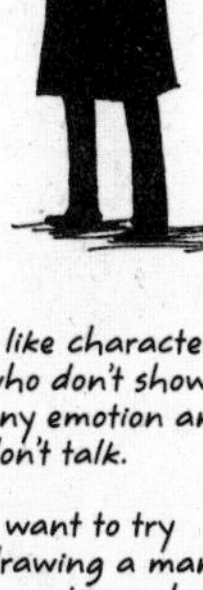

I like characters who don't show any emotion and don't talk.

I want to try drawing a manga some time where all the characters are like that.

An expressionless harem! What do you think? No good?

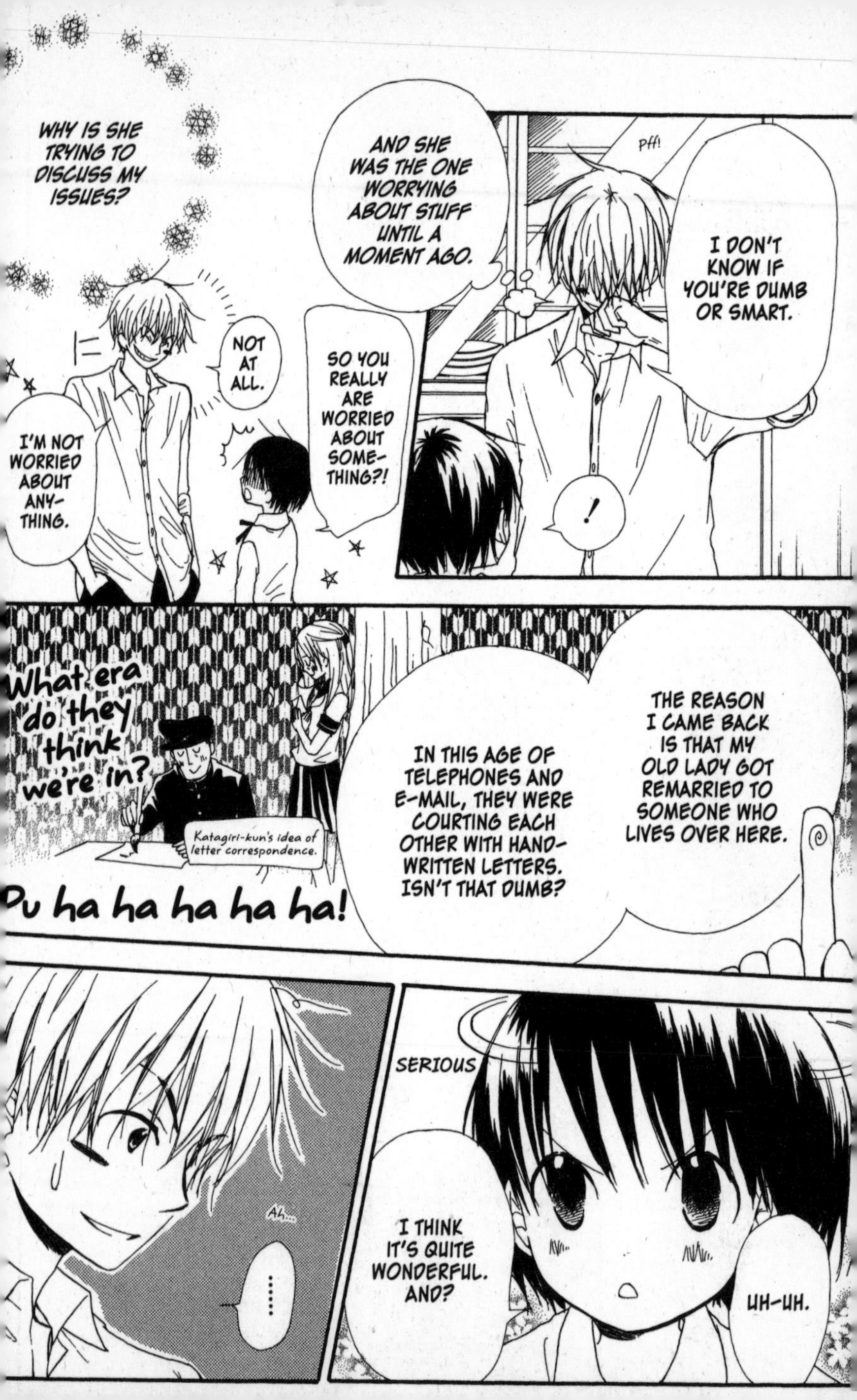

Pff!
I DON'T KNOW IF YOU'RE DUMB OR SMART.
!
AND SHE WAS THE ONE WORRYING ABOUT STUFF UNTIL A MOMENT AGO.
WHY IS SHE TRYING TO DISCUSS MY ISSUES?
SO YOU REALLY ARE WORRIED ABOUT SOME-THING?!
NOT AT ALL.
I'M NOT WORRIED ABOUT ANY-THING.
THE REASON I CAME BACK IS THAT MY OLD LADY GOT REMARRIED TO SOMEONE WHO LIVES OVER HERE.
IN THIS AGE OF TELEPHONES AND E-MAIL, THEY WERE COURTING EACH OTHER WITH HAND-WRITTEN LETTERS. ISN'T THAT DUMB?
What era do they think we're in?
Katagiri-kun's idea of letter correspondence.
Du ha ha ha ha ha!
SERIOUS
UH-UH.
I THINK IT'S QUITE WONDERFUL. AND?
Ah...
......

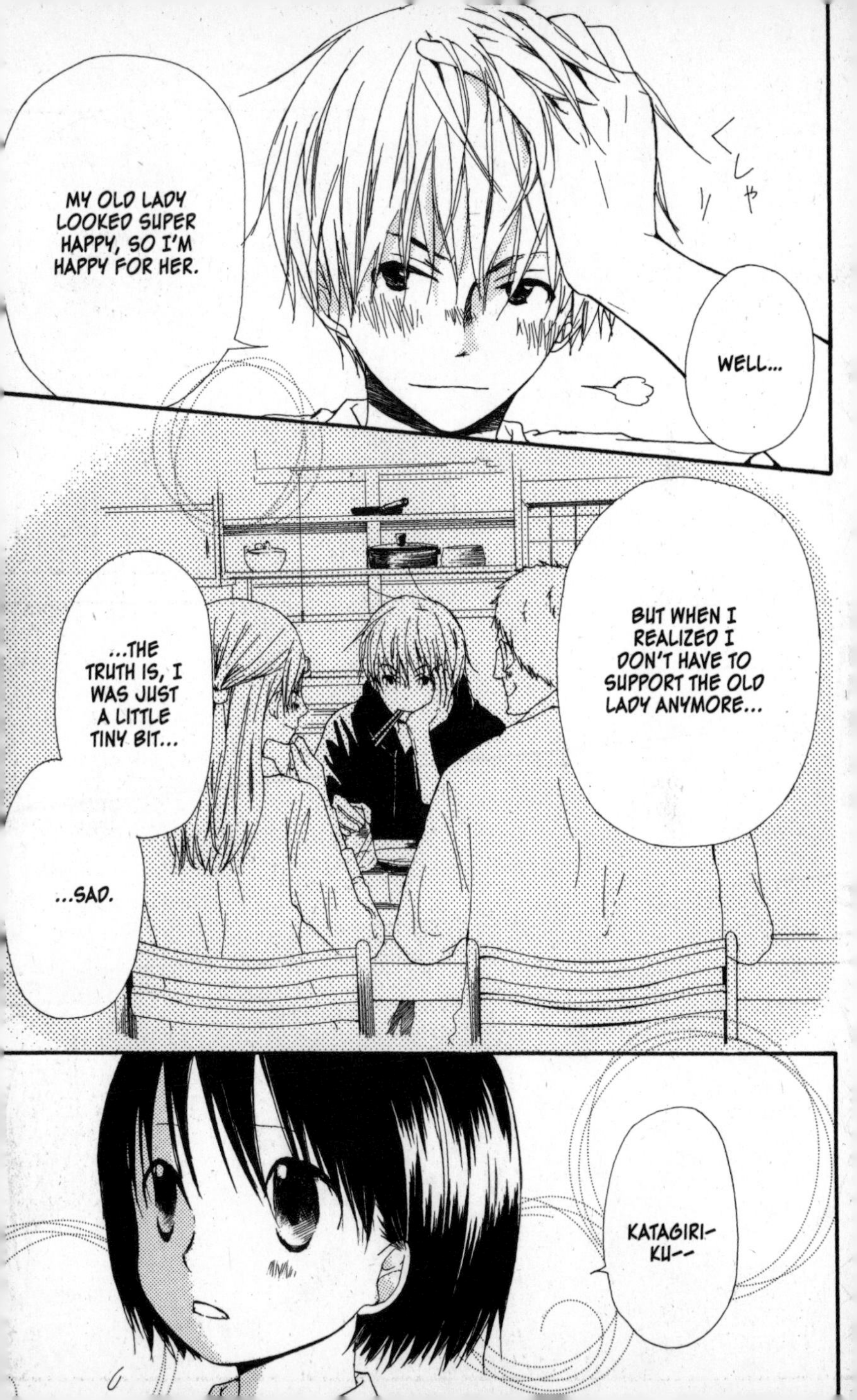
くしゃり
WELL...
MY OLD LADY LOOKED SUPER HAPPY, SO I'M HAPPY FOR HER.
BUT WHEN I REALIZED I DON'T HAVE TO SUPPORT THE OLD LADY ANYMORE...
...THE TRUTH IS, I WAS JUST A LITTLE TINY BIT...
...SAD.
KATAGIRI-KU--

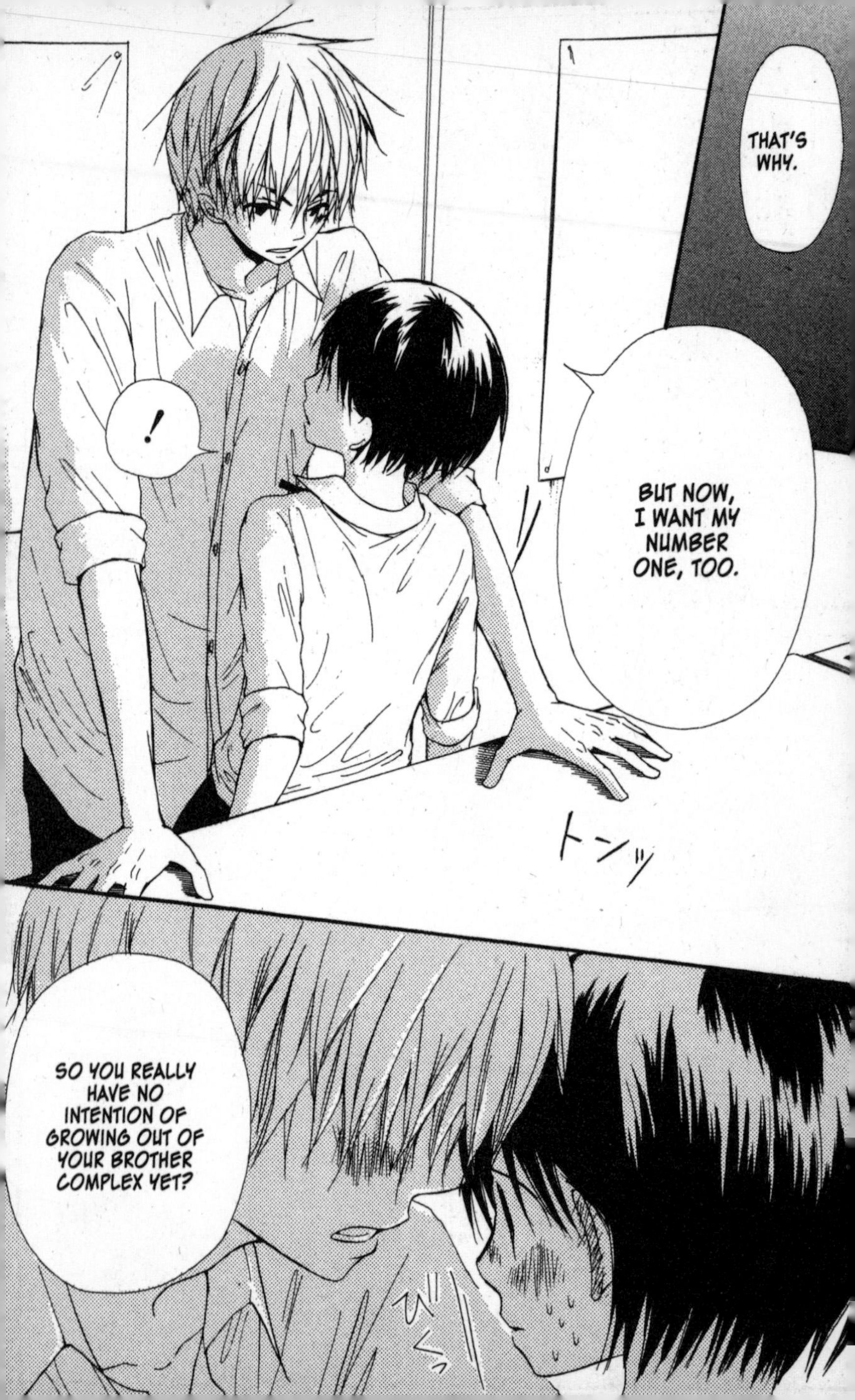
THAT'S WHY.
BUT NOW, I WANT MY NUMBER ONE, TOO.
!
トンッ
SO YOU REALLY HAVE NO INTENTION OF GROWING OUT OF YOUR BROTHER COMPLEX YET?
びくっ

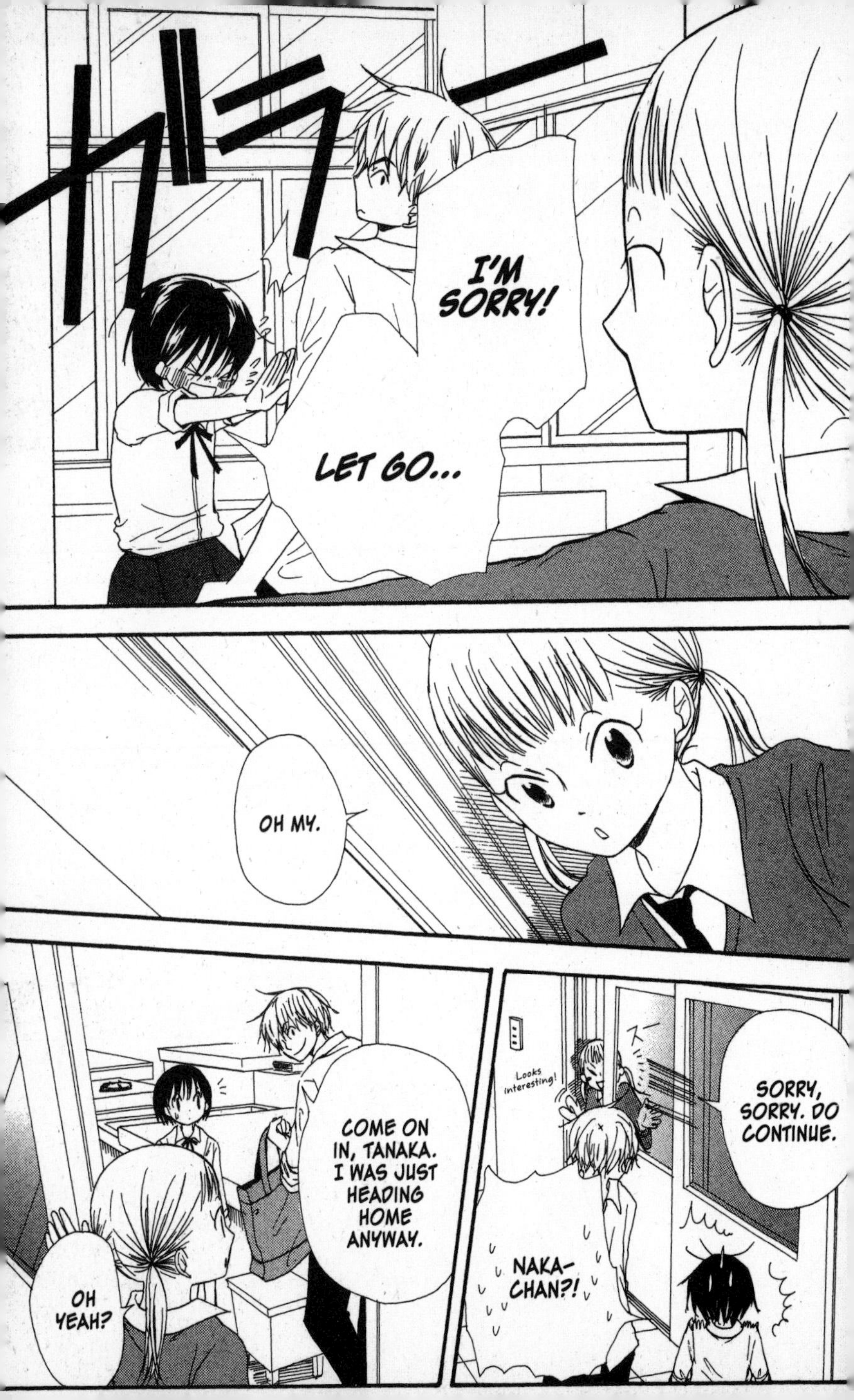
ガラー
I'M SORRY!
LET GO...
OH MY.
SORRY, SORRY. DO CONTINUE.
スー
Looks interesting!
NAKA-CHAN?!
COME ON IN, TANAKA. I WAS JUST HEADING HOME ANYWAY.
OH YEAH?

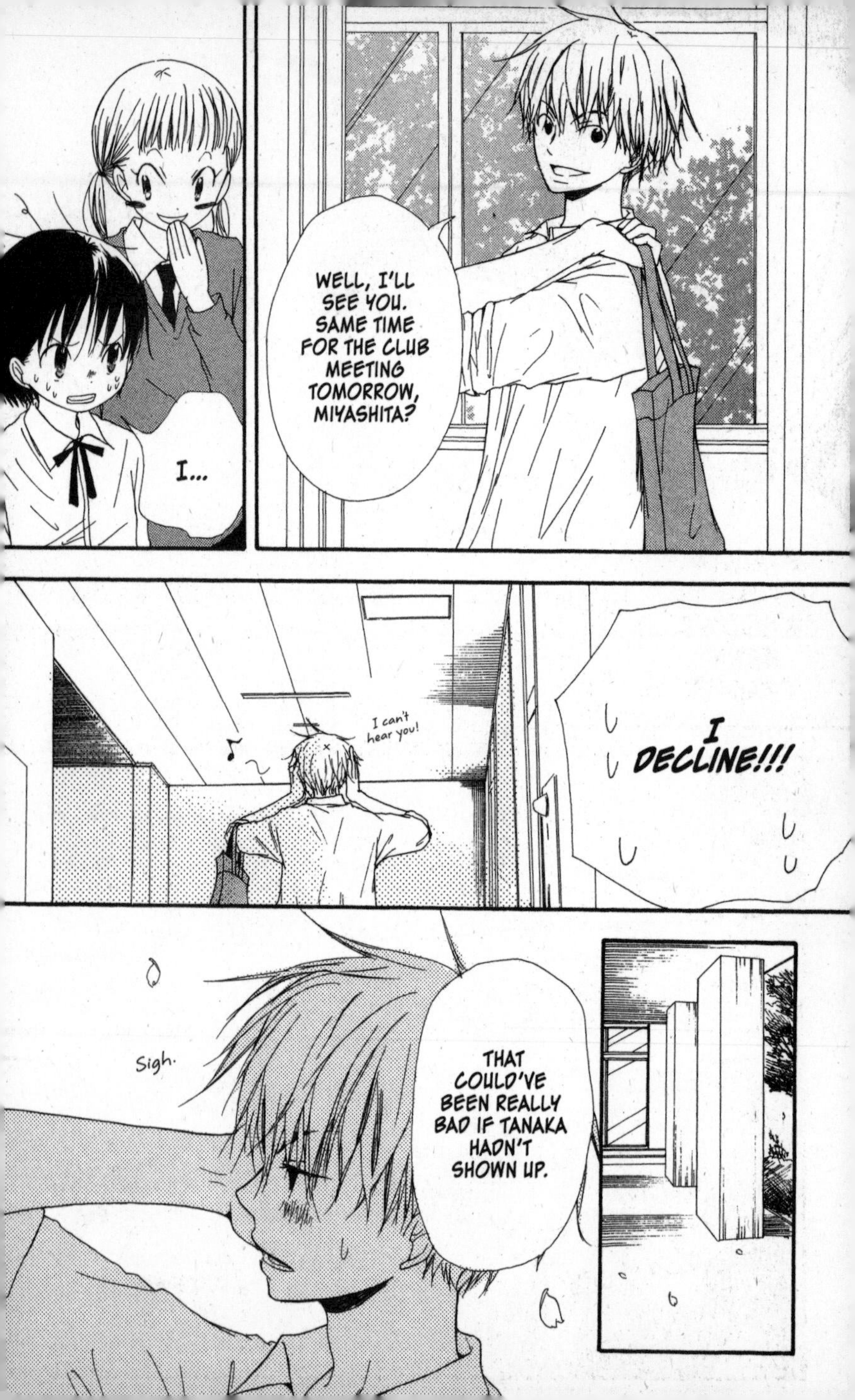
WELL, I'LL SEE YOU. SAME TIME FOR THE CLUB MEETING TOMORROW, MIYASHITA?
I...
I DECLINE!!!
I can't hear you!
THAT COULD'VE BEEN REALLY BAD IF TANAKA HADN'T SHOWN UP.
Sigh.

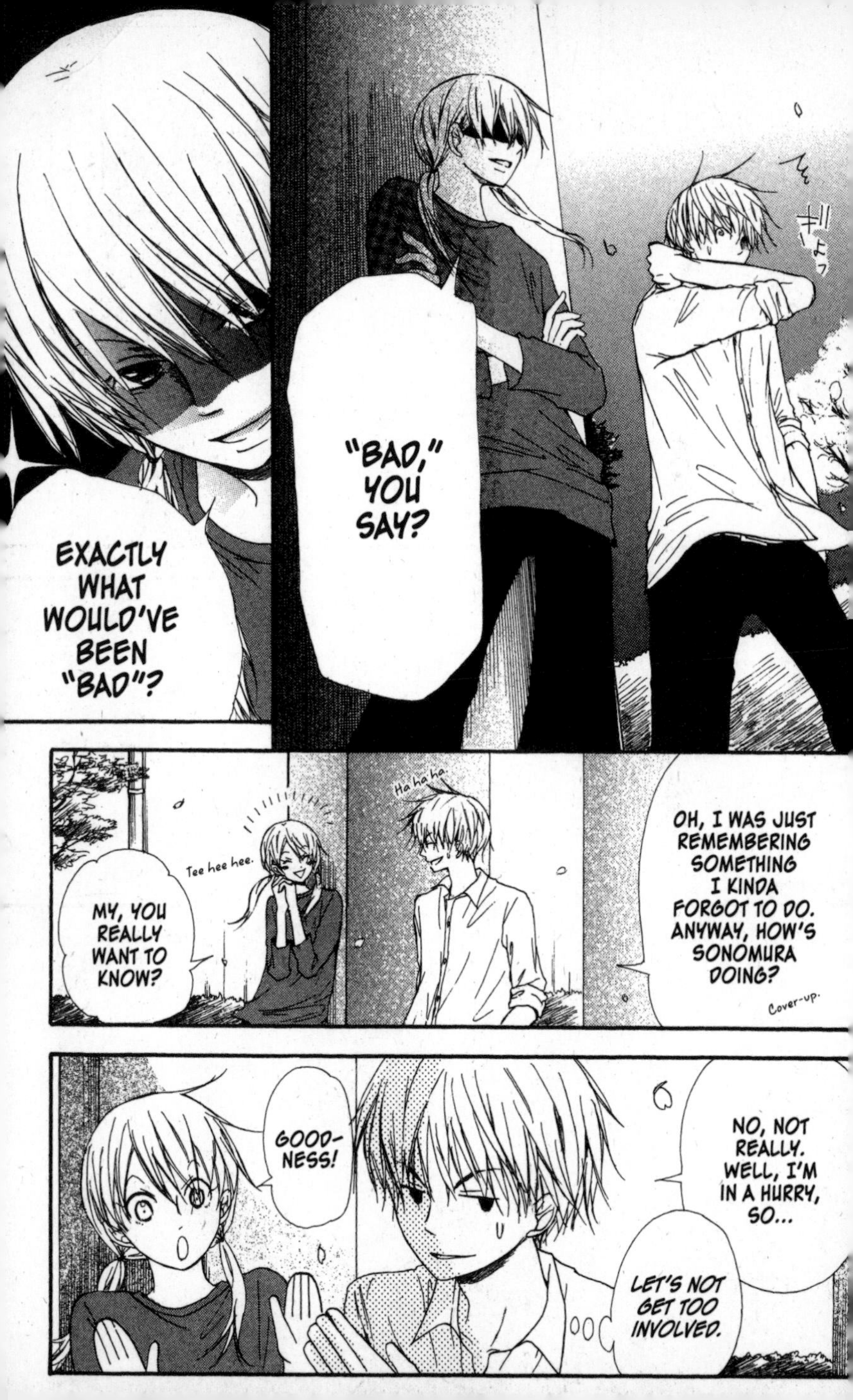
"BAD," YOU SAY?
EXACTLY WHAT WOULD'VE BEEN "BAD"?
OH, I WAS JUST REMEMBERING SOMETHING I KINDA FORGOT TO DO. ANYWAY, HOW'S SONOMURA DOING?
Cover-up.
Ha ha ha
Tee hee hee.
MY, YOU REALLY WANT TO KNOW?
NO, NOT REALLY. WELL, I'M IN A HURRY, SO...
LET'S NOT GET TOO INVOLVED.
GOOD-NESS!

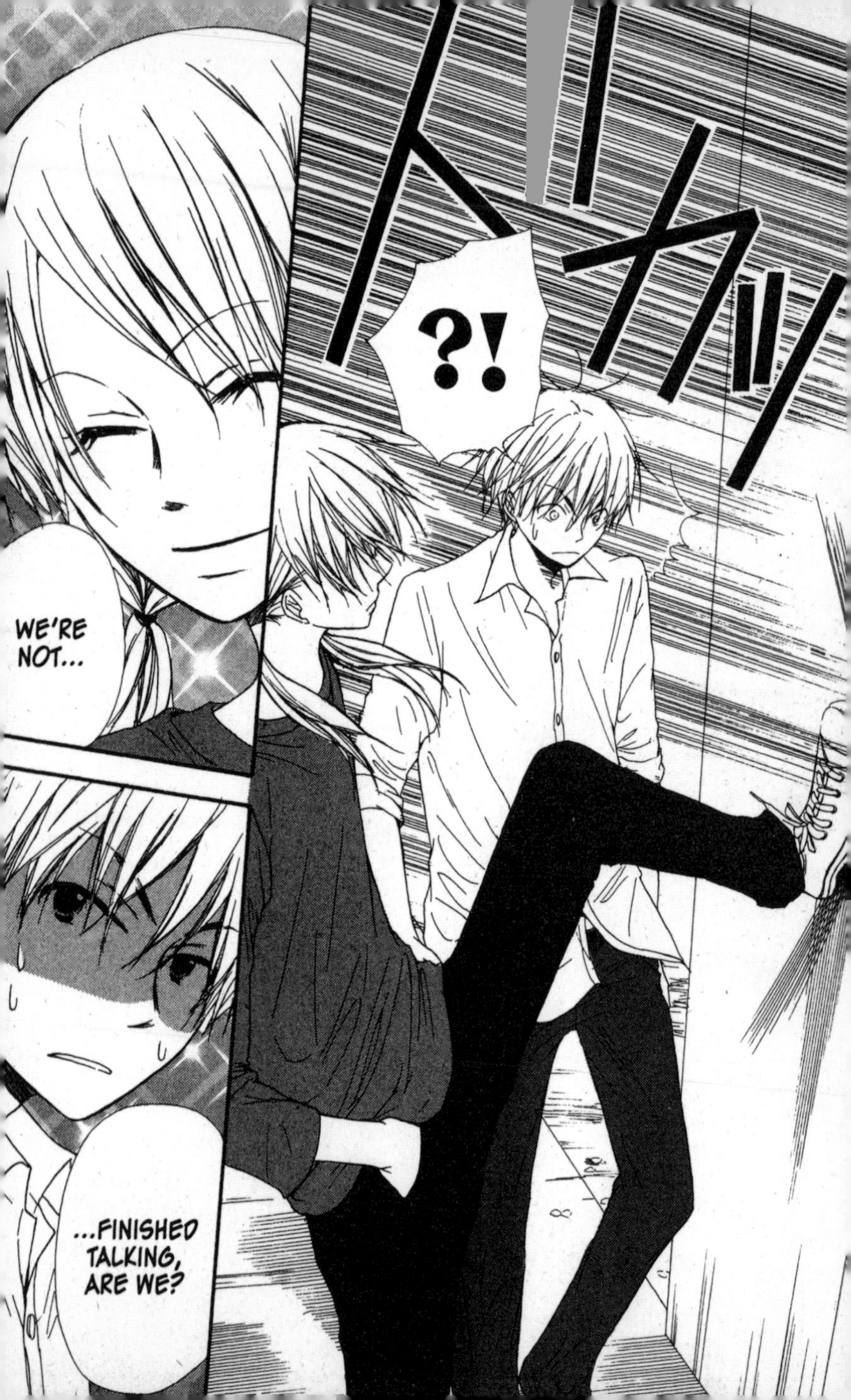
ドカッ
?!
WE'RE NOT...
...FINISHED TALKING, ARE WE?

Exaggerated expression.

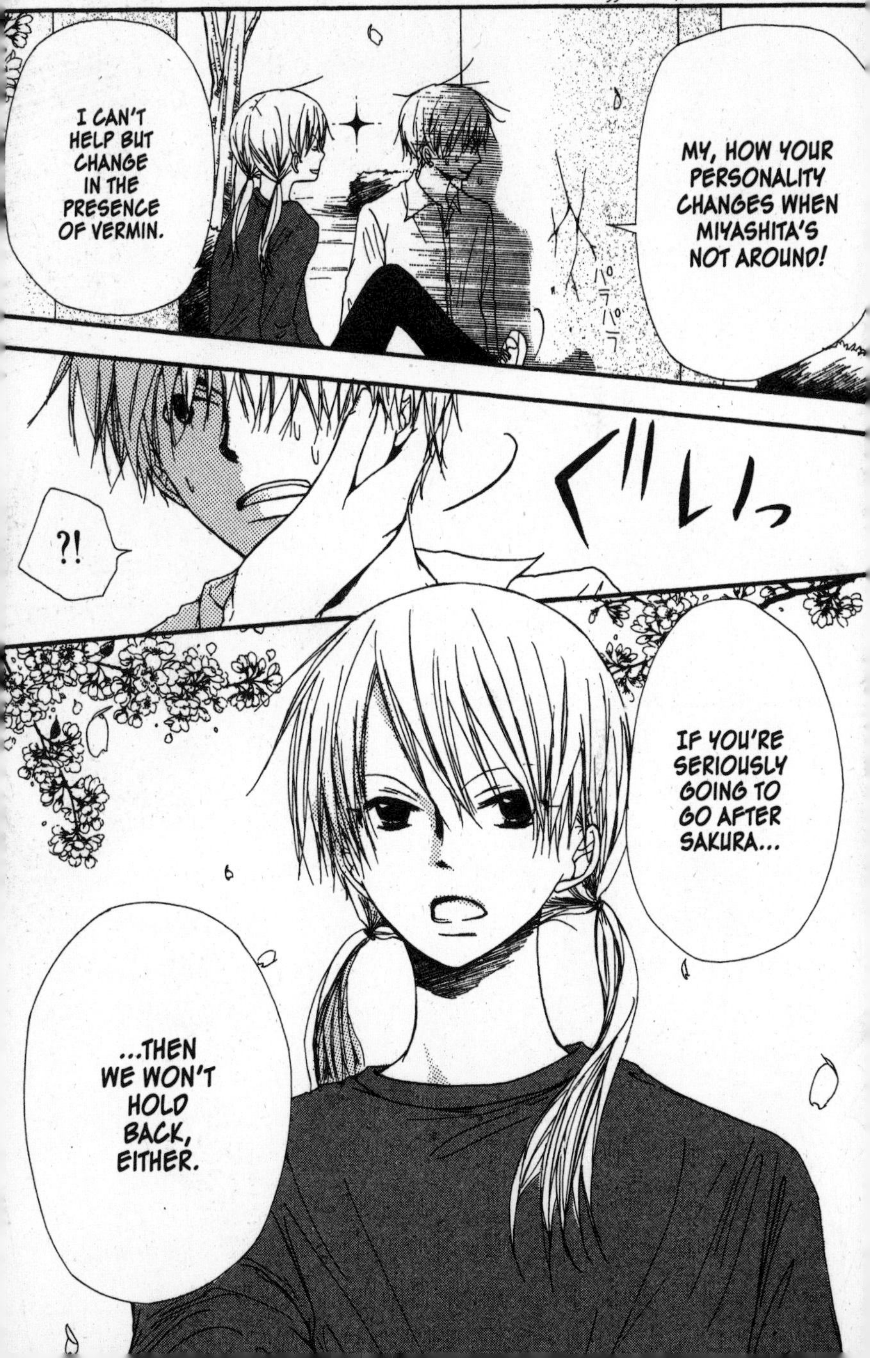
MY, HOW YOUR PERSONALITY CHANGES WHEN MIYASHITA'S NOT AROUND!
I CAN'T HELP BUT CHANGE IN THE PRESENCE OF VERMIN.
?!
IF YOU'RE SERIOUSLY GOING TO GO AFTER SAKURA...
...THEN WE WON'T HOLD BACK, EITHER.

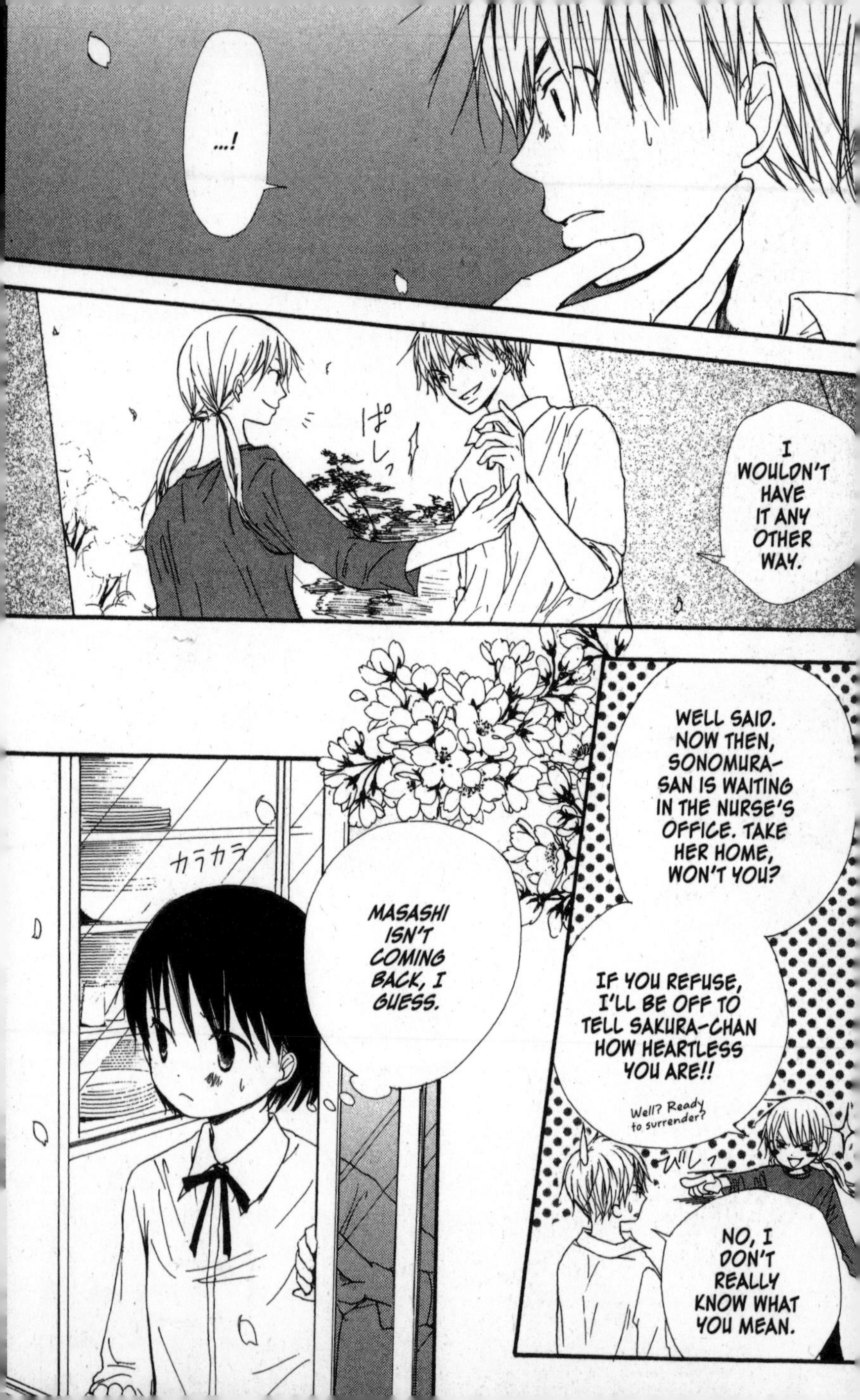
...!
ぱしっ
I WOULDN'T HAVE IT ANY OTHER WAY.
WELL SAID. NOW THEN, SONOMURA-SAN IS WAITING IN THE NURSE'S OFFICE. TAKE HER HOME, WON'T YOU?
IF YOU REFUSE, I'LL BE OFF TO TELL SAKURA-CHAN HOW HEARTLESS YOU ARE!!
Well? Ready to surrender?
びしっ
NO, I DON'T REALLY KNOW WHAT YOU MEAN.
カラカラ
MASASHI ISN'T COMING BACK, I GUESS.

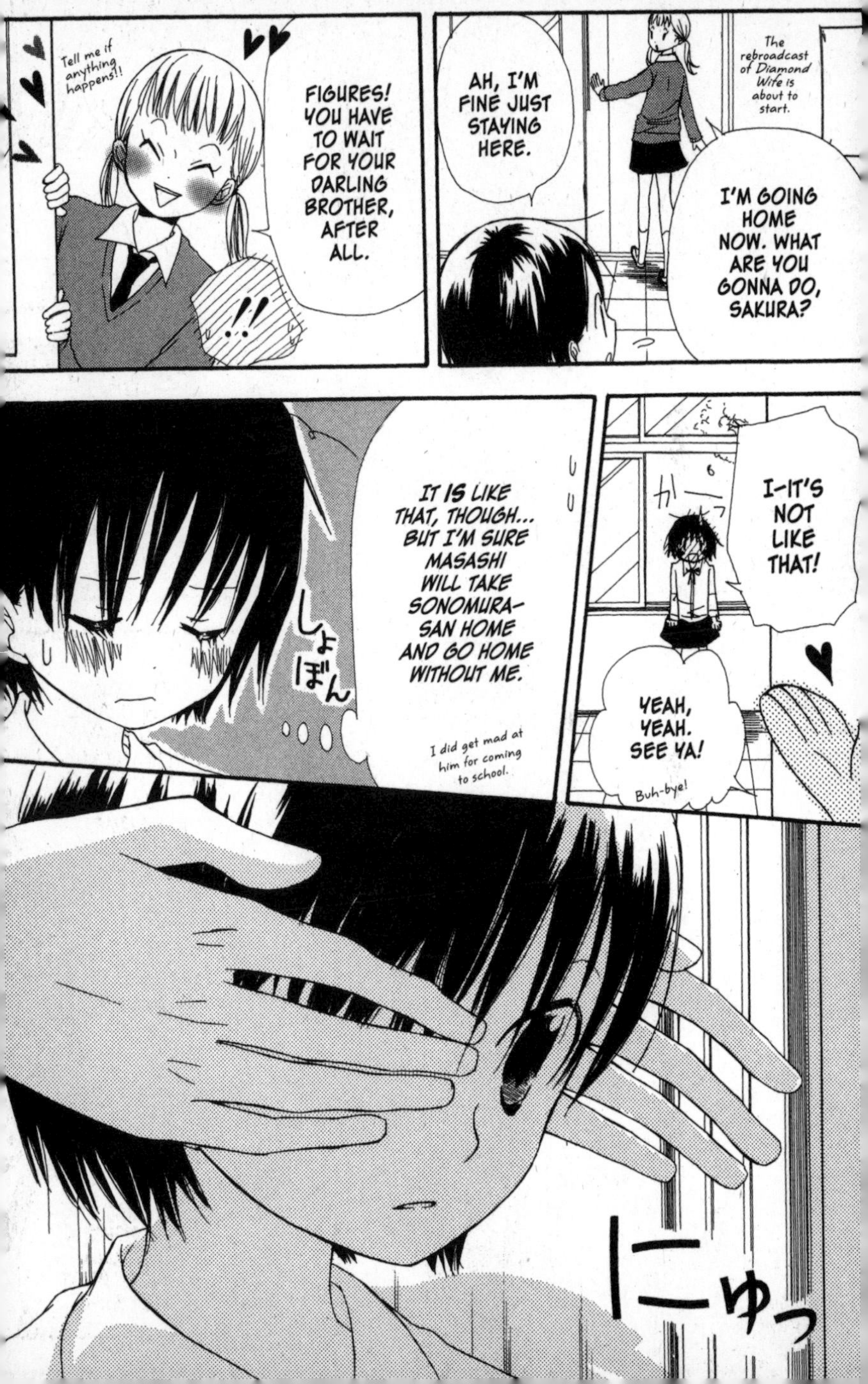
The rebroadcast of Diamond Wife is about to start.
I'M GOING HOME NOW. WHAT ARE YOU GONNA DO, SAKURA?
AH, I'M FINE JUST STAYING HERE.
FIGURES! YOU HAVE TO WAIT FOR YOUR DARLING BROTHER, AFTER ALL.
Tell me if anything happens!!
!!
I-IT'S NOT LIKE THAT!
YEAH, YEAH. SEE YA!
Buh-bye!
IT IS LIKE THAT, THOUGH... BUT I'M SURE MASASHI WILL TAKE SONOMURA-SAN HOME AND GO HOME WITHOUT ME.
I did get mad at him for coming to school.
しょぼん
にゅっ

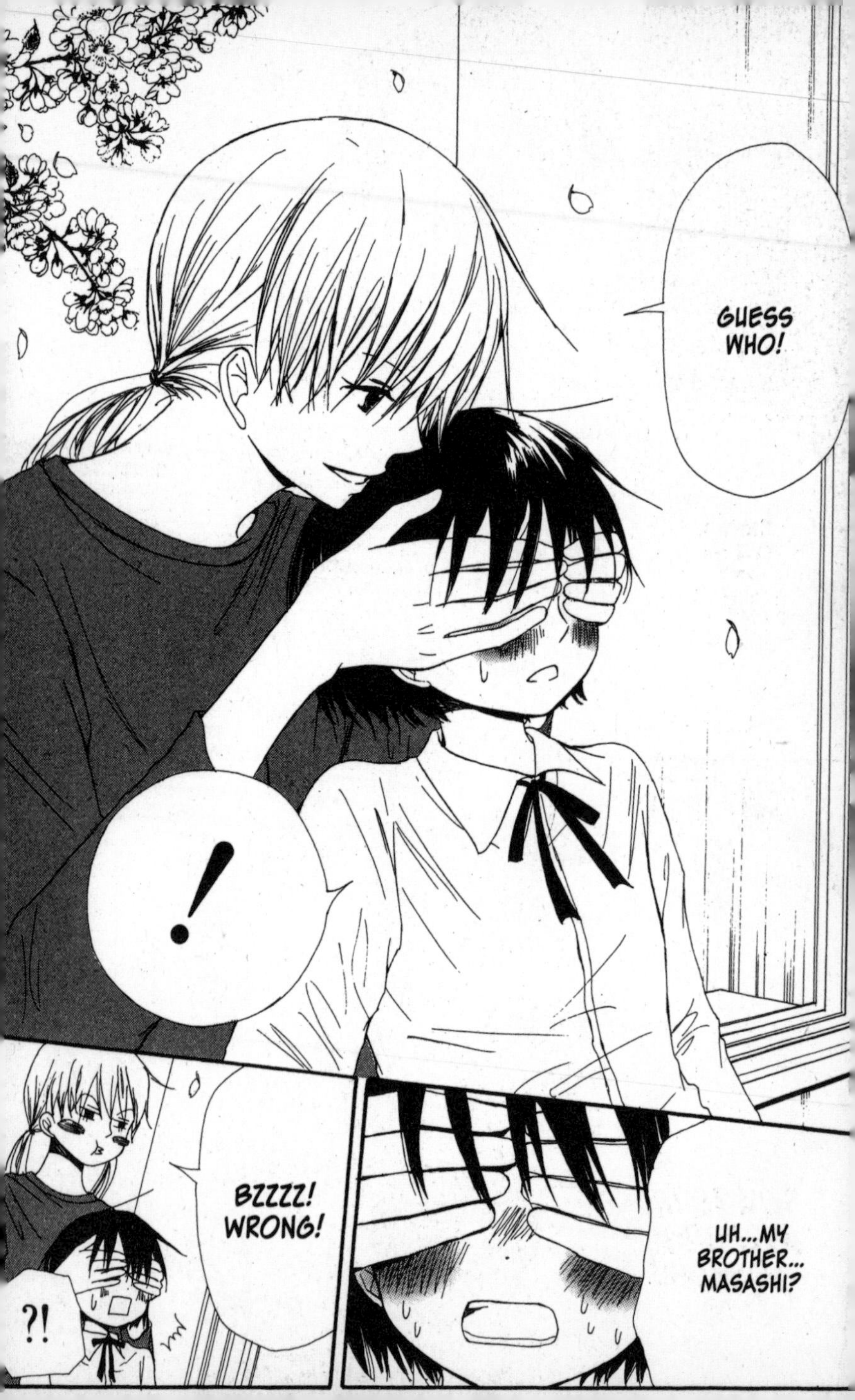
GUESS WHO!
!
UH...MY BROTHER... MASASHI?
BZZZZ! WRONG!
?!

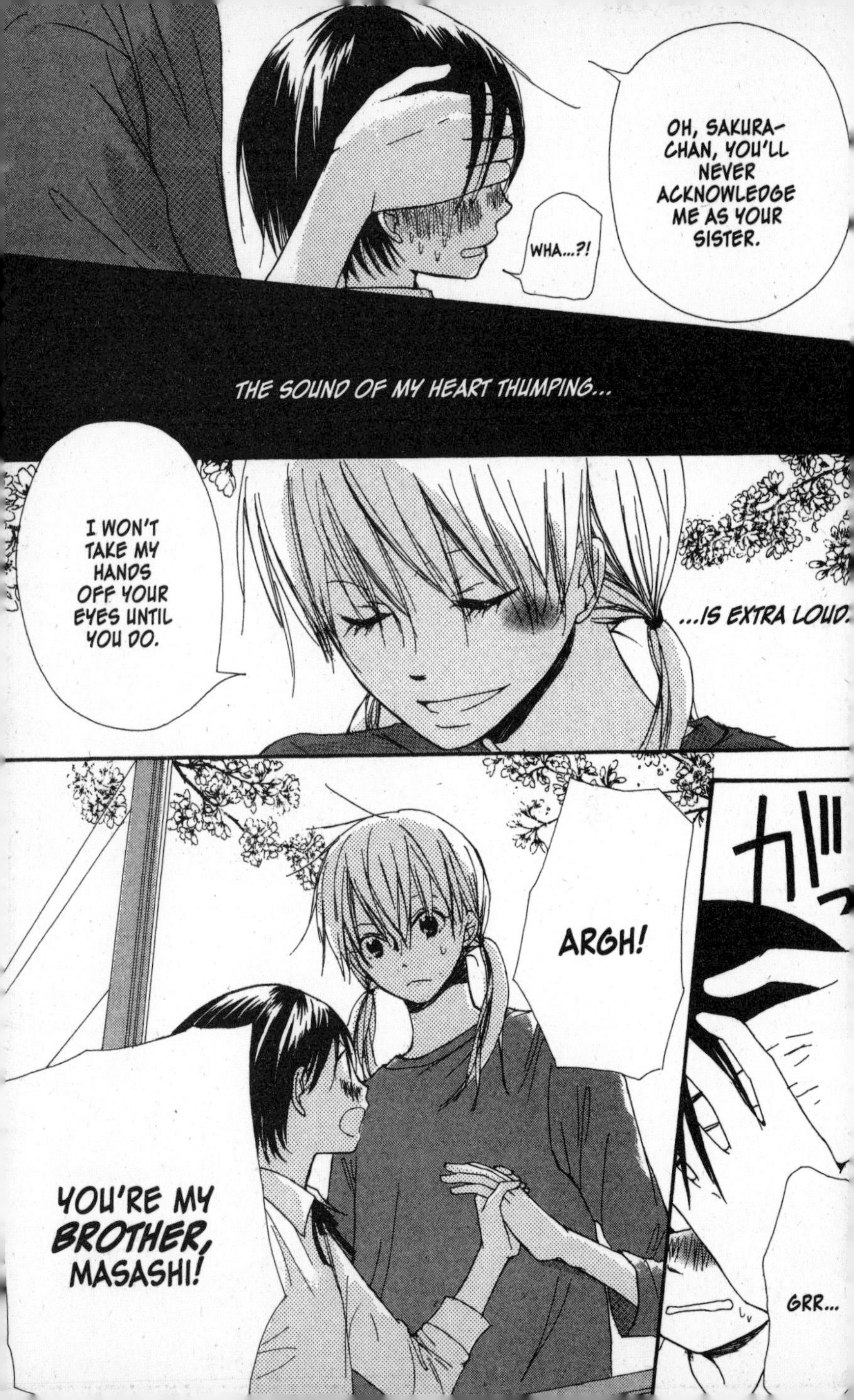
OH, SAKURA-CHAN, YOU'LL NEVER ACKNOWLEDGE ME AS YOUR SISTER.
WHA...?!
THE SOUND OF MY HEART THUMPING...
...IS EXTRA LOUD.
I WON'T TAKE MY HANDS OFF YOUR EYES UNTIL YOU DO.
GRR...
ARGH!
YOU'RE MY BROTHER, MASASHI!

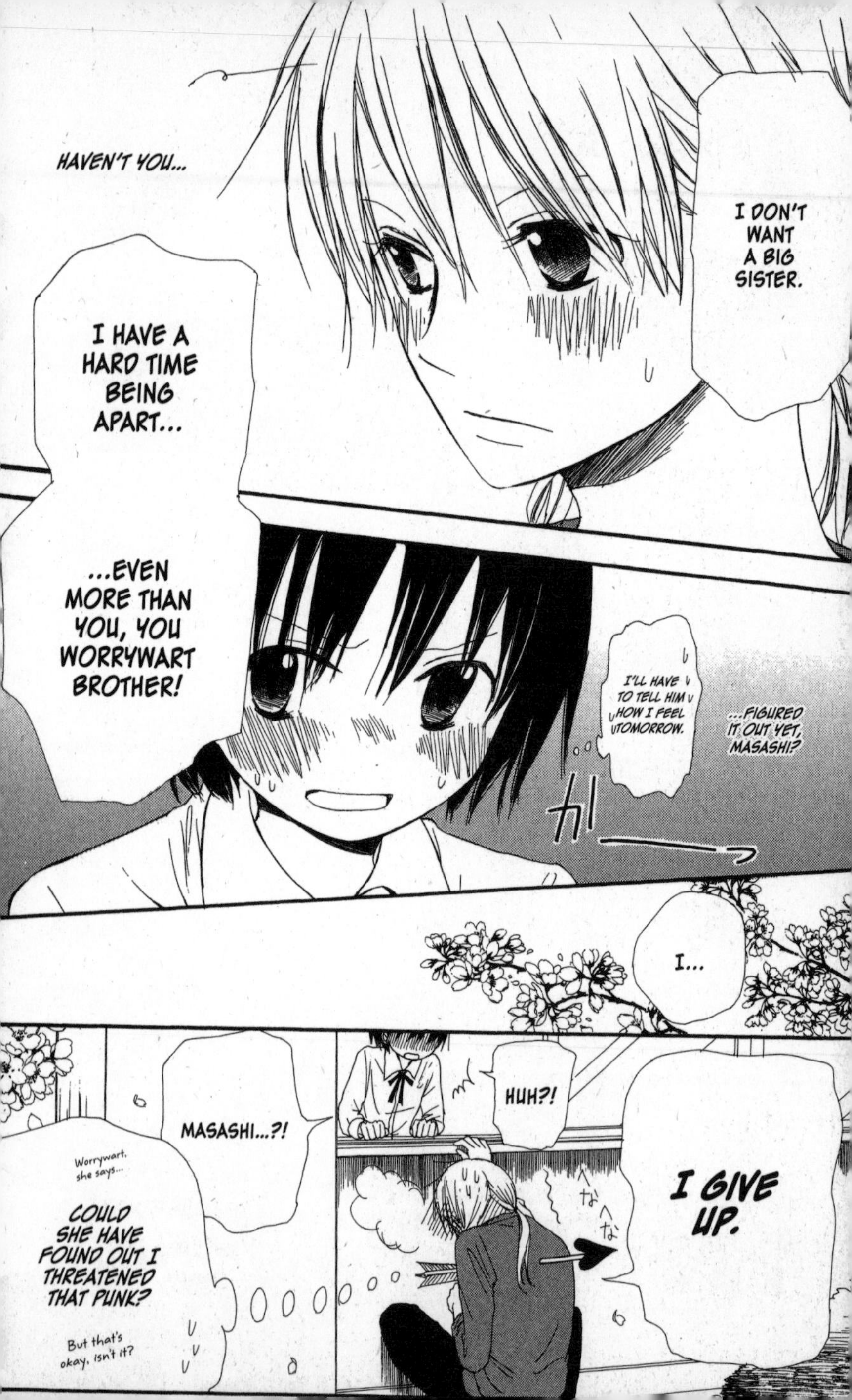
I DON'T WANT A BIG SISTER.
HAVEN'T YOU...
...FIGURED IT OUT YET, MASASHI?
I'LL HAVE TO TELL HIM HOW I FEEL TOMORROW.
I HAVE A HARD TIME BEING APART...
...EVEN MORE THAN YOU, YOU WORRYWART BROTHER!
I...
I GIVE UP.
HUH?!
へな へな
MASASHI...?!
Worrywart, she says...
COULD SHE HAVE FOUND OUT I THREATENED THAT PUNK?
But that's okay, isn't it?

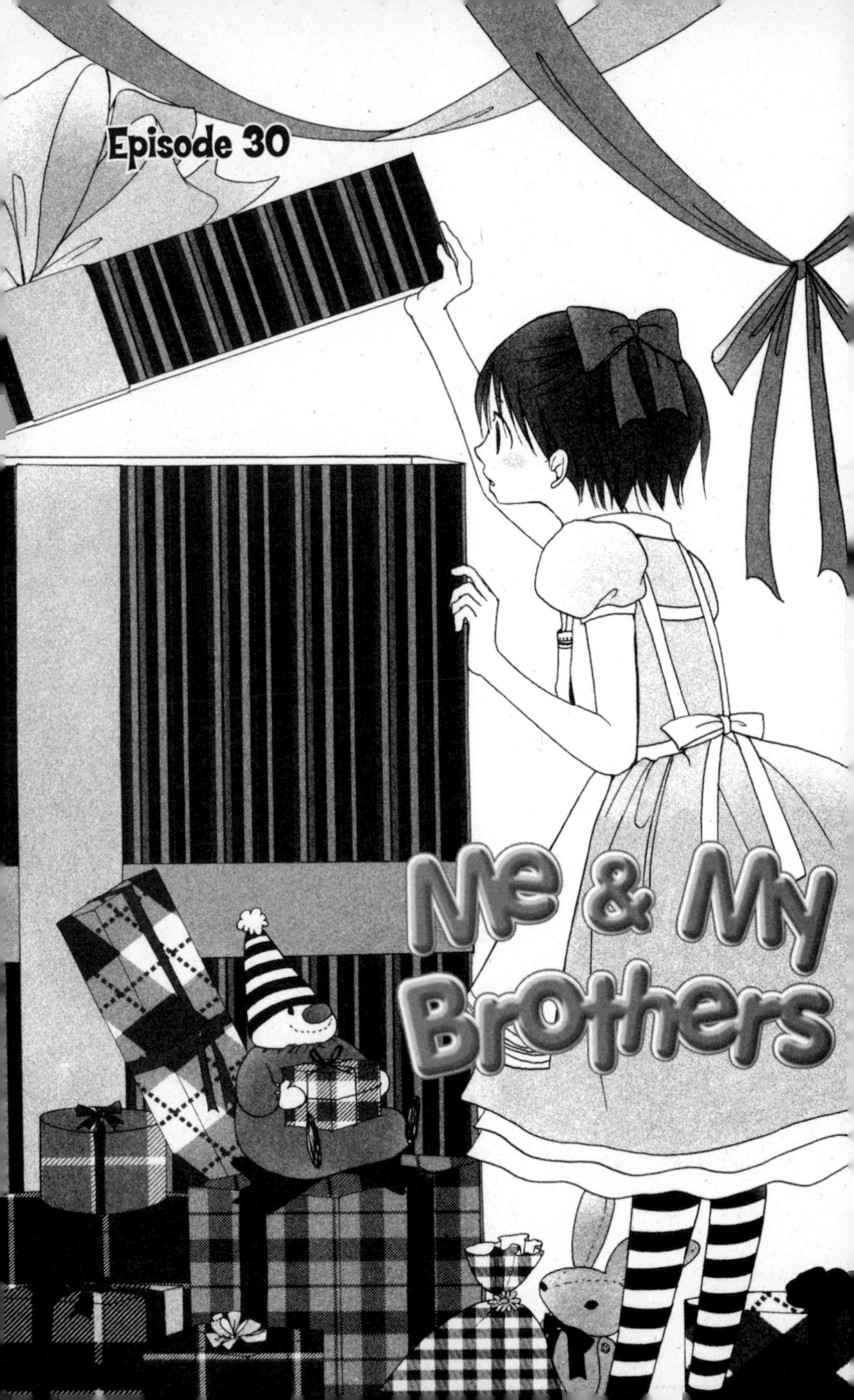
Episode 30
Me & My Brothers

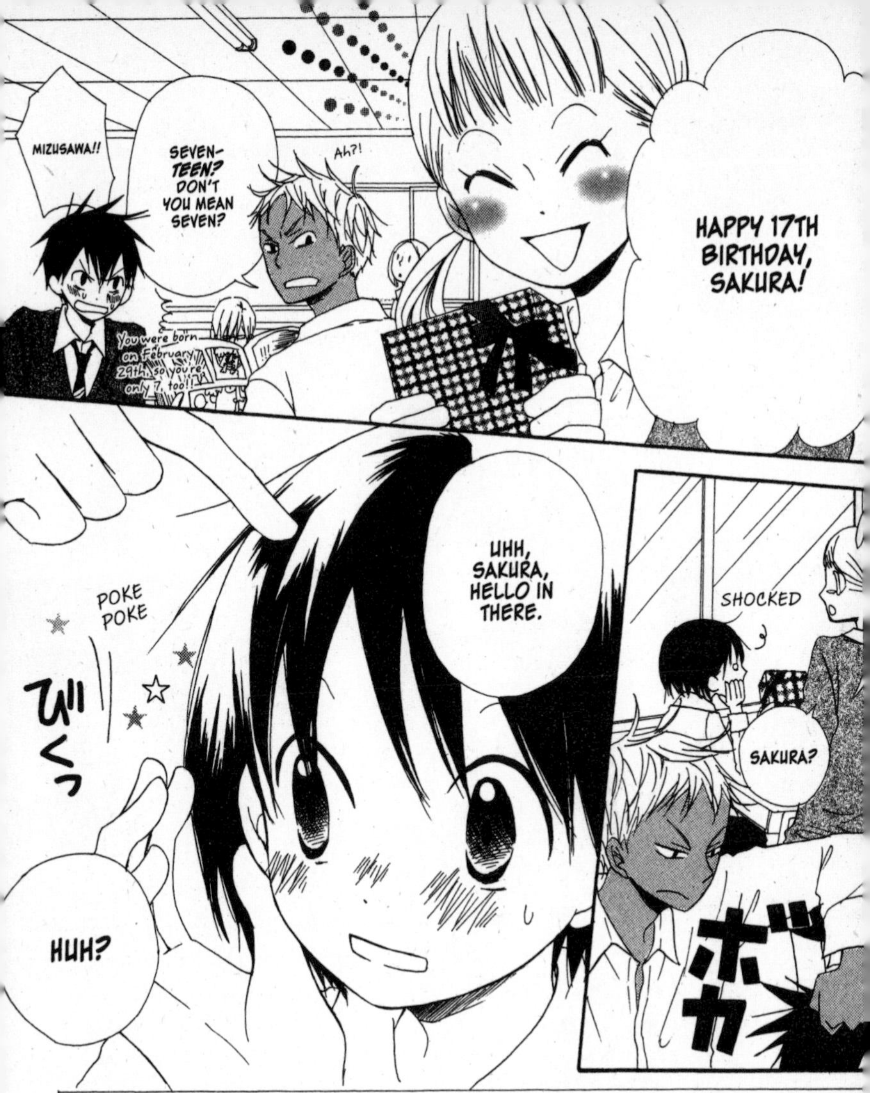
HAPPY 17TH BIRTHDAY, SAKURA!
Ah?!
SEVEN-TEEN? DON'T YOU MEAN SEVEN?
MIZUSAWA!!
You were born on February 29th, so you're only 7, too!!
SHOCKED
SAKURA?
ボカッ
UHH, SAKURA, HELLO IN THERE.
POKE POKE
びくっ
HUH?

Those of you who would like to tell me what you think, please send letters here:

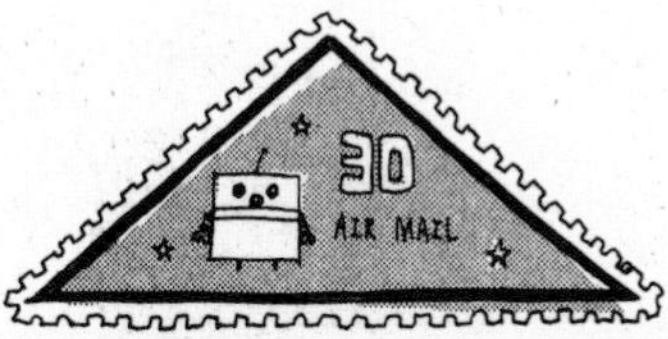
30
AIR MAIL

TOKYOPOP ↓
5900 Wilshire Blvd. Ste 2000
Los Angeles, CA 90036
c/o Hyun Joo Kim

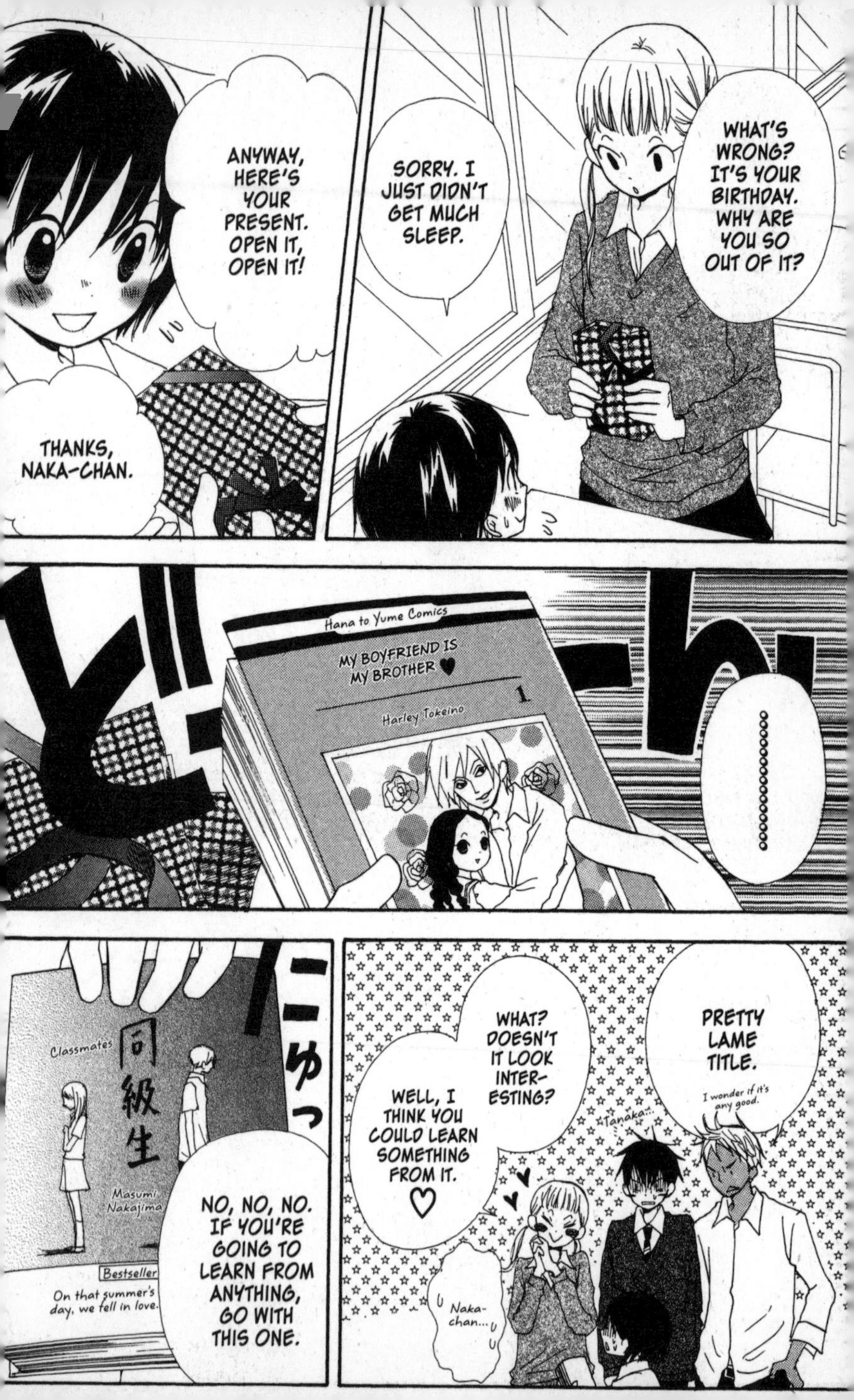
WHAT'S WRONG? IT'S YOUR BIRTHDAY. WHY ARE YOU SO OUT OF IT?
SORRY. I JUST DIDN'T GET MUCH SLEEP.
ANYWAY, HERE'S YOUR PRESENT. OPEN IT, OPEN IT!
THANKS, NAKA-CHAN.
Hana to Yume Comics
MY BOYFRIEND IS MY BROTHER ♥
1
Harley Tokeino
....
PRETTY LAME TITLE.
I wonder if it's any good.
WHAT? DOESN'T IT LOOK INTER-ESTING?
WELL, I THINK YOU COULD LEARN SOMETHING FROM IT. ♡
Tanaka...
Naka-chan...
にゅっ
Classmates
同級生
Masumi Nakajima
Bestseller
On that summer's day, we fell in love.
NO, NO, NO. IF YOU'RE GOING TO LEARN FROM ANYTHING, GO WITH THIS ONE.

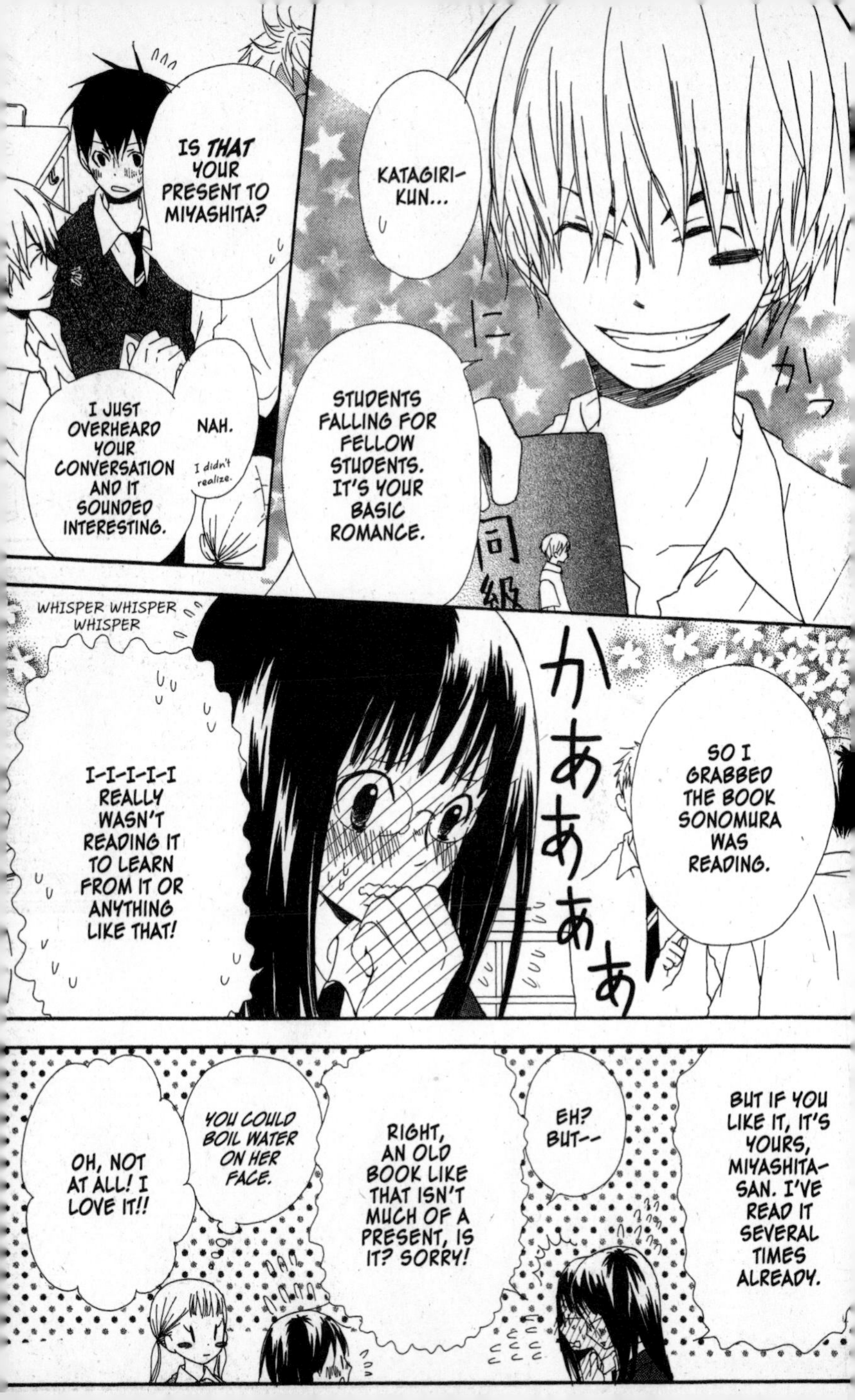
KATAGIRI-KUN...
STUDENTS FALLING FOR FELLOW STUDENTS. IT'S YOUR BASIC ROMANCE.
に
カッ
同級
IS THAT YOUR PRESENT TO MIYASHITA?
NAH.
I didn't realize.
I JUST OVERHEARD YOUR CONVERSATION AND IT SOUNDED INTERESTING.
SO I GRABBED THE BOOK SONOMURA WAS READING.
かああぁあ
WHISPER WHISPER WHISPER
I-I-I-I-I REALLY WASN'T READING IT TO LEARN FROM IT OR ANYTHING LIKE THAT!
BUT IF YOU LIKE IT, IT'S YOURS, MIYASHITA-SAN. I'VE READ IT SEVERAL TIMES ALREADY.
EH? BUT--
RIGHT, AN OLD BOOK LIKE THAT ISN'T MUCH OF A PRESENT, IS IT? SORRY!
YOU COULD BOIL WATER ON HER FACE.
OH, NOT AT ALL! I LOVE IT!!

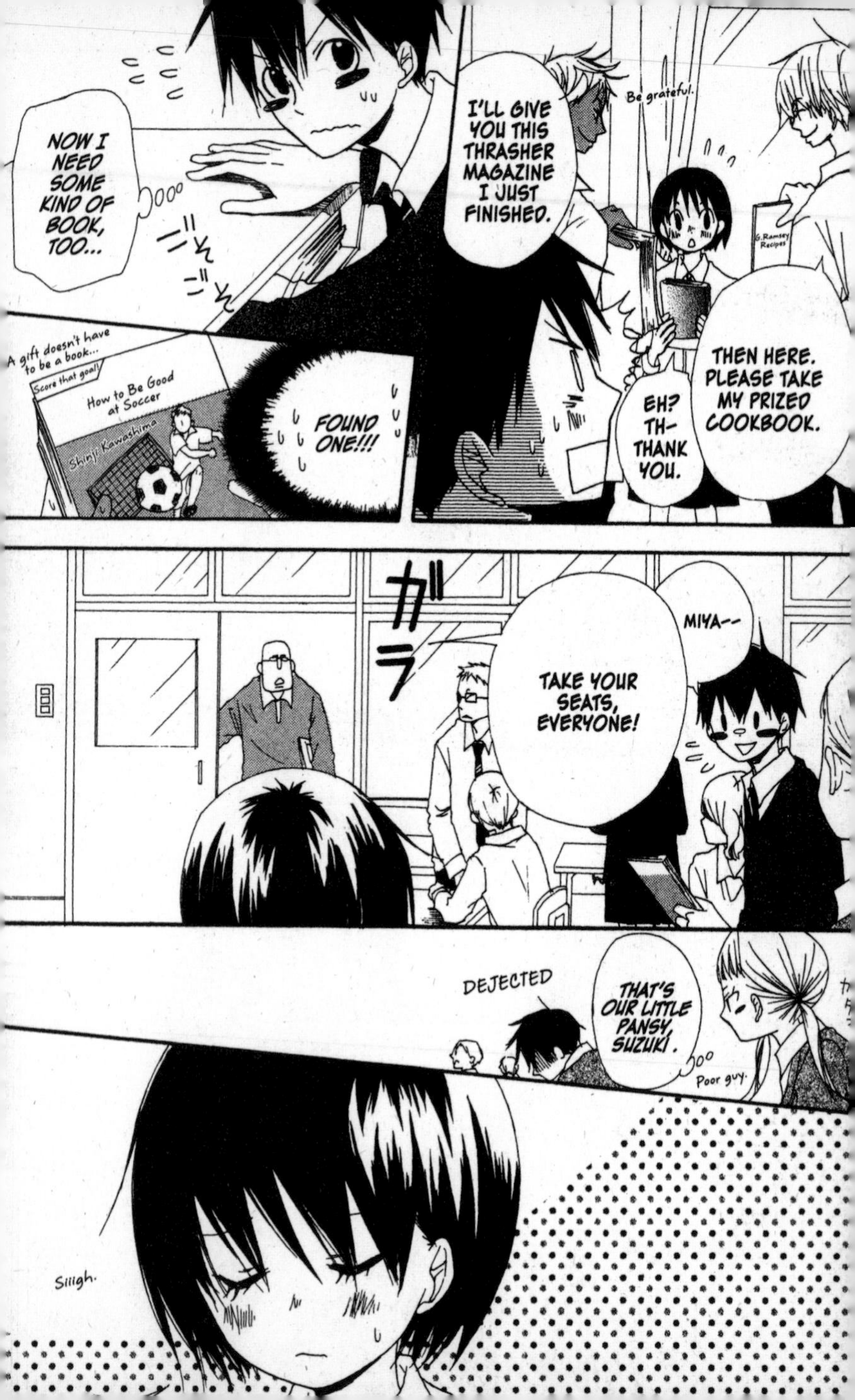

Be grateful.
I'LL GIVE YOU THIS THRASHER MAGAZINE I JUST FINISHED.
G.Ramsey Recipes
NOW I NEED SOME KIND OF BOOK, TOO...
THEN HERE. PLEASE TAKE MY PRIZED COOKBOOK.
EH? TH-THANK YOU.
FOUND ONE!!!
A gift doesn't have to be a book...
Score that goal!
How to Be Good at Soccer
Shinji Kawashima
MIYA--
TAKE YOUR SEATS, EVERYONE!
ガラ
THAT'S OUR LITTLE PANSY, SUZUKI.
Poor guy.
DEJECTED
Siiigh.

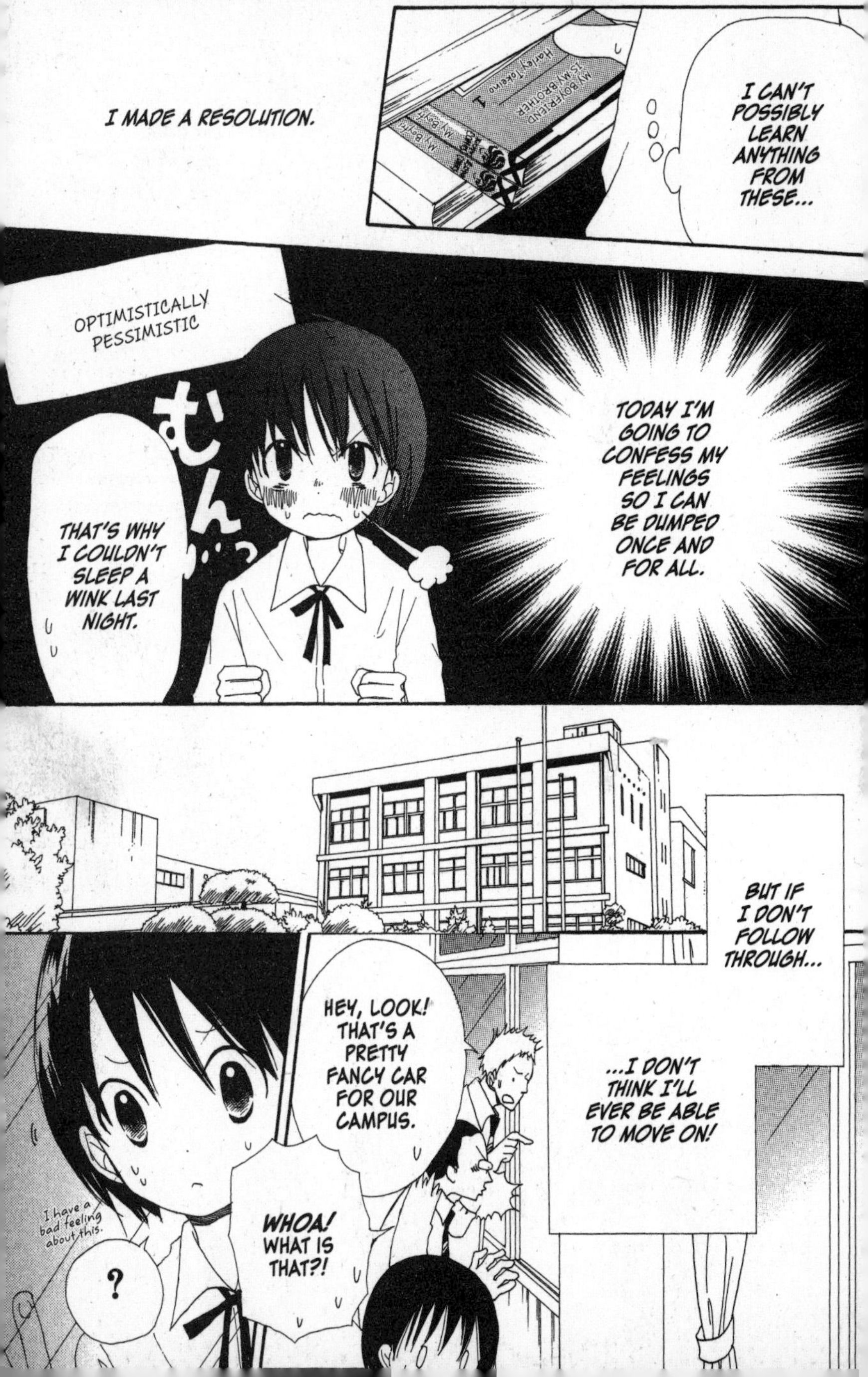
I CAN'T POSSIBLY LEARN ANYTHING FROM THESE...
MY BOYFRIEND IS MY BROTHER
Harley Tokeino
I MADE A RESOLUTION.
TODAY I'M GOING TO CONFESS MY FEELINGS SO I CAN BE DUMPED ONCE AND FOR ALL.
OPTIMISTICALLY PESSIMISTIC
むんっ
THAT'S WHY I COULDN'T SLEEP A WINK LAST NIGHT.
BUT IF I DON'T FOLLOW THROUGH...
...I DON'T THINK I'LL EVER BE ABLE TO MOVE ON!
HEY, LOOK! THAT'S A PRETTY FANCY CAR FOR OUR CAMPUS.
WHOA! WHAT IS THAT?!
?
I have a bad feeling about this.

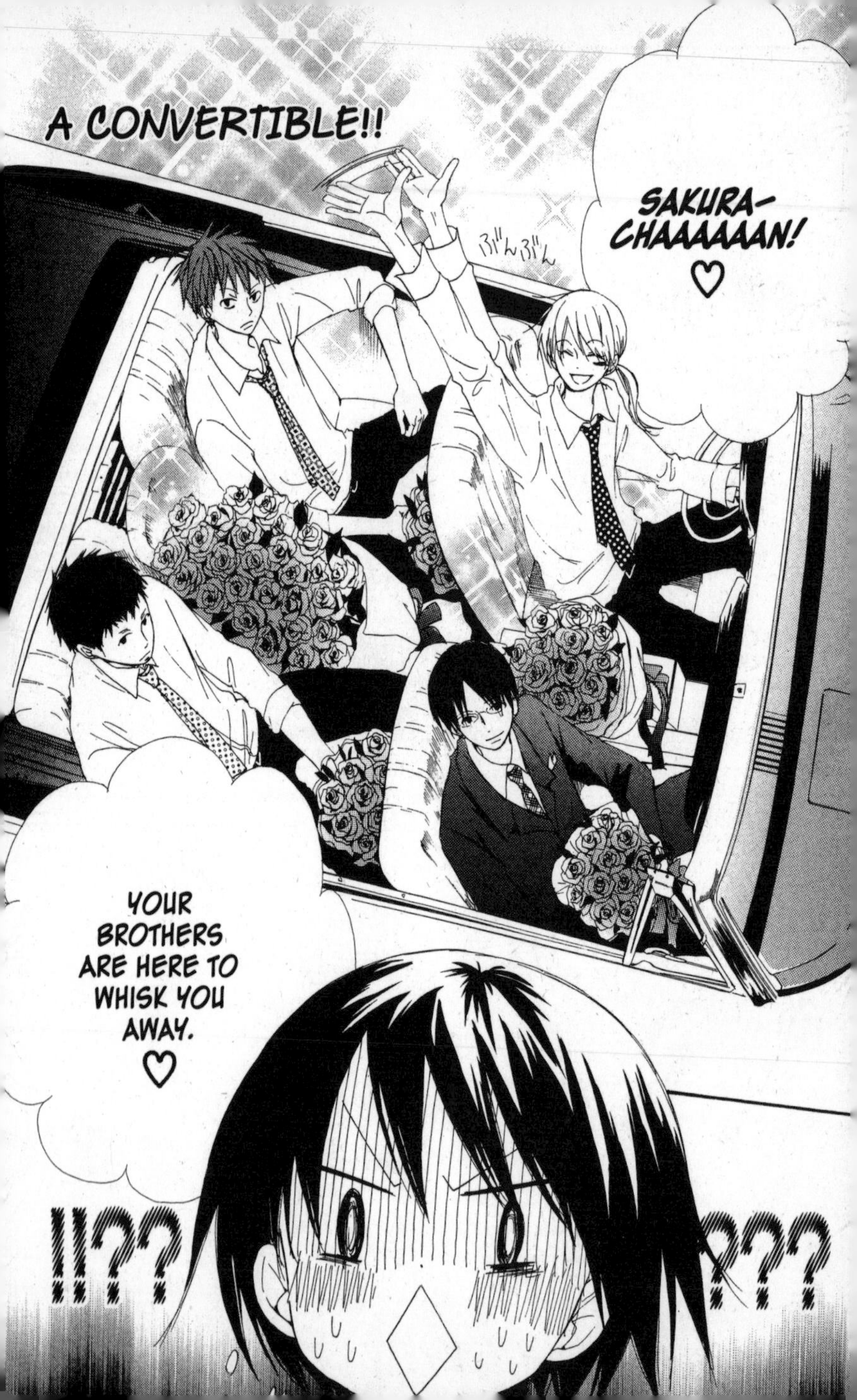

SAKURA-CHAAAAAAN! ♡
ぶんぶん
A CONVERTIBLE!!
YOUR BROTHERS ARE HERE TO WHISK YOU AWAY. ♡
???
!!??

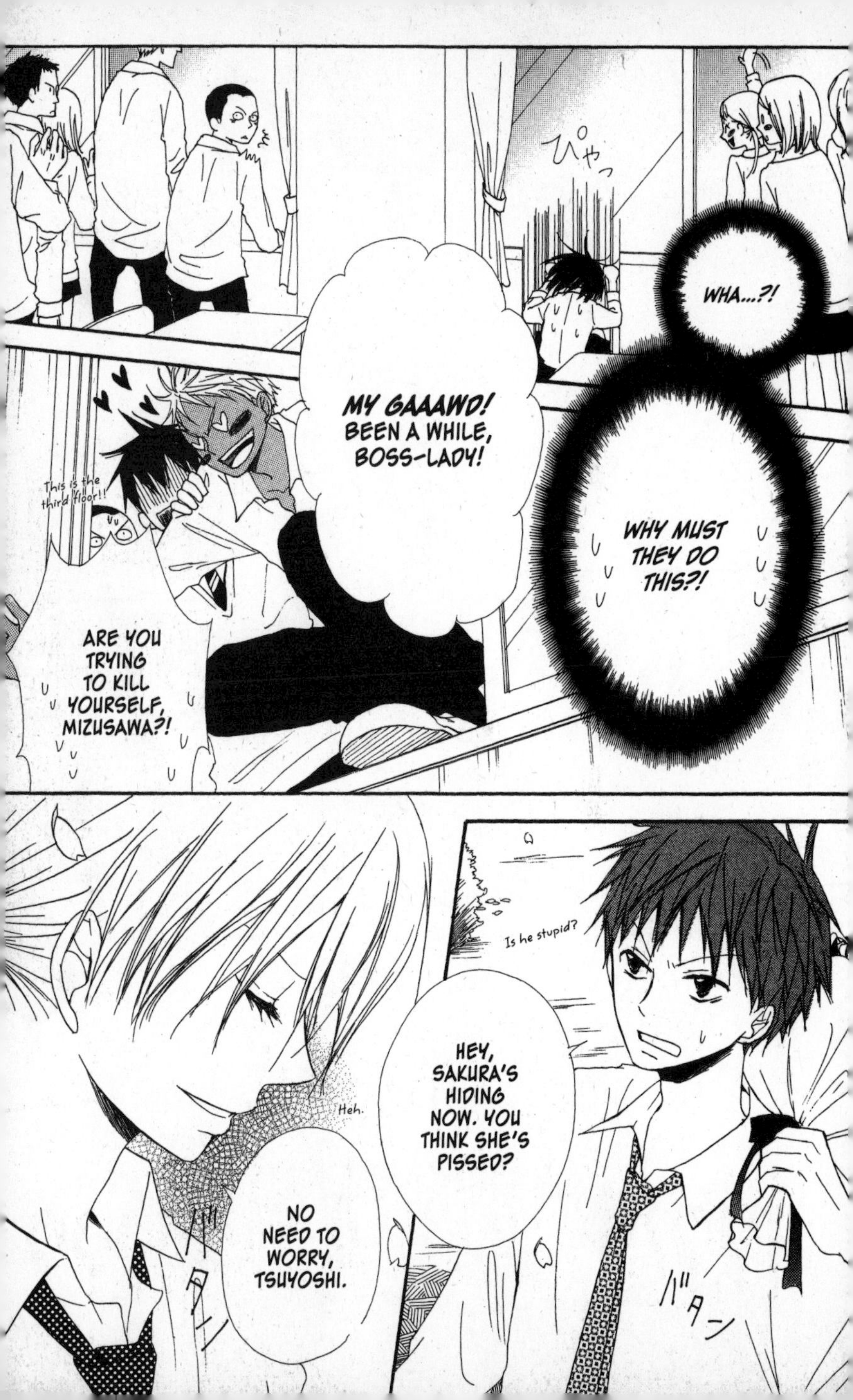
WHA...?!
WHY MUST THEY DO THIS?!
ぴゃっ
MY GAAAWD! BEEN A WHILE, BOSS-LADY!
This is the third floor!!
ARE YOU TRYING TO KILL YOURSELF, MIZUSAWA?!
Is he stupid?
HEY, SAKURA'S HIDING NOW. YOU THINK SHE'S PISSED?
バタン
Heh.
NO NEED TO WORRY, TSUYOSHI.

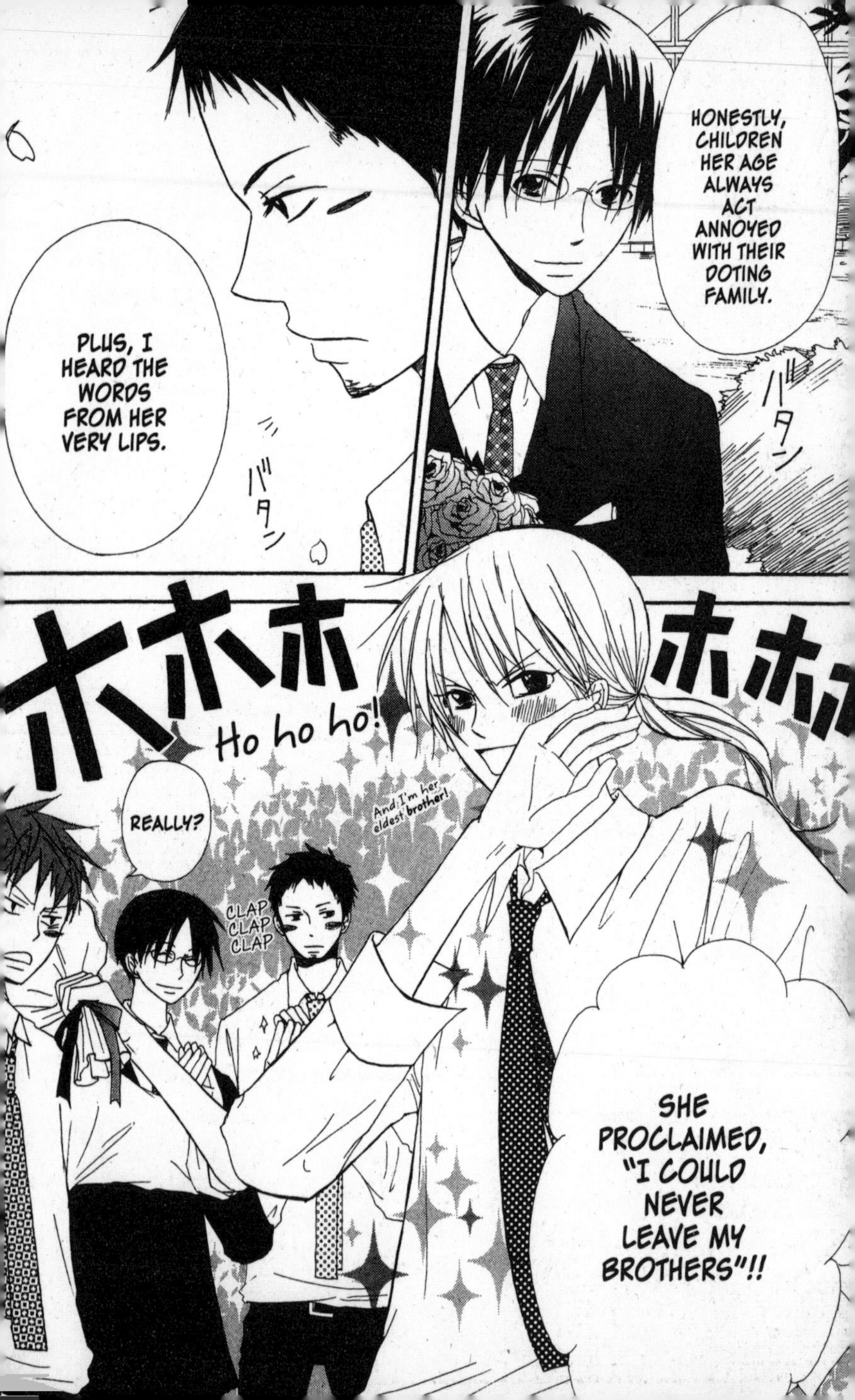

HONESTLY, CHILDREN HER AGE ALWAYS ACT ANNOYED WITH THEIR DOTING FAMILY.
バタン
PLUS, I HEARD THE WORDS FROM HER VERY LIPS.
バタン
ホホホ
ホホホ
Ho ho ho!
And I'm her eldest brother!
REALLY?
CLAP CLAP CLAP
SHE PROCLAIMED, "I COULD NEVER LEAVE MY BROTHERS"!!

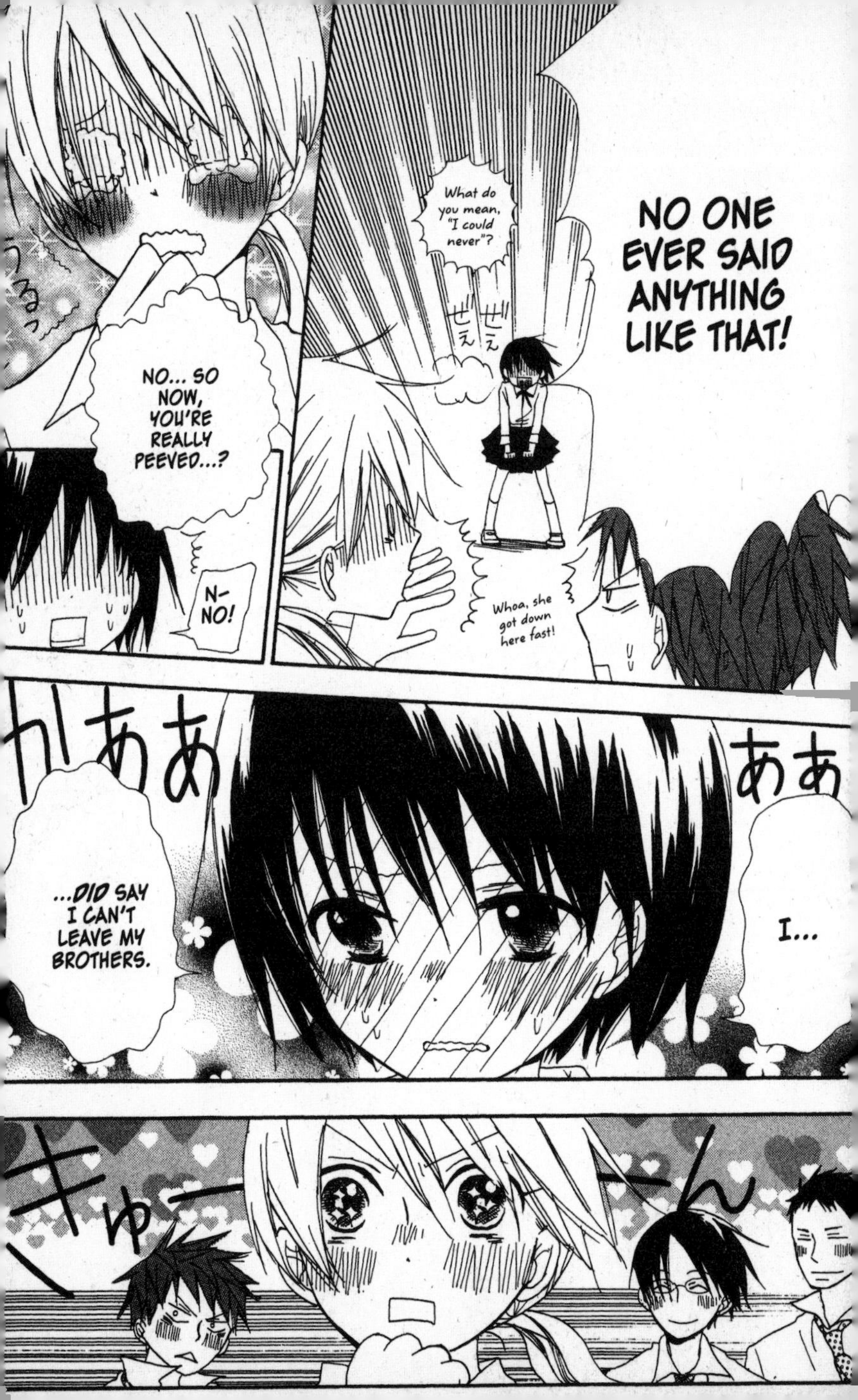
NO ONE EVER SAID ANYTHING LIKE THAT!
What do you mean, "I could never"?
ぜぇ ぜぇ
Whoa, she got down here fast!
うるっ
NO... SO NOW, YOU'RE REALLY PEEVED...?
N-NO!
かあああ ああ
I...
...DID SAY I CAN'T LEAVE MY BROTHERS.
きゅーーーん

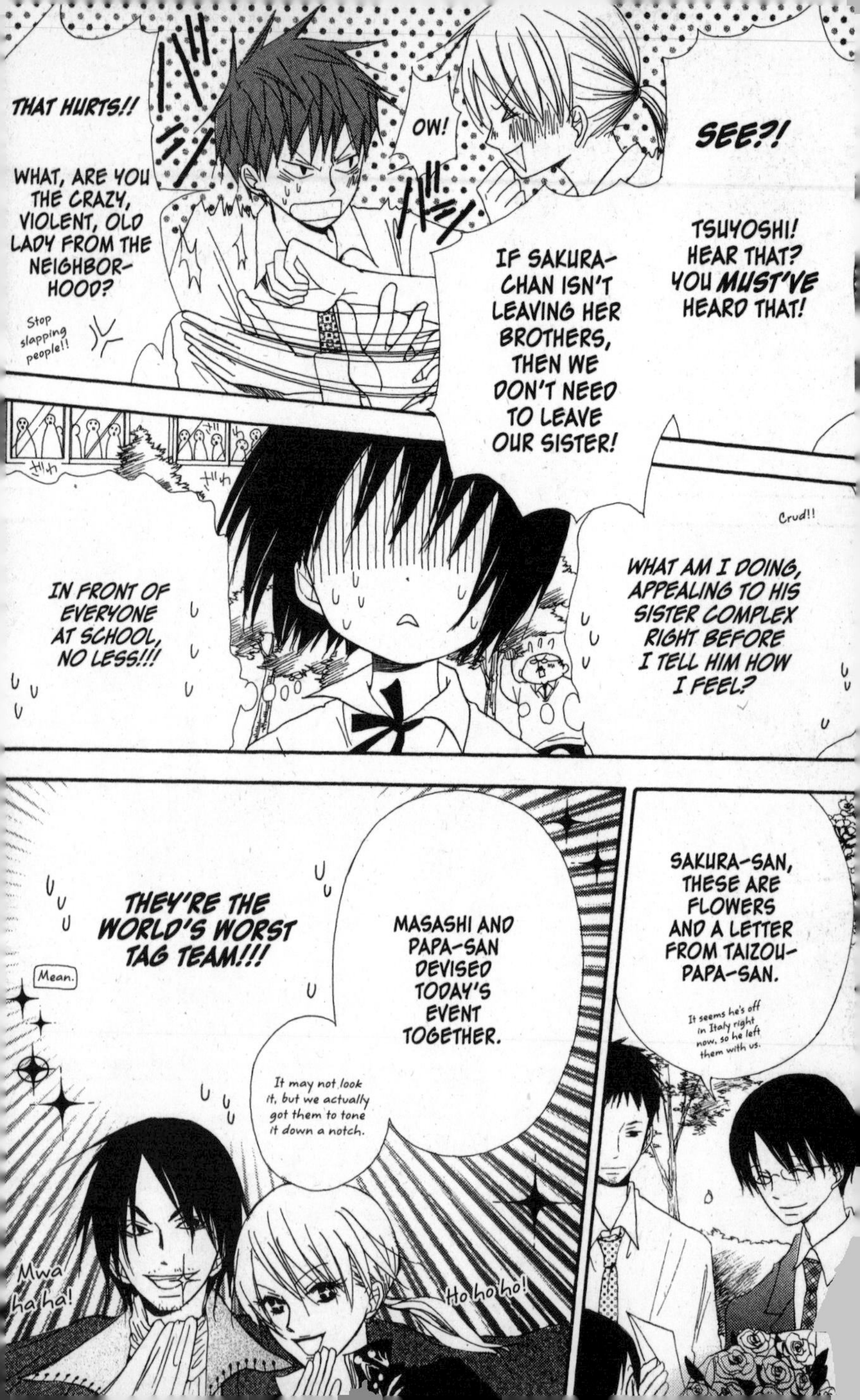
SEE?!
TSUYOSHI! HEAR THAT? YOU MUST'VE HEARD THAT!
OW!
IF SAKURA-CHAN ISN'T LEAVING HER BROTHERS, THEN WE DON'T NEED TO LEAVE OUR SISTER!
THAT HURTS!!
WHAT, ARE YOU THE CRAZY, VIOLENT, OLD LADY FROM THE NEIGHBOR-HOOD?
Stop slapping people!!
Crud!!
WHAT AM I DOING, APPEALING TO HIS SISTER COMPLEX RIGHT BEFORE I TELL HIM HOW I FEEL?
IN FRONT OF EVERYONE AT SCHOOL, NO LESS!!!
SAKURA-SAN, THESE ARE FLOWERS AND A LETTER FROM TAIZOU-PAPA-SAN.
It seems he's off in Italy right now, so he left them with us.
MASASHI AND PAPA-SAN DEVISED TODAY'S EVENT TOGETHER.
It may not look it, but we actually got them to tone it down a notch.
THEY'RE THE WORLD'S WORST TAG TEAM!!!
Mean.
Ho ho ho!
Mwa ha ha!

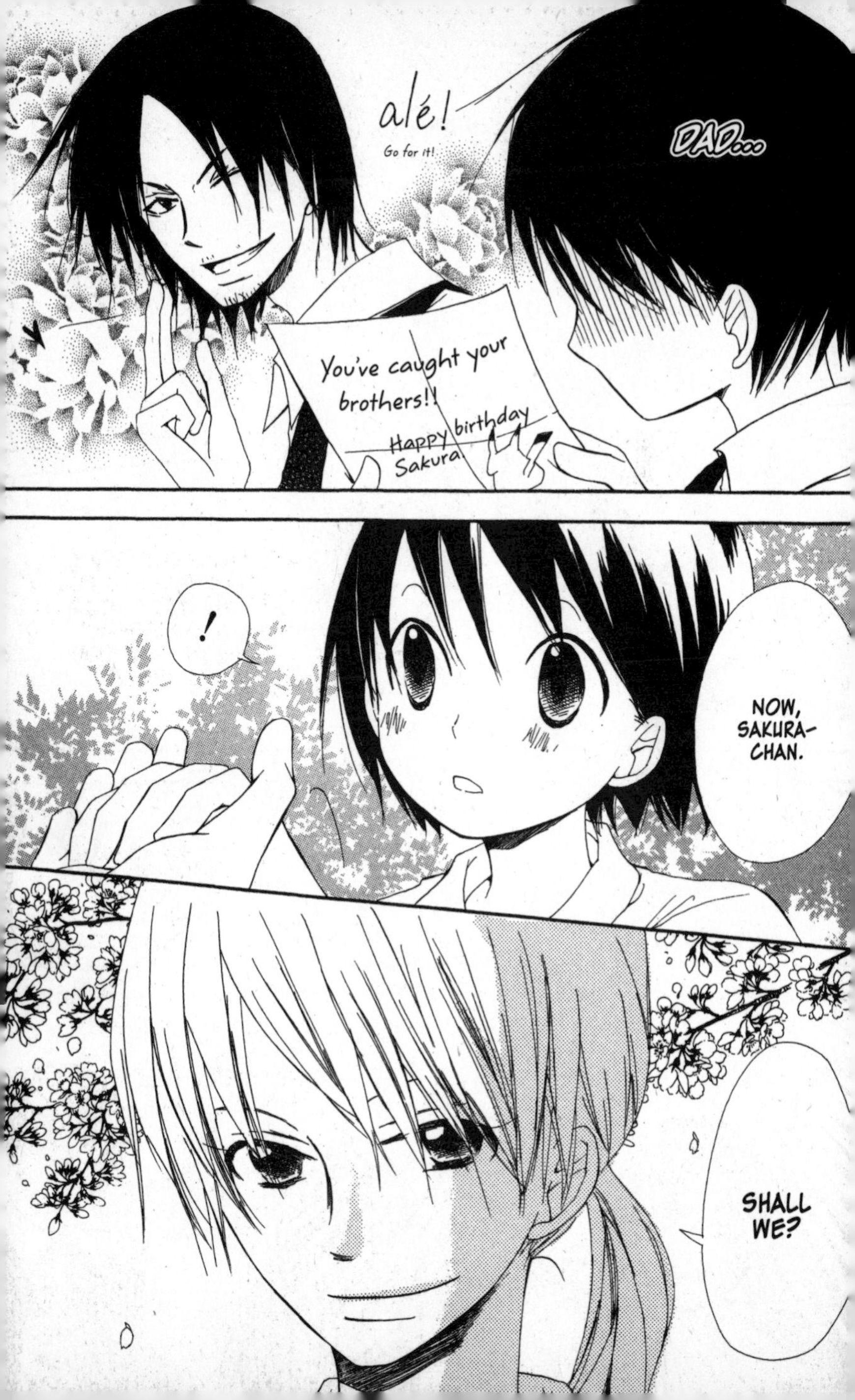
DAD...
alé!
Go for it!
You've caught your brothers!!
Happy birthday Sakura.
NOW, SAKURA-CHAN.
!
SHALL WE?

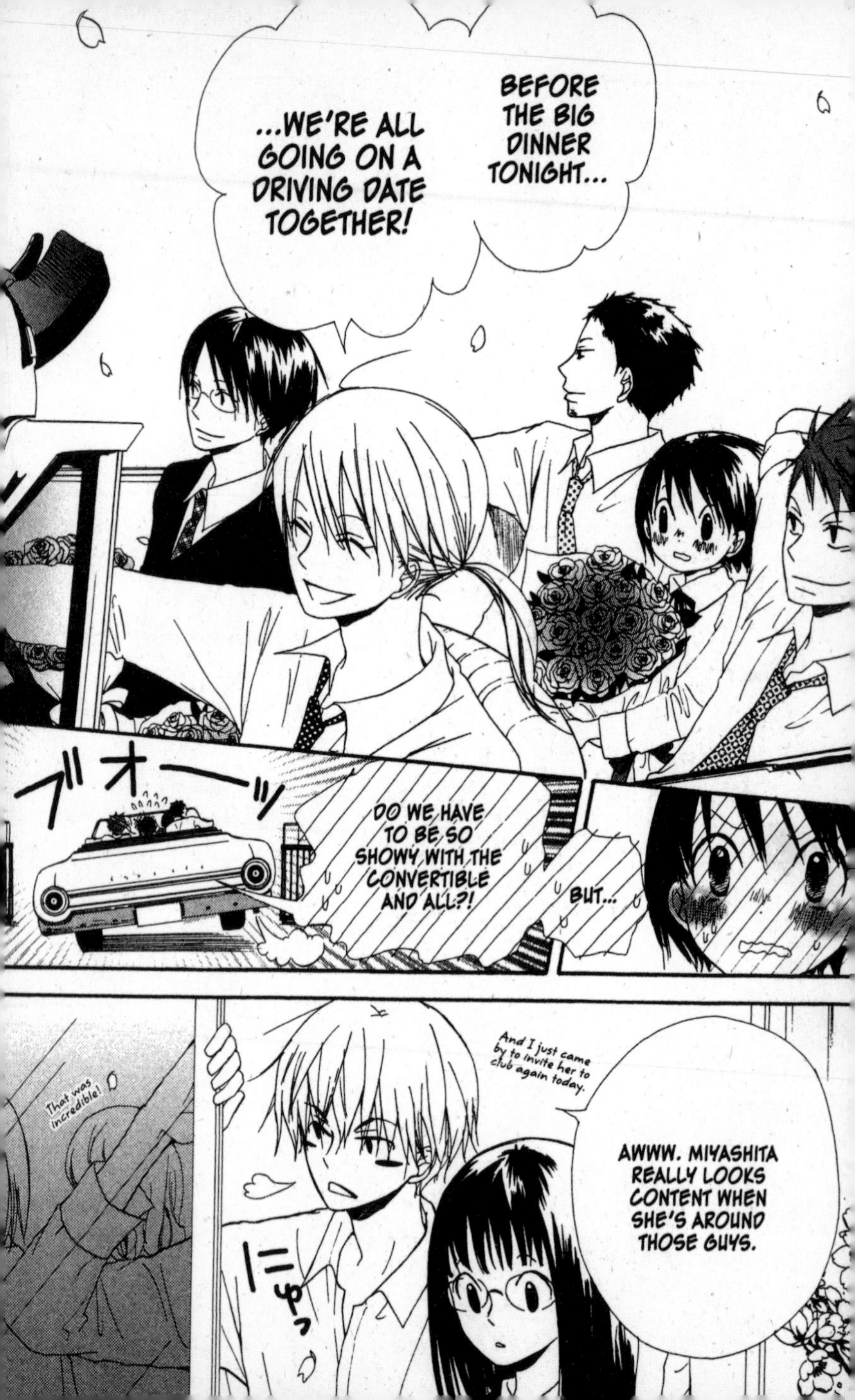
BEFORE THE BIG DINNER TONIGHT...
...WE'RE ALL GOING ON A DRIVING DATE TOGETHER!
ブオーーッ
DO WE HAVE TO BE SO SHOWY WITH THE CONVERTIBLE AND ALL?!
BUT...
AWWW. MIYASHITA REALLY LOOKS CONTENT WHEN SHE'S AROUND THOSE GUYS.
And I just came by to invite her to club again today.
にゅっ
That was incredible!

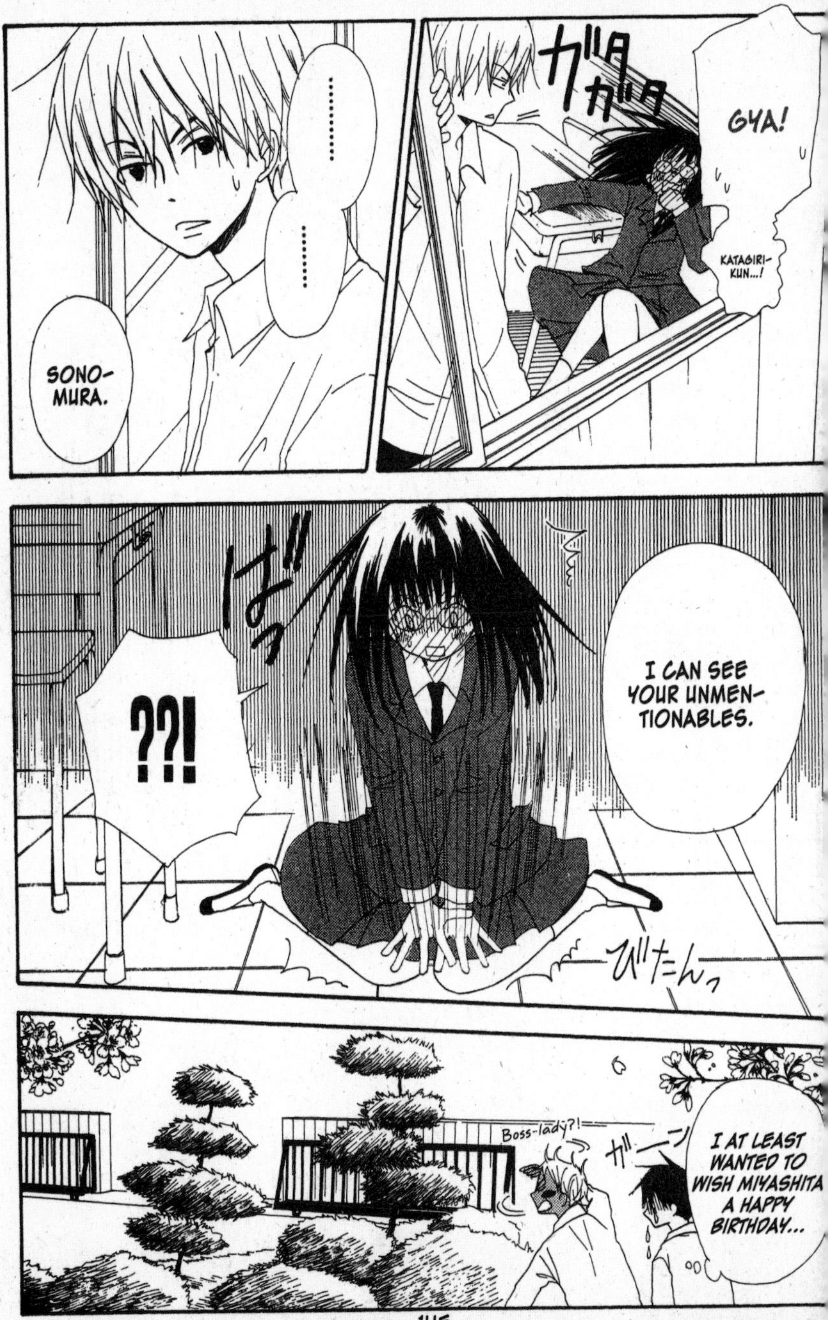
ガタガタ
GYA!
KATAGIRI-KUN...!
......
......
SONO-MURA.
I CAN SEE YOUR UNMENTIONABLES.
ばっ
??!
びたんっ
I AT LEAST WANTED TO WISH MIYASHITA A HAPPY BIRTHDAY...
ガーン
Boss-lady?!

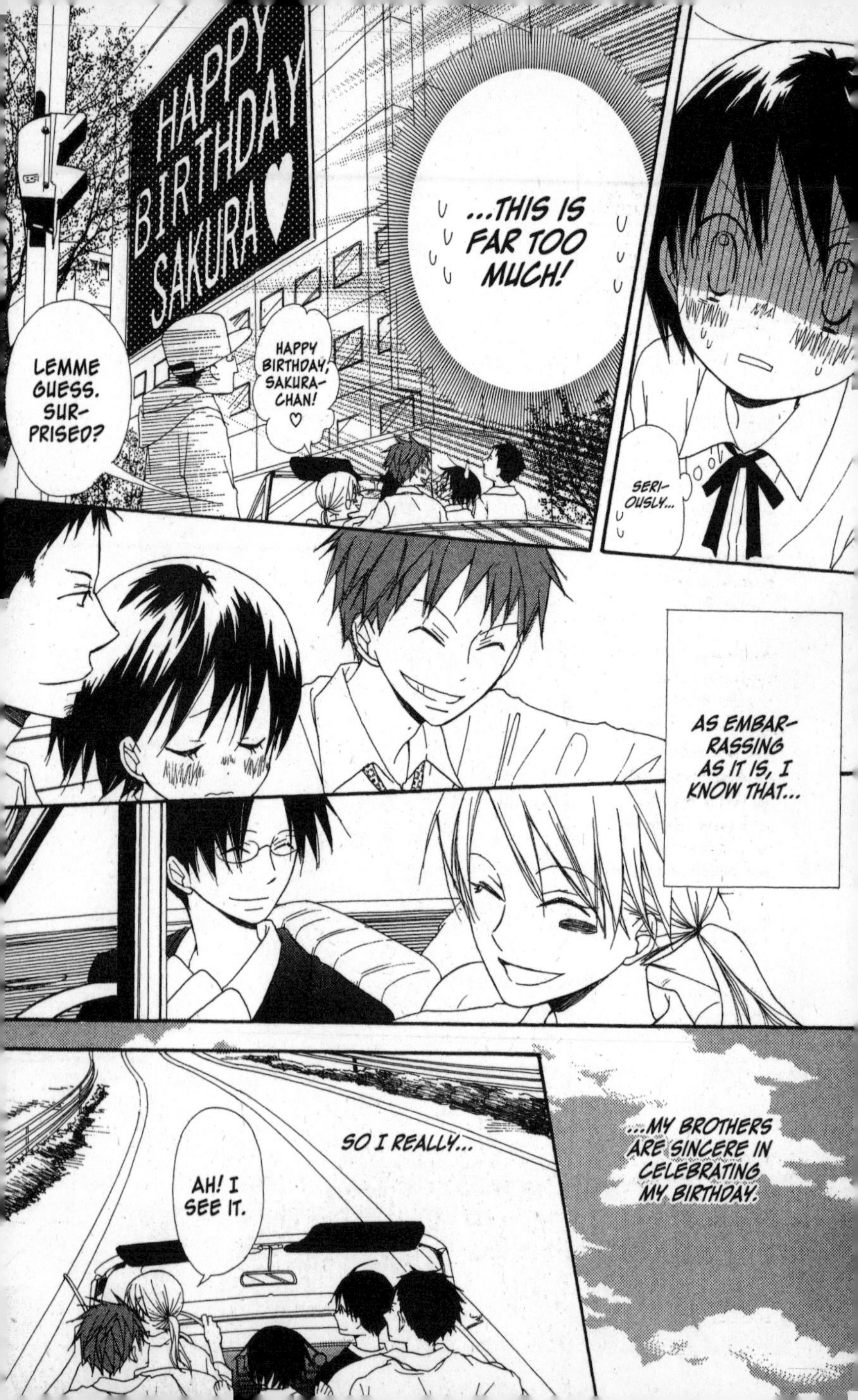
SERI-OUSLY...
...THIS IS FAR TOO MUCH!
HAPPY BIRTHDAY SAKURA ♥
HAPPY BIRTHDAY, SAKURA-CHAN! ♡
LEMME GUESS. SUR-PRISED?
AS EMBAR-RASSING AS IT IS, I KNOW THAT...
...MY BROTHERS ARE SINCERE IN CELEBRATING MY BIRTHDAY.
SO I REALLY...
AH! I SEE IT.

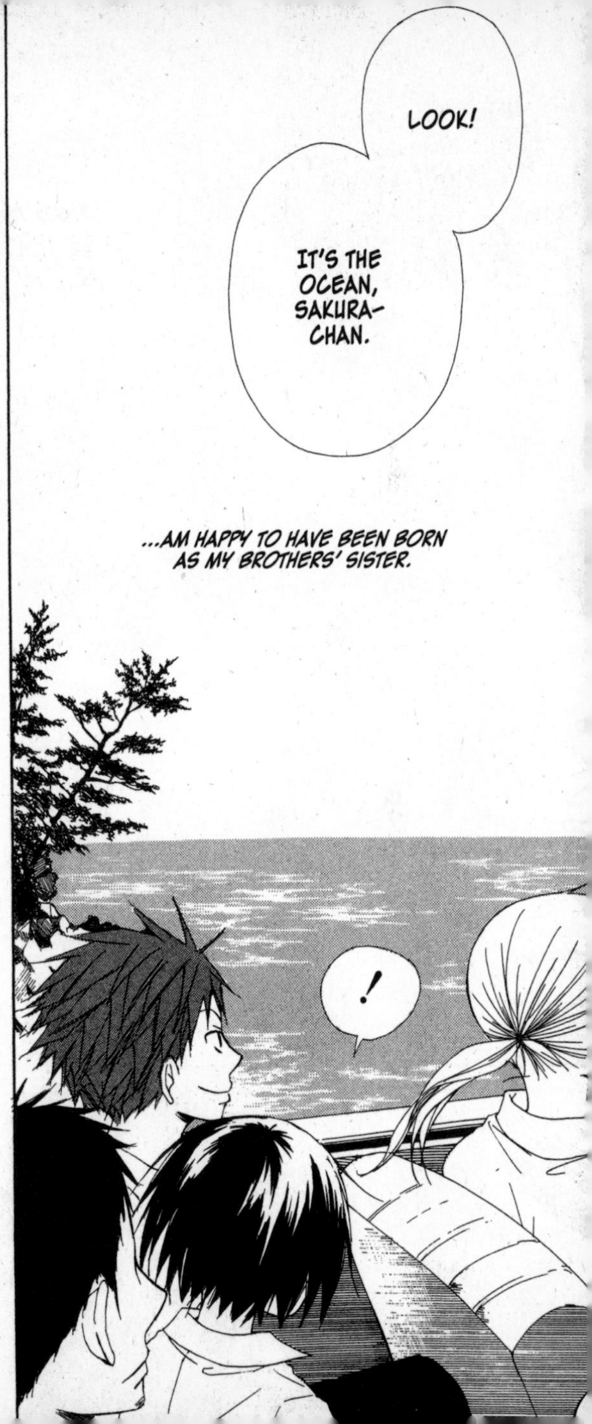
LOOK!
IT'S THE OCEAN, SAKURA-CHAN.
...AM HAPPY TO HAVE BEEN BORN AS MY BROTHERS' SISTER.
!

5

18th place:
All the middle-aged men

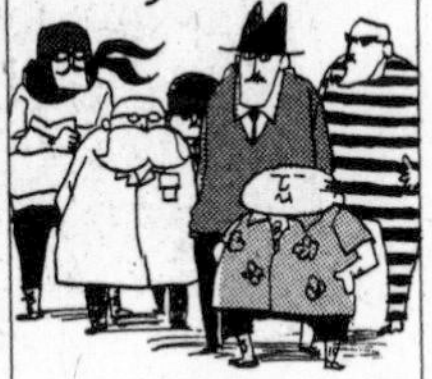

There were a few kind people who voted for the middle-aged men who show up in the columns and corners of this manga!! I'm so happy!!

Anyway, this concerns the results of the character contest, but they're all characters I came up with myself, so I was happy no matter who got what place.

At the same time, I was allowed to honor a few requests, and those are on the front page of Episode 26.

There were a lot of interesting suggestions. I hope I can draw them someday.

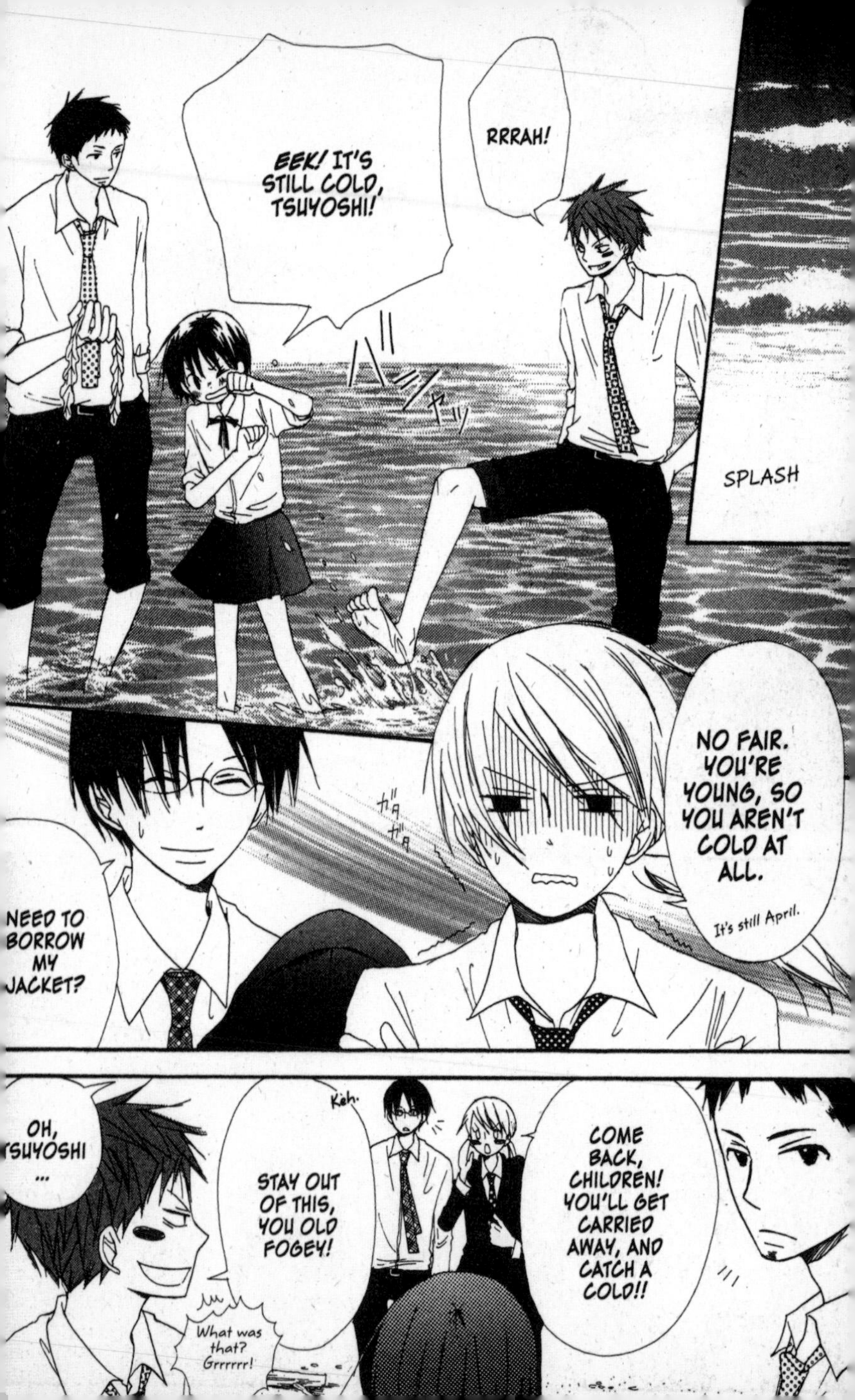
SPLASH
RRRAH!
EEK! IT'S STILL COLD, TSUYOSHI!
NO FAIR. YOU'RE YOUNG, SO YOU AREN'T COLD AT ALL.
It's still April.
NEED TO BORROW MY JACKET?
COME BACK, CHILDREN! YOU'LL GET CARRIED AWAY, AND CATCH A COLD!!
Keh.
STAY OUT OF THIS, YOU OLD FOGEY!
OH, TSUYOSHI ...
What was that? Grrrrrr!

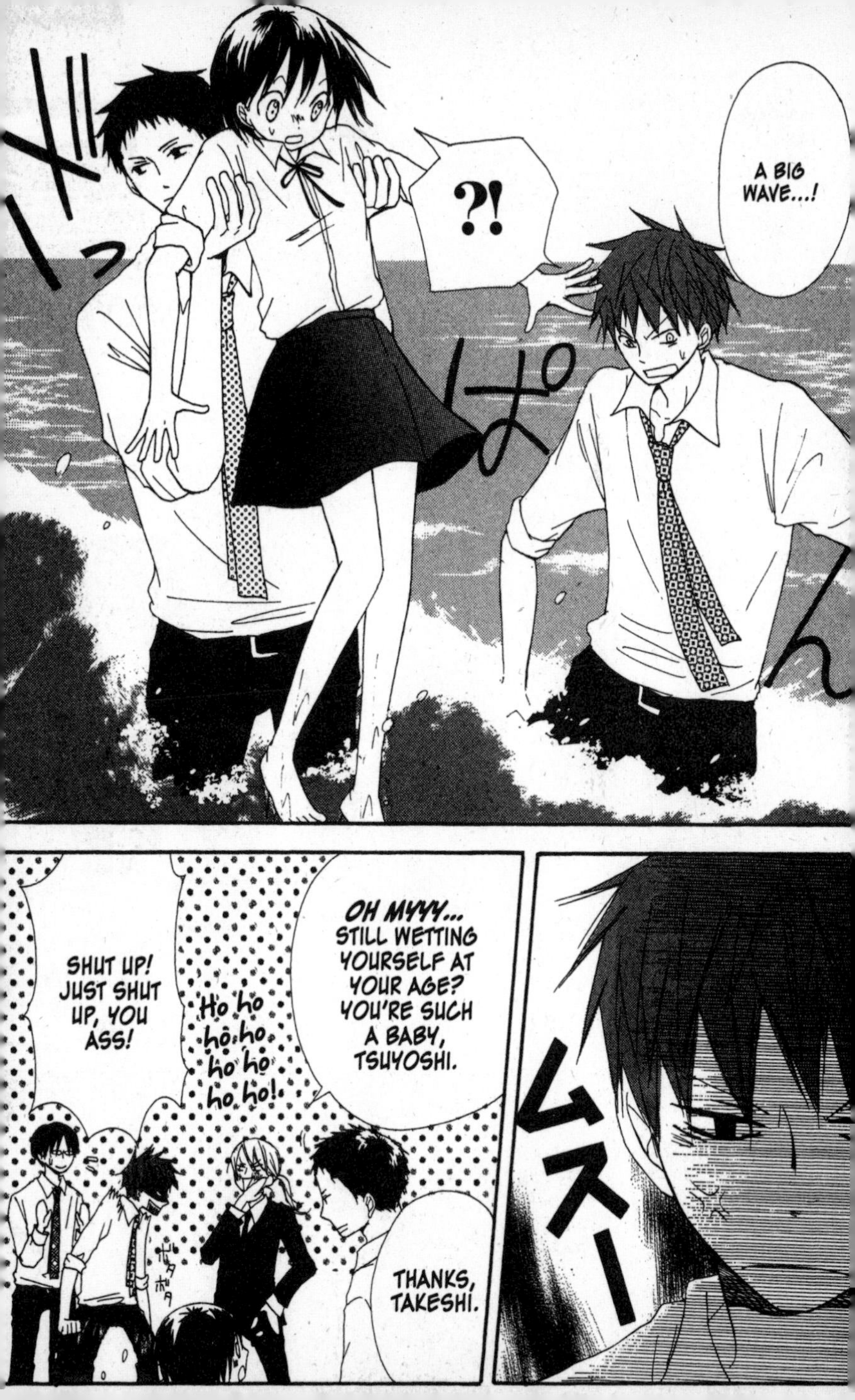
A BIG WAVE...!
?!
ムスー
OH MYYY... STILL WETTING YOURSELF AT YOUR AGE? YOU'RE SUCH A BABY, TSUYOSHI.
Ho ho ho ho ho ho ho ho!
SHUT UP! JUST SHUT UP, YOU ASS!
THANKS, TAKESHI.

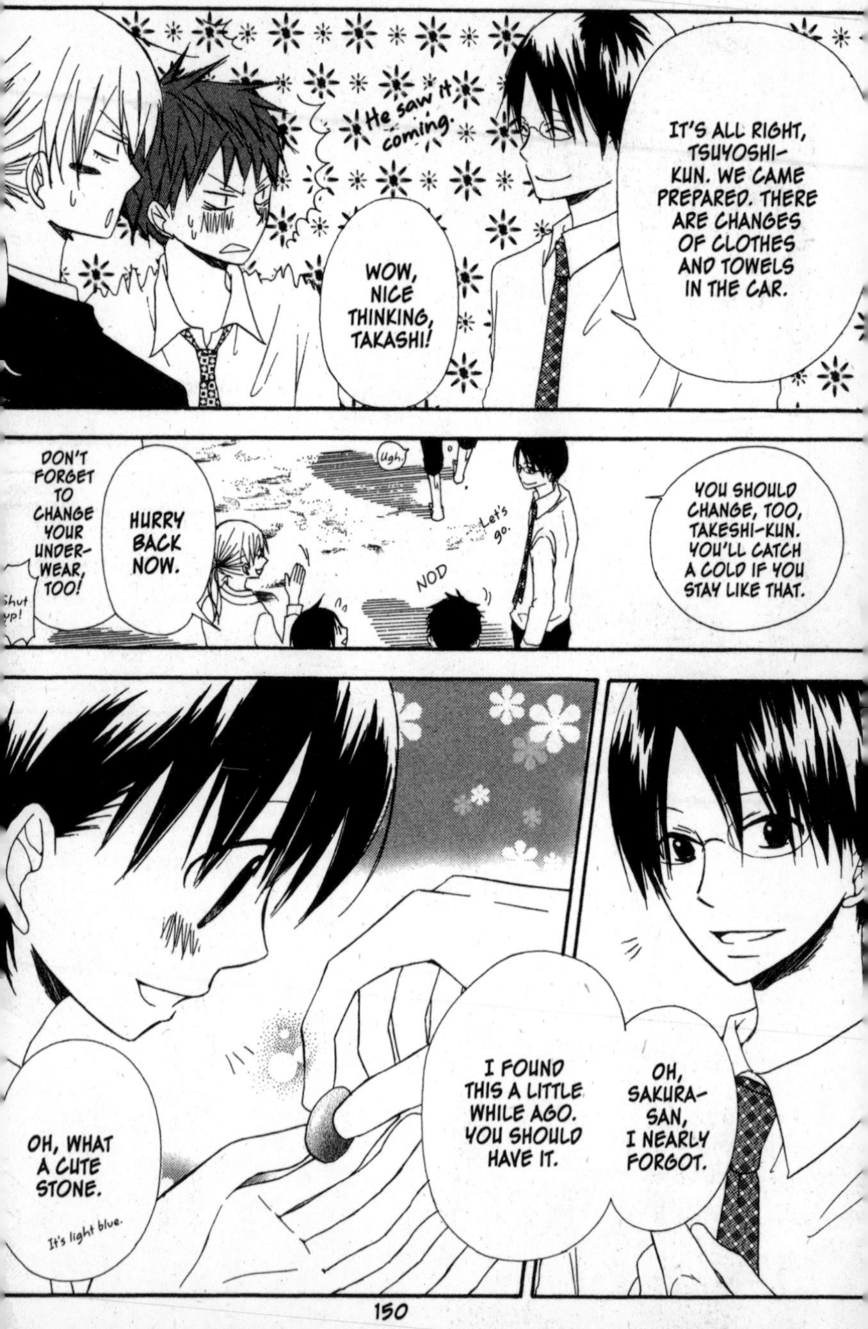
IT'S ALL RIGHT, TSUYOSHI-KUN. WE CAME PREPARED. THERE ARE CHANGES OF CLOTHES AND TOWELS IN THE CAR.
WOW, NICE THINKING, TAKASHI!
He saw it coming.
YOU SHOULD CHANGE, TOO, TAKESHI-KUN. YOU'LL CATCH A COLD IF YOU STAY LIKE THAT.
Let's go.
Ugh.
NOD
HURRY BACK NOW.
DON'T FORGET TO CHANGE YOUR UNDER-WEAR, TOO!
Shut up!
OH, SAKURA-SAN, I NEARLY FORGOT.
I FOUND THIS A LITTLE WHILE AGO. YOU SHOULD HAVE IT.
OH, WHAT A CUTE STONE.
It's light blue.

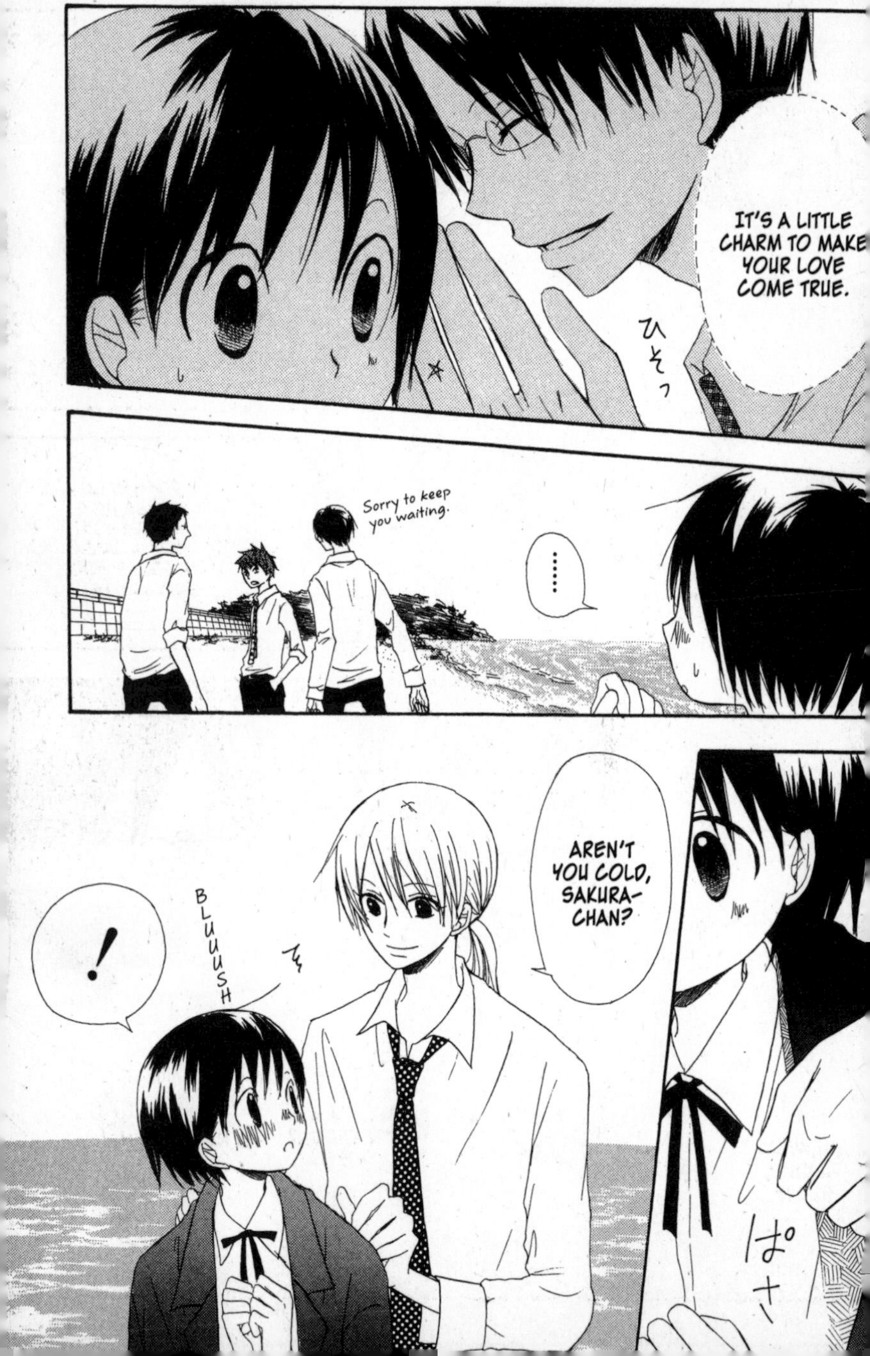
IT'S A LITTLE CHARM TO MAKE YOUR LOVE COME TRUE.
ひそっ
......
Sorry to keep you waiting.
ぱさ
AREN'T YOU COLD, SAKURA-CHAN?
BLUUUSH
!

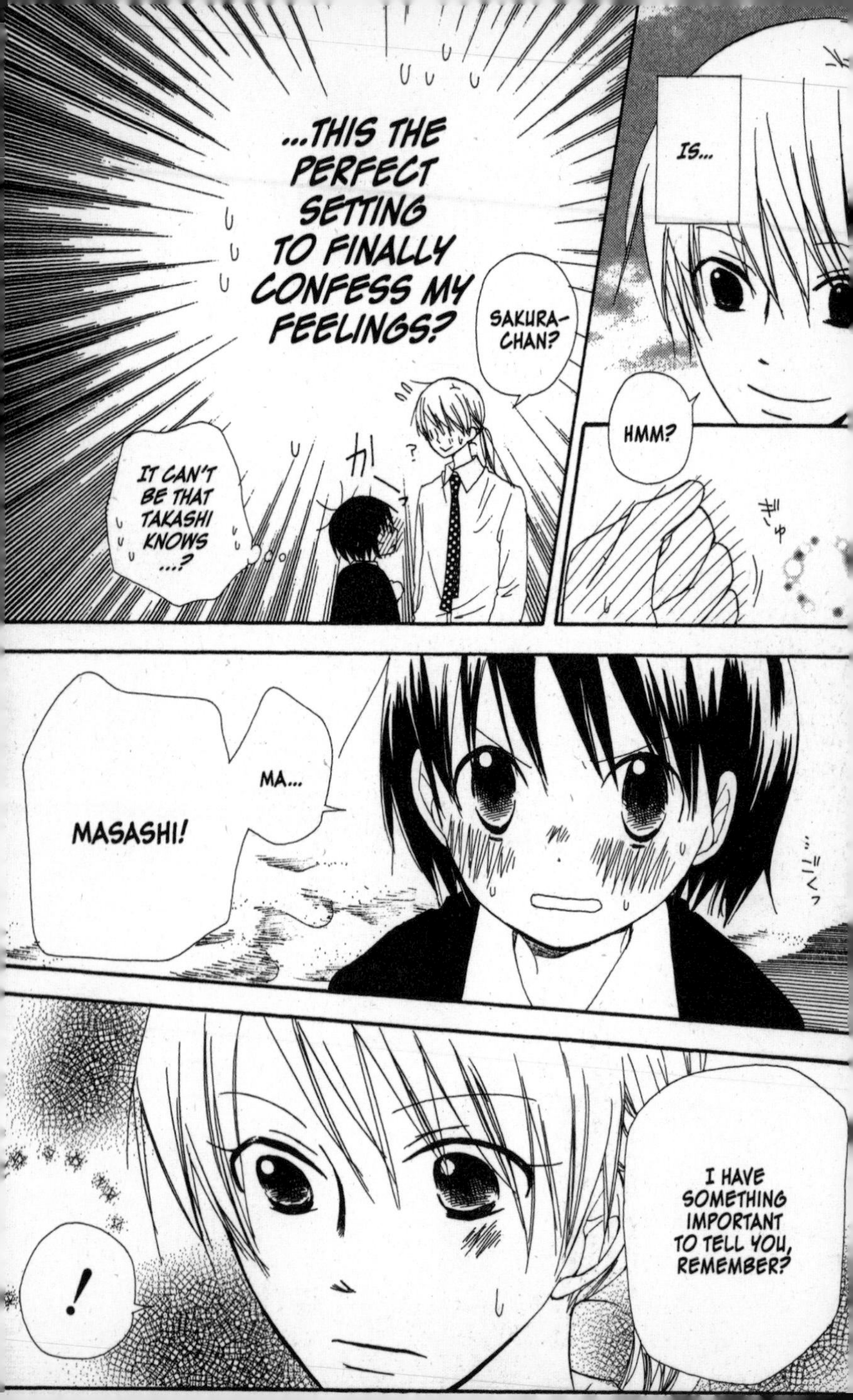
IS...
HMM?
ぎゅ
...THIS THE PERFECT SETTING TO FINALLY CONFESS MY FEELINGS?
SAKURA-CHAN?
IT CAN'T BE THAT TAKASHI KNOWS ...?
MA...
MASASHI!
I HAVE SOMETHING IMPORTANT TO TELL YOU, REMEMBER?
!

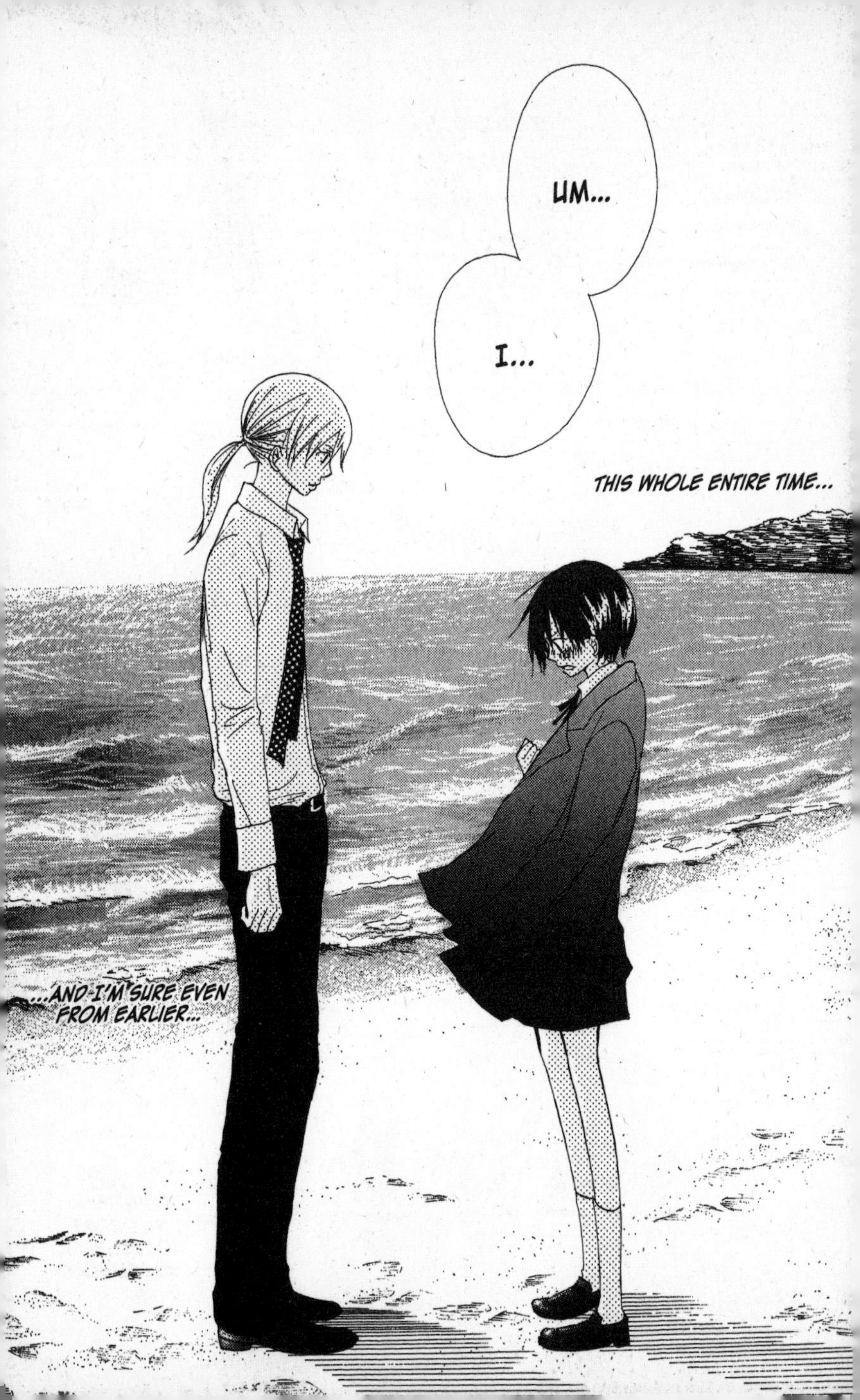
UM...
I...
THIS WHOLE ENTIRE TIME...
...AND I'M SURE EVEN FROM EARLIER...

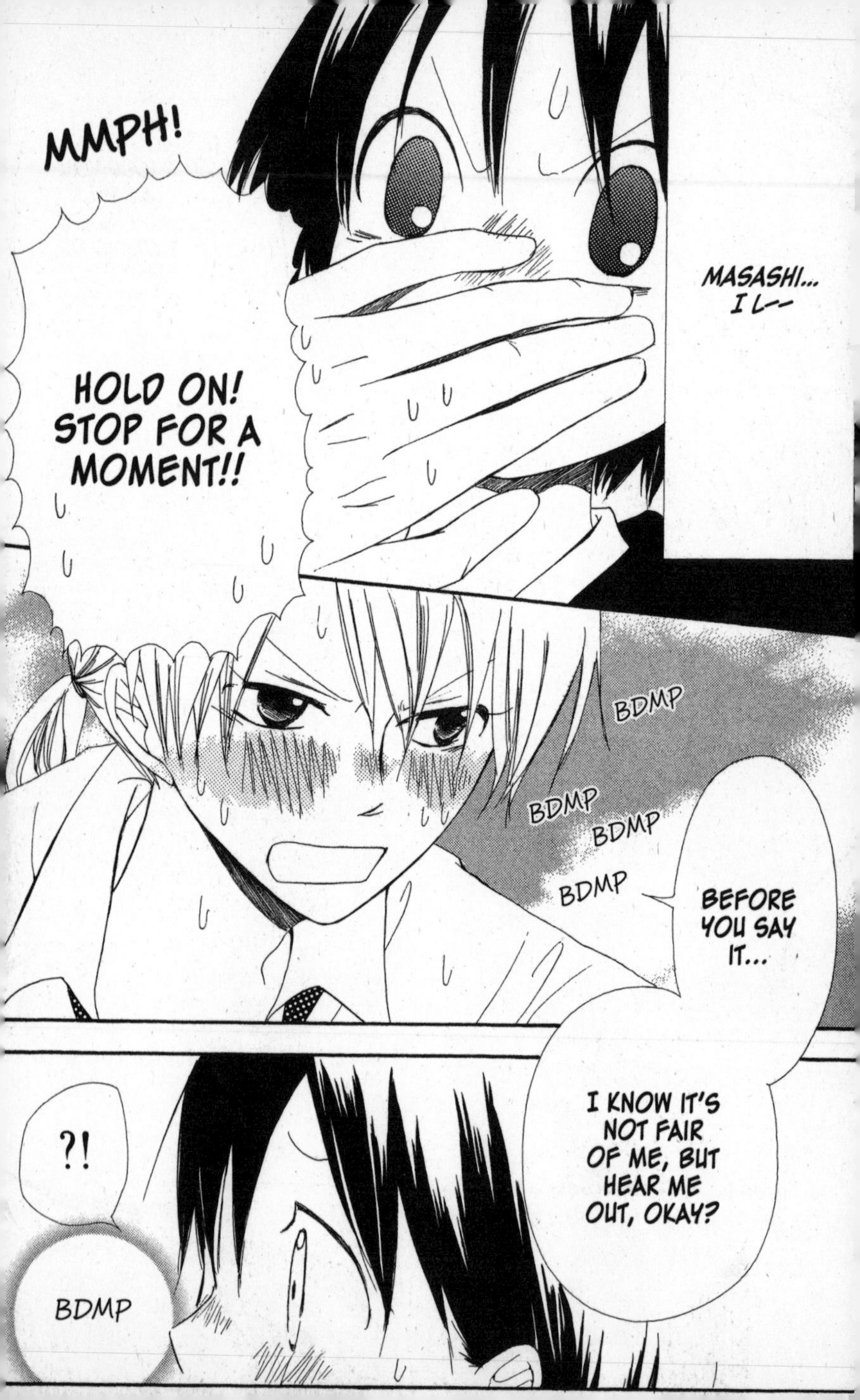
MASASHI... I L—
MMPH!
HOLD ON! STOP FOR A MOMENT!!
BDMP
BDMP
BDMP
BDMP
BEFORE YOU SAY IT...
I KNOW IT'S NOT FAIR OF ME, BUT HEAR ME OUT, OKAY?
?!
BDMP

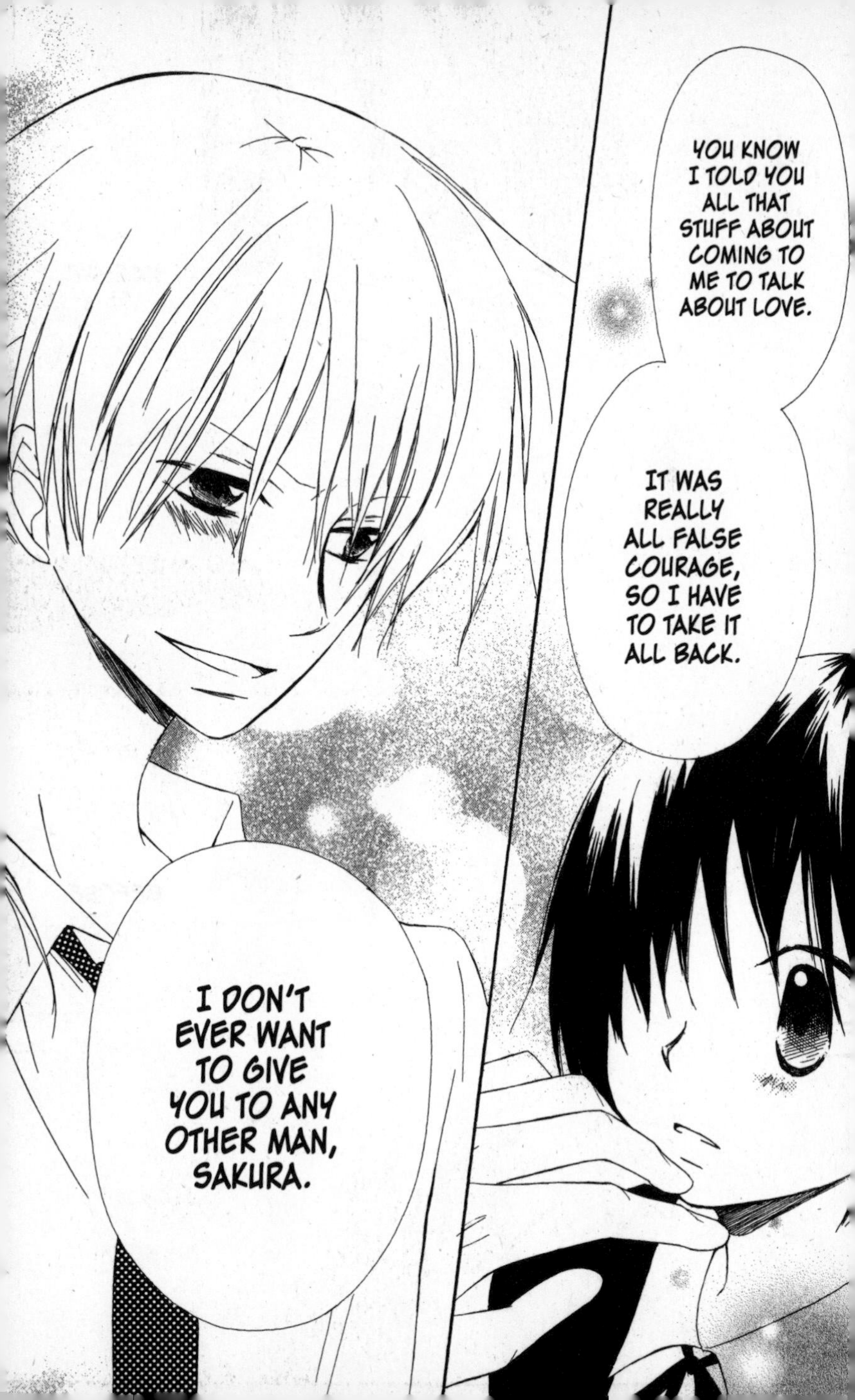
YOU KNOW I TOLD YOU ALL THAT STUFF ABOUT COMING TO ME TO TALK ABOUT LOVE.
IT WAS REALLY ALL FALSE COURAGE, SO I HAVE TO TAKE IT ALL BACK.
I DON'T EVER WANT TO GIVE YOU TO ANY OTHER MAN, SAKURA.

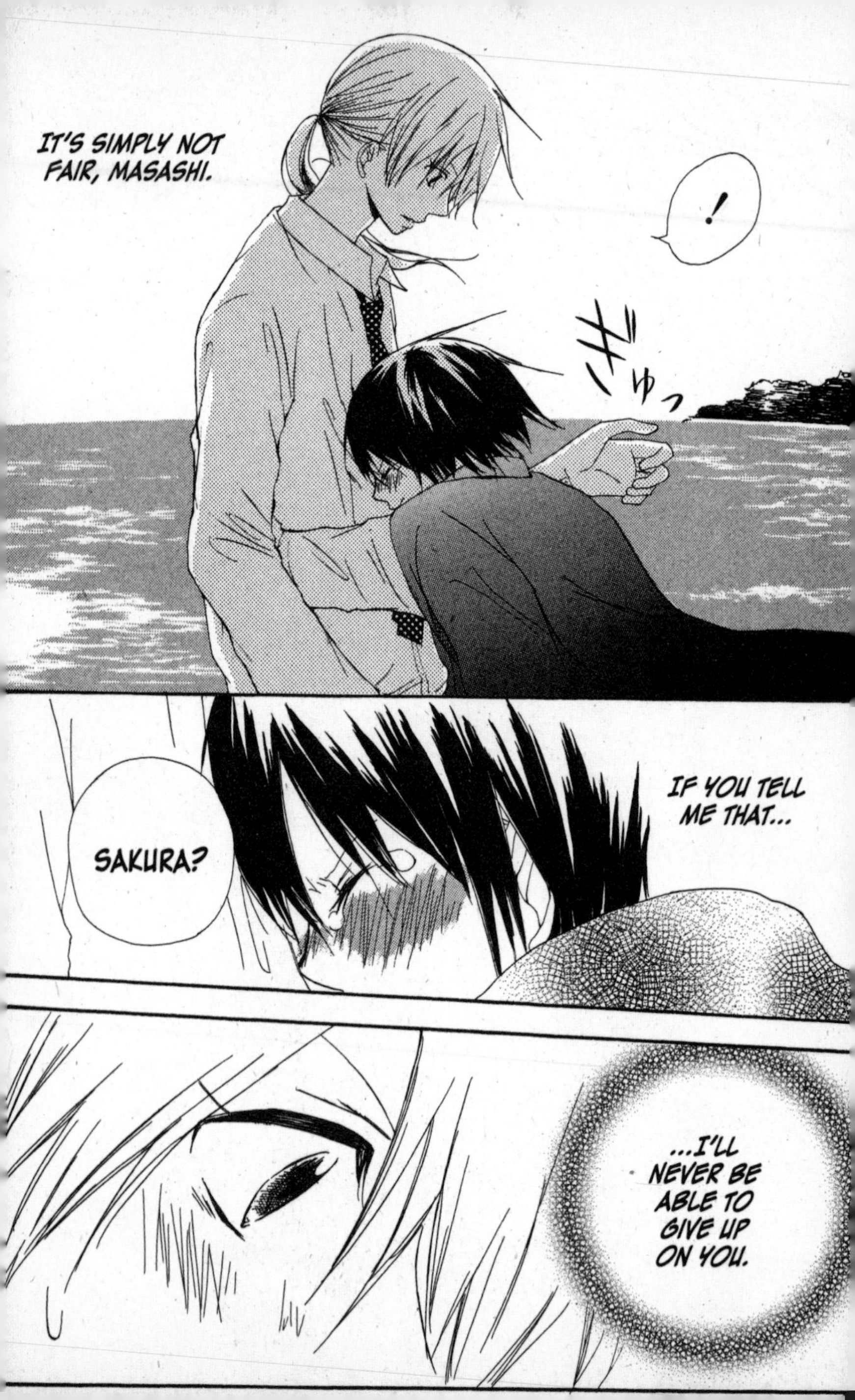
!
ぎゅっ
IT'S SIMPLY NOT FAIR, MASASHI.
IF YOU TELL ME THAT...
SAKURA?
...I'LL NEVER BE ABLE TO GIVE UP ON YOU.

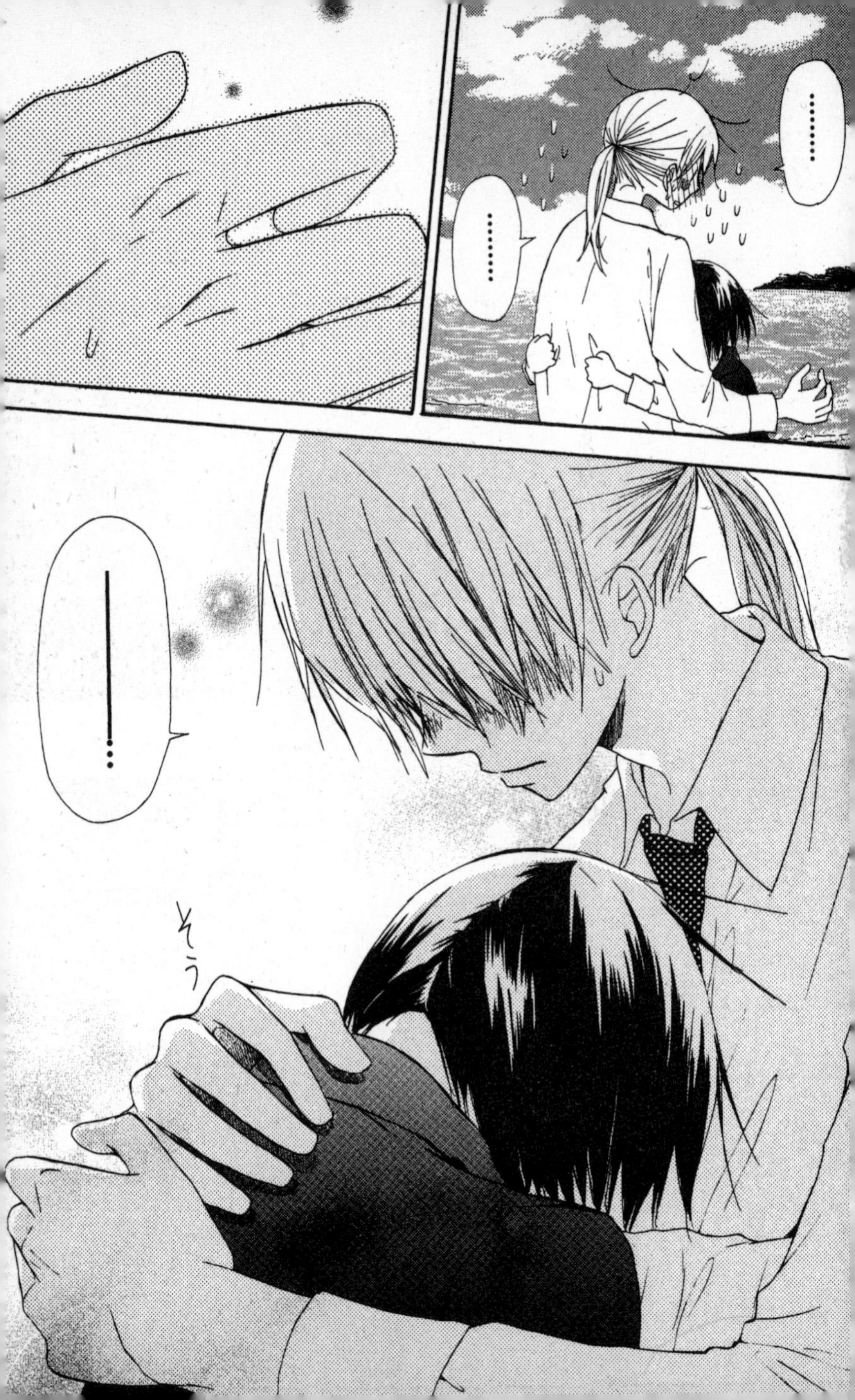
……
……
――…
そう

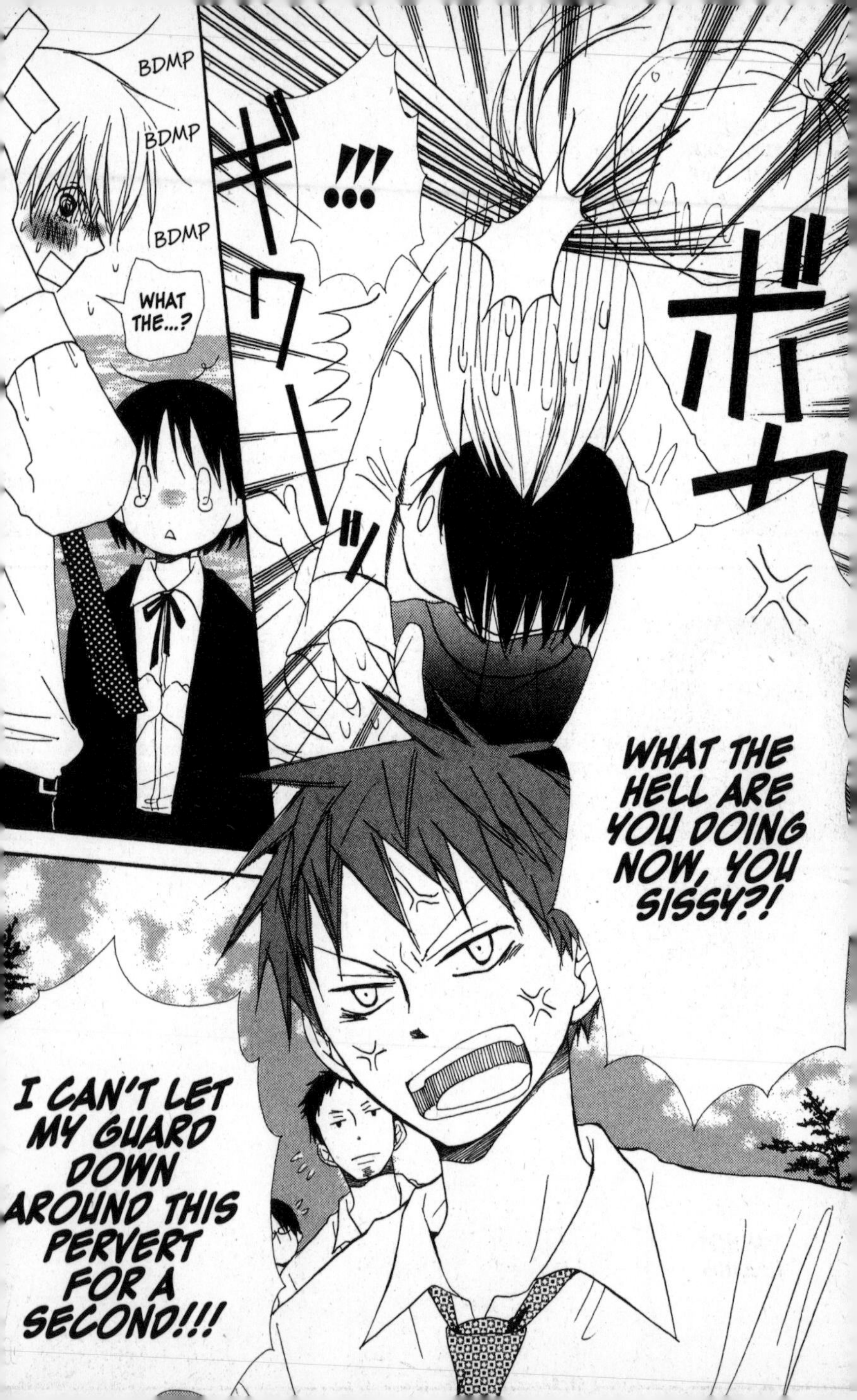
ボカ
!!!...
ギクーーッ
WHAT THE HELL ARE YOU DOING NOW, YOU SISSY?!
I CAN'T LET MY GUARD DOWN AROUND THIS PERVERT FOR A SECOND!!!
BDMP
BDMP
BDMP
WHAT THE...?

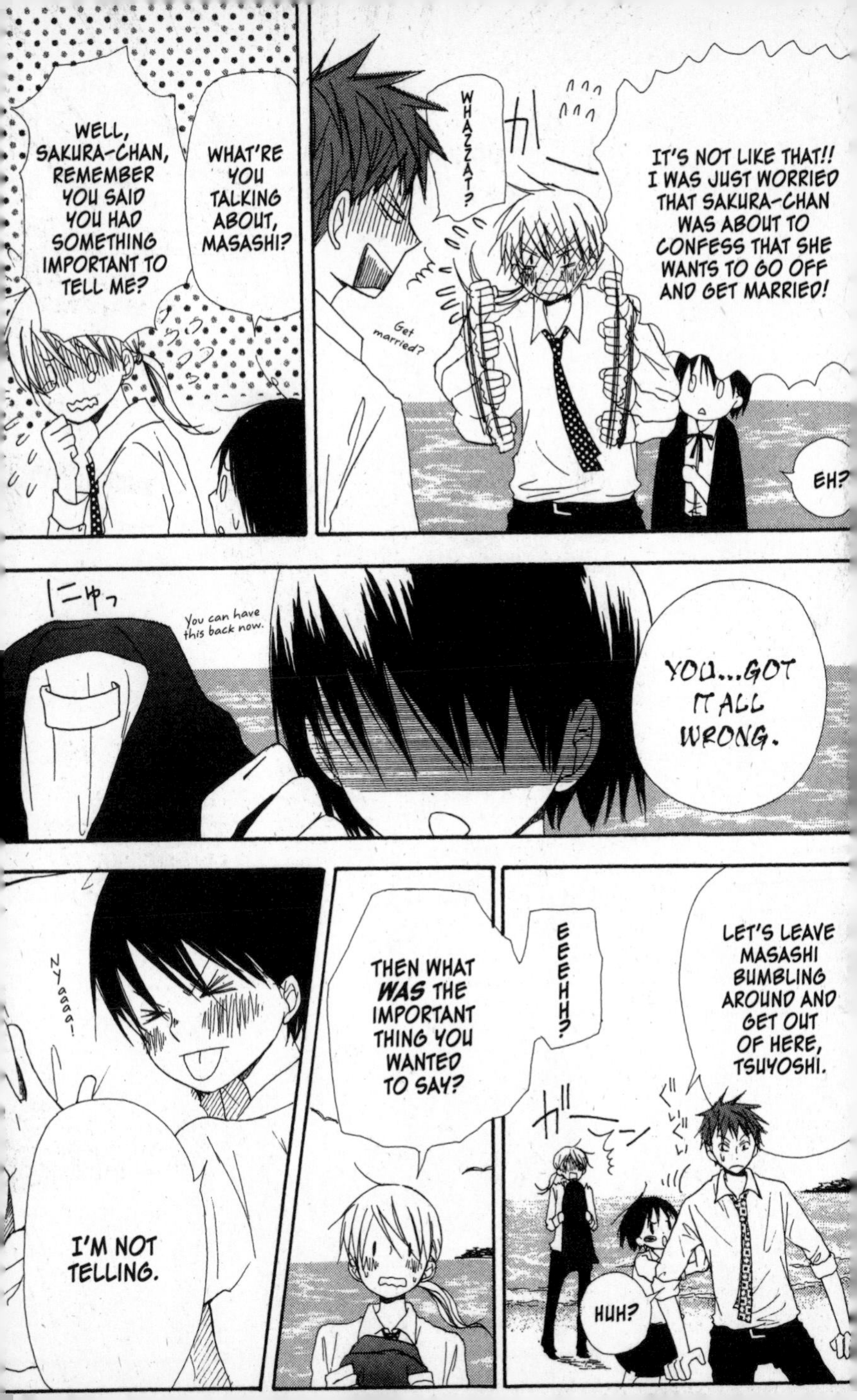
IT'S NOT LIKE THAT!! I WAS JUST WORRIED THAT SAKURA-CHAN WAS ABOUT TO CONFESS THAT SHE WANTS TO GO OFF AND GET MARRIED!
EH?
WHAZZAT?
Get married?
WHAT'RE YOU TALKING ABOUT, MASASHI?
WELL, SAKURA-CHAN, REMEMBER YOU SAID YOU HAD SOMETHING IMPORTANT TO TELL ME?
YOU...GOT IT ALL WRONG.
You can have this back now.
LET'S LEAVE MASASHI BUMBLING AROUND AND GET OUT OF HERE, TSUYOSHI.
HUH?
EEEEHH?
THEN WHAT WAS THE IMPORTANT THING YOU WANTED TO SAY?
NYaaaa!
I'M NOT TELLING.

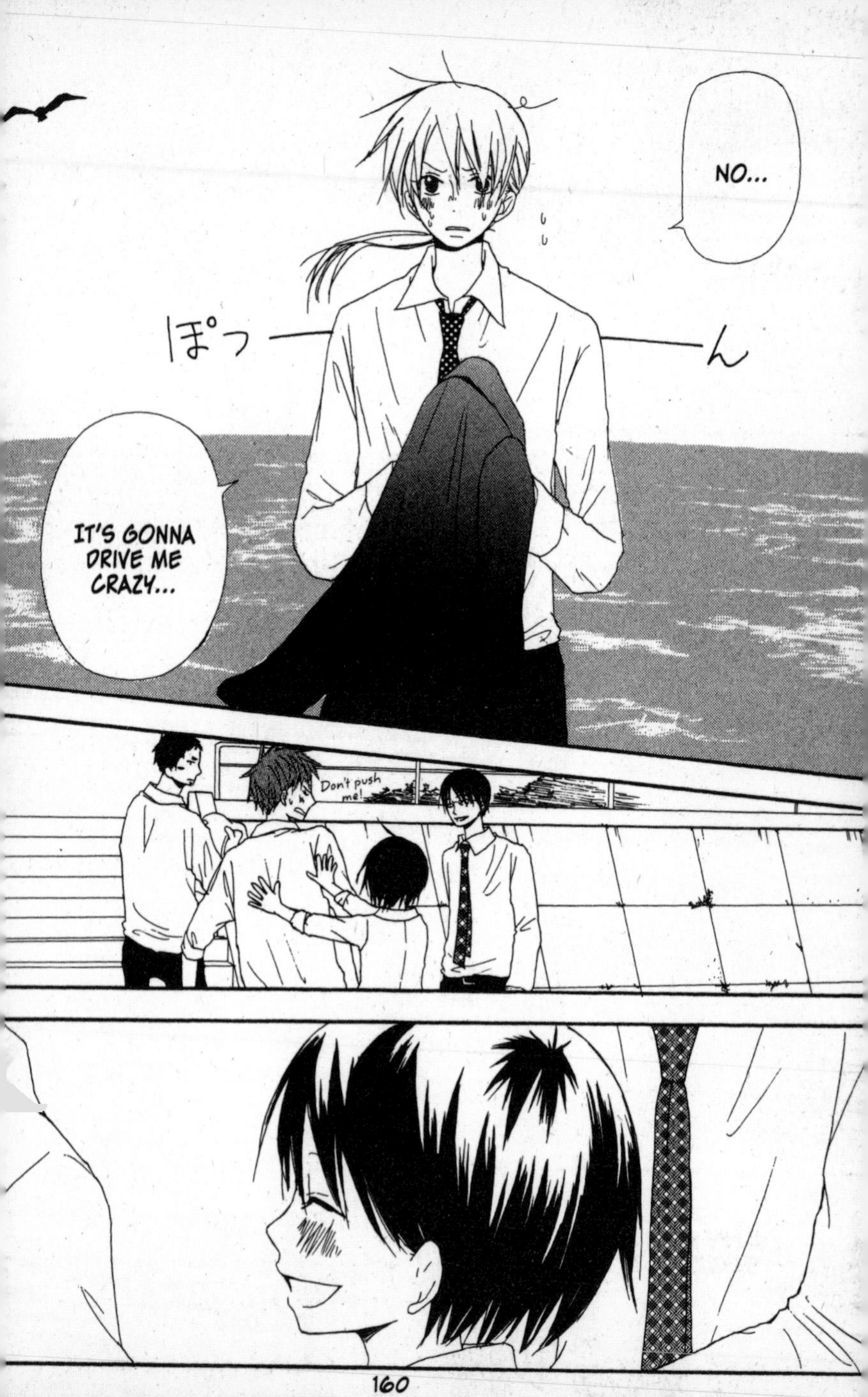
NO...
ぽっーーん
IT'S GONNA DRIVE ME CRAZY...
Don't push me!

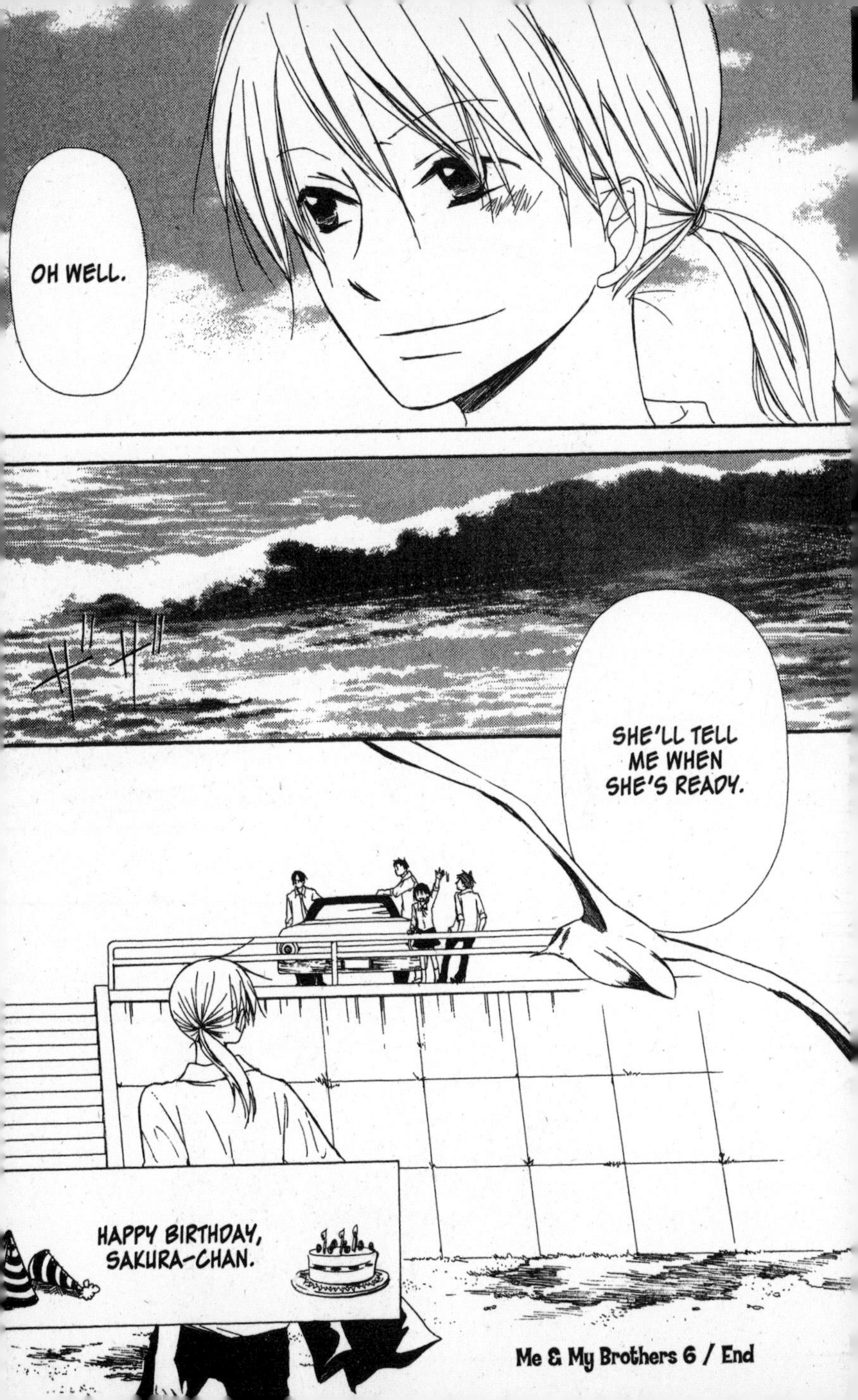
OH WELL.
SHE'LL TELL ME WHEN SHE'S READY.
HAPPY BIRTHDAY, SAKURA-CHAN.
Me & My Brothers 6 / End

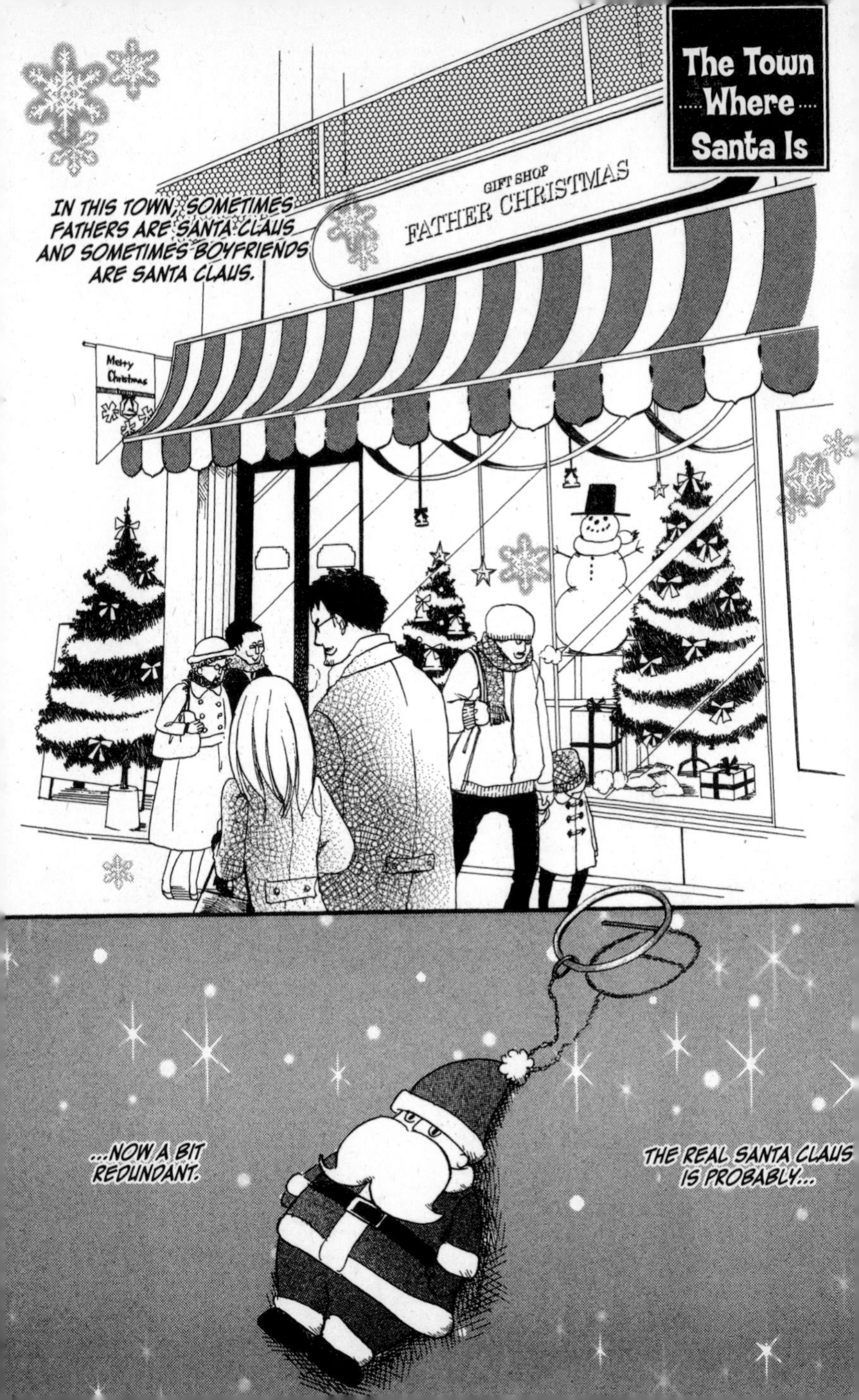
The Town Where Santa Is
GIFT SHOP
FATHER CHRISTMAS
IN THIS TOWN, SOMETIMES FATHERS ARE SANTA CLAUS AND SOMETIMES BOYFRIENDS ARE SANTA CLAUS.
Merry Christmas
THE REAL SANTA CLAUS IS PROBABLY...
...NOW A BIT REDUNDANT.

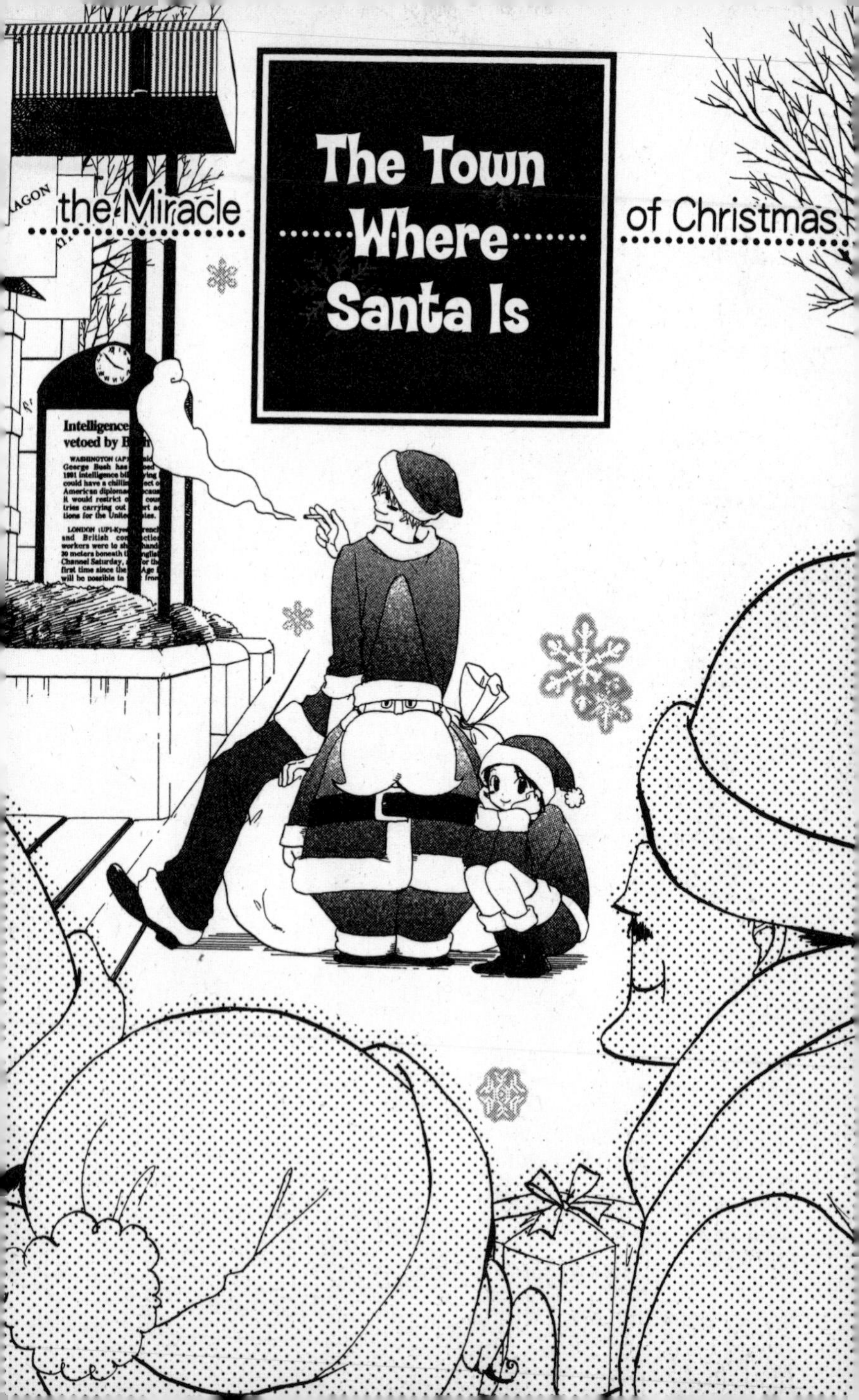
the Miracle
The Town Where Santa Is
of Christmas

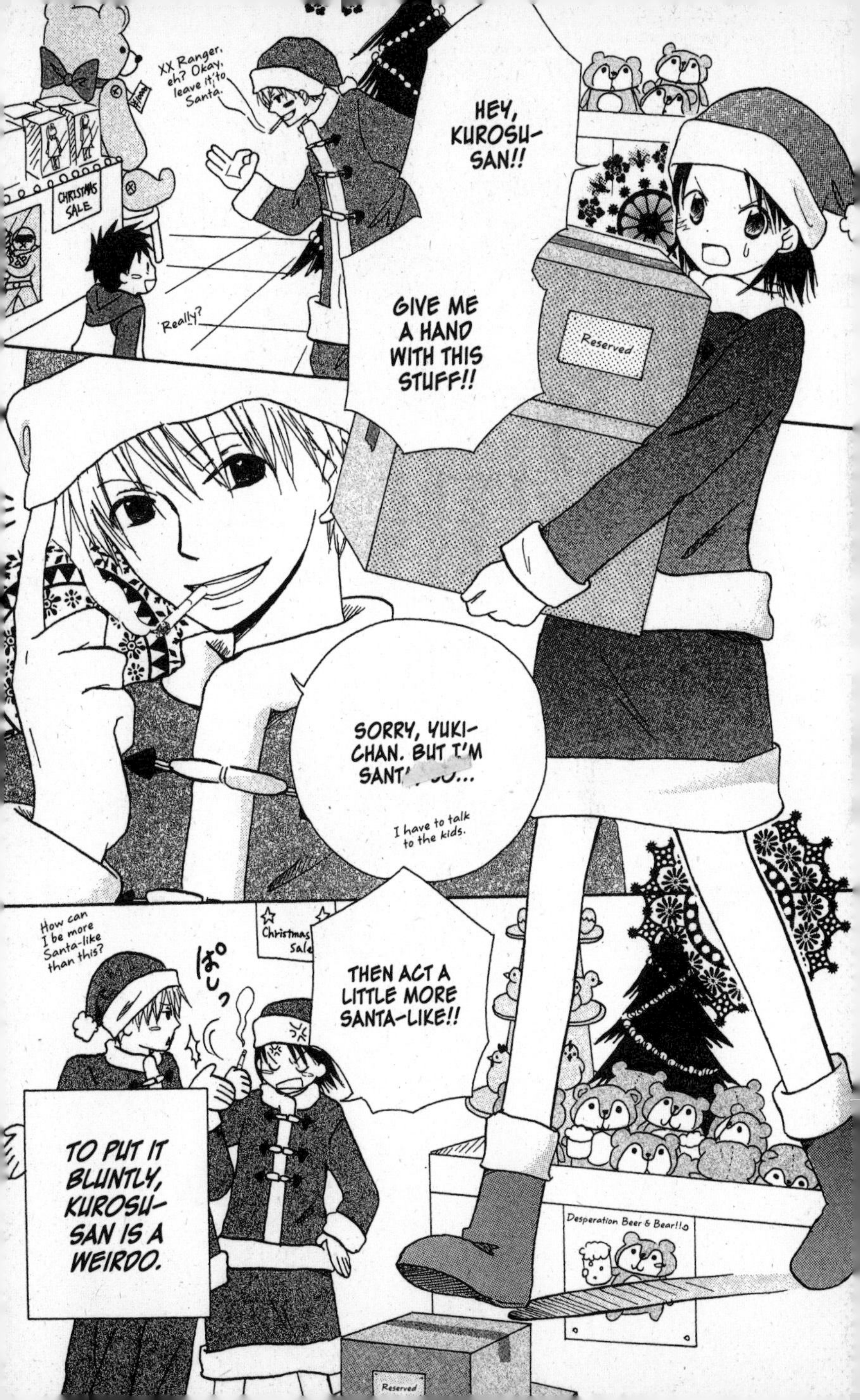
HEY, KUROSU-SAN!!
GIVE ME A HAND WITH THIS STUFF!!
Reserved
XX Ranger, eh? Okay, leave it to Santa.
CHRISTMAS SALE
Really?
SORRY, YUKI-CHAN. BUT I'M SANTA, SO...
I have to talk to the kids.
THEN ACT A LITTLE MORE SANTA-LIKE!!
Christmas Sale
How can I be more Santa-like than this?
ぱしっ
TO PUT IT BLUNTLY, KUROSU-SAN IS A WEIRDO.
Desperation Beer & Bear!!
Reserved

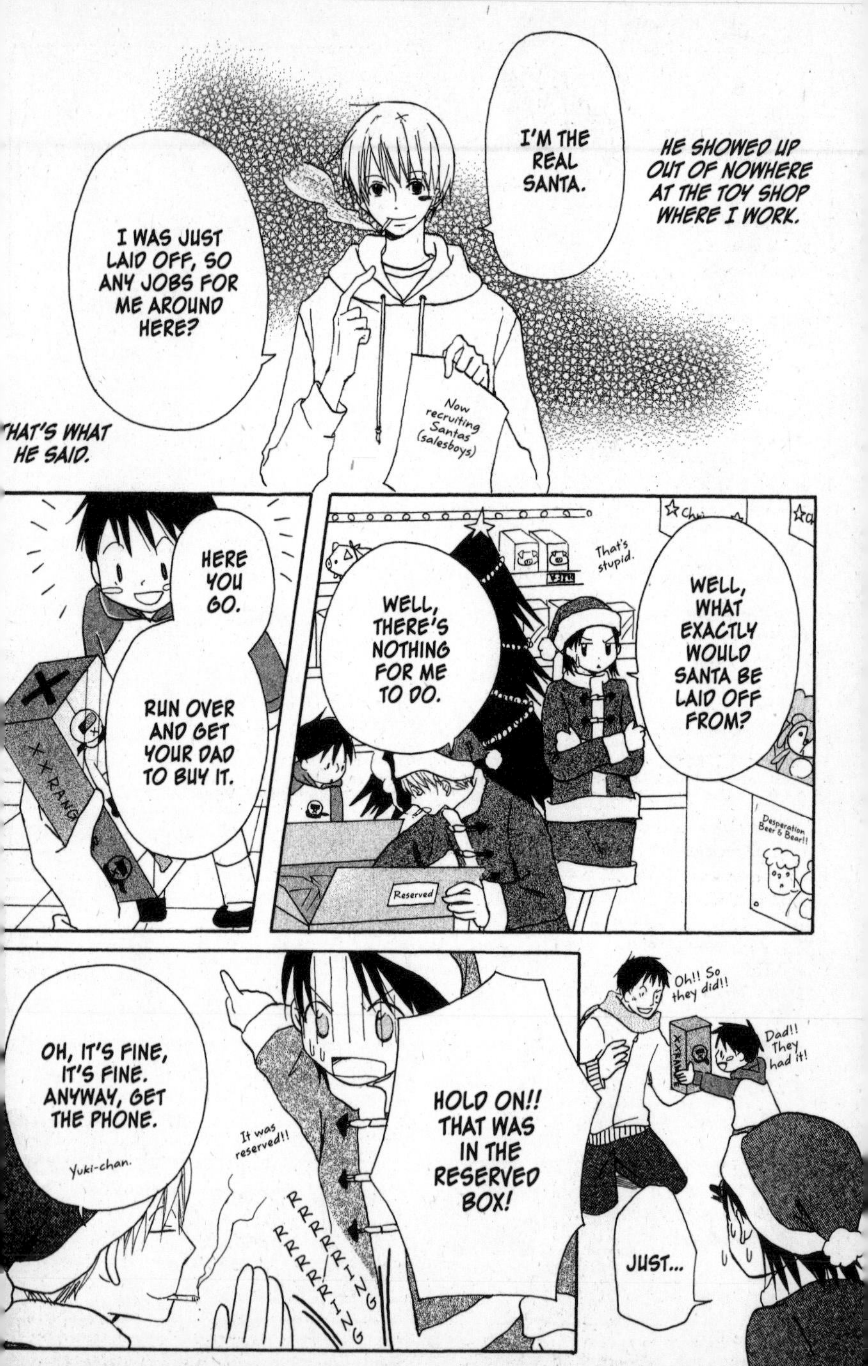
HE SHOWED UP OUT OF NOWHERE AT THE TOY SHOP WHERE I WORK.
I'M THE REAL SANTA.
I WAS JUST LAID OFF, SO ANY JOBS FOR ME AROUND HERE?
Now recruiting Santas (salesboys)
THAT'S WHAT HE SAID.
WELL, WHAT EXACTLY WOULD SANTA BE LAID OFF FROM?
That's stupid.
WELL, THERE'S NOTHING FOR ME TO DO.
Desperation Beer & Bear!!
Reserved
HERE YOU GO.
RUN OVER AND GET YOUR DAD TO BUY IT.
Dad!! They had it!
Oh!! So they did!!
JUST...
HOLD ON!! THAT WAS IN THE RESERVED BOX!
It was reserved!!
RRRRRING RRRRRING
OH, IT'S FINE, IT'S FINE. ANYWAY, GET THE PHONE.
Yuki-chan.

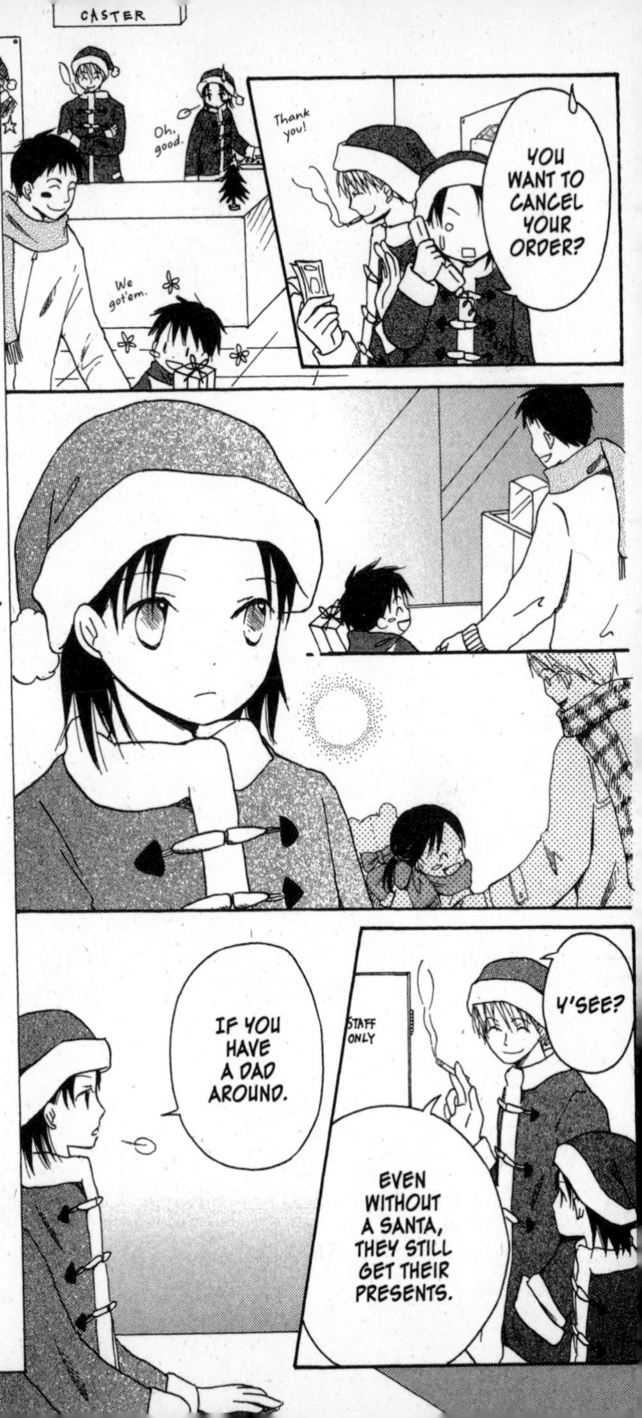

YOU WANT TO CANCEL YOUR ORDER?
Thank you!
CASTER
Oh, good.
We got'em.
STAFF ONLY
Y'SEE?
EVEN WITHOUT A SANTA, THEY STILL GET THEIR PRESENTS.
IF YOU HAVE A DAD AROUND.

6

"The Town Where Santa Is"

This short story was my debut work.

It's so old that I'm really embarrassed. So I impulsively made a lot of revisions and struggled like crazy, but all in vain.

But my editor taught me that with things like this, you enjoy seeing the differences between then and now.

That's quite right, so I changed my perspective, and the next opportunity I have to publish an old work, I think I'll have courage and leave it the way it is. Even though it's embarrassing...

Well then, really, thank you very much for picking up volume six!!

Hari Tokeino

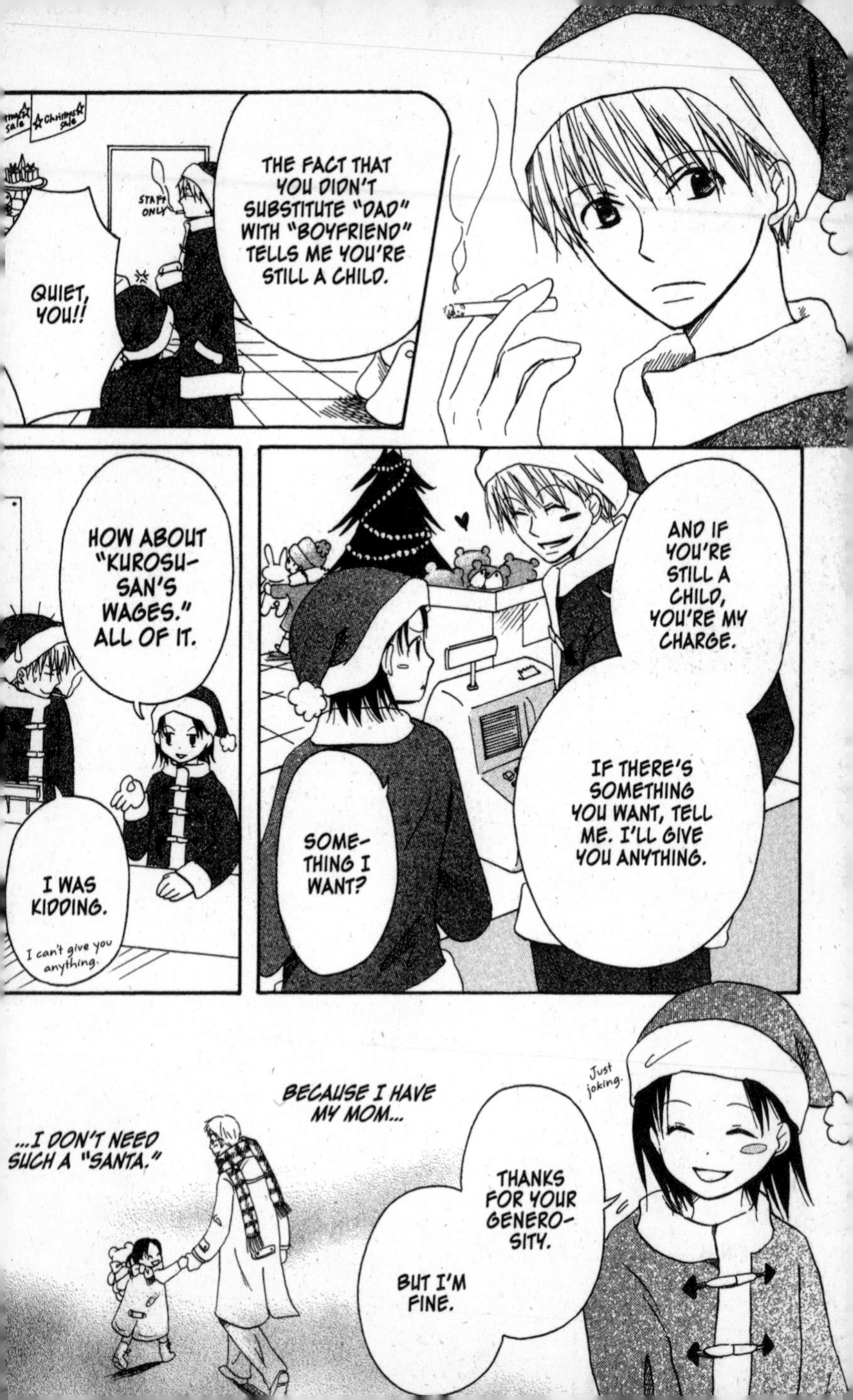
☆Christmas☆ sale
THE FACT THAT YOU DIDN'T SUBSTITUTE "DAD" WITH "BOYFRIEND" TELLS ME YOU'RE STILL A CHILD.
STAFF ONLY
QUIET, YOU!!
AND IF YOU'RE STILL A CHILD, YOU'RE MY CHARGE.
IF THERE'S SOMETHING YOU WANT, TELL ME. I'LL GIVE YOU ANYTHING.
SOMETHING I WANT?
HOW ABOUT "KUROSU-SAN'S WAGES." ALL OF IT.
I WAS KIDDING.
I can't give you anything.
Just joking.
THANKS FOR YOUR GENEROSITY.
BUT I'M FINE.
BECAUSE I HAVE MY MOM...
...I DON'T NEED SUCH A "SANTA."

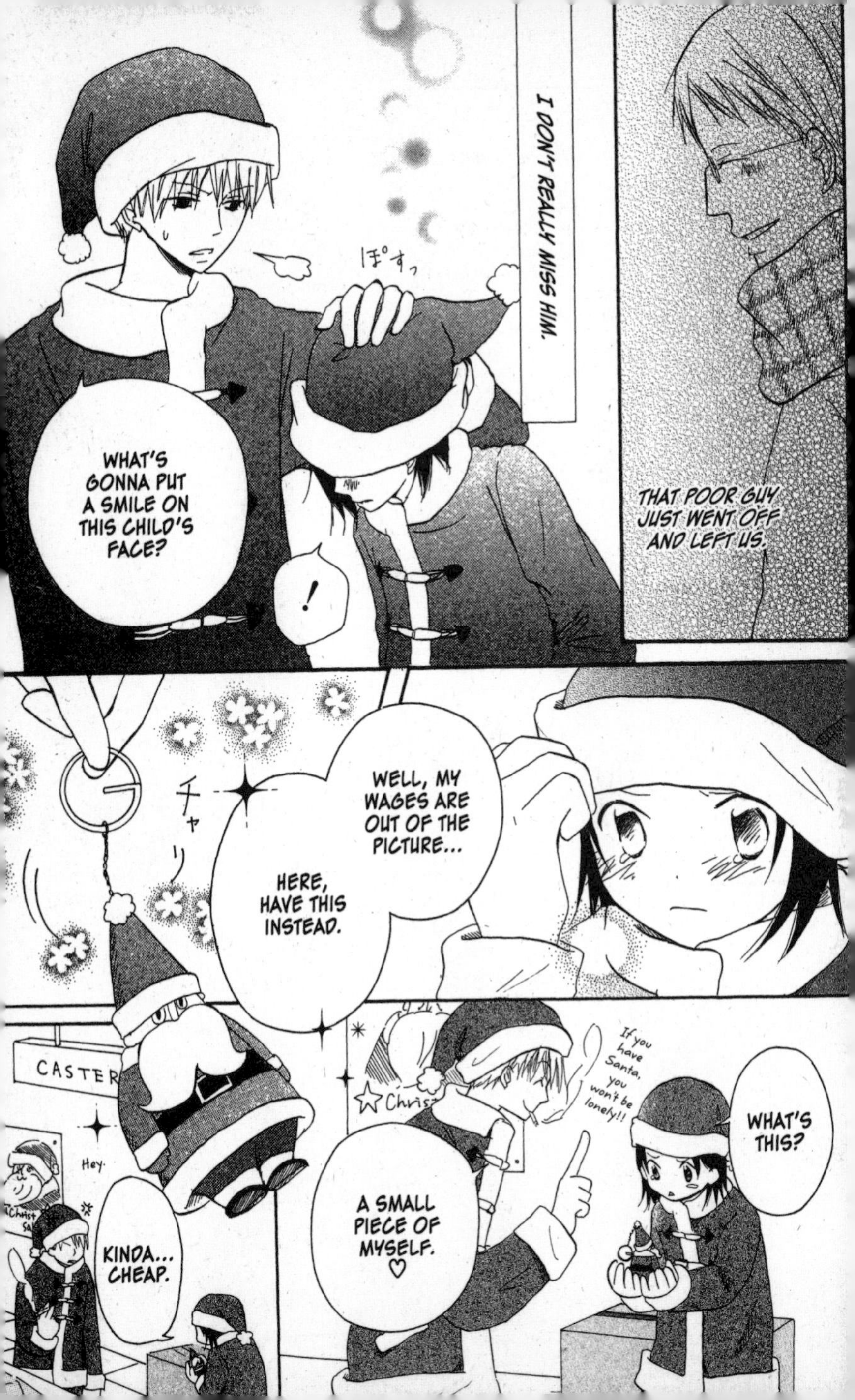
THAT POOR GUY JUST WENT OFF AND LEFT US.
I DON'T REALLY MISS HIM.
ぽすっ
WHAT'S GONNA PUT A SMILE ON THIS CHILD'S FACE?
!
WELL, MY WAGES ARE OUT OF THE PICTURE...
HERE, HAVE THIS INSTEAD.
チャリ
WHAT'S THIS?
If you have Santa, you won't be lonely!!
☆Christ
A SMALL PIECE OF MYSELF. ♡
CASTER
Hey.
KINDA... CHEAP.

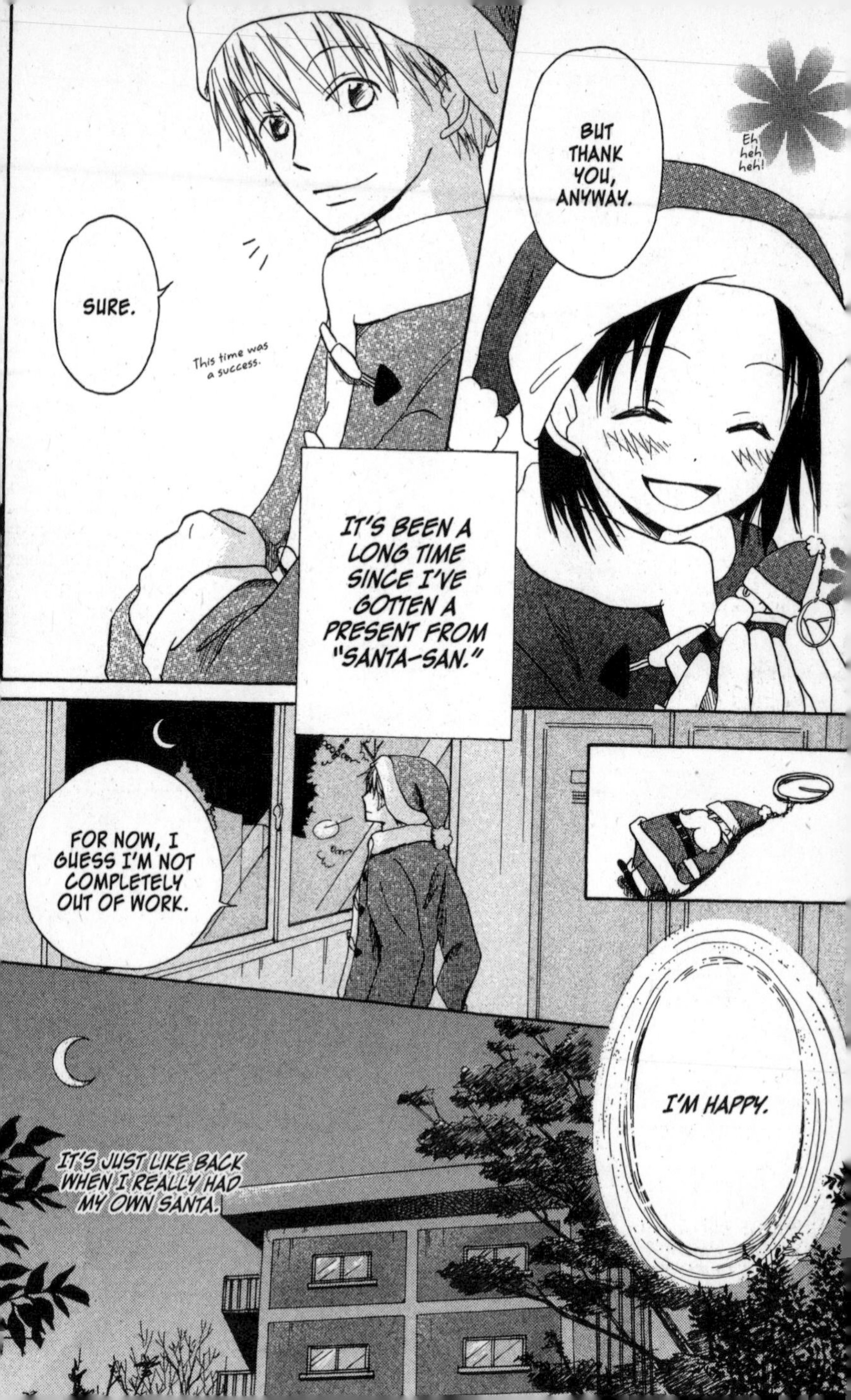
BUT THANK YOU, ANYWAY.
Eh heh heh!
SURE.
This time was a success.
IT'S BEEN A LONG TIME SINCE I'VE GOTTEN A PRESENT FROM "SANTA-SAN."
FOR NOW, I GUESS I'M NOT COMPLETELY OUT OF WORK.
I'M HAPPY.
IT'S JUST LIKE BACK WHEN I REALLY HAD MY OWN SANTA.

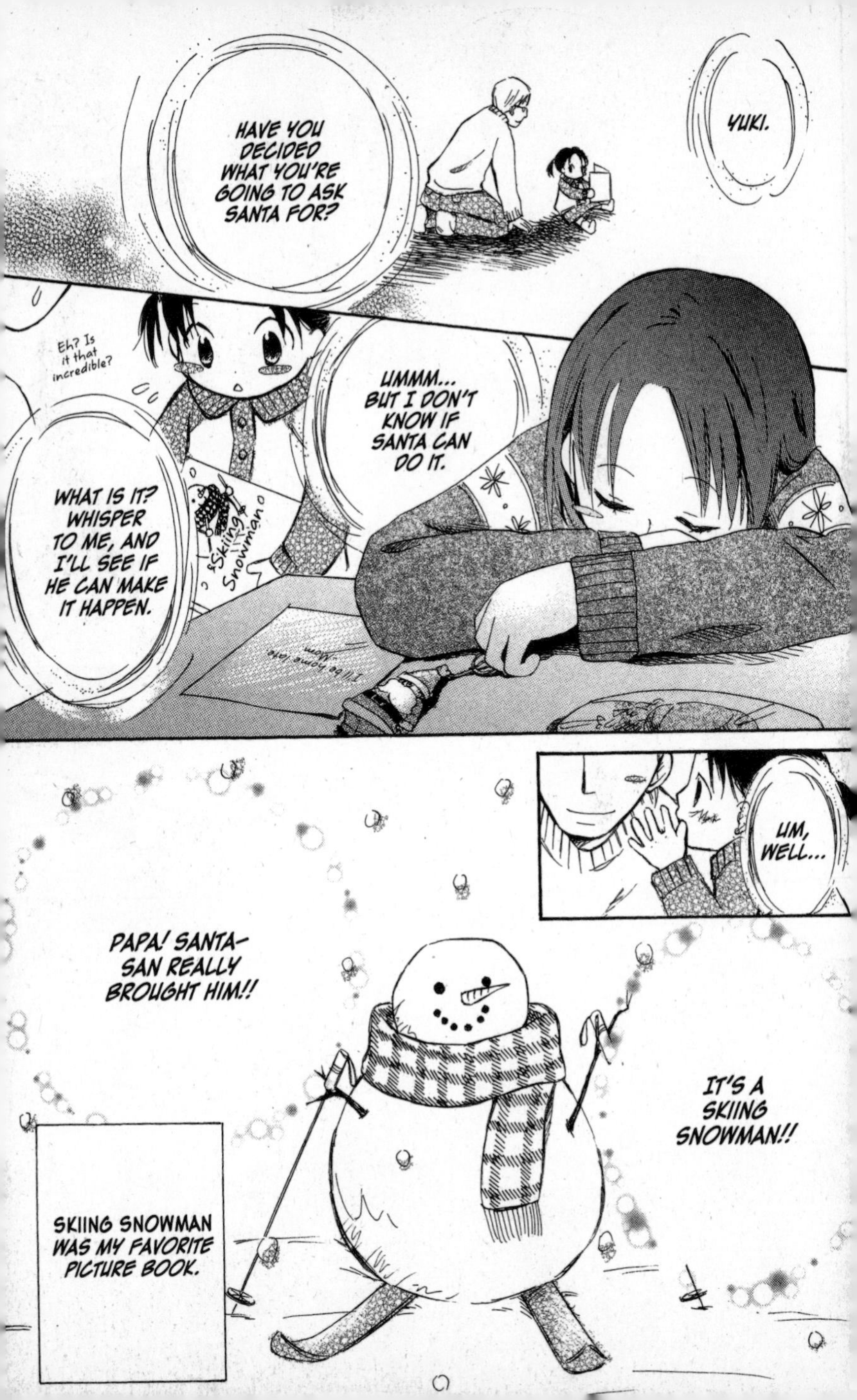
YUKI.
HAVE YOU DECIDED WHAT YOU'RE GOING TO ASK SANTA FOR?
UMMM... BUT I DON'T KNOW IF SANTA CAN DO IT.
Eh? Is it that incredible?
WHAT IS IT? WHISPER TO ME, AND I'LL SEE IF HE CAN MAKE IT HAPPEN.
Skiing Snowman
I'll be home late. Mom
UM, WELL...
PAPA! SANTA-SAN REALLY BROUGHT HIM!!
IT'S A SKIING SNOWMAN!!
SKIING SNOWMAN WAS MY FAVORITE PICTURE BOOK.

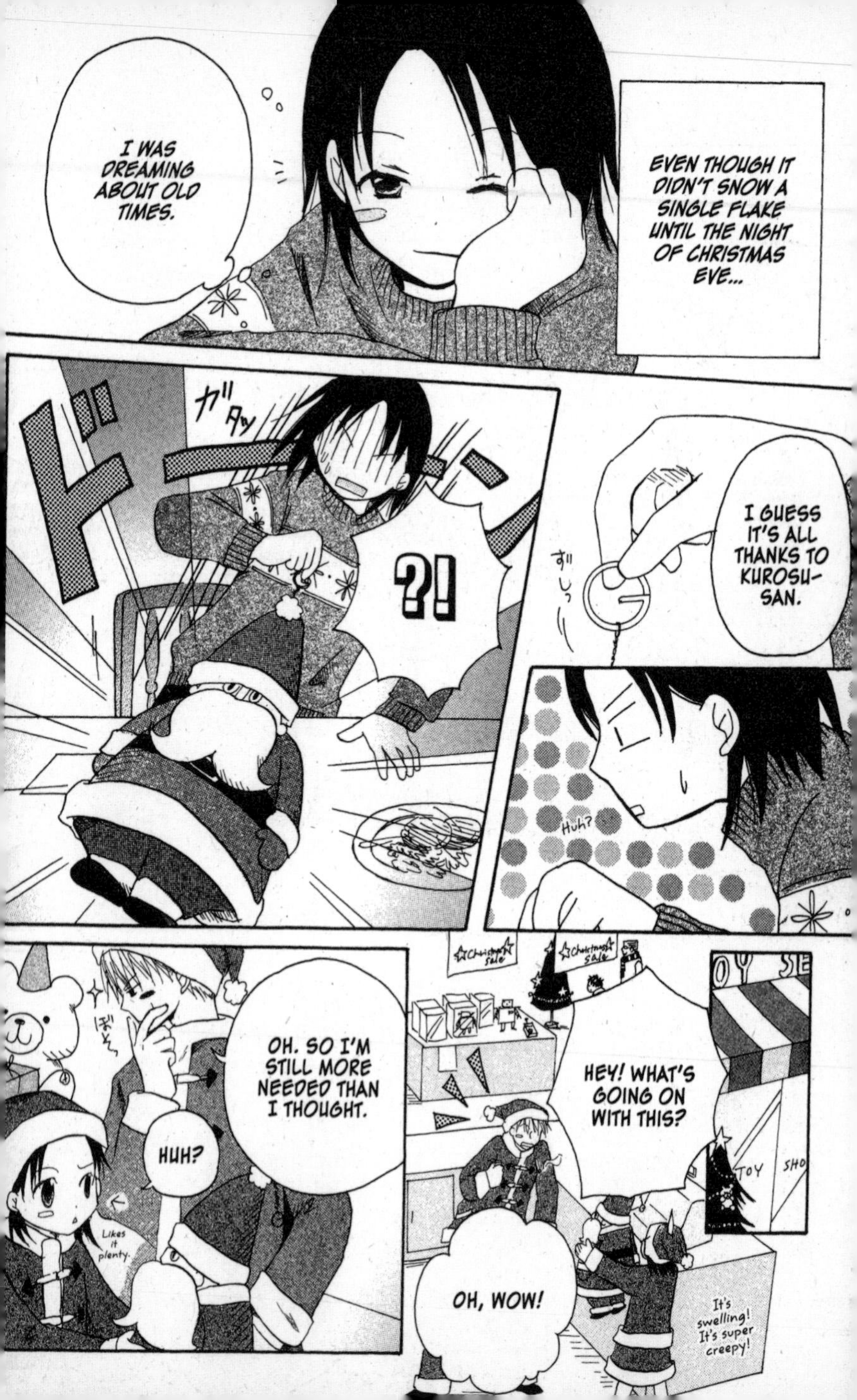
EVEN THOUGH IT DIDN'T SNOW A SINGLE FLAKE UNTIL THE NIGHT OF CHRISTMAS EVE...
I WAS DREAMING ABOUT OLD TIMES.
I GUESS IT'S ALL THANKS TO KUROSU-SAN.
Huh?
ガタッ
ドー
?!
HEY! WHAT'S GOING ON WITH THIS?
It's swelling! It's super creepy!
OH, WOW!
OH. SO I'M STILL MORE NEEDED THAN I THOUGHT.
HUH?
Likes it plenty.

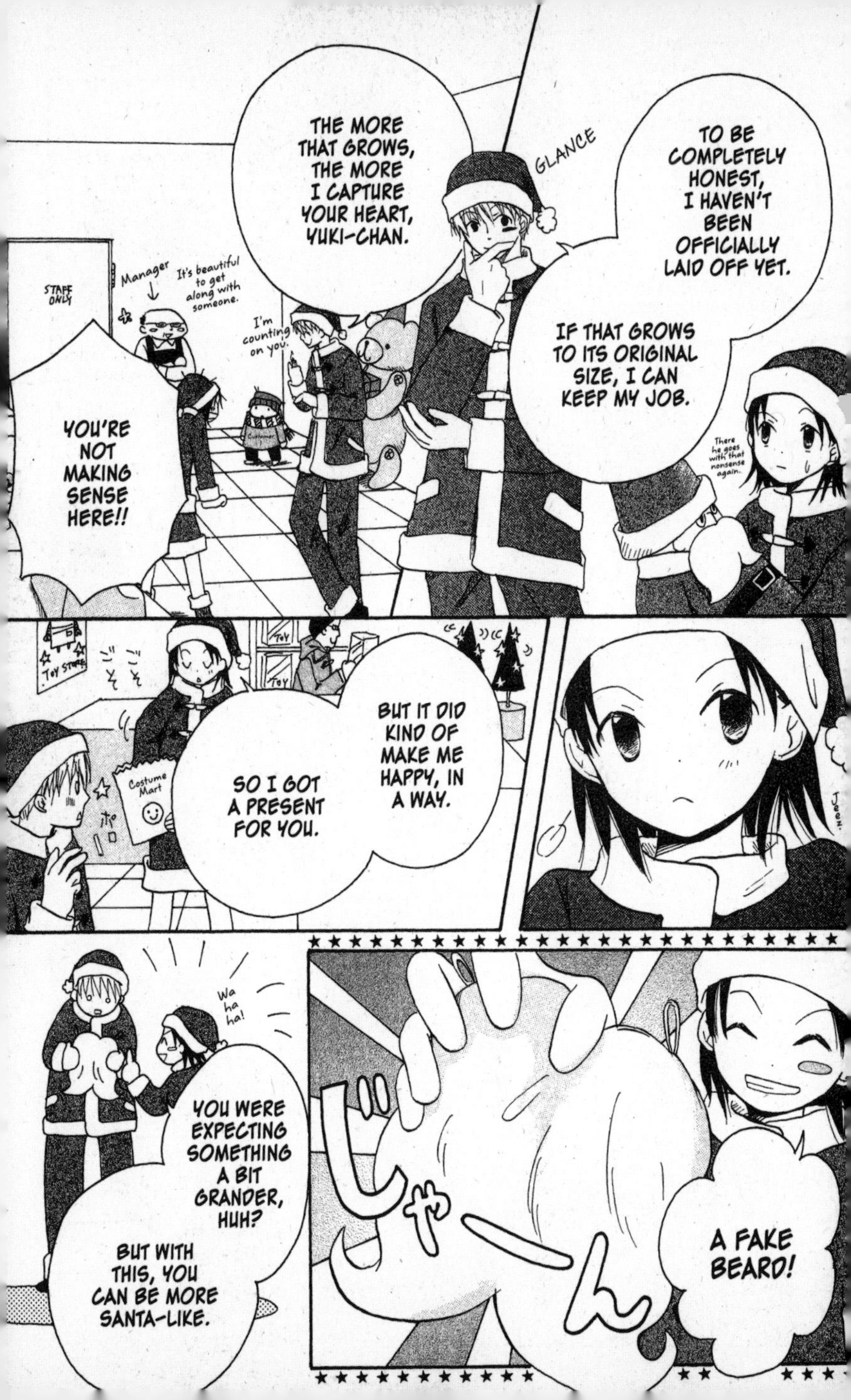
TO BE COMPLETELY HONEST, I HAVEN'T BEEN OFFICIALLY LAID OFF YET.
IF THAT GROWS TO ITS ORIGINAL SIZE, I CAN KEEP MY JOB.
There he goes with that nonsense again.
GLANCE
THE MORE THAT GROWS, THE MORE I CAPTURE YOUR HEART, YUKI-CHAN.
Manager
It's beautiful to get along with someone.
I'm counting on you.
STAFF ONLY
Customer
YOU'RE NOT MAKING SENSE HERE!!
Jeez.
BUT IT DID KIND OF MAKE ME HAPPY, IN A WAY.
SO I GOT A PRESENT FOR YOU.
TOY
TOY STORE
Costume Mart
A FAKE BEARD!
じゃーん
Wa ha ha!
YOU WERE EXPECTING SOMETHING A BIT GRANDER, HUH?
BUT WITH THIS, YOU CAN BE MORE SANTA-LIKE.

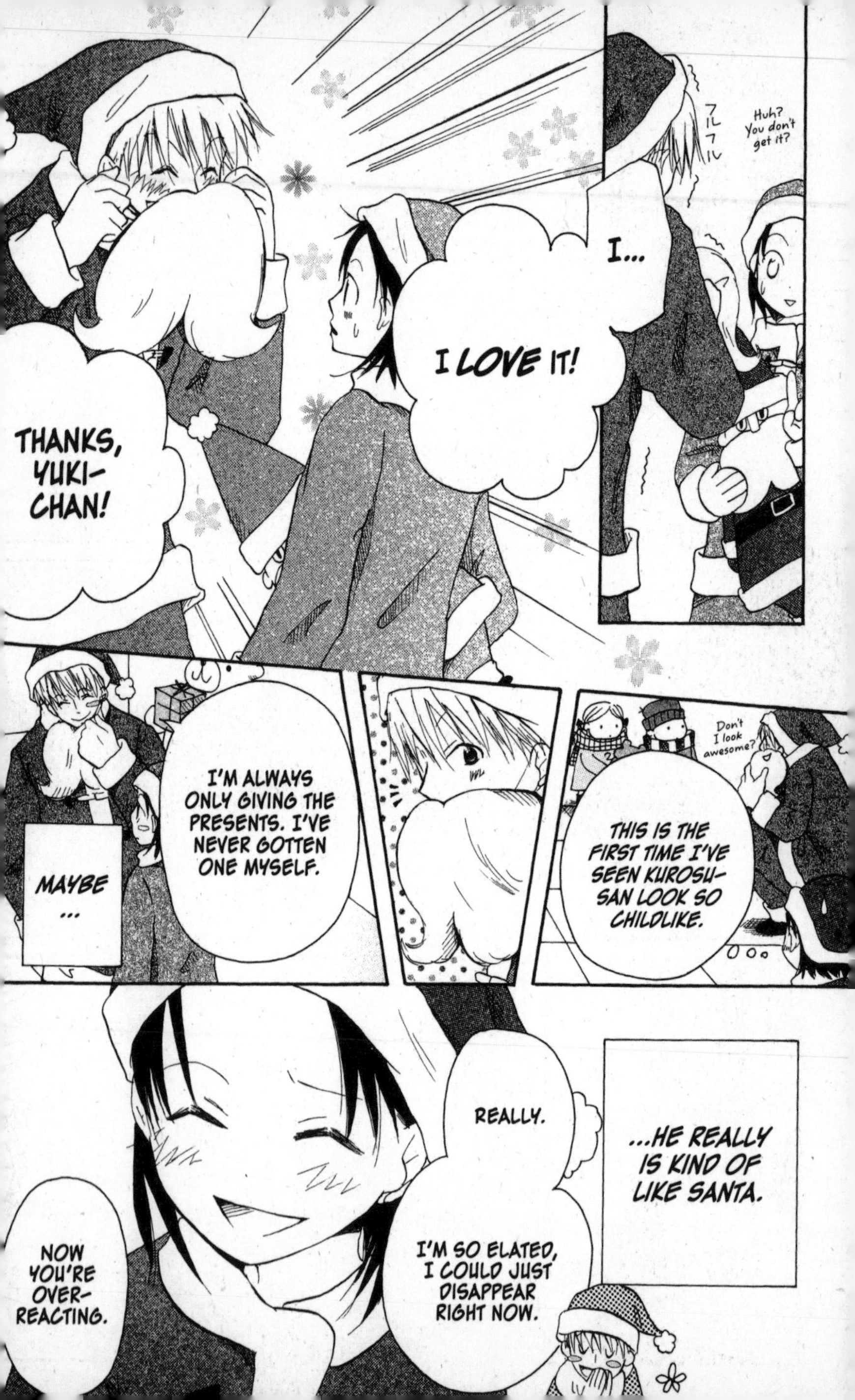
フルフル
Huh? You don't get it?
I...
I LOVE IT!
THANKS, YUKI-CHAN!
Don't I look awesome?
THIS IS THE FIRST TIME I'VE SEEN KUROSU-SAN LOOK SO CHILDLIKE.
I'M ALWAYS ONLY GIVING THE PRESENTS. I'VE NEVER GOTTEN ONE MYSELF.
MAYBE ...
...HE REALLY IS KIND OF LIKE SANTA.
REALLY.
I'M SO ELATED, I COULD JUST DISAPPEAR RIGHT NOW.
NOW YOU'RE OVER-REACTING.

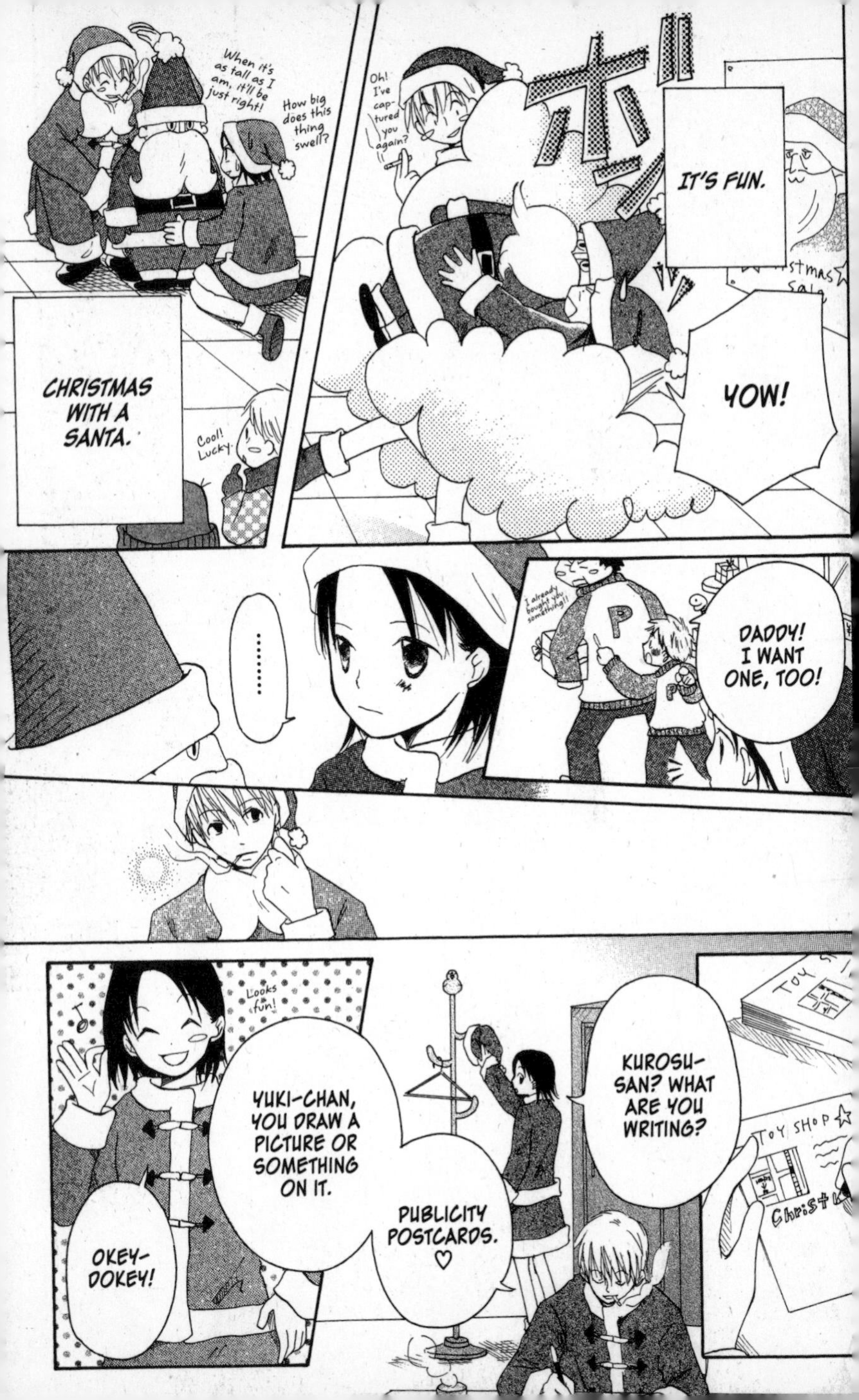
IT'S FUN.
YOW!
Oh! I've captured you again?
How big does this thing swell?
When it's as tall as I am, it'll be just right!
CHRISTMAS WITH A SANTA.
Cool! Lucky.
DADDY! I WANT ONE, TOO!
I already bought you something!!
......
KUROSU-SAN? WHAT ARE YOU WRITING?
TOY SHOP
PUBLICITY POSTCARDS. ♡
YUKI-CHAN, YOU DRAW A PICTURE OR SOMETHING ON IT.
Looks fun!
OKEY-DOKEY!

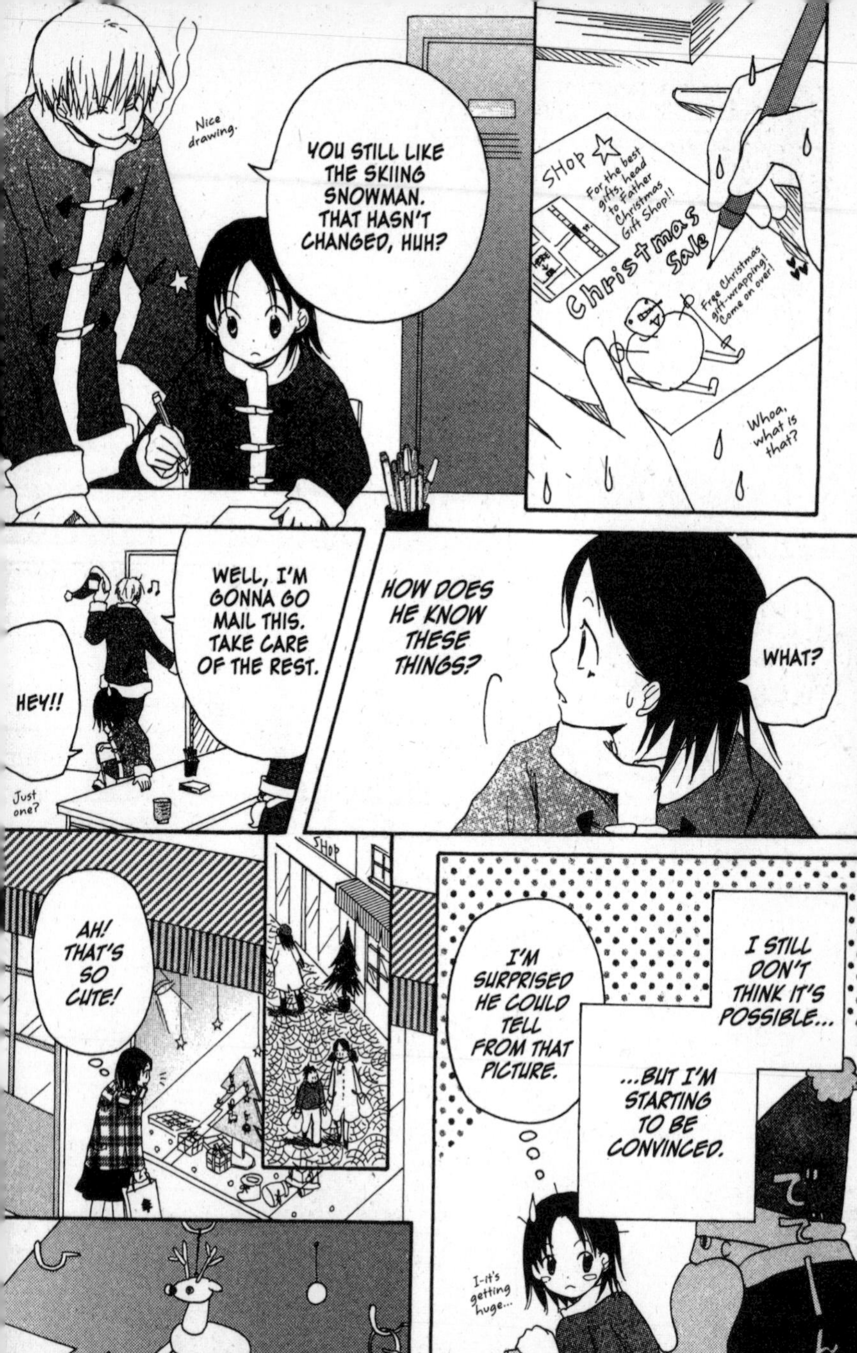
SHOP
For the best gifts, head to Father Christmas Gift Shop!!
Christmas Sale
Free Christmas gift-wrapping! Come on over!
Whoa, what is that?
YOU STILL LIKE THE SKIING SNOWMAN. THAT HASN'T CHANGED, HUH?
Nice drawing.
WHAT?
HOW DOES HE KNOW THESE THINGS?
WELL, I'M GONNA GO MAIL THIS. TAKE CARE OF THE REST.
HEY!!
Just one?
I STILL DON'T THINK IT'S POSSIBLE...
...BUT I'M STARTING TO BE CONVINCED.
I'M SURPRISED HE COULD TELL FROM THAT PICTURE.
I-it's getting huge...
SHOP
AH! THAT'S SO CUTE!
Reindeer keychain

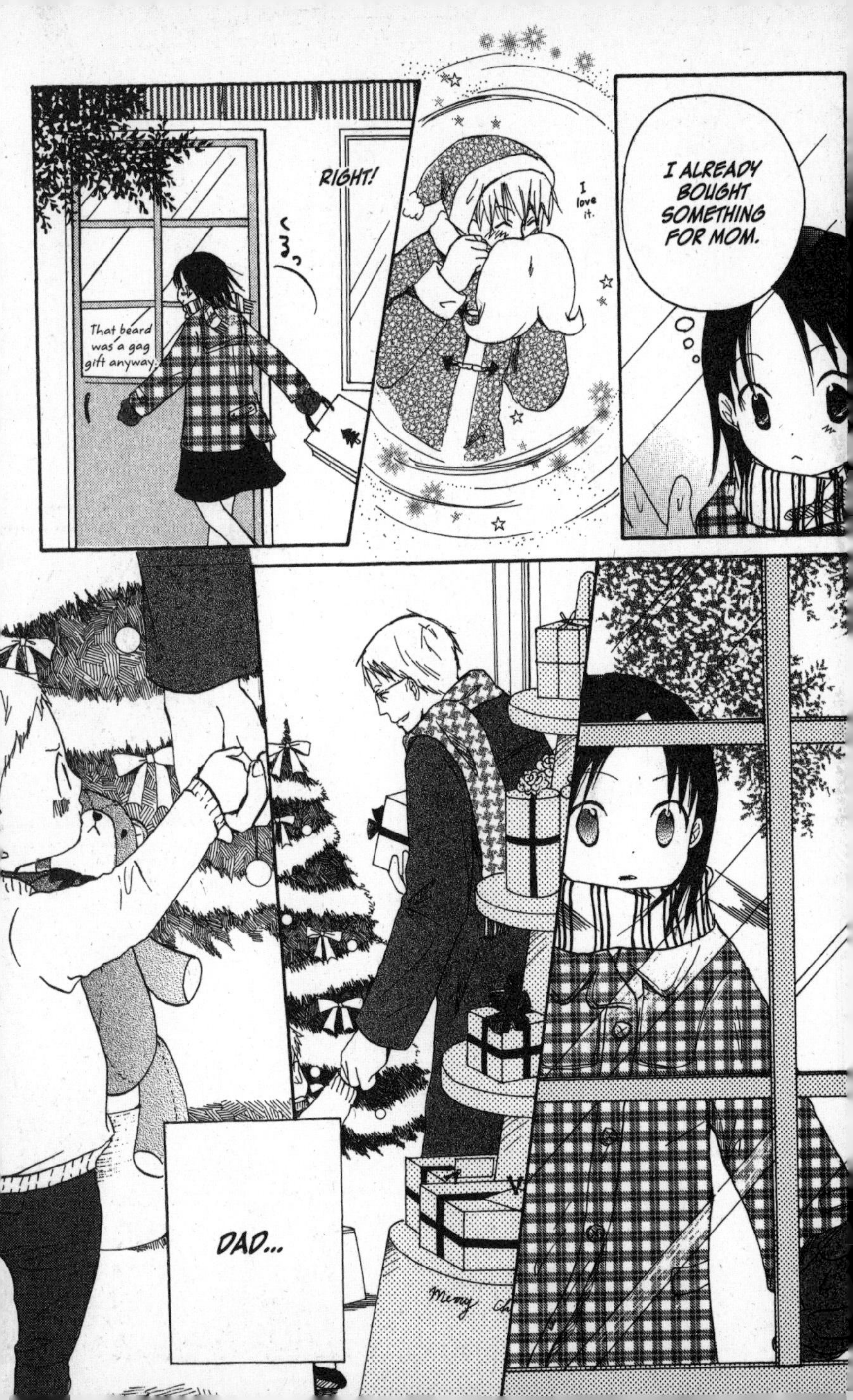
I ALREADY BOUGHT SOMETHING FOR MOM.
I love it.
RIGHT!
くるっ
That beard was a gag gift anyway.
DAD...

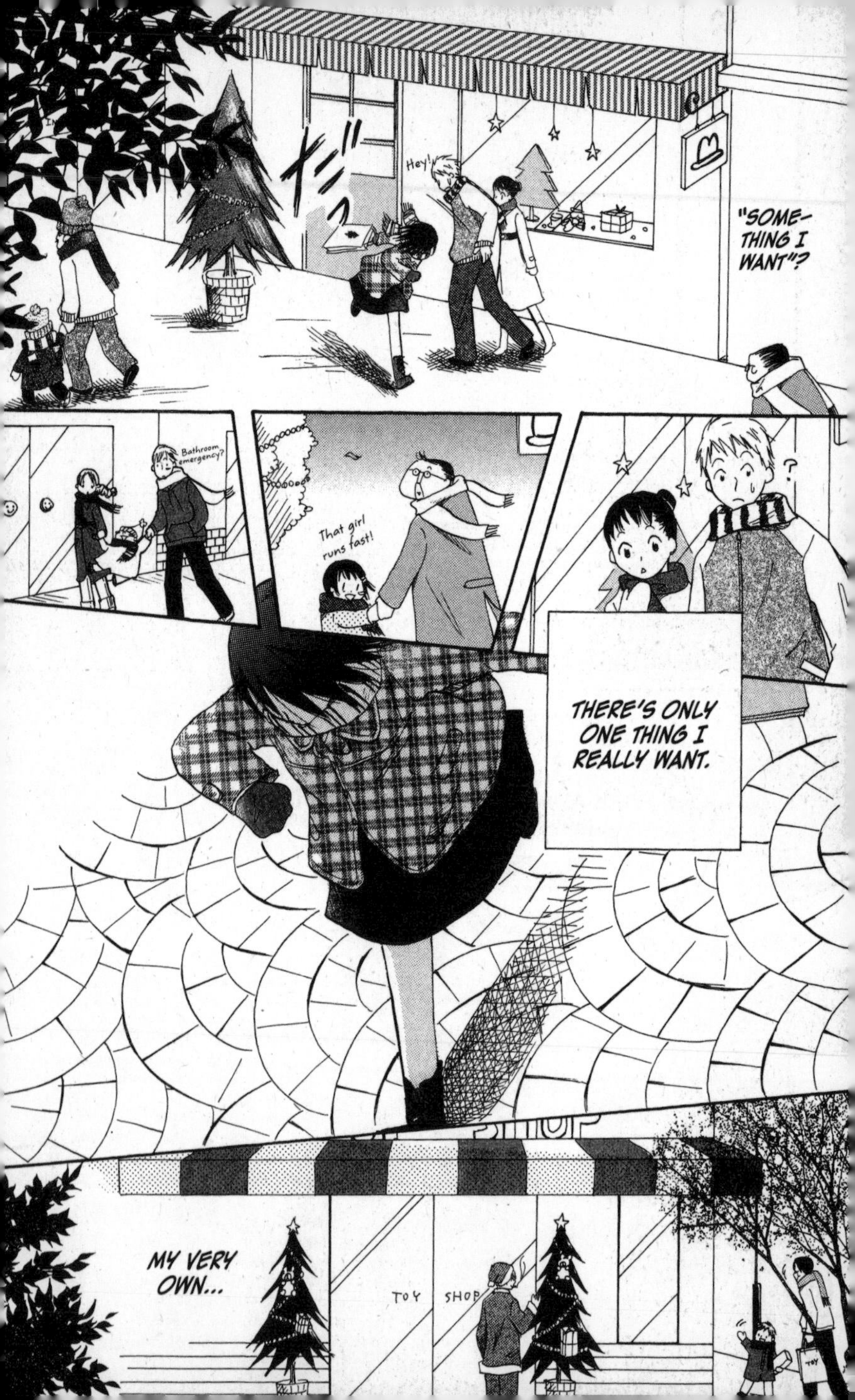
"SOME-THING I WANT"?
Hey!
That girl runs fast!
Bathroom emergency?
THERE'S ONLY ONE THING I REALLY WANT.
MY VERY OWN...
TOY SHOP

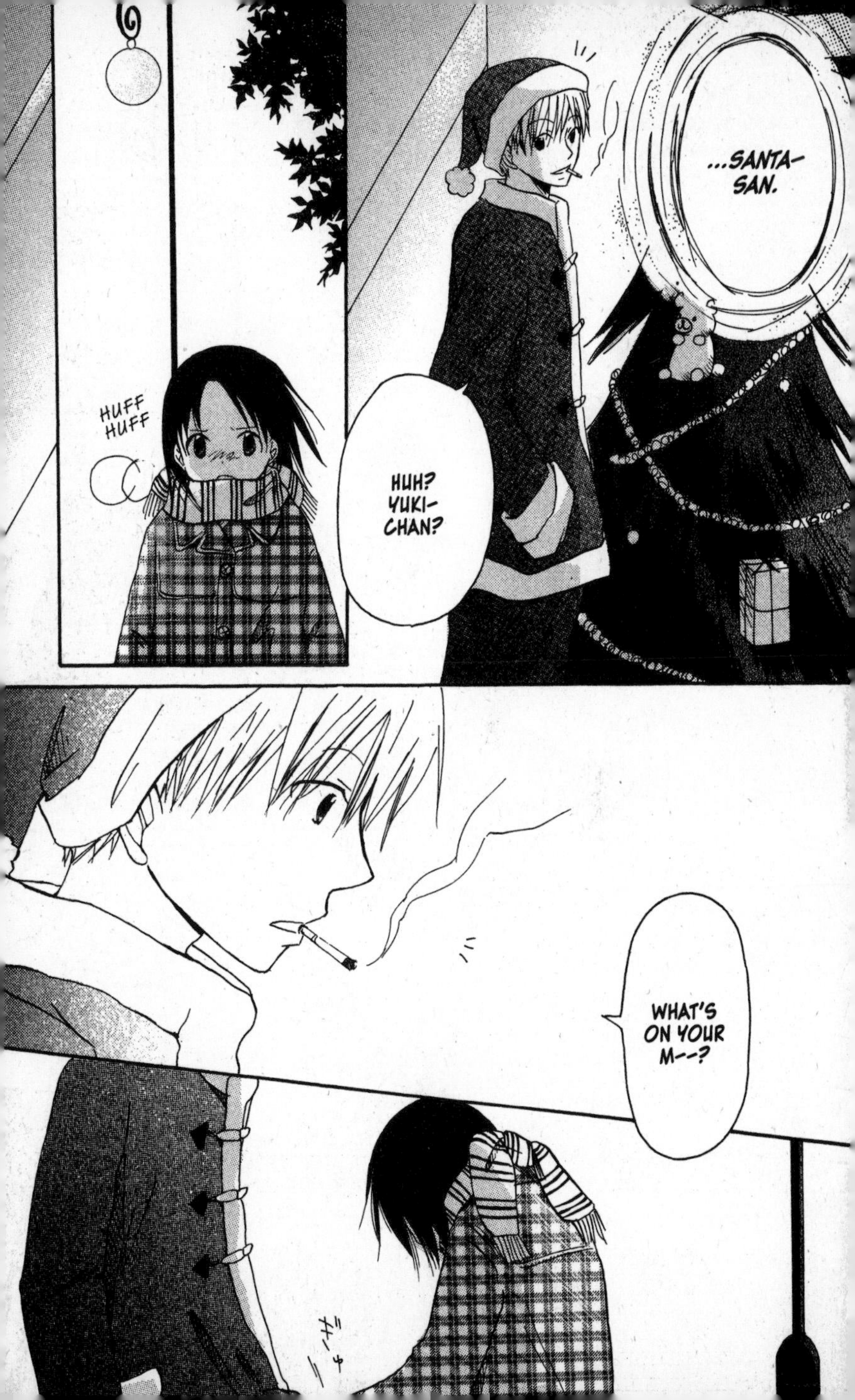
...SANTA-SAN.
HUH? YUKI-CHAN?
HUFF HUFF
WHAT'S ON YOUR M--?
ギュ

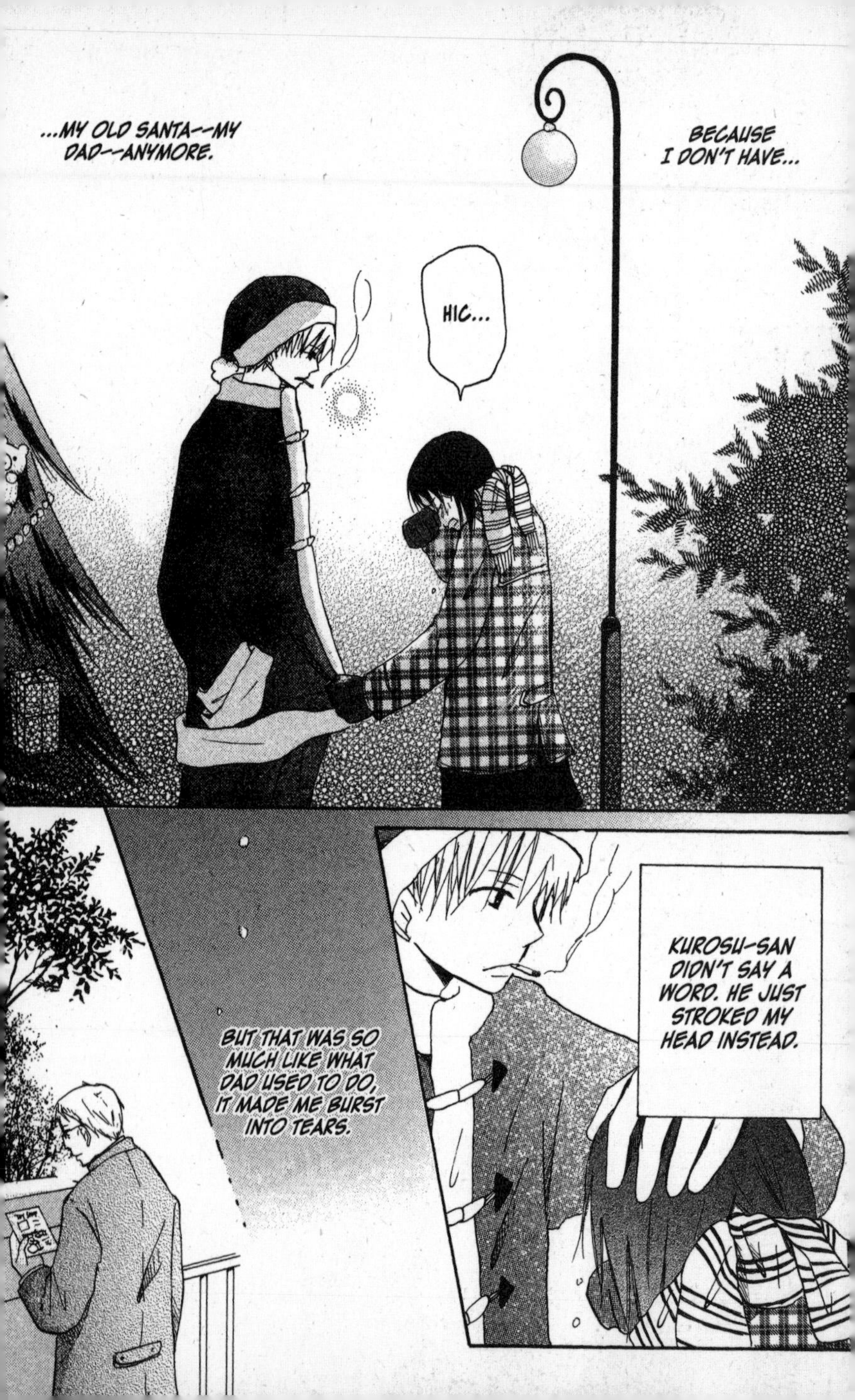
BECAUSE I DON'T HAVE...
...MY OLD SANTA--MY DAD--ANYMORE.
HIC...
KUROSU-SAN DIDN'T SAY A WORD. HE JUST STROKED MY HEAD INSTEAD.
BUT THAT WAS SO MUCH LIKE WHAT DAD USED TO DO, IT MADE ME BURST INTO TEARS.

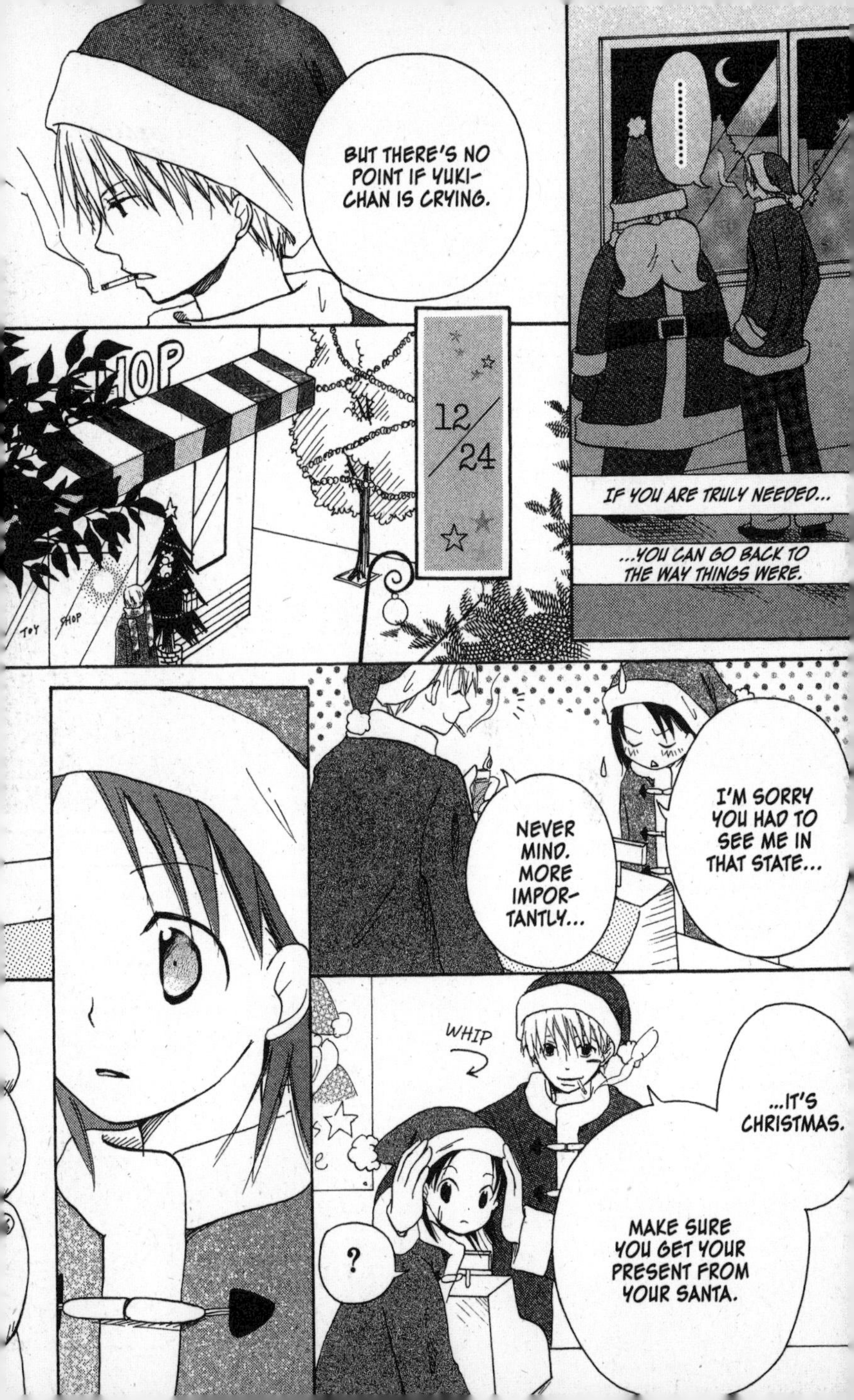

......
IF YOU ARE TRULY NEEDED...
...YOU CAN GO BACK TO THE WAY THINGS WERE.
BUT THERE'S NO POINT IF YUKI-CHAN IS CRYING.
12/24
TOY SHOP
I'M SORRY YOU HAD TO SEE ME IN THAT STATE...
NEVER MIND. MORE IMPOR-TANTLY...
...IT'S CHRISTMAS.
MAKE SURE YOU GET YOUR PRESENT FROM YOUR SANTA.
WHIP
?

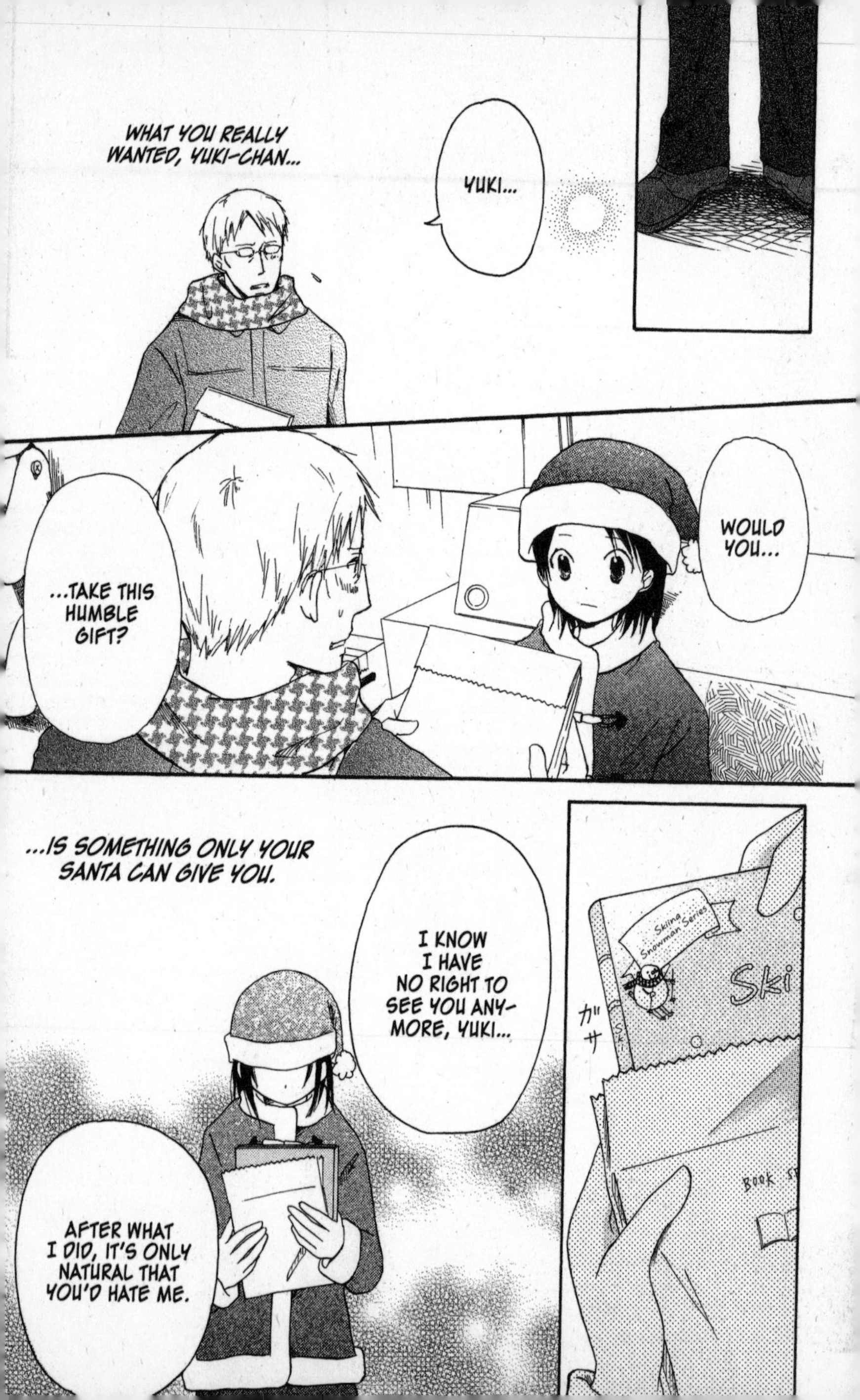
YUKI...
WHAT YOU REALLY WANTED, YUKI-CHAN...
WOULD YOU...
...TAKE THIS HUMBLE GIFT?
Skiing Snowman Series
Ski
ガサ
...IS SOMETHING ONLY YOUR SANTA CAN GIVE YOU.
I KNOW I HAVE NO RIGHT TO SEE YOU ANY-MORE, YUKI...
AFTER WHAT I DID, IT'S ONLY NATURAL THAT YOU'D HATE ME.

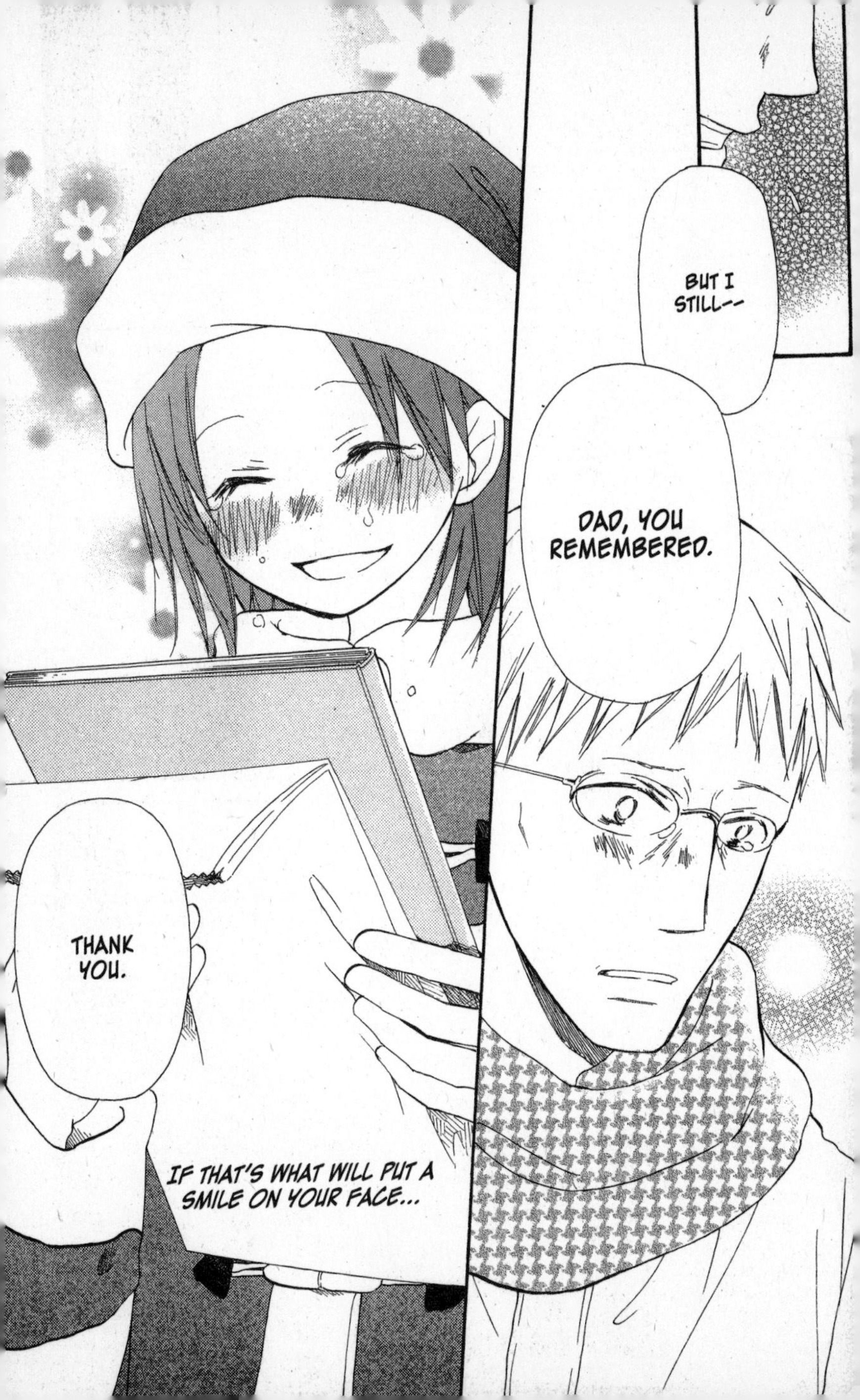
BUT I STILL--
DAD, YOU REMEMBERED.
THANK YOU.
IF THAT'S WHAT WILL PUT A SMILE ON YOUR FACE...

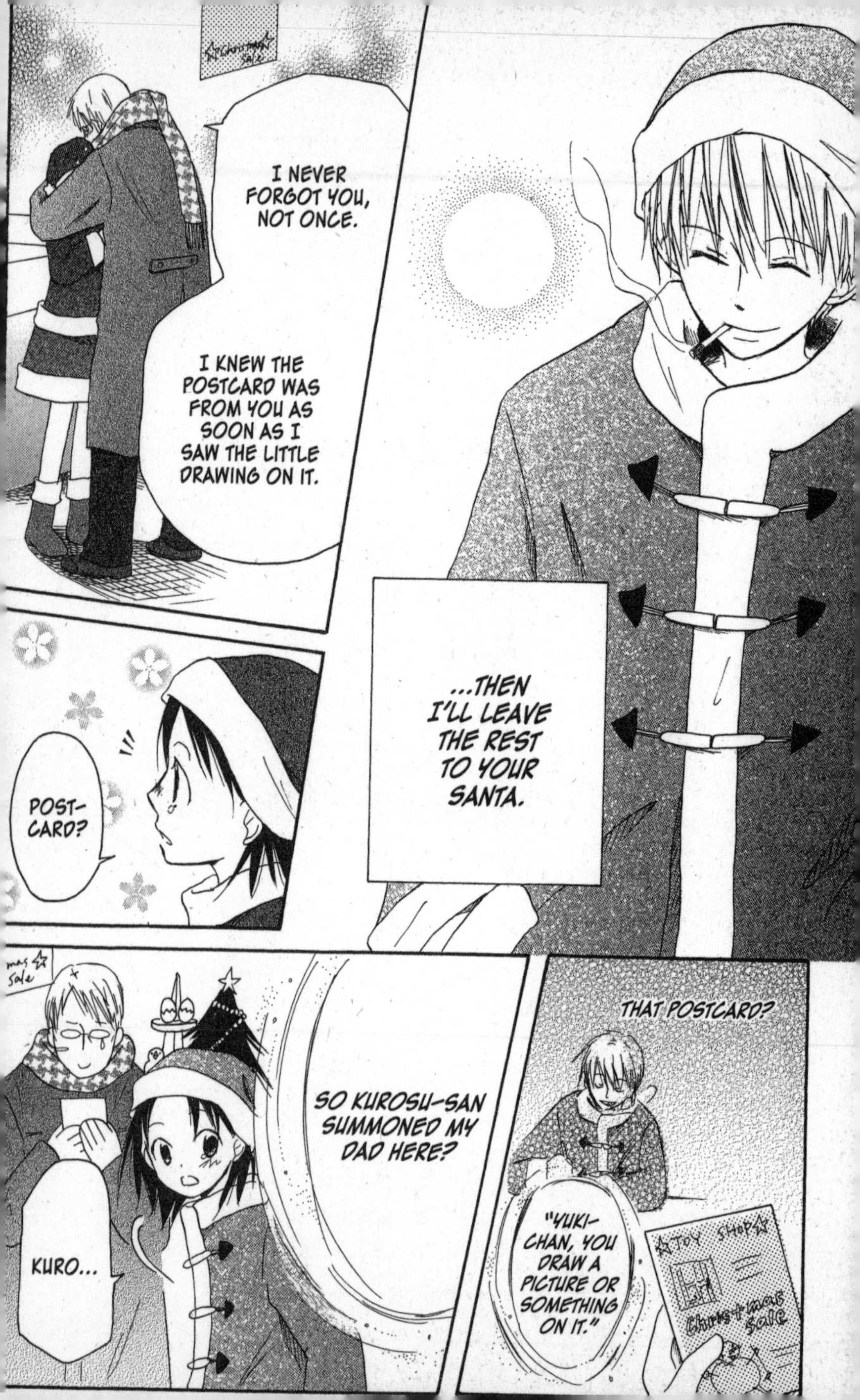
...THEN I'LL LEAVE THE REST TO YOUR SANTA.
I NEVER FORGOT YOU, NOT ONCE.
I KNEW THE POSTCARD WAS FROM YOU AS SOON AS I SAW THE LITTLE DRAWING ON IT.
POST-CARD?
THAT POSTCARD?
"YUKI-CHAN, YOU DRAW A PICTURE OR SOMETHING ON IT."
SO KUROSU-SAN SUMMONED MY DAD HERE?
KURO...

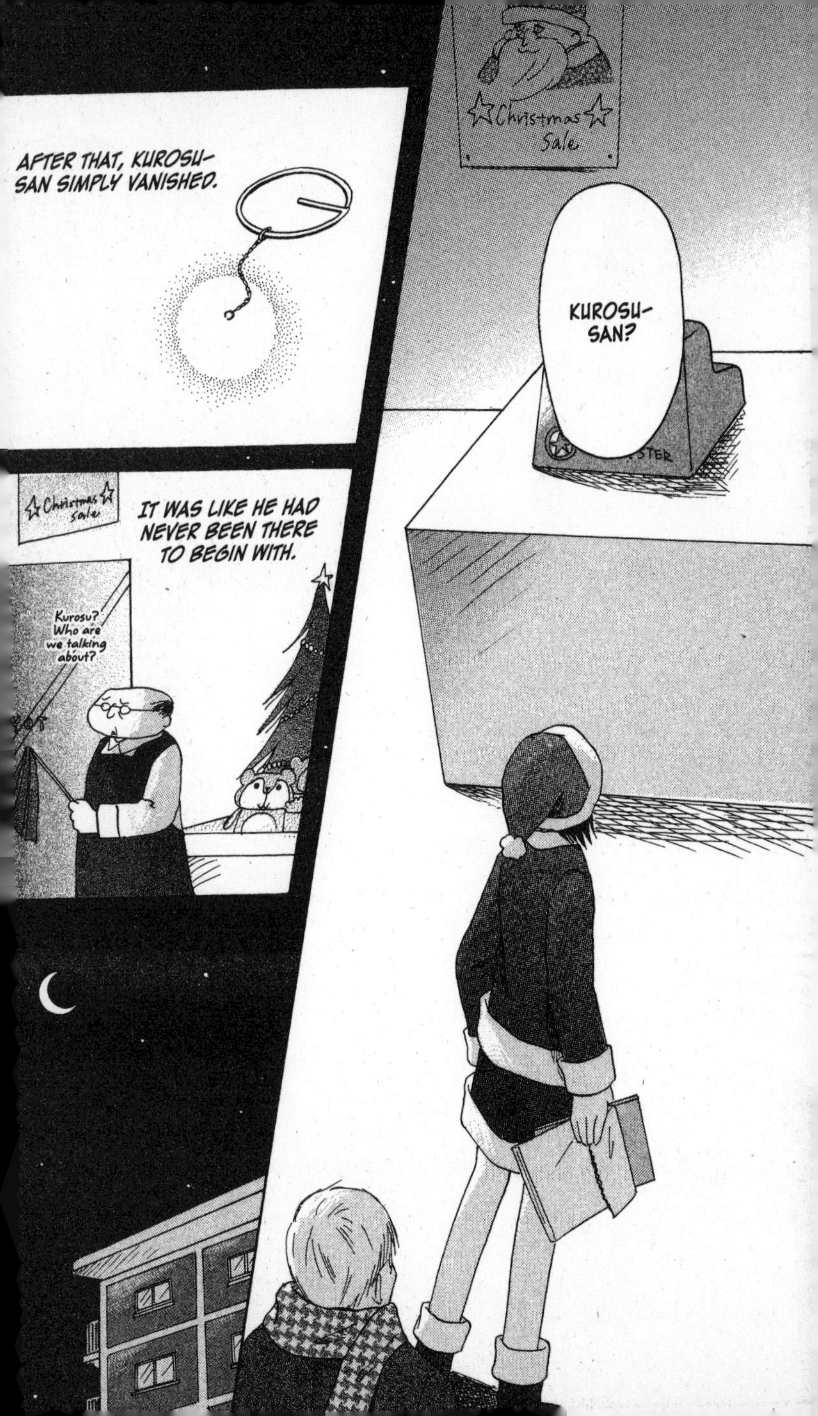
Christmas Sale
KUROSU-SAN?
AFTER THAT, KUROSU-SAN SIMPLY VANISHED.
Christmas sale
IT WAS LIKE HE HAD NEVER BEEN THERE TO BEGIN WITH.
Kurosu? Who are we talking about?

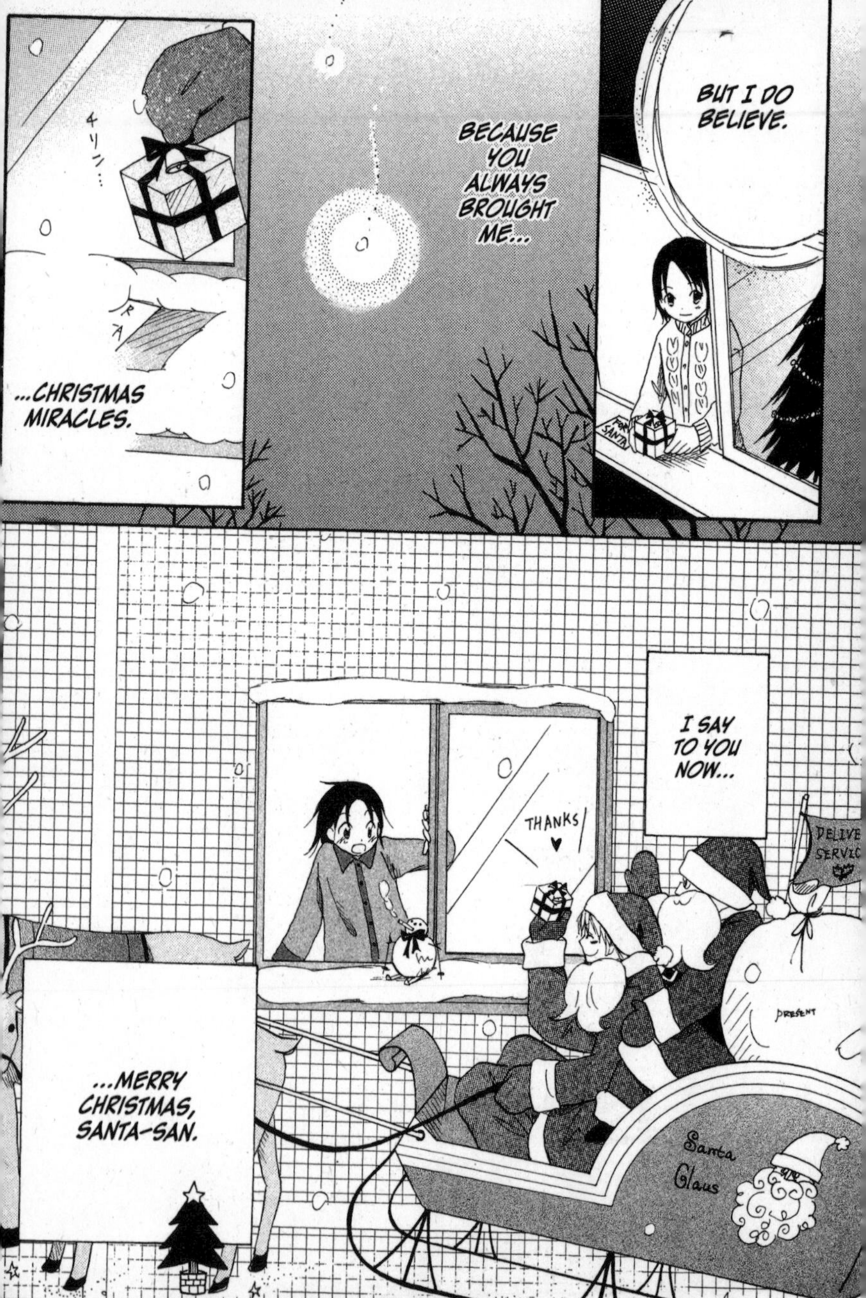
BUT I DO BELIEVE.
BECAUSE YOU ALWAYS BROUGHT ME...
...CHRISTMAS MIRACLES.
I SAY TO YOU NOW...
THANKS ♥
PRESENT
Santa Claus
...MERRY CHRISTMAS, SANTA-SAN.
The Town Where Santa Is /-End

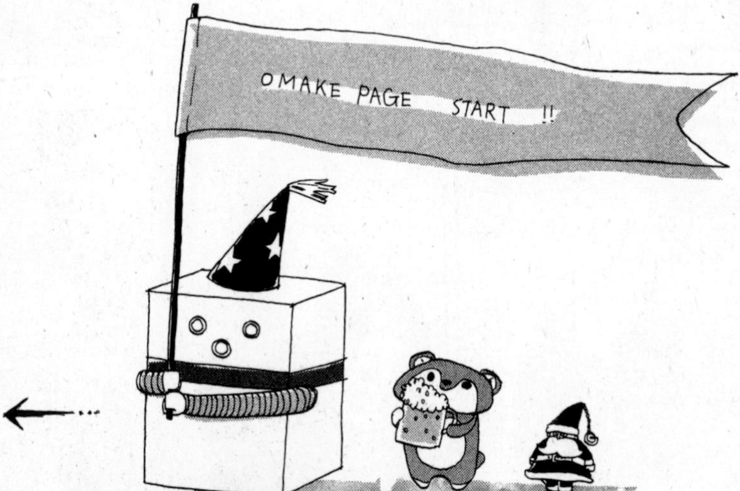
OMAKE PAGE START !!

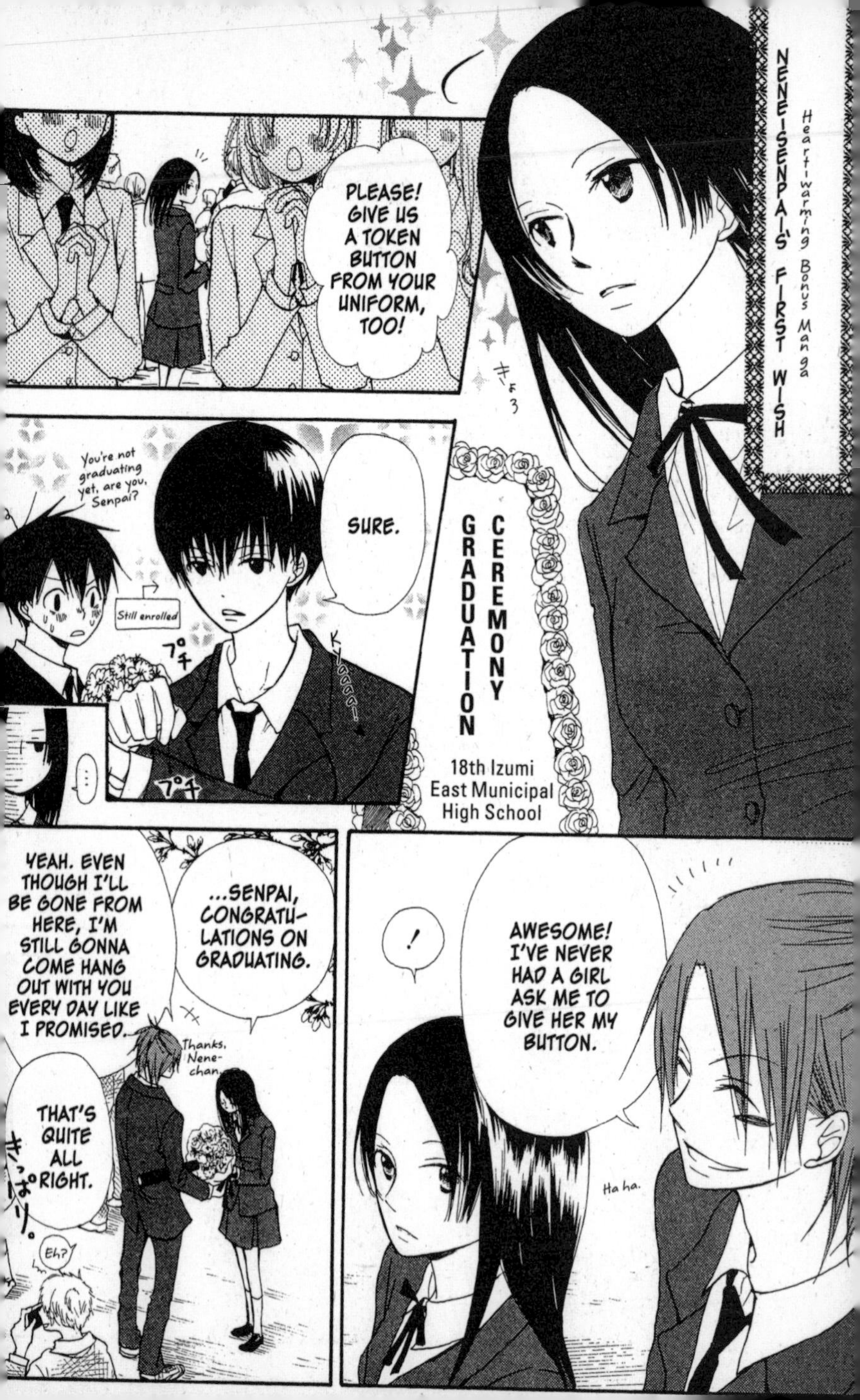
Heartwarming Bonus Manga
NENE-SENPAI'S FIRST WISH
GRADUATION CEREMONY
18th Izumi East Municipal High School
PLEASE! GIVE US A TOKEN BUTTON FROM YOUR UNIFORM, TOO!
SURE.
You're not graduating yet, are you, Senpai?
Still enrolled
プチ
プチ
...
!
AWESOME! I'VE NEVER HAD A GIRL ASK ME TO GIVE HER MY BUTTON.
Ha ha.
...SENPAI, CONGRATULATIONS ON GRADUATING.
YEAH. EVEN THOUGH I'LL BE GONE FROM HERE, I'M STILL GONNA COME HANG OUT WITH YOU EVERY DAY LIKE I PROMISED.
Thanks, Nene-chan.
THAT'S QUITE ALL RIGHT.
きっぱり。
Eh?

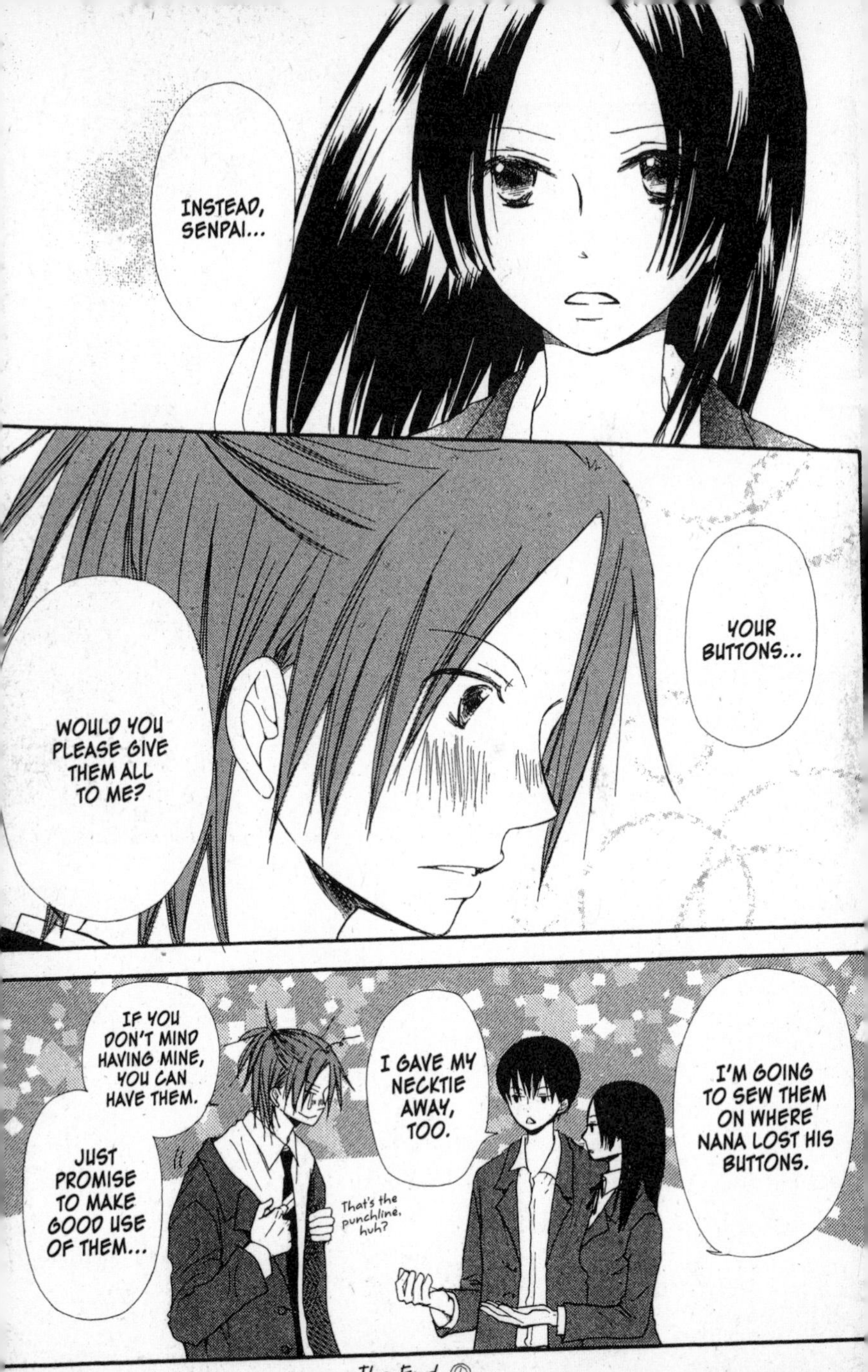
INSTEAD, SENPAI...
YOUR BUTTONS...
WOULD YOU PLEASE GIVE THEM ALL TO ME?
I'M GOING TO SEW THEM ON WHERE NANA LOST HIS BUTTONS.
I GAVE MY NECKTIE AWAY, TOO.
That's the punchline, huh?
IF YOU DON'T MIND HAVING MINE, YOU CAN HAVE THEM.
JUST PROMISE TO MAKE GOOD USE OF THEM...

The End

A Bonus to the Bonus

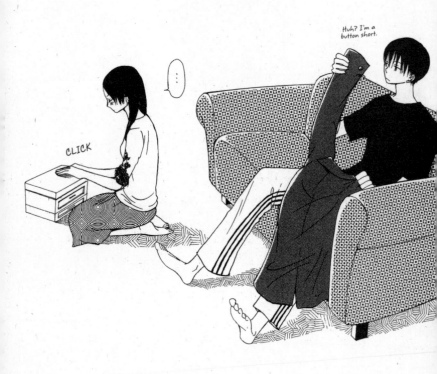

Huh? I'm a button short.

CLICK

...

THANKS !!

MIKAMI CHITO SAMA

NAKANO EMIKO SAMA

KONDOU SAMA

&

YOU !!!

TOKEINO HARI ⑭

Me & My Brothers

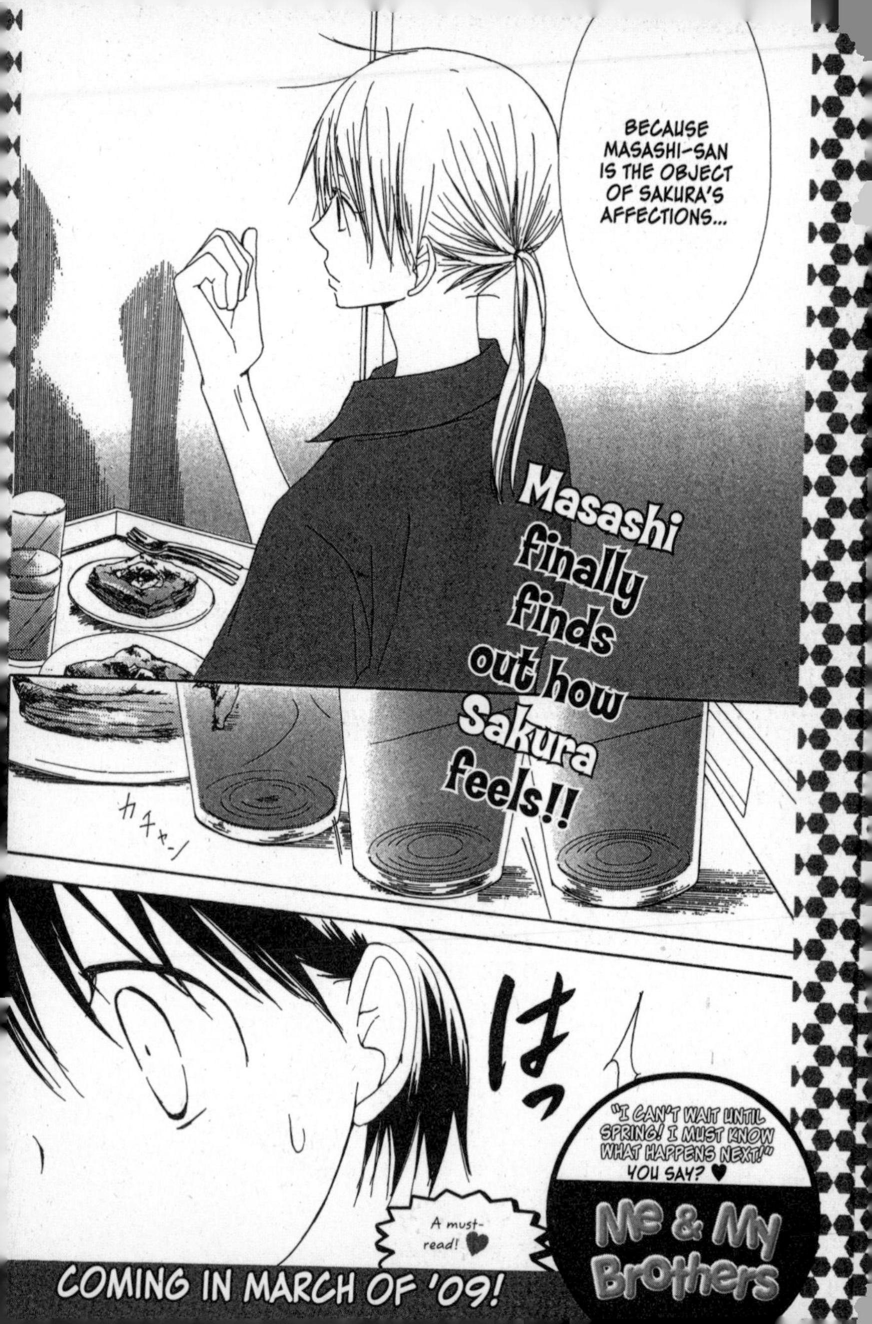
BECAUSE MASASHI-SAN IS THE OBJECT OF SAKURA'S AFFECTIONS...
Masashi finally finds out how Sakura feels!!
カチャーン
はっ
"I CAN'T WAIT UNTIL SPRING! I MUST KNOW WHAT HAPPENS NEXT!" YOU SAY? ♥
Me & My Brothers
A must-read! ♥
COMING IN MARCH OF '09!

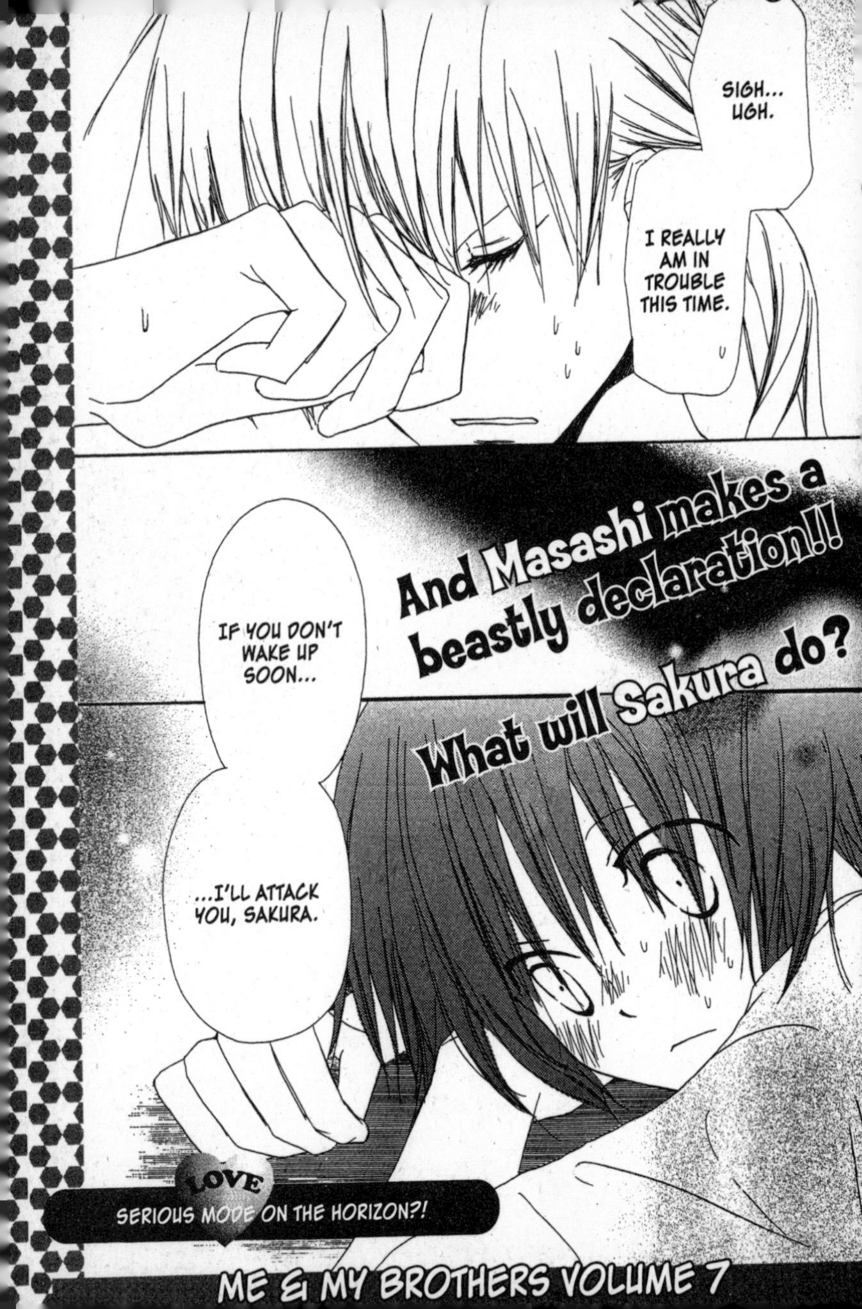
SIGH... UGH.
I REALLY AM IN TROUBLE THIS TIME.
And Masashi makes a beastly declaration!!
What will Sakura do?
IF YOU DON'T WAKE UP SOON...
...I'LL ATTACK YOU, SAKURA.
LOVE
SERIOUS MODE ON THE HORIZON?!
ME & MY BROTHERS VOLUME 7

Many Modes of Masashi

-Just in this volume alone!!

MAID-FOR-YOU MODE

HE'S SLIPPED INTO THIS MODE MANY TIMES THROUGHOUT THE SERIES. WE'D ALL LIKE TO HAVE A MAID/BROTHER HALF AS CUTE AS MASASHI!

I-STALK-BECAUSE-I-HAVE-TO MODE

STALKING SAKURA IS ONE OF MASASHI'S FAVORITE ACTIVITIES, IT SEEMS. IT GETS HIM INTO ALL KINDS OF ODD COSTUMES AND POSITIONS.

EXTRA-CUTE-IN-TEARS MODE

HE IS OFTEN SEEN IN THIS MODE. HE GETS TEARY EYED WHEN SAKURA OR TSUYOSHI YELLS AT HIM. LIKE I SAID, HE IS OFTEN SEEN LIKE THIS.

I'M-VERY-JUDGMENTAL-WHEN-IT-COMES-TO-FASHION MODE

WHETHER HE'S SHOPPING WITH SAKURA OR TRYING TO DECIDE WHAT FRILLY OUTFIT TO WEAR TO DINNER, MASASHI GETS ALL SERIOUS WHEN PRETTY CLOTHING IS INVOLVED.

YOU'LL-BE-SLEEPING-WITH-THE-FISHES MODE

THIS ONLY SURFACES WHEN HE'S AROUND GUYS SAKURA'S AGE. WHEN A PROSPECTIVE BOYFRIEND GETS WITHIN 30 YARDS OF HER, MASASHI'S THERE. DEATH STARE AND ALL.

I'M-UPPING-MY-GAME MODE

THIS MODE IS AN UPGRADED VERSION OF HIS OTHER MODES. THIS PARTICULAR VOLUME, HE UPGRADED HIS I-STALK-BECAUSE-I-HAVE-TO MODE BY RECRUITING A SIDEKICK (SAKURA).

SAKURA'S-SISTER-AND-BFF MODE

DOESN'T REQUIRE ANY ADDITIONAL EXPLANATION, DOES IT?

JUST-CALL-ME-MOTHER-MIYASHITA MODE

ON TOP OF PLAYING SISTER TO SAKURA, MASASHI MUST ALSO PLAY MOTHER TO HIS ENTIRE FAMILY. HE'S ONE BUSY GUY. IS IT ANY WONDER HE NEVER SEEMS TO GET HIS WRITING WORK DONE ON TIME?

We love
them all!!

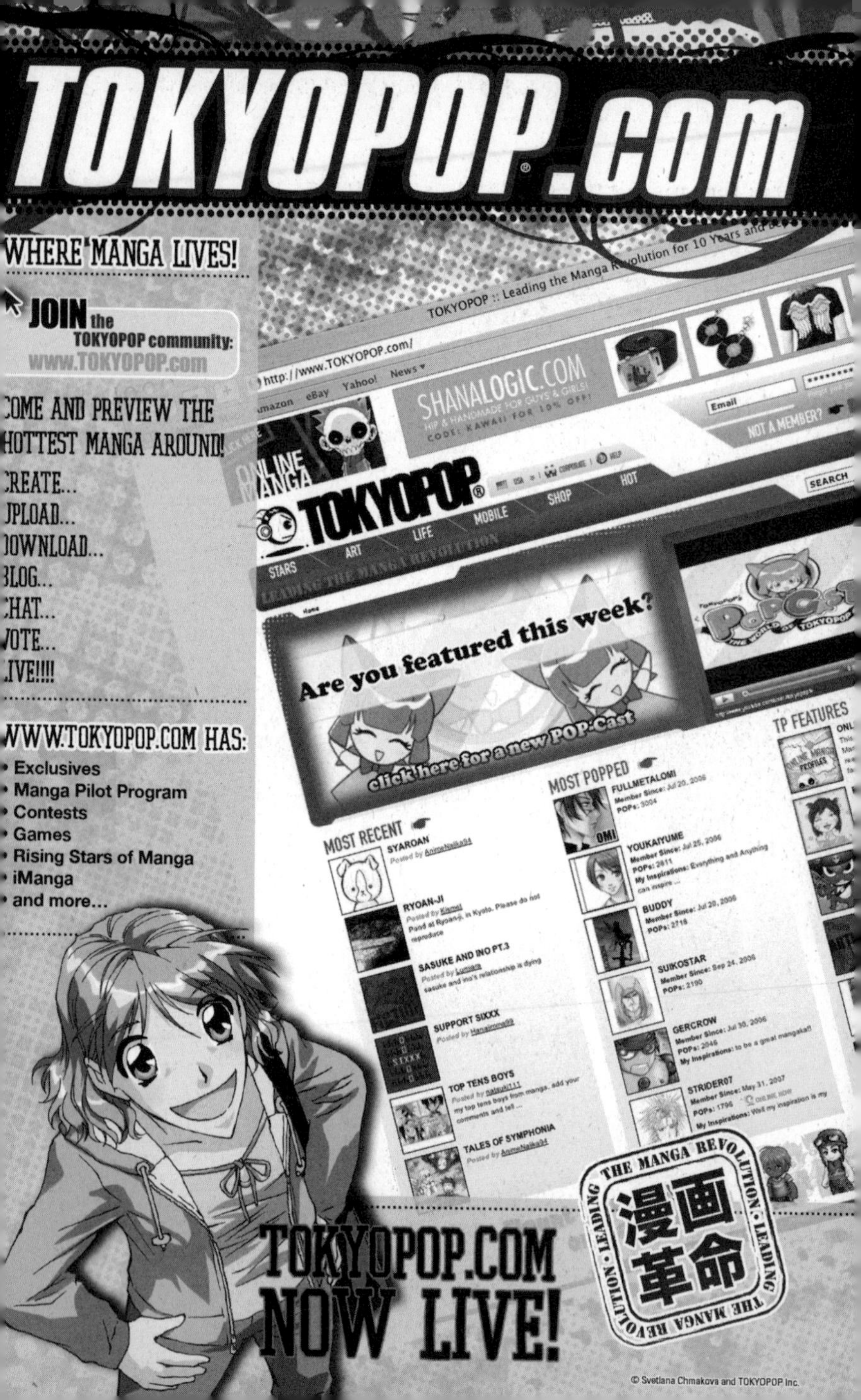
TOKYOPOP®.com
WHERE MANGA LIVES!
JOIN the TOKYOPOP community:
www.TOKYOPOP.com
COME AND PREVIEW THE HOTTEST MANGA AROUND!
CREATE...
UPLOAD...
DOWNLOAD...
BLOG...
CHAT...
VOTE...
LIVE!!!!
WWW.TOKYOPOP.COM HAS:
• Exclusives
• Manga Pilot Program
• Contests
• Games
• Rising Stars of Manga
• iManga
• and more...
TOKYOPOP :: Leading the Manga Revolution for 10 Years and Beyond
http://www.TOKYOPOP.com/
SHANALOGIC.COM
NOT A MEMBER?
ONLINE MANGA
TOKYOPOP®
STARS
ART
LIFE
MOBILE
SHOP
HOT
SEARCH
Are you featured this week?
click here for a new POP-Cast
MOST RECENT
MOST POPPED
TP FEATURES
THE MANGA REVOLUTION · LEADING
漫画革命
TOKYOPOP.COM NOW LIVE!
© Svetlana Chmakova and TOKYOPOP Inc.

INCLUDES A PREVIEW OF FRUITS BASKET VOL. 22 (MARCH 2009)

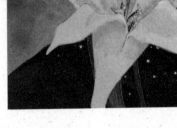

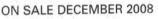

TOKYOPOP MANGA SUPPLEMENT

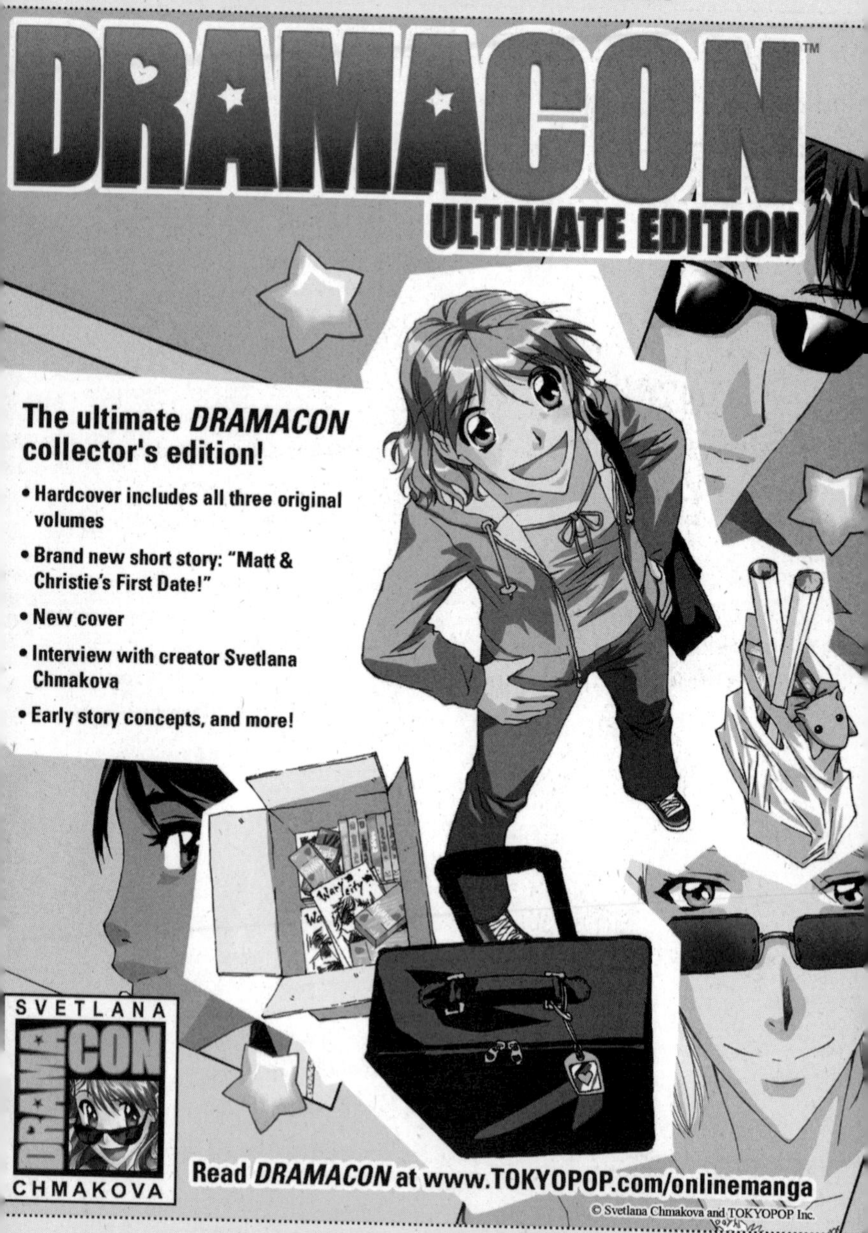
DRAMACON™
ULTIMATE EDITION
The ultimate DRAMACON collector's edition!
• Hardcover includes all three original volumes
• Brand new short story: "Matt & Christie's First Date!"
• New cover
• Interview with creator Svetlana Chmakova
• Early story concepts, and more!
SVETLANA
DRAMACON
CHMAKOVA
Read DRAMACON at www.TOKYOPOP.com/onlinemanga
© Svetlana Chmakova and TOKYOPOP Inc.

BUY IT AT WWW.TOKYOPOP.COM/SHOP

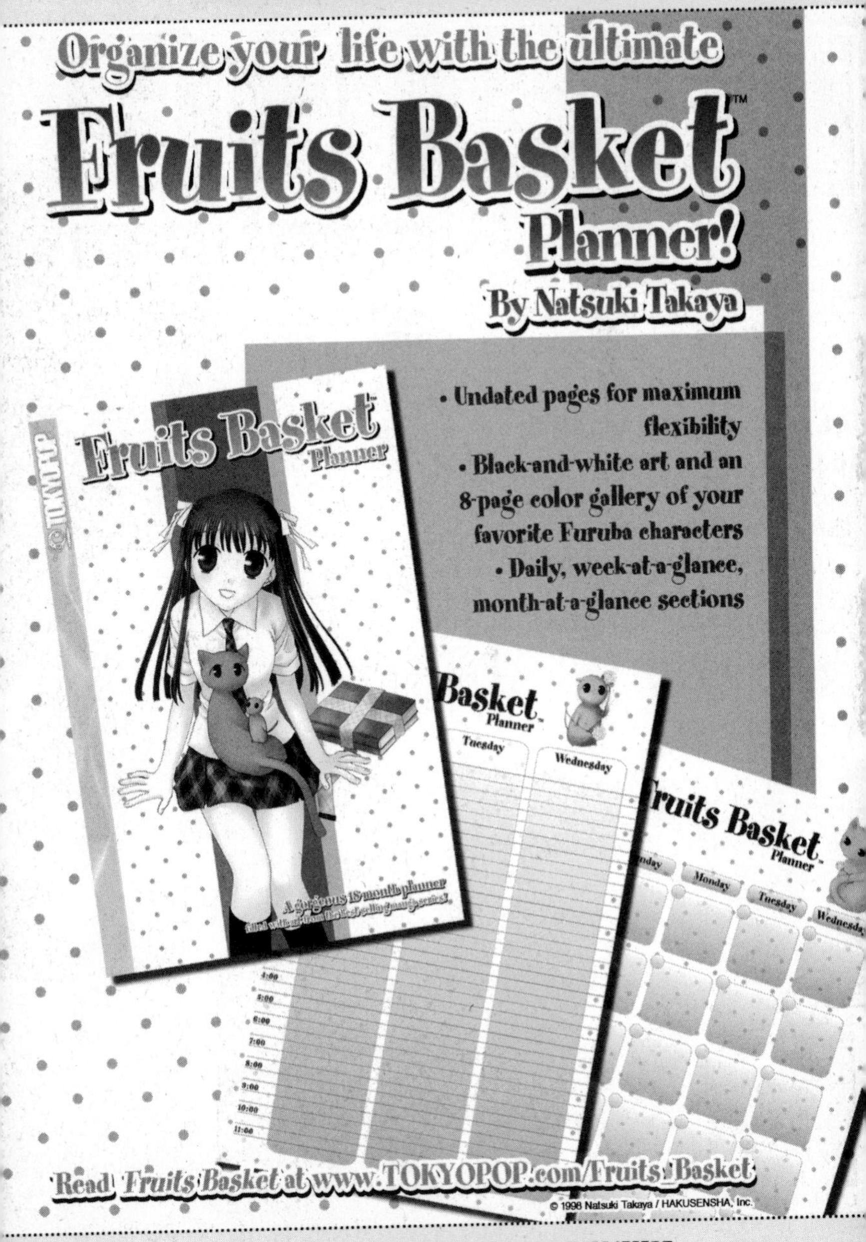
Organize your life with the ultimate
Fruits Basket™ Planner!
By Natsuki Takaya
• Undated pages for maximum flexibility
• Black-and-white art and an 8-page color gallery of your favorite Furuba characters
• Daily, week-at-a-glance, month-at-a-glance sections
Fruits Basket Planner
TOKYOPOP
A gorgeous 18-month planner filled with art from the best-selling manga series!
Basket Planner
Tuesday
Wednesday
Fruits Basket Planner
Monday
Tuesday
Wednesday
Read Fruits Basket at www.TOKYOPOP.com/Fruits_Basket
© 1998 Natsuki Takaya / HAKUSENSHA, Inc.

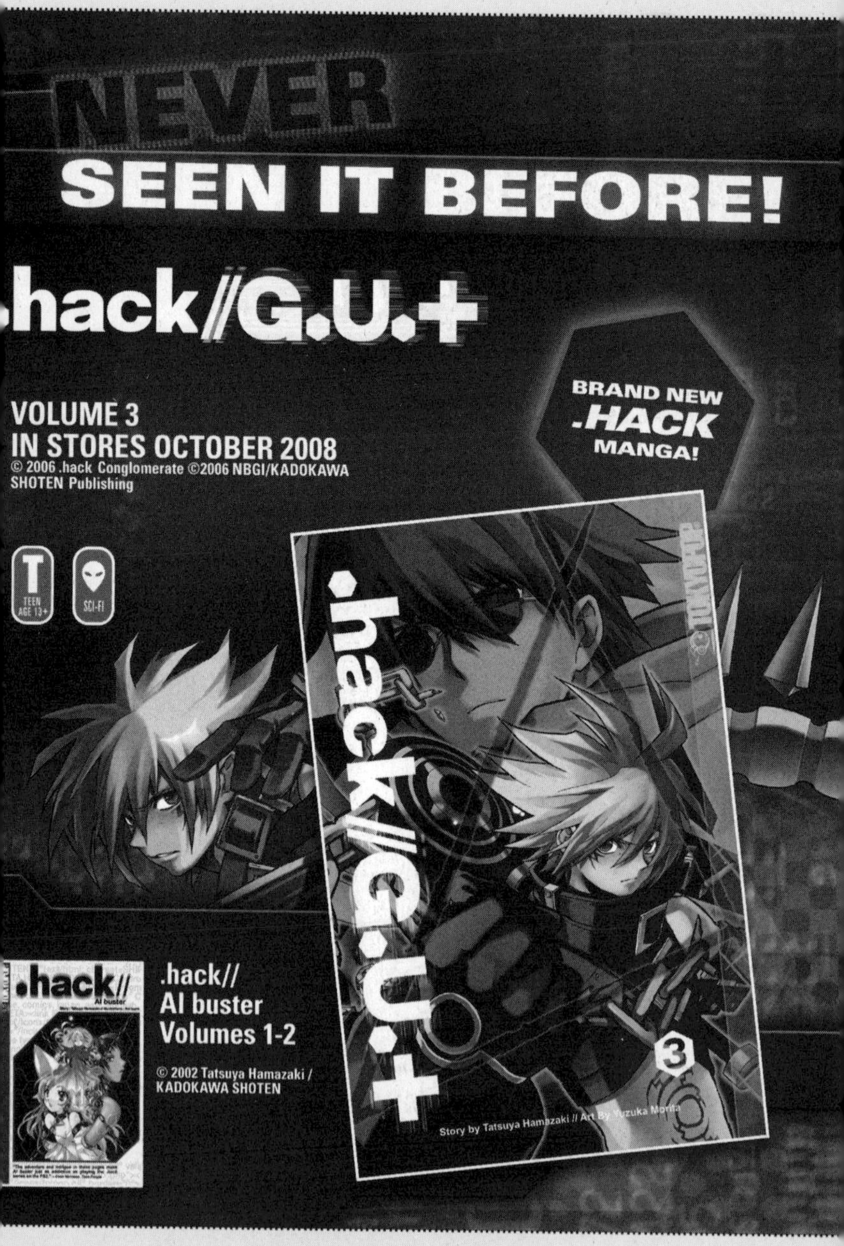
NEVER
SEEN IT BEFORE!
.hack//G.U.+
VOLUME 3
IN STORES OCTOBER 2008
© 2006 .hack Conglomerate ©2006 NBGI/KADOKAWA SHOTEN Publishing
BRAND NEW .HACK MANGA!
T TEEN AGE 13+
SCI-FI
.hack//G.U.+
3
Story by Tatsuya Hamazaki // Art By Yuzuka Morita
.hack// AI buster
.hack//
AI buster
Volumes 1-2
© 2002 Tatsuya Hamazaki / KADOKAWA SHOTEN

.HACK UNIVERSE

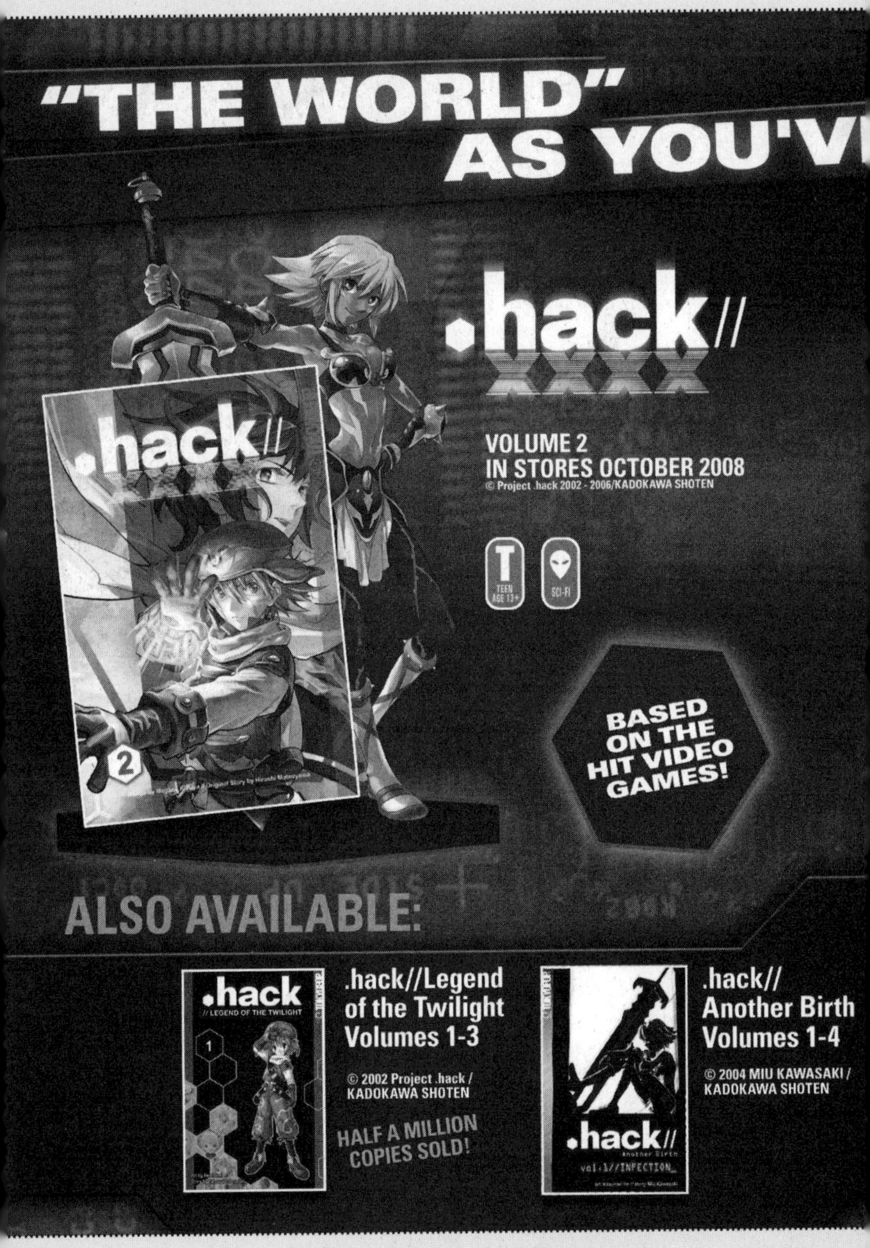
"THE WORLD"
AS YOU'V
.hack//
XXXX
VOLUME 2
IN STORES OCTOBER 2008
© Project .hack 2002 - 2006/KADOKAWA SHOTEN
T
TEEN AGE 13+
SCI-FI
.hack//
2
BASED ON THE HIT VIDEO GAMES!
ALSO AVAILABLE:
.hack
// LEGEND OF THE TWILIGHT
1
.hack//Legend of the Twilight Volumes 1-3
© 2002 Project .hack / KADOKAWA SHOTEN
HALF A MILLION COPIES SOLD!
.hack//
Another Birth
vol.1//INFECTION
.hack// Another Birth Volumes 1-4
© 2004 MIU KAWASAKI / KADOKAWA SHOTEN

FOR MORE INFORMATION VISIT:

STOP!

This is the back of the book.
You wouldn't want to spoil a great ending!

This book is printed "manga-style," in the authentic Japanese right-to-left format. Since none of the artwork has been flipped or altered, readers get to experience the story just as the creator intended. You've been asking for it, so TOKYOPOP® delivered: authentic, hot-off-the-press, and far more fun!

DIRECTIONS

If this is your first time reading manga-style, here's a quick guide to help you understand how it works.

It's easy... just start in the top right panel and follow the numbers. Have fun, and look for more 100% authentic manga from TOKYOPOP®!